Snapshots *of* GOD

A Daily Devotional

RICHARD W. COFFEN

REVIEW AND HERALD® PUBLISHING ASSOCIATION
Since 1861 | www.reviewandherald.com

The Review and Herald® Publishing Association publishes biblically based materials for spiritual, physical, and mental growth and Christian discipleship.

The author assumes full responsibility for the accuracy of all facts and quotations as cited in this book.

This book was
Edited by Steven S. Winn
Copyedited by James Cavil
Designed by Trent Truman
Cover photo composite: © iStockphoto.com / joshblake / nico blue / evirgen
Interior design by Heather Rogers
Typeset: Cartier Book 11/13

PRINTED IN U.S.A.
13 12 11 10   5 4 3 2 1

Library of Congress Cataloging-in-Publication Data
Coffen, Richard W.
  Snapshots of God: a daily devotional / Richard W. Coffen.
     p. cm.
  1. Devotional calendars—Seventh-day Adventists. I. Title.
  BV4811.C63 2009
  242'.2—dc22
                          2009012474

ISBN 978-0-8280-2460-0

Also by Richard W. Coffen: *Where Is God When You Hurt?*
To order, call **1-800-765-6955**.

Visit us at **www.reviewandherald.com**
for information on other Review and Herald® products.

Dedicated to Mother,
who devours the daily devotional books

～

A Few Words Before We Begin . . .

How does one go about organizing a daily devotional book? What theme or themes should one accept as worthy of emphasis in such an important book? There are, of course, many ways to organize a book, including daily devotionals. And there are many themes important enough for a year's worth of inspirational messages.

From the time I was a child I viewed the Bible as the most important book in the world. Mother and Father taught me that. Sabbath school teachers taught me that. Elementary and secondary school teachers taught me that. College teachers taught me that. And seminary professors taught me that.

So it's only natural, I suppose, that the organizing principle for this daily devotional book should be Scripture itself. It seemed to me appropriate to select cogent biblical passages from Genesis to Revelation for meditation. A little calculation indicated that between five and six passages would be needed from each Bible book to cover 365 days in the year. Of course, since some books are more easily gleaned than others, you'll find more than five devotional readings for some books and fewer than five for others.

But what should I emphasize in this book? Should every reading be a variation on one theme? That could get boring after the first few days! So you'll find various themes stressed in this devotional book. I perceive the Bible as a photo album of sorts—with snapshots of God, of the disposition His people should exemplify, and of life itself.

The biblical passages selected for this book are extremely diverse. Although I've included many much-loved texts, some of the passages chosen aren't what most of us would consider personal favorites. Nonetheless, they've played an important role in my thinking about spiritual matters—about who God is, His relationship with us, and our relationship with Him. I hope that you'll find these scriptural passages significant for your spiritual growth also.

I found it a challenge to encapsulate my understanding of a Bible verse or story in under 400 words, and some of what I've discovered in Scripture may come as a surprise to you—just as it astonished me. However, I've tried to adhere strictly to what the biblical writers said, drawing implications from the details.

I now commit this photo album of God and His people into your hands. Most of all, I hope that these readings will help you spiritually. The book will also be a success if some readings stimulate you intellectually. A daily devotional book that speaks to both heart and mind should surely be worth reading. May God's Spirit make it so!

—*Richard W. Coffen*

Do You Get It?

Now all these things happened unto them for ensamples: and they are written for our admonition, upon whom the ends of the world are come.
1 Cor. 10:11.

It may have happened in geometry class. The teacher explained a theorem, and Henry mumbled, "I don't get it." The teacher tried again, and Henry beamed, "Oh, I get it!" Or perhaps a classmate told a joke, and everyone laughed but Sally, who whimpered, "I don't get it." Someone had to explain the joke, and Sally finally announced, "Oh, I get it!"

Sometimes when I read a philosophy book, I'll say to myself, "I don't get it." Other times a light will flood the shadows of my dim mind, and I'll think, *I get it!* Good books are like that—even a good story book. At the end readers should say, "Oh, I get it!"

Writers have a point of view to get across. When we read what they wrote, we should have an "encounter with the text." We should be able to "get" what they intended. Sometimes, through interaction with the text, we may even "get" more than what was intended. And we will probably lay the book down with a different "take-away" than someone else; benefits vary from person to person. We call the writing/giving and the reading/taking "communication."

There should always be some "take-away" for us—something that challenges us, influencing our lives. And that's especially true when it comes to reading the Bible. We who believe that it is God's Word should find valuable "take-away" as a result of our study. Ideally, when we "get it," we've come to understand the author's intended point, though we often walk away with much more. I suspect that's what makes Scripture the living Word of God, despite its having been encoded with ink on paper. Paul said Scripture was given to us as an example and for our admonition. When we read it, we should end up saying, "Oh, I get it!"

In the pages of this book I'm going to share with you some of my "take-away" from Scripture. I'm not a Bible scholar; I reserve that term for my friends who have devoted their lives to that discipline. Although a pastor by training and an editor by vocation, I've also had some training in biblical interpretation. I hope that what I "get" from reading the Bible just might help you exclaim, "Oh! I get it!"

God Is Our
First Truth

*In the beginning God created
the heaven and the earth.
Gen. 1:1.*

When we begin reading God's Word, we notice that the writers assumed God's existence. We find no philosophical discussions about whether or not He exists. Such pursuits were the domain of Greek philosophers and their successors. What we do find, however, are insights into the character of the Hebrew God known as YHWH ("Lord"). Think of the Bible as an album of snapshots of God "taken" by the various writers. Some of the pictures may be clearer than others, but they all afford us insights into what God is like.

Yes, the authors of Scripture took God's existence for granted. Everything they said—and did—was predicated on the idea that God *is*. (And that's the way believers have behaved ever since, including those of us who read these daily devotional books.) God for those ancient Hebrews—and for us—is what philosophers call a "first truth." And when it comes to everyday living, we, as well as the Bible writers, live in His presence.

In addition to presupposing God's existence, the opening verse of Holy Writ asserts that He created. All of us recognize that scientists and even theologians have invested a lot of time and energy into arguing over when and how Planet Earth was made. Yet even those biblical scholars whom we might call "evolutionists" affirm that God is Creator.

Whatever else we may mean when we identify God as Creator, at the least that claim entails that we and our environment are contingent. Our existence depends on Another. We did not originate ourselves. Neither we nor any other life form on earth made our environment, our world, our cosmos. (Now that it exists we can, of course, affect it for good or evil, thereby transforming it into a better and safer or worse and more dangerous place to live.)

The truth that God is Creator helps us to see ourselves in proper perspective. On the one hand, we can legitimately conclude that we have value because God Himself made us. On the other hand, we should recognize that we aren't all that independent! We aren't self-originating or self-sustaining. As the apostle Paul told the Athenians: "In [God] we live, and move, and have our being" (Acts 17:28).

God—not you or I—is the Creator. Let us rejoice!

God at Work, 1

And God said, Let there be light: and there was light.
And God saw the light, that it was good. . . . And the
evening and the morning were the first day.
Gen. 1:3-5.

You know the rest of the story, of course. The same pattern recurs. It's almost boring! Can you hear the metronome ticking away in the background as you read this Creation story?

Everything happens like clockwork. God speaks. Light appears. It is good. It is the first day. Tick tock. God speaks. The waters are gathered together, and dry land appears. It is good. It is the second day. Tick tock. God speaks. Plants sprout. It is good. It is the third day. Tick tock. God speaks. The heavenly bodies appear. It is good. It is the fourth day. Tick tock. God speaks. Life forms fill the waters. It is good. It is the fifth day. Tick tock. God speaks. Air and land animals appear, including humans. It is good. It is the sixth day. Tick tock.

This account makes God's work as Creator sound too easy! He merely utters a few words, and the elements essential for life on our planet appear. The God portrayed here is powerful. His creative work takes place effortlessly. What could involve the expenditure of less energy than merely enunciating a few words that then have a miraculous effect?

And this Creator God is so proficient! Despite the intricate ecosystems and life forms that sprang into existence at His word, there was no trial and error. There was no, "Oops! That elephant needs only one trunk. Let's try that again." At the end of each creative session He was so pleased with the result of His command of "Let there be . . ." that His inspection always ended with ". . . it was good."

Oh, that I could be so efficient! I struggle to make things. I experience many false starts—even when I think that I've thought things through in advance. In my workshop there's a lot of waste, and the results of my efforts are quite crude. I'm a klutz!

But not so with the God pictured in the first chapter of Genesis. He's the complete expert, the connoisseur of perfection—an unimaginably powerful genius! His creativity results in a biosphere that is good in all respects. And He does it all without breaking a sweat! That's the kind of God we worship!

God at Work, 2

The Lord God formed man of the dust of the ground, and breathed into his nostrils the breath of life. . . . And out of the ground the Lord God formed every beast of the field, and every fowl of the air; and brought them unto Adam to see what he would call them.
Gen. 2:7-19.

Now events happen more casually; the colors seep outside the precise lines of Genesis 1.

In chapter 1 God appears aloof, speaking all into existence as He stands somewhere in remote space. But in Genesis 2 He kneels in the dirt and becomes intimately involved in the creative process.

In Genesis 1 these verbs represent God's creativity: "created," "said," "saw," "divided," "called," "made," "set," and "blessed." Genesis 2 uses stronger verbs: "formed" (molded), "breathed," "planted," "put" (set down), "made" (caused to sprout), "took" (settled), "commanded," "brought" (carried or led), "caused" (knocked out), "closed up," "made" (built), and "brought."

God does a lot of talking in chapter 1. But in chapter 2, much more active, He says little, speaking only twice—once to Himself and once commanding the first man.

And unlike God's gratification in Genesis 1 that all was good, here when God reviewed the situation, it was "not good" (Gen. 2:18), because the first person was alone. So He set about to rectify the situation. How? We all know that He made a woman from a rib He cut out of the first man. But most of us overlook that this was God's *final* attempt to change the "not good" into the "good." Prior to that last—and successful—attempt, God started molding from the dirt (the same process by which He created the first man) animals and birds. "But for Adam there was not found an help meet for him" (verse 20).

Each of these stories provides an important snapshot of God.

Genesis 1 shows us a wise, sedate, powerful Technician. In Genesis 2 we see a God who is intimately and personally involved in His creative work, getting His hands dirty molding the first man, and the animals and birds, from clay. He even gets His fingers bloodied as He cuts open Adam, removing a rib and building (yes, that's the word used here) Eve from it. He is a personal, hands-on, roll-up-your-sleeves Do-it-Yourselfer personally involved with each of us.

Bad News

And the Lord God called unto Adam, and said unto him, Where art thou? Gen. 3:9.

Scripture calls the garden where God placed Adam and Eve "Eden," which means "pleasure." Their new home was blissful, until . . . Having been enticed by the serpent, Eve ate the forbidden fruit in violation of the one and only prohibition in the garden of delight. And when she shared the fruit with her husband, he tasted it also.

What a small thing—a mouthful of fruit! Yet despite the "size" of their disobedience, the first pair instantly felt guilt, swiftly followed by a series of strange—even bizarre—effects.

First, they became aware of their nakedness. Where would they have gotten the idea that there was something deficient in being nude? That condition, after all, was all they knew.

Second, when God came to visit them, they hid in the woods.

Third, when He asked what they'd done, they refused to accept personal accountability. Adam blamed Eve, whom God had given him, as the troublemaker. She insisted that it was the serpent's fault.

Fourth, after God had made them clothing from animal pelts and decided to expel them from the garden of delight, He had to *drive* them from Eden (verse 24). This is the same verb that elsewhere describes what hornets would do to the Hivites—force them to flee (Ex. 23:28). Apparently the guilty couple didn't leave Eden freely!

Fifth, having seen their truculence, God felt that He must station cherubim to "keep the way of the tree of life" (Gen. 3:24) so that Adam and Eve would not sneak back into the garden and gain access to the tree of life.

Sixth, once Cain and Abel had matured, in a fit of rage Cain murdered Abel. And by the time of Noah, "every imagination . . . was only evil continually" (Gen. 6:5).

I can't understand how perfect people could degenerate so quickly. The effects seem disproportionate to their cause. Yet whenever we watch the evening news the results of the Fall are obvious; the reality of evil has become one of the most often used arguments against God's existence!

Thankfully, God didn't immediately inflict the death penalty upon humanity. Instead, He initiated the "plan of salvation." And *that* is truly good news!

Almost Obedient

Abram departed, as the Lord had spoken unto him.
Gen. 12:4.

Terah, an idolater (Joshua 24:2, 14), lived in Chaldean Ur—a center for the worship of the moon god Sin. For some untold reason, Terah decided to move his entire clan to Canaan (Gen. 11:31). However, the trip got delayed when they reached the Mesopotamian city of Haran, another center of moon worship. While there, Terah died at age 205 (verse 32).

Following his father's death, Abram received specific instructions from YHWH. Abram was to do three things, and God would do five things. Abram was to (1) go from his native land, (2) leave his relatives, and (3) depart Terah's household. God would (1) guide Abram to a new land, (2) turn his offspring into a great nation, (3) bless Abram, (4) give him a great name, and (5) bless Abram's allies and curse his enemies (Gen. 12:1-3). Abram was to turn his back on his national identity, kinfolk, and a high standard of living. He was about to be uprooted from all that was near and dear.

Abram made the necessary plans, packed all his possessions, and at 75 years of age headed out on a 450-mile trek to Canaan. "This is the first human journey that is not a punishment" (David W. Cotter, *Berit Olam, Genesis*, p. 89).

"Abram departed, *as the Lord had spoken unto him*" (verse 4). But wait! Something isn't quite right here. Whereas Abram's physical *departure* may have been in harmony with YHWH's command, Abram didn't obey to the letter. The next part of the verse tells us that "Lot went with him" (see also verse 5). Lot was, as you recall, Abram's fatherless but adult nephew, who also owned large herds. Abram didn't leave him behind with the rest of the kinfolk, as God had instructed.

This was, however, merely the first time that Abram didn't obey YHWH explicitly and took matters into his own hands. Yet God remained true to Abram/Abraham. Despite Abram's less-than-perfect obedience during his remaining 100 years as he roamed throughout Canaan, he and God became so close that Abram was later given the nickname "friend of God" (James 2:23; 2 Chron. 20:7; Isa. 41:8). And those of us who love Jesus can also rest assured that God is our friend (John 16:27; the verb used here is *philéo*, friend)—despite our shortcomings.

Abraham Teaches God a Lesson in Ethics

Why, you would be treating the innocent and the guilty exactly the same! Surely you wouldn't do that! Should not the Judge of all the earth do what is right? Gen. 18:25, NLT.

A braham was enjoying a siesta in the door of his tent when suddenly he looked up and saw three "men" standing there—God Himself and two angels, out and about in the noontime sun.

Abraham, with understatement and self-deprecation, invited them to linger while he fetched "a *little* water" for their grimy feet and a "*morsel* of bread" "to comfort [their] hearts" (verses 4, 5).

Abraham's household shifted into high gear to prepare a feast. Sarah used 20 quarts of semolina to make pita bread. Abraham rounded up a fattened calf, handing it to a slave to butcher and roast. Along with cheese (curds) and milk, Abraham set the huge piles of flatbread and veal before the guests.

After eating and drinking their fill, God and the two angels stood up to continue their journey. Abraham accompanied them for a distance—to show them the way. The two angels turned and headed toward Sodom, but God and Abraham remained together. God explained that He'd come to investigate Sodom, with the intent to destroy it.

Since Lot and his family resided there, Abraham became deeply concerned. Surely God had forgotten His morals! It wouldn't be right to destroy good people along with the bad. So Abraham figured he'd better teach God a lesson in ethics. He did so by reminding God that it would be morally repugnant to destroy people without regard to their character. That's the whole idea behind Abraham's carefully chosen words, which he said twice, "Far be it from thee." And he added, "Shall not the Judge of all the earth do right?" (verse 25).

Abraham then extracted from God promise after promise that if 50, 45, 30, 20, or even 10 good people lived in Sodom, He'd spare the entire city. Then "the Lord went on his way . . . , and Abraham returned to his tent" (verse 33, NLT).

What an interesting snapshot of God! He willingly let Abraham lecture Him on ethics! And God granted concession after concession upon Abraham's persistence. And that's the God we serve. He listens . . . to reason . . . from His creatures.

God's Strange Command and Its Stranger-Yet Fallout

Take your son, your only son, Isaac, whom you love, and go to the region of Moriah. Sacrifice him there as a burnt offering.
Gen. 22:2, NIV.

Can you imagine receiving a command from God in the middle of the night to offer your child as a sacrifice? I can't.

Since we're familiar with this gut-wrenching story, I won't go into the details. However, we often overlook the details of geography embedded in this story and its immediate context.

When Abraham received these instructions, he resided at Beer-sheba (Gen. 21:33). God told him to go to Moriah. If Moriah was in the vicinity of Jerusalem, as some believe, Abraham and Isaac's trip covered about 50 miles. Scripture tells us it involved a three-day journey. After the episode at Moriah, Abraham retraced his steps to Beer-sheba, where he continued to live (Gen. 22:19).

The next geographical tidbit is found in Genesis 23:1, 2, which tells us that Sarah died when she was 127 years old . . . in the town of Kirjath-arba, which later was known as Hebron. "Abraham *came* to mourn for Sarah" (verse 2), from which it's possible to infer that he made the 30-mile trip from Beer-sheba, where he dwelt, to Hebron, where Sarah died.

Scripture says nothing about Isaac's being there to help bury his mother. We do learn, though, another piece of geographical information in chapter 24. Isaac was living at Beer Lahai-roi (verse 62). It's possible, maybe even probable, that the site known as 'Ain-Gedeirat (also known as 'Ain Qedeis) is ancient Kadesh. It's situated 47 miles southwest of Beer-sheba.

Do you get the picture? Abraham returned to Beer-sheba; Sarah died at Hebron, 30 miles north of Beer-sheba, so Abraham had to "come" or "go" there (the Hebrew verb in 23:2 can mean either); and Isaac lived at Beer Lahai-roi, 47 miles south of Beer-sheba.

Apparently after the episode at Moriah, Abraham's family split up. He stayed at Beer-sheba, Sarah headed some 30 miles north, and Isaac settled nearly 50 miles south. Might it be that Abraham's obedience to God's command was more than the family could endure?

Religious commitment sometimes has that effect. Jesus said, "If any man come to me, and hate not his father, and mother, and wife, and children, and brethren, and sisters, yea, and his own life also, he cannot be my disciple" (Luke 14:26). How strong is your faith . . . and obedience?

Deceiver on the Lam

*This is none other but the house of God,
and this is the gate of heaven.
Gen. 28:17.*

Isaac spoiled Esau; Rebekah spoiled Jacob. As the boys grew older, they chose different lifestyles. Esau, a rough and ready hunter, married heathen girls: Judith, Basemath, and Mahalath. Jacob, a shepherd, married two Mesopotamian cousins: Leah and Rachel.

Esau disregarded his birthright, which he sold to Jacob for a bowl of lentil stew. Later when Isaac thought he was dying, he asked Esau to hunt down and prepare venison, at which time he'd bless the older twin. But while Esau was doing his father's bidding, Rebekah schemed to have Jacob impersonate Esau.

With Mother's help, Jacob brought food to blind Isaac, who suspected a ruse. Jacob, however, kept misleading his father by insisting that he was indeed Esau. Isaac, still apprehensive, felt and smelled Jacob, who felt and smelled like Esau, thanks to Rebekah's help. Isaac ate the meat and uttered a generous blessing over Jacob, assuming that Jacob was Esau.

Hardly had Jacob left Isaac's presence, having received the lavish blessing, than Esau arrived. Both Isaac and Esau felt deeply upset over the hoax that Jacob had perpetrated, but there was no retracting the blessing. Seventy-seven-year-old Esau bawled like a baby, and Isaac managed to concoct a lame blessing for him.

Esau vowed to murder Jacob, so Rebekah and Isaac came up with the charade that Jacob must flee to Haran so that he could find a wife there among his kinfolk. Just before Jacob started his long trek, Isaac blessed him a second time. Just how many blessings did Jacob need? He'd wangled the birthright from Esau, and now he'd received two blessings from Father.

More than 50 miles from home Jacob settled down for the night at Bethel. He dreamed of a ramp (or staircase) that connected earth to heaven, upon which angels were gliding up and down. YHWH stood at the top and promised Jacob that he was the recipient of the blessings previously given to Abraham.

God chooses the most unlikely heroes! Jacob, who had grown up in a dysfunctional family, had taken advantage of his twin brother, and had deceived Isaac, would carry on the covenant God had made with Abraham.

With that in mind, surely there's hope for you and me!

Prayer Warrior

You have fought with God . . . and have prevailed.
Gen. 32:28, NET.

Jacob was returning to Canaan from Haran and about to meet Esau, and Jacob was downright scared! The thought of this imminent encounter drove him to his knees—not a bad idea for Jacob or for us, especially if fear is not our only motivator for speaking with God.

In anguish of mind Jacob pleaded, "O Lord, please rescue me from my brother, Esau. I am afraid that he is coming to kill me, along with my wives and children. But you promised to treat me kindly and to multiply my descendants" (verses 11, 12, NLT).

Having offered this petition, Jacob separated his family into two groups, sent them across the river Jabbok, and spent the night by himself on the other shore of the Jabbok. Sensing the presence of someone else in the darkness, Jacob tackled the Intruder. All night long they wrestled. First one and then the other would gain the ascendancy, grappling with half nelsons, full nelsons, hammerlocks, piledrivers, and other maneuvers.

Just before dawn God conceded the match to Jacob, who in awe said afterward, "I have seen God face to face" (verse 30).

What do we make of this unparalleled wrestling contest in which 97-year-old Jacob bested God? I suppose much could be said.

However, I regard this encounter as being the embodiment of irony. First, Jacob had been met by angels (verse 1). Second, he'd asked for deliverance. And third, God appeared in person to him. Have you ever had God appear in the flesh, so to speak, after you've asked Him for deliverance? I doubt it. But that's what happened in this story.

And did Jacob welcome God with open arms? No. Instead he put Him in a wrestling hold, earning him the title of a prayer warrior. Actually, I dislike that term because it makes it sound as though in prayer we have to pummel God into submission. Jacob, the original prayer warrior, fought with God . . . and won! But he needn't have done that. God had come in response to his prayer.

How many times do we not recognize God's answer to our prayers, refusing to acknowledge it for what it is?

Why So Sheepish?

*Esau ran to meet him, and embraced him,
and fell on his neck and kissed him.
Gen. 33:4, NRSV.*

The news that Esau was approaching with a posse of 400 was disconcerting. So Jacob, feeling insecure, decided to send Esau a present—550 animals, including goats, sheep, camels, cows, and donkeys! But Jacob didn't deliver them all at once; he sent them in nine waves—one herd, then a gap, another herd, followed by another gap, etc.

Having inundated Esau with livestock, Jacob kept bowing himself "to the ground seven times, until he came near" (verse 3). But Esau, weeping, ran to his twin brother and hugged him.

When Esau asked about the farm animals sent to him, Jacob called him his master and explained that they were a gift of peace. Esau replied, "I have enough, my brother; keep what you have for yourself" (verse 9, NKJV).

Jacob begged, "If I find favor with you, then accept my present . . . ; for truly to see your face is like seeing the face of God" (verse 10, NRSV).

Esau accepted the gift, but he proposed that they travel together, with his 400 scouts leading the way. Jacob, however, refused Esau's bighearted gesture. Esau then offered to lend him some of the 400 men, but Jacob turned that down also. Then he lied to Esau (what else was new?), saying that he'd meet him in Seir (verse 14). "But Jacob journeyed to Succoth" (verse 17, NRSV). And the brothers met again only at Isaac's funeral.

Esau genially bent over backwards, constantly offering to assist his brother. But every time he reached out to Jacob, his graciousness was spurned—even though Jacob had been begging Esau to be gracious toward him!

There may be many reasons Jacob behaved that way—even in the face of Esau's forgiving spirit. It seems clear to me, though, that although Esau had forgiven Jacob, Jacob hadn't forgiven himself. His overly self-effacing actions tell me that Jacob was still nursing a guilty conscience, which is always a barrier to reconciliation. Forgiveness has two aspects—what others do to and for the guilty, and what the guilty do to and for themselves.

Spoiled Rotten

Israel loved Joseph more than all his other
sons, for he was the son of his old age,
and he had a decorated tunic made for him.
Gen. 37:3, New Jerusalem.

Joseph was Jacob's pet, and the most obvious evidence of Jacob's bias was the robe that he had tailored for his darling son. The Hebrew expression for this garment has been variously translated as "coat of many colours" (KJV), "long tunic" (NAB), "richly ornamented robe" (NIV), "long robe with sleeves" (NRSV), etc. E. A. Speiser has pointed out that "there [is not] anything remarkable about either colors or sleeves" (*Genesis, Anchor Bible*, p. 289). Colored clothing and long robes with or without sleeves were commonplace in the ancient Near East.

What was this special attire? The only other time the same Hebrew words (*k͑tonet passīm*) appear in Scripture is in a passage about King David's daughter. She wore the same garment, which was what all the king's virgin daughters wore (2 Sam. 13:18, 19). Cuneiform documents refer to a piece of clothing called *kitû* (or *kutinnû*) *pišannu*. During religious ceremonies this robe was wrapped around the shoulders of female idols.

In short, the only known instances of this expression referred to women's clothing, making one wonder if Jacob's favoritism had the effect of effeminizing Joseph, who had to wear what might have looked like showy female clothing with sequins attached.

Seventeen-year-old Joseph's behavior was also offensive. He ratted on his brothers Dan, Naphtali, Gad, and Asher (Gen. 37:2). Later he had two dreams in which his brothers and parents bowed down to him. And instead of keeping his mouth shut, Joseph blabbed to everyone about his dreams. Even Jacob got upset and scolded his child (verse 10).

People have argued for centuries about what shapes one's personality—nature or nurture. Today we recognize that both genetics *and* environment are important to the formation of one's personality. Here and in the next reading we focus on Joseph's upbringing, which surely must have been a handicap for him. However, we aren't prisoners to either DNA or surroundings, as powerful as they are. God created us with free will, which means there's yet another factor that contributes to who we are. Here's the formula: chromosomes + circumstances + choices = character.

Look on the Bright Side

*Tell my father about all the honor accorded me
in Egypt and about everything you have seen.
And bring my father down here quickly.*
Gen. 45:13, NIV.

Poor Joseph! First, his father spoiled him. Second, his brothers hated him. Third, his doting father bawled him out. Fourth, his brothers threw him into a dried-up cistern to die. Fifth, they changed their minds and sold him to itinerant merchants. Sixth, in Egypt the merchants auctioned him off as a slave to Potiphar. Seventh, Potiphar's wife falsely accused Joseph. Eighth, Potiphar threw him—an innocent man—into the dungeon. Ninth, the butler, who held Joseph's only "Get Out of Jail Free" card, forgot about him for "two full years" (Gen. 41:1). Have I forgotten anything?

Joseph's conditions couldn't have been much worse. However, as a result of exercising his power of choice, combined with providence, he ended up as vizier of Egypt. Second only to Pharaoh himself, Joseph was given an Egyptian name, Zaphnath-paaneah, as well as the king's signet ring, a gold collar, and royal vestments woven from fine linen (verse 42). He rode about in the royal chariot, accompanied by a herald who commanded all bystanders to kneel (verse 43).

Because of Joseph's prudent administration, the Egyptians survived an unusually severe famine that scourged the ancient Near East for seven years. "Moreover, all the world came to Joseph in Egypt to buy grain" (verse 57, NRSV).

Eventually 10 of Joseph's brothers trekked to Egypt to buy food rations. And when they appeared before the "Egyptian" vizier, they "bowed themselves before him with their faces to the ground" (Gen. 42:6, NRSV). For Joseph, uh, Zaphnath-paaneah, it was déjà vu. And after two trips into Egypt for provisions, accompanied by hair-raising events resulting from the vizier's machinations, Joseph's entire family—66 persons in all (Gen. 46:26)—moved to Egypt.

Regardless of the details in the chain of cause-and-effect circumstances throughout Joseph's life, God in His amazing creativity brought good out of what seemed to be misfortune. Joseph may have been a spoiled brat. He may have "asked for it" by the way he treated his brothers. Nevertheless, when divine will and human will unite, we can surmount our circumstances—even compensating for our faulty genetics.

The Miracle Workers

Now there arose a new king over Egypt,
who did not know Joseph.
Ex. 1:8, NKJV.

Let the good times roll! Joseph was alive. Jacob and family moved to Egypt. Pharaoh insisted that they settle in the "best of the land" (Gen. 47:6).

Then came a pharaoh "who did not know Joseph" (Ex. 1:8, NKJV). The Israelite men were forced into the corvée. (Later, when Moses told Pharaoh to let God's people go, he made them scrounge around for straw for the bricks they manufactured.)

Still the Hebrews multiplied like proverbial rabbits. So Pharaoh summoned the Israelite midwives, Shiphrah and Puah, ordering them to kill all newborn males (verses 15, 16). Yet despite his "best" efforts at population control, the Hebrew population burgeoned. Pharaoh then told the Israelite parents that they must toss their neonatal boys into the Nile River.

This was no time to get pregnant, but Jochebed and Amram learned they were to have yet another baby. This Hebrew family despised infanticide, so they hid the baby boy. Eventually the child began making so much noise that they could no longer conceal him. To avoid trouble, they complied with the letter of Pharaoh's injunction—they put the baby in the Nile. Oh, but I failed to mention one small detail. The baby was secure in a watertight basket.

We usually crave big, spectacular miracles. We admire magnificent miracle workers such as Elijah and Elisha and Jesus, who performed stunning feats that leave us amazed. But that's not what happened in this first story of the book of Exodus.

Oh, there were miracles aplenty, but they were executed by run-of-the-mill people going about their ordinary everyday lives. Puah and Shiphrah were gutsy enough to disobey Pharaoh, and when he called them to account they blew him away with their rejoinder about Hebrew women being robust. Amram and Jochebed hid their newborn rather than toss him to the Nile crocodiles. Miriam watched over the baby in the basket floating on the river. Pharaoh's daughter went to the Nile for her daily bath, fell in love with the baby in the basket, and adopted him. Jochebed served as wet nurse for the pharaoh's new "grandson."

And so Moses' life was spared by one tiny miracle after another performed by average men and women. God can use you and me to perform miracles also as we go about our routine daily living.

The Doer

*Looking this way and that and seeing no one in sight,
he killed the Egyptian and hid him in the sand.
Ex. 2:12, New Jerusalem.*

Some people are thinkers; some, doers. In just a few minutes thinkers can dream up enough ideas to overwhelm the rest of us. A healthy profit depends upon new products and innovative ways of convincing people to purchase them. The spinning of ideas is essential.

But how does a company design and manufacture new goods and prepare successful marketing and advertising campaigns? Doers make it happen. Doers, however, sometimes get into trouble and even *make* trouble. Doers have no toes, you see, because they pull the trigger before they draw their handgun from its holster. They've shot off all their toes!

Moses was a doer. At 40 years of age he was touring the section of Egypt where the Israelites worked, and "he saw an Egyptian beating a Hebrew" (verse 11, NRSV). Such treatment was not uncommon. Slaves were made to be beaten! There was a time that schoolchildren were beaten to help them "learn." Egyptian scribe Wenemdiamun said to his teacher, "You beat my back; your teaching entered my ear" (*Papyrus Lansing*). "The beating of a boy is like manure to the garden" (*Aramaic Proverbs of Ahiqar* [Syriac version]).

Moses' anger boiled over. "Looking this way and that and seeing no one in sight, he killed the Egyptian and hid him in the sand" (verse 12, New Jerusalem). Like so many criminals, Moses just *had* to revisit the scene of the felony, and found two Hebrews fighting each other. Moses accosted the man who had started the fight, remonstrating, "What do you mean by hitting your kinsman?" (verse 13, New Jerusalem).

The man's retort shocked Moses into realizing that despite his precautions the previous day, someone *had* witnessed the murder: "Do you intend to kill me as you killed the Egyptian?" (verse 14, New Jerusalem). And it wasn't just this aggressive Hebrew who knew what Moses had done. Somehow word reached Pharaoh, who unilaterally pronounced Moses worthy of the death penalty. So he fled Egypt, ending up in the land of Midian (verse 15).

Yes, Moses was a doer. Like most doers he could be rash, but in his impulsiveness he could get things done! God seems to like doers. He chooses them to work for Him. If you're a doer, God most surely has a place for you, but pray that He'll harness your impulsiveness.

The Burning Bush

*"Come no nearer." . . . "Take off your sandals, for
the place where you are standing is holy ground."*
Ex. 3:5, New Jerusalem.

When Moses, a fugitive from justice, arrived in the land of Midian, he
stopped by a well. He had two good reasons for doing so: (1) he was de-
hydrated from his flight through the desert, so it was a good place to slake
his thirst, and (2) wells were places where people gathered, so it was a good
place to meet the locals.

After having defended the seven daughters of a priest of Midian from
bullies at the well, Moses was invited by their father to join their household.
Moses accepted the invitation, and ultimately married Zipporah, one of
Jethro's seven daughters. Caring for his father-in-law's sheep, Moses stayed in
Midian for 40 years.

On a stint with the flock in the wilderness, Moses ended up at Horeb,
"the mountain of God" (verse 1), another name for Sinai. There he saw a
shrub aflame. As he got closer to the spectacle, he noticed that the fire
wasn't consuming the bush.

God's voice boomed from the blaze, telling Moses to remove his sandals
because this was holy ground. He introduced Himself as "the God of thy
father, the God of Abraham, the God of Isaac, and the God of Jacob" (verse
6). Moses removed his footwear and fell on his face.

What do you suppose made the vicinity holy? Had the rocky ground
been holy before the fire flared? Did the ground remain holy once God left
and the fire flickered out? Superstition holds that some places are naturally
hallowed, and the ancient Near East had many such spots.

In Scripture something becomes holy when it's set apart for religious
purposes. Before dedicatory rituals, a person, place, or thing is profane; afterward it's sacred. But we can infer from Scripture another "cause" for holiness.
Something previously unhallowed became holy when God's presence appeared. For instance, the tent tabernacle, which Moses later constructed, became a "sanctuary"—a sacred place—when God's glory hovered over the ark
of the covenant.

And that's how an ordinary person becomes a "saint," a holy person.
Christians become holy not because they've been set aside for religious pur-
poses or because they are sinless, but because God's Holy Spirit indwells them.
And that includes you . . . and me!

19

Within God's Will

*I am sending you to Pharaoh to bring
my people the Israelites out of Egypt.
Ex. 3:10, NIV.*

Among evangelicals, we hear much talk about "being in God's will." The expression implies that because God has from eternity past willed everything that will ever take place, Christians must discover that will and live within it.

Whether one is Calvinistic or Wesleyan, the fruit of this odyssey is often personal vexation. How can I learn what God's precise will is for me? Suppose I don't continuously live within that divine will?

But wait! There's another perspective, one that leads to serenity. Because God is infinite and all-wise, He isn't stymied by our behavior—especially when we open ourselves to His blessing. God is creative enough to achieve His ends even when we exercise our free will in less-than-ideal ways.

That's the way it was with Moses. For most of his first 40 years he was absorbed into the Egyptian lifestyle. He matured in Pharaoh's household. He mastered the Egyptian language. He knew the indigenous mores. He learned the etiquette of the sovereigns. He had an insider's access to the imperial family. He knew what made the pharaohs "tick." To paraphrase what Mordecai later told Esther (Esther 4:14), Moses could say, "Who knoweth whether I am come to the kingdom for such a time as this?"

If he ascended the throne, he could easily have freed the Hebrew slaves. If he never became pharaoh but remained in the court, surely as an insider he could have finessed the exodus of the Israelites from Egypt, without bloodshed and with Egyptian tolerance.

But Moses rashly murdered an Egyptian and had to flee for his life. There could now be no Pharaoh Moses to rescue the Israelites. There could now be no insider leverage for the emancipation of the Hebrew people. And for another 40 years Moses learned how to herd sheep. Possibly, when God sent him back to Egypt, his first 40 years as a royal insider would still put him in good stead, but God would have to bring about the exodus with different methods.

Whatever the means, Moses would be doing God's will. And so He can work with *our* decisions, finding ways to incorporate them within His plans. Divine will can work with human will to bring about ultimate good.

Reticent Prophet

But Moses protested again, "Look, they won't believe me! They won't do what I tell them. They'll just say, 'The Lord never appeared to you.'"
Ex. 4:1, NLT.

M oses was in an argumentative mood.
Moses: "How can you expect me to lead the Israelites out of Egypt?" (Ex. 3:11, NLT). **God:** "I will be with you" (verse 12, NLT). **Moses:** "They will ask, 'Which god are you talking about?'" (verse 13, NLT). **God:** "Tell them, 'I AM has sent me'" (verse 14, NLT).

Moses: "They won't believe me!" (Ex. 4:1, NLT). **God:** "What do you have there in your hand?" (verse 2, NLT). **Moses:** "A shepherd's staff" (verse 2, NLT). **God:** "Throw it down" (verse 3, NLT). It became a viper. "Put your hand inside your robe" (verse 6, NLT). It became leprous.

Moses: "I'm just not a good speaker" (verse 10, NLT). **God:** "Who makes mouths?" (verse 11, NLT). **Moses:** "Send someone else" (verse 13, NLT). **God:** "Aaron will be your spokesman" (verse 16, NLT).

And Jethro, Moses' father-in-law, responded, "Go with my blessing" (verse 18, NLT).

God had won . . . finally.

"Moses took his wife and sons, put them on a donkey, and headed back to . . . Egypt. In his hand he carried the staff of God" (verse 20, NLT). Moses and Aaron teamed up, explaining to the Hebrews God's intention to deliver them. "After this presentation to Israel's leaders, Moses and Aaron went to see Pharaoh. They told him, 'This is what the Lord, the God of Israel, says: "Let my people go"'" (Ex. 5:1, NLT).

It isn't wicked to quarrel with God. Abraham argued with Him overlooking Sodom. Jacob wrestled with God at Jabbok. Moses wrangled with Him here and would do it again when God would say He'd wipe out the Israelites. Mary and Martha scolded Jesus.

We should be honest with God. He knows our innermost feelings anyway, so why not be open? We can't hide our concerns from the all-knowing God! Scripture portrays a Deity who respects candor. Prayer is talking to God as to a friend, and friends sometimes squabble. God expects openness from His friends.

If we're open *with* and *to* God, He'll be open *with* and *to* us.

The Divine Name(s)

To Abraham, Isaac and Jacob I appeared
as El Shaddai, but I did not make my
name Yahweh known to them.
Ex. 6:3, New Jerusalem.

God's name YHWH probably came from an old Hebrew verb for "to be" and may mean "I am who I am," "I will be who I will be," "He causes to be what exists," "the Eternal One," or "the Self-existent One." But He also went by other names.

El and Elohim—These two names are the singular and plural forms of the generic name for god. *El* was also used for the gods of the Mesopotamians, Canaanites, Egyptians, etc.

El Shaddai—Associated with the patriarchs, this name is usually translated "God Almighty." It means God of breasts but with the understanding that breasts here refer to mountains, as in the name Grand Teton National Park. In the ancient Near East, gods were associated with mountains, where they supposedly lived.

El Elyon—Originally it was the name of the god worshipped in heathen Jerusalem before David conquered it. The term means "God most high." Once Jerusalem became the "City of David," *El Elyon* was applied to the Israelite God.

El Olam—This was the name for the Canaanite god worshipped in the vicinity of Beer-sheba. It means "God of eternity." Once Beer-sheba became part of Israelite territory, the name was used of the God of Scripture.

El Berith—This proper name means "God of the covenant." It was the name for the local Canaanite god of Shechem. Like *El Olam,* it came to refer to the biblical God.

Other names for God also appear in the Old Testament.

Early Adventists found the names of the days of the week offensive because they contained the names of heathen deities—*Sun*day, *Moon*day, etc., so they spoke of the first day, second day, third day, etc. Some Adventists today are bothered because Christmas and Easter have pagan roots.

Some Christians make a lot over the various divine names, unaware of the origin of these terms. It seems to me that the names for God show how "liberal" He was, absorbing to Himself the names of heathen deities. Indeed, the biblical God is "liberal" enough to take the names of heathen gods.

The Passover

The blood will be a sign for you on the houses where you are. When I see the blood I shall pass over you, and you will escape the destructive plague when I strike Egypt. Ex. 12:13, New Jerusalem.

After executing signs before Pharaoh and nine devastating plagues upon the land, the time had come for the ultimate showdown between YHWH, the Hebrew God, and Pharaoh.

The tenth plague was imminent—a plague with such shock value that the other plagues looked almost trivial.

The Israelites were to set aside a lamb, which they were to slaughter on the fourteenth of the Hebrew month Nisan. They were to sprinkle the blood on the doorframe, roast the lamb, and at suppertime eat it with bitter herbs. Everyone in the family was to eat this meal standing up, ready to begin their trek to the Promised Land at a moment's notice. Any leftovers were to be burned the next morning.

God threatened: "I will execute judgment against all the gods of Egypt, for I am the Lord" (verse 12, NLT).

"The Israelites then went away and did as Yahweh had ordered Moses and Aaron" (verse 28, New Jerusalem). At midnight the angel of death killed every firstborn in Egypt, man and beast. "And loud wailing was heard throughout the land of Egypt. There was not a single house where someone had not died" (verse 30, NLT).

But as God meted out His judgment upon the Egyptians, the firstborn children of the Israelites were spared. God saw the blood on their doorframes and passed over them. From that time since, Jews have celebrated the Passover annually. And each year they repeat the same words: "Next year in Jerusalem."

Fanny J. Crosby wrote the gospel song "Pass Me Not, O Gentle Savior," which pleads with Jesus to not pass us by, but this was one time God's people hoped and prayed that God would pass by—pass over them.

Paul wrote: "Christ, our Passover Lamb, has been sacrificed for us" (1 Cor. 5:7, NLT). When the blood of Jesus Christ marks our lives, then we can face God's judgment with confidence. The judgment is not something to fear—unless one is not protected by the blood of Jesus. For the saved, the record of sins and their punishment is passed over.

The Song of Moses

Who is like you, O Lord, among the gods?
Who is like you, majestic in holiness,
awesome in splendor, doing wonders?
Ex. 15:11, NRSV.

Pharaoh, who had urged the Hebrews to leave Egypt ASAP, decided he should drag them back as prisoners of war. He thought he had them between a rock and a hard place at the Red Sea (sea of reeds). However, the Israelites crossed to the other side by walking on a dry path through the lake bed, but when Pharaoh's troops followed suit, the waters collapsed on them.

After this spectacular deliverance, Moses—the man who had a hard time with words—burst into song!

Verse 3 sounds a bit strange to our ears at first: "The Lord is a man of war." First, we don't normally refer to YHWH as a "man," but that's what the Hebrew says. Second, we often feel uncomfortable thinking about God as a warrior. We find a similar thought, though, in Isaiah 42:13: "[YHWH] shall stir up His zeal like a man of war. . . . He shall prevail against His enemies" (NKJV). And Psalm 24:8 refers to Him as "the Lord mighty in battle." This really shouldn't surprise us. Often in Scripture God is called the "Lord of hosts." The Hebrew word used is *tsaba'*, which means armed forces.

This picture of a violent deity continues in Moses' song: He "shattered the enemy" (Ex. 15:6, NRSV). He "fell [His] assailants" (verse 7, New Jerusalem). Additionally, Moses sang of God's powerful right hand (verse 6), of the blast of God's nostrils (verse 8), and of His wrath that burned the Egyptians like stubble (verse 7).

But the same violent God is protective of His people. "In [His] faithful love [He] led out the people [He] had redeemed" (verse 13, New Jerusalem). He would "bring them in and plant them on the mountain" (verse 17, New Jerusalem).

The word translated "faithful love" in verse 13 is *hesed*. This Hebrew word is used often of God and refers to His faithfulness to the covenant that He made with His people. He had promised Abraham that he would have many descendants and possess much land. And God repeated these promises when He spoke to Moses (Ex. 6:4-8). God said, "I have remembered my covenant" (verse 5). The time had come for God to make good on His promises.

He keeps His promises. Do you?

The Ten Commandments

Moses was there with the Lord forty days and forty nights. . . . And he wrote on the tablets the words of the covenant—the Ten Commandments. Ex. 34:28, NIV.

Scripture refers to the Decalogue as the covenant God made with the Israelites. Christians call it the moral law—God's revealed will that is universally applicable. Let's take a quick survey to see if the commandments are generic enough to transcend time and culture.

"Thou shalt have no other gods before me. Thou shalt not make unto thee any graven image. . . . Thou shalt not bow down thyself to them" (Ex. 20:3-5). These verses deal with worship, emphasizing the supremacy of YHWH and banning idolatry. Suppose, however, the Decalogue were more specific, commanding the worshipper to offer a lamb. How could Eskimos, who know only about dogs, seals, walruses, whales, and polar bears, worship? How could people in Papua New Guinea and in Amazonia worship? They know nothing about sheep or goats or bulls.

"Remember the sabbath day, to keep it holy. . . . In it thou shalt not do any work" (verses 8-10). Suppose it commanded worshipping at the Mosaic tabernacle or later at the Temple. How could people keep the Sabbath if they didn't live in Jerusalem? Suppose that the fourth commandment defined work. What is work? Is taking a shower work? How about brushing one's teeth or washing dishes? This commandment also is sufficiently nonspecific so that it can apply everywhere.

"Thou shalt not kill" (verse 13). Every time the Hebrew verb translated "kill" is used, it refers to taking human life—murder or manslaughter. Suppose this commandment were more explicit and referred to killing any living thing. We'd not be able to drive our vehicles, because insects hit the windshield and die. We couldn't swat mosquitoes without violating the commandment.

Because of their generality the commandments don't define the prohibited actions. For instance, the local culture must determine what is work, homicide, adultery, and robbery, and what it means to honor parents.

The Decalogue speaks in generalities. Therefore, its prohibitions can be universally applied, because the banned behavior must be defined by and within one's culture. The Decalogue leaves much up to us to define, providing us with a snapshot of God's wisdom and versatility.

A Repentant God

*The Lord repented of the evil which
he thought to do unto his people.
Ex. 32:14.*

A biblical scholar commented: "In Scripture God does more repenting than His people." That may be an overstatement, but there's a core of truth in it. Exodus is only the second book of the Bible, yet God has already repented: "It repented the Lord that he had made man" (Gen. 6:6).

While Moses was atop Mount Sinai, receiving the Decalogue carved into stone, the people at its base became anxious. So they said to Aaron, "Make us some gods who can lead us. This man Moses . . . has disappeared" (Ex. 32:1, NLT).

Aaron suggested that they hand him their earrings, and they readily complied. From this jewelry he carved a golden calf, and the Israelites proclaimed, "O Israel, these are the gods who brought you out of Egypt!" (verse 4, NLT). They hadn't yet seen the stone tablets, but had already violated one of its commandments. The next day they sacrificed "burnt offerings and peace offerings [to the calf]. After this, they celebrated with feasting and drinking, and indulged themselves in pagan revelry" (verse 6, NLT).

God saw what was happening and told Moses that he should descend the mountain. The Israelites "have defiled themselves" (verse 7, NLT), He said. The word God used means they had become rotten. Furthermore, God intended to kill them. "Leave me alone," He told Moses, "so my anger can blaze against them and destroy them all. Then I will make you, Moses, into a great nation instead of them" (verse 10, NLT).

A compliant person would have run. But Moses brazenly began arguing with God, trying to convince Him to not overreact. "Why are you so angry . . . ?" Moses scolded. "The Egyptians will say, 'God tricked them . . . so he could kill them and wipe them from the face of the earth'" (verses 11, 12, NLT). Then Moses spouted some orders! "Turn away from your fierce anger. Change your mind about this terrible disaster you are planning against your people!" (verse 12, NLT). Finally, he urged God to consider His ancient pact. "Remember your covenant with your servants—Abraham, Isaac, and Jacob" (verse 13, NLT).

And God changed His mind! Why? Because Moses spoke up and urged God to cool off and keep His promises. Prayer changes things.

God From Behind

The Lord, . . . merciful and gracious, slow to anger, and abounding in steadfast love and faithfulness, . . . forgiving iniquity.
Ex. 34:6, 7, NRSV.

M oses had brazenly asked: "Show me your glory" (Ex. 33:18, NRSV). God consented, although He explained He could show Moses only His back.

God is *merciful*. The Hebrew comes from the root word for womb. God is described as having a uterus. I suppose we shouldn't take this literally, but the idea is that God resembles a mother, whose gut feeling is that of tender love toward her child(ren). He is "wombish."

God is *gracious*. Whenever this Hebrew adjective is used, it refers to God. It refers to the goodwill a Superior might show toward an inferior. Because the word may come from a word meaning to bow down, it reverses normal courtesy—instead of inferiors prostrating themselves before the Superior, the Superior does the condescending. Anyone with this attribute shows goodwill and favor.

God is *slow to anger*. The Hebrew literally says that God has a long nose. In Hebrew when people got angry, they snorted through their nose. God isn't quick to do this. He puts up with His people for a long time, tolerating their foibles, stupidity, and nastiness.

God *abounds* in . . . The Hebrew word means that God's character teems with the adjectives that follow. They are like the sea in magnitude.

God abounds in *steadfast love*. The Hebrew word means enduring kindness and can be translated "grace" and "cordial assistance." It also means covenant loyalty.

God also abounds in *faithfulness*. The concept is that of firmness or reliability, which makes it similar to "steadfast love." God's love is permanent, although He sometimes must punish.

God *forgives*. The Hebrew word used here means to lift up or to carry. God removes His people's iniquities, transgressions, and sins, carrying them away Himself. Instead of His people having to lug about their load of sin, bearing their own guilt, God lifts it from them, hauling it away Himself.

This is truly a remarkable snapshot of God, especially when we realize that this isn't even His best side!

The Tent of Meeting

The Lord summoned Moses and spoke to him from the tent of meeting, saying: Speak to the people of Israel. Lev. 1:1, NRSV.

The book of Leviticus "sounds" foreign to us. Why?

First, it was a handbook for Hebrew priests, which we aren't. (Despite its title, the book wasn't addressed to the Levites, but to the priests. The book mentions Levites only once, in Leviticus 25:32-34.)

Second, we no longer offer animal sacrifices, and would consider it repugnant if God suddenly were to tell us that we should do exactly as Leviticus specifies. Although Leviticus explicitly states that atonement and forgiveness result from the slaughter of animals, to us it appears to be a disgustingly violent means to achieve those ends.

Nonetheless, if we put our minds to it, we can gain a "blessing" when we read Leviticus.

In the first verse of Leviticus YHWH is active. He "summoned Moses" (NLT). The Hebrew verb is the one used when someone was cowering in fear. Why might Moses have been cringing? After all, He was always quite bold with God. Exodus 40:34 helps us understand why Moses was acting so out of character: "The cloud covered the tent of meeting, and the glory of the Lord filled the tabernacle" (RSV). The construction work was completed. Now the visible sign of God's acceptance—His presence—descended like a cloud, filling the tabernacle with His glory and thereby turning the tabernacle (dwelling place) into the sanctuary (holy place).

God's voice boomed from "the tent of meeting." In the ancient Near East, tents were used as housing for gods. In Canaan, where the Israelites were headed, El (their chief deity) lived in a tent. El also had an assembly that met with him from time to time—probably in the tent where he lived. In the case of the Hebrew people, YHWH resided in the tent Moses had built, but instead of it being a place where God conferred with a congress of supernatural beings, it was here where He met with Moses and the Israelites.

The Mosaic tabernacle, with the Shekinah presence of YHWH hovering over the ark of the covenant in the Most Holy Place, visibly said, "God is with us." And the sense was twofold. First, "God is with us" can imply physical presence—God is here . . . in this place. Second, "God is with us" can have a psychological sense—God is on our side . . . He's for us.

The Message
From the Tent

Bring [your sacrificial animal] . . .
for acceptance in your behalf.
Lev. 1:31, NRSV.

L et's briefly summarize the tent of meeting and its furnishings.

First, the courtyard was inside a fabric wall. Outside the curtain, the land had no particular significance. Inside, the land was where the Hebrews brought their animal offerings.

Second, there was a curtained-off room called the holy place. This area was considered more sacred than the courtyard. Only priests could enter the holy place.

Third, the Most Holy Place was the holiest of the three sacred spaces. Whereas any priest could minister in the holy place, only the High Priest had access to the Most Holy Place, and only once a year on the Day of Atonement.

Each special area had its own furnishings.

A large bronze altar of burnt offering stood within the courtyard. Here the slaughtered animals were burned. Between this altar and the draped entryway to the holy place was a bronze laver, a basin in which the priests washed their hands and feet prior to their ministrations.

The holy place contained three ritual items made of gold: a table of showbread (bread of the presence), an altar of incense, and a lampstand. With no windows in the fabric walls, the holy place was quite dark, illuminated (making the ministrations of the priests possible) only with light from the flickering oil lamps, possibly symbolizing the Holy Spirit, who makes possible the work of salvation. The cakes of showbread were changed each Sabbath and apparently symbolized God, the source of life. Incense was burned on the golden altar as an accompaniment to prayers.

The Most Holy Place housed a single piece of furniture—the ark of the covenant. Inside the ark were the stone tables of the Decalogue. The ark was covered with a lid on which stood two cherubim with bowed heads—the "mercy seat," a symbol of God's throne.

Much speculation has gone into the "meaning" of the elements constituting the sanctuary. Some interpretation is pure allegorization. Perhaps it's better to paint with a larger brush. The sanctuary (later the Temple) indicates that all heaven is organized for our salvation, and maybe that's all we need to know.

Atonement and Forgiveness

*"The burnt offering . . . shall be
acceptable." "You shall be forgiven."
Lev. 1:4; 5:10, NRSV.*

L eviticus provides details about the Hebrew sacrificial system—which animals to offer, how the carcasses should be disposed of, and how the sacrificial blood should be ministered.

In our most sober moments we shudder at such a "primitive" system of
rituals that included slitting the throat of an animal, dismembering it, burning most of the carcass, and splashing its blood around. It's true, of course,
that the offering of animals as sacrifices is not only archaic but also not
unique to the Hebrew people. Even in certain indigenous religions today animals are still ritually slaughtered.

At this remove, we sometimes disparage the sacrificial system, suggesting that it was in reality ineffective. We may assume that such barbaric pro-
cedures are unproductive. But that's not the testimony found in the book of
Leviticus, where again and again we read that as a result of sacrificing an animal, atonement was effected and people experienced forgiveness. We may
disagree with that judgment, but in doing so, we're at variance with the explicit statements of Leviticus.

Also among some Adventists I've known, there has been a rather romantic view of the Mosaic tabernacle and the later Temple(s). With all the shim-
mering of gold and glistening of bronze and wafting of incense, people have
a tendency to idealize these institutions.

In reality, however, the Israelite center of worship was a stinking, messy place.

Animal flesh was incinerated on the altar of burnt offerings. Have you ever
smelled burning flesh? (If your physician has ever cauterized one of your body
parts, you understand what I mean.) And the incense could be overpowering. (If
you've attended a Mass in which incense was burned, you know what I'm talking about.) The Israelite incense must have perfused the air for miles around!

Priests splashed blood on the horns of the altar of burnt offering and
poured it around the base of the same altar, splattered it onto the veil separating the holy place from the Most Holy Place, and sprinkled it over the
mercy seat on the Day of Atonement.

The sanctuary was gross! Dealing with sin is not cute or pretty. Just think
of Jesus hanging on the cross!

Unclean Foods

I am the Lord your God; . . . be holy, for I am holy. You shall not defile yourselves with any swarming thing that moves on the earth.
Lev. 11:44, NRSV.

The Israelites were allowed to eat (1) mammals that had cloven hooves and chewed the cud, (2) fish with both fins and scales, and (3) specifically identified flying creatures. Various explanations have been proposed to explain these rules, but each appears to be flawed.

Some argue that "unclean" creatures cause disease. But wait! Pork may cause trichinosis, but only if it isn't thoroughly cooked. Animals identified as "clean" have also produced illnesses. Others suggest that the banned animals are unaesthetic, having dirty habits. "Unclean" pigs wallow in mud. Yet what can be dirtier than "clean" sheep with fecal-matted wool? Another explanation is that the proscribed birds eat carrion. But so do chickens, which are "clean."

Leviticus gives the reason for the distinction. The Israelites were to eat only "clean" animals because they were to be holy as God is holy—a religious reason. But how could dividing animals into clean and unclean categories promote holiness?

Some have pointed out that differentiating between "clean" and "unclean" helps maintain the order of the cosmos. Dirt is matter out of place. Holiness means keeping everything in its place. The taboo animals are atypical and are thereby out of place. By not eating them, the Israelites helped to maintain the divinely ordered cosmos. Details of this explanation have also come under severe criticism. However, the point that holds is that maintaining a differentiation between the "clean" and "unclean" animals was one way the Israelites would be holy.

Early Adventists argued over the ongoing validity of Leviticus 11. Stephen Haskell urged compliance with these rules. James White reasoned that Christ did away with the distinction between "clean" and "unclean" meat. Wouldn't acceptance of the "clean" and "unclean" distinctions in chapter 11 logically require us to abide by the other "clean" and "unclean" distinctions elsewhere in Leviticus? After a long struggle, consensus was that we should eat the "clean" and not eat the "unclean" meats, although Adventists haven't officially held that flesh foods should be "kosher" in the strictest sense.

Those of us who have chosen a vegetarian diet need not worry if ignoring the "clean" and "unclean" differentiation is sinful.

Covenant Remembered

Then will I remember my covenant with Jacob;
I will remember also my covenant with Isaac
and also my covenant with Abraham.
Lev. 26:42, NRSV.

God spelled out positive and negative reinforcements for conformity to His covenant.

Positive reinforcements—"If you . . . keep my commandments . . . , I will give you your rains in their season, and the land shall yield its produce" (Lev. 26:3, 4, NRSV).

There would be peace in the land (verse 6). Predatory animals would vanish (verse 6). If war broke out, ratios of victory would be astounding: one Hebrew would rout 20 and pursue 100 (verse 8). The number of Israelites would mushroom (verse 9). God would pitch His tent with them, walking among them (verse 11).

Negative reinforcements—If they broke the covenant, diseases would plague them (verse 16). They would plant crops, but their enemies would reap them (verse 16). Foreign soldiers would overrun the land (verse 17). Drought would cause crop failures (verses 19, 20). Ravaging beasts would kill children and livestock (verse 22). God's people would resort to cannibalism to fend off starvation (verse 29). The land would turn desolate, and the people would be scattered to other countries (verses 32, 33). Displaced Israelites would be so paranoid that a rustling leaf would terrify them (verse 36).

However, regardless of how degenerate they would become, God remained alert for repentance. "If they confess their iniquity . . . then will I remember my covenant with Jacob . . . with Isaac . . . and . . . with Abraham, and I will remember the land" (verses 40-42, NRSV).

All these blessings and cursings depended on the land having its sabbaths. Land was precious because there was only a finite amount. It was regarded as a limited good. YHWH claimed to own the land, but He allowed it to be parceled out among His stewards. To mistreat the land (by not observing its sabbaths), therefore, was tantamount to insulting God.

Having land meant having a livelihood. Voluntary forfeiture of land resulted only from desperation and wasn't to be a permanent condition. They held the land with an enduring lease. That's why even today religious Jews in Israel feel strongly about ownership of the land.

In certain Christian circles the enduring promise of land is spiritualized, referring to heaven and the new earth.

The Priests

Appoint Aaron and his sons, and they
shall attend to their priesthood.
Num. 3:10, NKJV.

A priest had to meet rigorous qualifications. First, he needed to be descended from Aaron. He had to be anointed with oil and blood. He could marry only Israelite virgins. Additionally, he—yes, priests were all male—was to have no blindness, lameness, disfigurement, deformation, broken leg, broken arm, hunchback, dwarfism, eye discoloration, scarring, etc.

Priestly duties included, among other things: approaching God for man—the ministration of the sacrificial carcass and blood, corporate praying, pronouncing blessings, and consulting the Urim and Thummim. They also wore special clothing that could not be worn by the run-of-the-mill Hebrew.

Some argue that ordained ministers are the contemporary equivalent of the ancient priests. Therefore, women pastors mustn't be ordained. They are not male, so fail to qualify. This rationale might be valid *if* pastors truly functioned as priests. But . . .

Pastors differ in numerous ways from the Hebrew priests. Pastors are ordained, not anointed; ordination doesn't involve application of oil and blood. Although some functions of pastors may resemble those of priests—such as praying corporately and teaching—pastors don't offer sacrifices and administer the carcasses and blood. (Roman Catholic priests *do* offer the sacrifice of the Mass.)

The chief role of pastor seems more like that of prophet—approaching the people for God and speaking in God's behalf by interpreting and explaining Scripture. If pastors more closely resemble prophets than priests, then the argument against ordination of women falters, as there *were* female prophets in both the Old and New Testaments.

Furthermore, if Adventist pastors were indeed the counterpart of priests, then shouldn't *all* the necessary qualifications be applied—regulating whom pastors marry, requiring special attire, and disallowing all with a physical deformity?

Maybe the current furor over not ordaining women is nothing more than a tempest in a teapot. "There is no longer male and female; for all of you are one in Christ Jesus" (Gal. 3:28, NRSV).

When the Wife Strays

Such is the ritual in cases of suspicion, when a woman has gone astray and made herself unclean while under her husband's authority. Num. 5:29, New Jerusalem.

When a Hebrew husband suspected his wife of adultery but had no confirming witnesses, there was a procedure for determining her guilt or innocence.

1. He brought her, along with an offering, two quarts of barley meal, to the priest, who escorted her "before the Lord."

2. The priest mixed a potion of water and debris scraped from the sanctuary "floor."

3. The priest disheveled (Num. 5:18, NRSV) her hair and had her hold the barley meal.

4. The priest uttered an oath that if she was innocent, she'd survive the ordeal, but if guilty, she'd be cursed. He wrote the curses with ink and washed them into the "water of bitterness and cursing" (verse 18, New Jersalem).

5. The suspected adulterer drank the water.

6. The priest took the barley meal and waved it "before the Lord."

7. If the wife remained healthy after drinking the brew, she was deemed innocent. If her reproductive organs withered (verse 27, New Jerusalem), she was guilty and considered cursed.

What can we make of this trial by ordeal? It all sounds so primitive . . .

Notice that God commanded no comparable ordeal for unfaithful husbands. But what should we expect in a patriarchal society? Women were regarded as potentially dangerous. It was *they* who had the most potential of bringing shame to the family. It was *they* who seduced men into adultery. It was *they* who were "unclean" for about half of the time (during menstruation). And when it came to monetary worth, females were less valuable than males.

Trial by ordeal was not unheard-of in the ancient Near East, so this passage wouldn't have shocked them as it does us. Yet despite our distress over such a passage, perhaps it gives us insight into how in Holy Writ God accommodated Himself to culture. "God committed the preparation of His divinely inspired Word to finite man" (*Selected Messages*, book 1, p. 16). Scripture "is not God's mode of thought and expression. It is that of humanity. . . . The Bible . . . does not answer to the great ideas of God" (*ibid.*, pp. 16, 21, 22). Nevertheless, it is our privilege to take the Bible "just as it is" (*ibid.*, p. 17).

The Priestly Blessing

May Yahweh bless you and keep you. May Yahweh let his face shine on you and be gracious to you.
Num. 6:24, 25, New Jerusalem.

L et's take a closer look at the priestly benediction.

"May Yahweh bless you." The verb expresses a desire—the yearning that YHWH will bless His people. But perhaps it's even more than that. It expresses what God does . . . because He has promised to bless. Uttering a blessing in the ancient Near East was performative speech. That means the mere act of speaking the words would produce the desired effect.

"And keep you." The first use of this Hebrew verb is in Genesis 2:15, which tells us that Adam was to tend the garden where God placed him. It was also used to describe what shepherds do—guard their sheep. The connotation is that of careful, compassionate attention.

"May Yahweh let his face shine on you." The picture is that of daybreak, when light dawns and floods the countryside. When YHWH's face shines on us, it's a sign of favor. When He hides His face, He's showing His disapproval. God is portrayed as beaming in love upon His children.

"May Yahweh . . . be gracious to you." The word used describes how a benevolent superior relates to an underling. More than half the times that the word appears as a verb in the Old Testament, it refers to God's attitude, and the adjective from the same root always describes God. God looks kindheartedly upon His people. When a king has this attribute, he listens to his subjects' grievances.

"May Yahweh show you his face." This is similar to having God's face shine upon His people. Although in the most literal sense no human can see God's face, in this metaphorical sense we *can* see it. The verb used has God lifting up His face for His people so that they can know Him personally.

"May Yahweh . . . bring you peace." The verb has the sense of placing or putting something somewhere. In this instance the thing God bestows upon His people is *shalom*. Although this noun is usually translated into English as "peace," the sense behind the word is much more than the absence of war. *Shalom* includes health, safety, and serenity. It has overtones of being happily whole.

35

The Firstborn

*For all the firstborn among the Israelites are
mine, both human and animal. On the day
that I struck down all the firstborn in the land
of Egypt I consecrated them for myself.*
Num. 8:17, NRSV.

What's your birth order? Were you a firstborn? lastborn? middle child?
Because God killed the Egyptian firstborn at the onset of the Exodus
yet spared the Israelite firstborn, He claimed the firstborn as His.

"All the firstborn of your livestock that are males shall be the Lord's. . . .
Every firstborn male among your children you shall redeem. When in the future your child asks you, 'What does this mean?' you shall answer, '. . . When
Pharaoh stubbornly refused to let us go, the Lord killed all the firstborn in
the land of Egypt. . . . Therefore I sacrifice to the Lord every male that first
opens the womb, but every firstborn of my sons I redeem'" (Ex. 13:12-15,
NRSV).

Furthermore, the firstborn son automatically received the birthright—
twice as much inheritance as given to the rest of the children combined.

It got a bit tricky, however, with twins. Normally we think of twins as
being equal in age, and if they're identical, equal pretty much in all aspects.
After all, they're genetically alike. Nonetheless, the firstborn twin was the
one to inherit the birthright. That's why Hebrew midwives carefully marked
which twin exited the womb first. (In the case of Jacob and Esau, Jacob's little hand emerged first, but Esau actually was born ahead of his brother.)

Now we can return to the question asked at the outset: Are you a firstborn? Careful, now! Before you answer, consider the following. Paul says that
Jesus is the "firstborn of all creation" (Col. 1:15, NRSV), a text some have mis-
construed to mean that even the preexistent Son of God was a created being.
In Romans, Paul calls Jesus the "firstborn within a large family" (Rom. 8:29,
NRSV), thus acknowledging the priority of Jesus Christ. He is also the "firstborn from the dead" (Col. 1:18, NRSV). Very impressive!

But there's more. Hebrews 12:23 says we're members of the "church of
the firstborn" (NIV) or "Church of first-born sons" (New Jerusalem). So all
Christians are firstborn, including you, regardless of how many your siblings.
I suppose that's because we're all in Christ, who was the preeminent firstborn. We are privileged indeed!

On the Road Again

At the command of the Lord they would camp, and at the command of the Lord they would set out. Num. 9:23, NRSV.

Many who aren't country music fans know Willie Nelson's song "On the Road Again," which he wrote for the 1980 motion picture *Honeysuckle Rose*. Traveling seems to get "in the blood" of some people. As the child of a Seventh-day Adventist pastor, I began feeling the wanderlust after we'd stayed at a place for three years.

It's not always easy to know when it's the right time to move—or to make any other kind of change.

When I attended Atlantic Union College, the pastor received a call to another conference but decided the call came from the devil. (If he'd thought the call had come from God, he would have had to accept it, and he didn't want to move.) On one occasion my father-in-law, another Adventist pastor, accepted three calls to other conferences at the same time. He watched for indications of God's will.

The Israelites spent 40 years trekking from Egypt to Canaan. Whether they should move on or remain at a site came at God's bidding with a visible sign. A pillar of fire by night and cloud by day were visible signs of God's leading. "Whenever the cloud lifted from over the [tabernacle], then the Israelites would set out; and in the place where the cloud settled down, there the Israelites would camp" (Num. 9:17, NRSV).

If only we had such a concrete omen to help us decide what to do—move to another city, state, or country; change jobs; choose which house to purchase; decide on a course of treatment for disease . . . The list, I suppose, could go on ad infinitum.

Prayer, of course, is important when we're faced with a decision. Even then, it's not always clear which course God wants us to take. It seems that decision-making doesn't come easily to many of us. Sometimes we even get torn up inside when confronted with decisions.

We don't have a pillar of light by night and a cloud by day to direct our lives, so we're left with Bible study, prayer, advice from others, and the exercise of our God-given free will. When we use these in unison, we can confidently step out in faith.

Moses' Turn to Whine

*I am not able to carry all this people
alone, for they are too heavy for me.
Num. 11:14, NRSV.*

L eading the Israelites to the Promised Land was no cakewalk! Moses
sensed that from the start and argued long and hard with God at the
burning bush. Ultimately God won out. Moses trudged back to Egypt, where
things went from bad to worse—for both the Israelites and the Egyptians.

At times, Moses could be like a pit bull—defensive of God's people.
That's how he was at Mount Sinai when the people worshipped the golden
calf. God decided He'd wipe them out, but Moses lectured God, convincing
Him to repent of His plans for destruction.

Sooner or later, however, leadership responsibilities wear one down to
the point of sheer desperation. That seems to be what happened with Moses.
The people began whining about their diet; manna had become boring.
They wanted the fish, cucumbers, melons, onions, and garlic they ate in
Egypt.

Soon both God and Moses got fed up with all their fussing. This time it
was Moses who reached the breaking point. Listen to his sarcastic words:
"Wherefore have I not found favour in thy sight, that thou layest the burden
of all this people upon me? Have I conceived all this people? have I begotten
them, that thou shouldest say unto me, Carry them in thy bosom, as a nursing father beareth the sucking child . . . ? I am not able to bear all this people alone, because *it is* too heavy for me. . . . Kill me, I pray thee . . . if I have
found favour in thy sight" (verses 11-15).

Moses did what many leaders do. He bore the burdens alone. God had a
better idea—delegate authority. (Moses' father-in-law also made the same
suggestion.) "Gather for me seventy of the elders of Israel. . . . I will take some
of the spirit that is on you and put it on them; and they shall bear the burden of the people along with you" (verses 16, 17, NRSV).

You're most likely a leader of some sort—Sabbath school teacher, parent, etc. So don't whine as you do all the work yourself. Try God's solution—
delegation. You can hand over age-appropriate responsibilities to your
children. Even God needed help and turned to Moses.

Drudgery is not a divine gift! Remember that trite but true proverb:
"Many hands make light work."

Generosity Is a
Sign of Meekness

*Are you jealous for my sake? Would that all
the Lord's people were prophets, and that the
Lord would put his spirit on them!
Num. 11:29, NRSV.*

Smart man, Moses was. He took God's counsel to heart, selecting 70 men
who could bear leadership responsibilities. And the funk in which Moses
had been wallowing apparently dissipated. The idea of sharing responsibility
with 70 other individuals must have eased Moses' stress level considerably.

Of course, Moses would have to trust the 70 he appointed. It wouldn't
be good for him to have 70 aides who had nothing to do. His level of frustration would soar again, and the only thing the appointees would soon be sharing would be his aggravation!

God helped by sending His Spirit on the 70 as they gathered at the sanctuary. "The Lord . . . took some of the spirit that was on [Moses] and put it
on the seventy elders" (Num. 11:25, NRSV). Surely, now there was no question
about their qualifications. The same Spirit who inspired Moses was now
theirs.

If there was still a lingering doubt, it should have abated when "they
prophesied" (verse 25, NRSV). The Hebrew word for prophesying has various
aspects. In 1 Samuel 19:24 King Saul's prophesying involved lying naked all
day and all night. First Chronicles 25:1, 3 speaks of men prophesying with
lyres, harps, and cymbals, so it could involve making music. In Ezekiel 12:27
(and other places) it refers to making predictions. Ezekiel 37 presents it in the
context of giving a command. In Jeremiah 19:14 it seems to mean preaching.

That 70 additional men started to prophesy should have caused awe
among the rest of the Israelites. But not so. Even a man as dedicated as
Joshua became concerned—not for himself but for Moses. He urged Moses
to prohibit Eldad and Medad (who were among the 70 but had for some reason absented themselves from the tabernacle) from prophesying.

Moses' response to Joshua shows his true character. "Would that all the
Lord's people were prophets, and that the Lord would put his spirit on
them!" (verse 29, NRSV). He didn't know what professional jealousy was!

You see, it's not enough to delegate. If we truly want peace of mind, we
need to be humble enough to support those who help us. That's real leadership!

Twelve Secret Agents

We came unto the land whither thou sentest us,
and surely it floweth with milk and honey;
and this is the fruit of it. Nevertheless . . .
Num. 13:27, 28.

God had described Canaan as flowing with milk and honey (Ex. 3:8). Had God exaggerated? A firsthand report would prove helpful, so Moses selected 12 secret agents to spy out the land. "See what the land is like, and whether the people who live in it are strong or weak, whether they are few or many, . . . and whether the land is rich or poor, and whether there are trees in it or not. . . . And bring some of the fruit of the land" (Num. 13:18-20, NRSV). Big assignment!

These undercover agents spent 40 days scoping out the land. Upon completing their mission they returned, as Moses had asked, with a sampling of fruit. They had found one bunch of grapes so enormous that they had to put it on a pole carried by two men. (The Hebrew word to describe the pole indicated that it was quaking and/or bending under the weight as the men hiked back to camp.) They also brought back some pomegranates and figs.

They returned with a majority and a minority report. All agreed that the land truly was productive. God hadn't overstated matters. Canaan was pleasing. They proudly showed off the fruit. Can't you just imagine various people sampling the grapes, pomegranates, and figs?

But there the accord stopped. The majority account indicated that the Amalekites, Hittites, Jebusites, Amorites, and Canaanites occupied the land. All the people living there were huge, but the gigantic Anakim also lived there, so dwarfing the Hebrew scouts that the 12 men looked like grasshoppers!

Caleb and Joshua's minority report espoused a confident viewpoint: "Let us go up at once . . . , for we are well able to overcome it" (verse 30, NRSV). "The Lord is with us" (Num. 14:9).

The people rejected this minority report, demanding the death of the two dissidents. YHWH flew into a rage—again. And Moses—again—argued Him out of His anger. God relented . . . somewhat. Caleb and Joshua would actually enter Canaan. The other spies died shortly from a plague. The rest of the masses would die en route, except for the children.

None of us need be a Pollyanna, but negativism in the face of God's leading is especially demoralizing and can have far-reaching fallout. Let us shun it!

Gung Ho!

Why do you continue to transgress the command of the Lord? That will not succeed.
Num. 14:41, NRSV.

M oses told the people that the 10 spies would die from the plague and that the rest of the people would perish on the way to Canaan. Additionally, the "congregation" would ramble about in the desert for 40 years, one year for each day the spies had spent scoping out the Promised Land.

Hearing that their trip would be unnecessarily prolonged, "the people mourned greatly" (Num. 14:39). The Hebrew verb "mourn" comes from a root that means "wither, dry up." The terminology could refer to both a physiological condition (shriveling) and to a psychological state (remorsefulness). It has overtones of self-abasement. It was a pretty devastated bunch of people who crawled into bed that night. Already about 14 months had elapsed since they'd fled Egypt.

Few slept well that night, you can be sure. No doubt they constantly rehearsed in their minds what had taken place the previous day and what they should have done differently. After tossing and turning all night, "they rose up early in the morning" and admitted, "We have sinned" (verse 40).

Honor and shame were significant concerns in the ancient Near East. People, especially men, did all in their power to maintain honor and avoid shame. Indeed, even today in the Middle East, a man is reluctant to declare guilt. Instead of admitting that he'd not gotten up in time to catch the train, he will say, "The train left without me." So it was a serious matter for those ancient Hebrews to admit they had sinned.

The remorseful Israelites struck out for Canaan on their own despite Moses' warning, "That will not succeed" (verse 41, NRSV). They were determined to abide by God's will—His earlier will. They overlooked that God's plan had changed because of their bad attitude. And what happened? "The Amalekites and the Canaanites who lived in that hill country came down and defeated them" (verse 45, NRSV). God's will isn't inflexible. What we do *can* shape it. It pays neither to lag behind God in reticence nor to run ahead of Him in fervor. The challenge for us, of course, is to be ever sensitive to His desires.

The Boomerang Effect

Edom said to him, "You shall not pass through, lest I come out with the sword against you."
Num. 20:18, RSV.

Blood feuds are common when preserving honor and avoiding shame are foundational values. Vengeance is a key method for preserving or regaining honor. A man who doesn't even the score loses yet more honor. Typically people in these cultures have very long memories.

As the Israelites continued their march toward Canaan, one of the more or less direct routes went through the territory of Edom. Edom, you recall, was a nickname for Esau, so the Edomites were distant cousins of the Israelites. So it was that "Moses sent messengers . . . to the king of Edom, 'Thus says your brother Israel: You know . . . how . . . the Egyptians oppressed us . . . ; and when we cried to the Lord, he . . . brought us out of Egypt; and here we are in Kadesh, a town on the edge of your territory. Now let us pass through your land. We will not pass through field or vineyard, or drink water from any well; . . . not turning aside to the right hand or to the left until we have passed through your territory'" (Num. 20:14, NRSV).

The request sounded reasonable enough, but the response wasn't level-headed: "You shall not pass through, lest I come out with the sword against you" (verse 18, RSV).

The Israelites countered: "We will stay on the highway; and if we drink of your water, we and our livestock, then we will pay for it. It is only a small matter; just let us pass through on foot" (verse 19, NRSV).

Again Edom's answer was negative, this time backed by a show of force. So the Hebrew people pursued an alternate route.

Centuries had elapsed since Jacob and Esau had parted ways, but one cannot help wondering if Edom's response would have been more gracious had Jacob: (1) not taken advantage of Esau's hunger, thereby buying the birthright for some stew; (2) not deceived Isaac, thereby stealing Esau's blessing; and (3) not refused Esau's kindly offers of help, thereby going separate ways after Jacob once again lied to Esau. Jacob's ongoing deviousness had not been forgotten despite the passing of hundreds of years.

His descendants were now experiencing the boomerang effect. And who can justifiably blame the Edomites?

The Bronze Snake

The Lord told him, "Make a replica of a poisonous snake and attach it to the top of a pole. Those who are bitten will live if they simply look at it!"
Num. 21:8, NLT.

O nce again the Israelites became discouraged. (Who can blame them?) In their pique they rebelled against Moses and even against YHWH Himself. This was clearly mutiny. "There is nothing to eat here and nothing to drink. And we hate this wretched manna!" (Num. 21:5, NLT).

The verb they used meant they felt revulsion toward the manna. They went so far as to call the manna "wretched" or "putrid," using a very strong adjective, which was based on a root that meant "lightness." In short, they were insisting that the manna was of no account, contemptible. Furthermore, their "soul" revolted at the thought of this yucky food from heaven. They were implying that whenever they thought about manna, they wanted to throw up! They sound like some children I've heard, who've said the very same thing about their food! No wonder they were called the *children* of Israel!

YHWH "sent poisonous snakes among them, and many were bitten and died" (verse 6, NLT). The KJV calls the snakes "fiery," which is a literal translation. The venom caused burning inflammation and was fatal. Many lost their lives.

Moses turned to God, who told him to construct from bronze the likeness of a fiery serpent. Whenever anyone was bitten, they were to look at the image and be healed.

Ancient Near Easterners knew all about snakebite. In Mesopotamia there were specific magic rituals for turning poisonous serpents into nonpoisonous snakes. Another common practice is what some call "sympathetic magic," in which an image resembling the problem was made, supposedly having curative power.

Frequently prayer and magic went hand in hand, because both were based on the belief that deity was behind it. But even good things—sacred things—can sometimes turn out to be stumbling blocks. Over the centuries the bronze snake became more and more an object of idolatry and was called "Nehushtan." So King Hezekiah had it destroyed.

In Scripture "bad" things can become "good" (as when God adopted the names of pagan deities) and "good" things can become "bad" (as with Nehushtan). God give us the wisdom to know the difference!

War Booty

Only the young girls who are virgins
may live; . . . keep them for yourselves.
Num. 31:18, NLT.

The Israelites declared war on the Midianites, remote relatives who had descended from Abraham's son Midian. In the conflict all the Midianite men were killed, and the Israelite warriors "burned all the towns and villages where the Midianites had lived" (Num. 31:10, NLT). If we take the report literally, this was clearly genocide.

The Hebrews returned with "plunder," all that the individual soldiers took as their own, and the "spoils of war," all that was taken corporately as communal chattel. The Israelite troops had returned home with mind-boggling quantities of spoils: 675,000 sheep; 72,000 cattle; 61,000 mules; 32,000 virgins; and much jewelry, about 420 pounds of gold—worth more than $3.3 million (at $540 per troy ounce).

When Moses saw the booty, he became irate about the females and children brought back as prisoners of war. Moabite women afforded a source of idolatry. So he commanded: "Kill all the boys and all the women who have slept with a man" (verse 17, NLT). When the grisly task had been completed, 32,000 Moabite virgins remained. Moses further commanded that a certain percentage of the spoils go to the Levites, which amounted to 6,750 sheep, 720 cattle, 610 mules, and 320 virgins. Another percentage went to YHWH (via Eleazar the priest), amounting to 675 sheep, 72 cattle, 61 mules, and 32 virgins.

The question arises, What did God do with His 32 virgins? And even if Eleazar received them in YHWH's behalf, what did *he* do with them?

The entire scenario is troubling. All Moabite cities and towns had been razed. Genocide had taken place. A scant 32,000 virgins had remained alive, and they had been "thingified," doled out among the Israelite men like chattel. But how did their virginity avoid the problem of idolatry? And, of all things, 32 of the virgins went to YHWH!

Once again—as so often happens—we're confronted with the human element in the Bible. As with the Incarnation, the divine became human. The Word—both the living and the written words—have become flesh. God works through defective vehicles, which includes you and me.

Justice for All

You must be perfectly fair at all times, not only to fellow Israelites, but also to the foreigners. . . . Never favor those who are rich; be fair to lowly and great alike. Deut. 1:16, 17, NLT.

M oses needed help administering the Israelites. So he told each tribe to select someone to assist him, advising them on how they should render decisions: "Be perfectly fair at all times" (Deut. 1:16, NLT). First, they were to "hear," to use the ears to pay attention to someone's grievance. Second, they were to "judge." The word means not only to make judicial decisions and govern but also to deliver.

The helpers were to decide "righteously." The idea is that of fairness that restores the good life of the innocent. The combination of the verb "to judge" with the adverb "righteously" indicates that the peace (*shalom*) had been broken by someone acting aggressively toward another. If complainants had legitimate grievances, the arbitrators should decide in their favor. If antagonists were innocent, then the complainants would be dealt with. The result would reestablish tranquillity.

Most significantly, elsewhere in Scripture this is how God judges His people. Scripture doesn't speak about Him hearing praises, though He surely does. Rather God hears the problems of His people and then gives a righteous verdict, making a decision that restores peace.

According to Moses these aides should be fair "not only to fellow Israelites, but also to the foreigners living among you" (verse 16, NLT). ("Foreigners" were typically slaves.) Regardless of who the accusers and accused were—relatives or not—the judges were to make just decisions on behalf of the grieved party. Moses' assistants must "never favor those who are rich; [but] be fair to lowly and great alike" (verse 17, NLT). The judges must not be biased because of someone's social status. Everyone must be treated evenhandedly.

Finally, Moses told his aides, "Don't be afraid of how they will react" (verse 17, NLT). Literally, they weren't to dwell (sojourn) on man's face. Brooding over the likely emotional reactions of plaintiffs or defendants mustn't taint decisions.

Although Moses was addressing the 12 deputized arbitrators, his advice is appropriate for any who deal with others, in other words, all of us. The objective of any pronouncements we make must be the restoration of peace, and our decision-making must be free from favoritism.

Not a Square Foot

*Do not provoke them to war, for I will not give you
any of their land, not even enough to put your foot on.
I have given Esau the hill country of Seir as his own.
Deut. 2:5, NIV.*

God promised land and many descendants to Abraham. God, as Creator, owned the land, but He parceled it out among the nations. "The Most High gave the nations their inheritance" (Deut. 32:8, NIV).

But not all of Abraham's descendants were part of this covenant, renewed with Isaac and Jacob. Nonetheless, true to His promise, YHWH blessed even the offspring of Abraham who didn't worship Him.

For instance, God promised: "As for Ishmael . . . I will surely bless him. . . . I will make him into a great nation" (Gen. 17:20, NIV).

But a special portion of the land He promised to give to Abraham and his descendants who were part of the everlasting covenant. So when the Israelites were ready to take possession of Canaan, God offered some surprising warnings about which land they should take and which they shouldn't take.

When the time came for them "to pass through the territory of your brothers the descendants of Esau" (Deut. 2:4, NIV), they were to "be very careful" (verse 4, NIV). Why? Because this was not the land God intended to give to His covenant people. "I will not give you any of their land, not even enough to put your foot on. I have given Esau the hill country of Seir as his own" (verse 5, NIV).

God gave similar instructions regarding the land of the Ammonites (and Moabites), who had descended from Lot, Abraham's nephew. "Do not harass them or provoke them to war, for I will not give you possession of any land belonging to the Ammonites. I have given it as a possession to the descendants of Lot" (verse 19, NIV).

YHWH was willing to live with the consequences of Lot's incestuous relationship, of Abraham's do-it-yourself attempt to have progeny, and of Esau's cavalier attitude toward the birthright. God honors His vows, even though doing so might not always be convenient, and He expects His people to keep their promises also. "When a man . . . takes an oath to obligate himself . . . , he must not break his word" (Num. 30:2).

Covenant Promises

Oh, that their hearts would be inclined to fear me and keep all my commands always, so that it might go well with them and their children forever!
Deut. 5:29, NIV.

When YHWH appeared atop Sinai to reestablish His covenant with the Israelites, it was an awesome occasion.

Rudolf Otto in his book *The Idea of the Holy* has said that we behave simultaneously in two ways when in the presence of the holy: (1) we feel repelled, wanting to flee, and (2) we feel fascinated, wanting to linger. "Boundless awe" springs from a sense of the uncanniness of the experience, and "boundless wonder" comes from a sense of fascination with the holy.

The content of the covenant that "the Lord our God made . . . with us at Horeb" (Deut. 5:2, NIV) was the Ten Commandments, which Moses repeated in Deuteronomy 5. God had spoken these words from the fire, cloud, and darkness. Moved by this supernatural event, the people urged Moses to serve as their representative with YHWH.

The covenant God made with Abraham, Isaac, Jacob, and the Israelites included several promises that He Himself made: (1) many descendants, (2) land, (3) He would be their God and they His people, and (4) the nations would be blessed through them.

Part of this renewal of the covenant at Mount Sinai included stipulations regarding how the Israelites were to honor YHWH and their neighbors. The Decalogue spelled out these covenantal stipulations.

The Israelites, after hearing the 10 provisions, pledged their allegiance to YHWH's covenant. "Tell us everything that Yahweh our God has told you; we shall listen and put it into practice!" (verse 27, New Jerusalem). In other words, they would comply with the specifications, thereby keeping covenant with YHWH.

God heard their pledge of allegiance and said, "Everything they said was good. Oh, that their hearts would be inclined to . . . keep all my commands always" (verses 28, 29, NIV).

"The covenant that God made with His people at Sinai is to be our refuge and defense. . . . This covenant is of just as much force today as it was when the Lord made it with ancient Israel" (*The Seventh-day Adventist Bible Commentary*, Ellen G. White Comments, vol. 1, p. 1103).

The Shema'

Hear, O Israel: The Lord our God, the Lord is one!
Deut. 6:4, NKJV.

Our verse is called the Shema'. We should note three peculiarities in this passage.

First, it refers to YHWH ("Lord"), ignoring the many other names that God went by. In fact, YHWH appears twice in the passage.

Second, the word translated "one" (*'echâd*) can also mean "alone"—with the sense of "only."

Third, often Hebrew grammar doesn't require the verb "to be." So a sentence might literally read "I want a firefighter when I grow up." The reader or translator supplies the verb: "I want *to be* a firefighter when I grow up." (In the KJV such supplied words are printed in italics to alert readers that the italicized words are not in the original text.)

With these three points in mind, it's grammatically possible to translate the verse with four variations: (1) "YHWH [is] our God; YHWH [is] one" (see NASB); (2) "YHWH [is] our God, YHWH alone" (see NRSV and NLT); (3) YHWH our God [is] one YHWH (see NIV and RSV); (4) YHWH our God, YHWH [is] one" (see NKJV).

According to Moshe Weinfeld (*Deuteronomy 1-11, Anchor Bible*), the first two options don't fit the grammatical patterns of Deuteronomy and so would be uncharacteristic uses in their present context. The last option, he says, is awkward, which leaves the third rendering as making the most sense: "YHWH our God [is] one YHWH."

Traditionally, the verse is taken as the foundation for monotheism, understanding *'echâd* in a strictly numerical sense, and so it's translated as "one." On this reading, which is used in an exclusive way, it singles out YHWH as the sole deity. However, it can also be understood as referring to God's nature—He is an undivided unity. Theologians can thus speak of God's person being "simple."

Trinitarians need to decide if the Shema', with its use of *'echâd*, rules out worshipping a God consisting of three persons. Apparently not. Genesis 2:24 indicates that in marriage husband and wife become one (*'echâd*) flesh. Genesis 11:6 and 34:16 refer to a crowd of people being one (*'echâd*). So it's possible for the word to refer to the unity that exists between multiple persons. Thus, we don't think our belief in the triune God disagrees with the Shema'.

Lest You Forget

Do not forget the Lord, who brought you out of the land of Egypt.
Deut. 6:12, NRSV.

The exodus was God's great act in salvation history. "Search all of history, from the time God created people on the earth until now. Then search from one end of the heavens to the other. See if anything as great as this has ever happened before" (Deut. 4:32, NLT).

First, the miracles lay in where they'd come from. Twice Pharaoh initiated measures to reduce the Hebrew population—infanticide. The Hebrew men became slave laborers. After Moses showed up demanding their release, Pharaoh ordered that they'd have to find their own straw to bind together the clay for the bricks they were to make, yet he didn't reduce the production quota. Then came horrendous plagues as Pharaoh refused to let the Israelites go. When they were told to leave ASAP, they became hemmed in between the Red Sea and the Egyptian military forces. Yes, the exodus was a stupendous miracle.

Second, the miracles lay in where they were headed. With YHWH fighting on their side, they would evict the peoples of Canaan and settle into their cities. They would enjoy "flourishing cities [they] did not build, houses filled with all kinds of good things [they] did not provide, wells [they] did not dig . . . vineyards and olive groves [they] did not plant . . . [and would] . . . eat and [be] satisfied" (Deut. 6:10, 11, NIV).

If this hadn't been God's doing, one might fairly accuse the marauding Hebrews of being leeches. Like parasites they got to enjoy the results of others' labors—municipalities, abodes, furnishings, water supplies, gardens, food aplenty.

Moses painted an idyllic picture, of course. The Israelites needed to remember that this luxury was not something they earned but was a gift from YHWH, Creator, Sustainer, and Redeemer. "Be careful that you do not forget the Lord" (verse 12, NIV).

When every bounty falls into one's lap, it's easy to become lackadaisical. But laziness isn't a virtue. And one needn't suffer from Alzheimer's disease to experience spiritual memory loss. The longer we enjoy prosperity, basking in the good times, the easier it becomes to forget God, "from whom all blessings flow." It's human nature.

Have *you* forgotten God's beneficence? Have *I*? Surely every day should be Thanksgiving Day.

Remember the Poor

If there are any poor people in your towns . . .
do not be hard-hearted or tightfisted toward them.
Deut. 15:7, NLT.

The word translated "hard-hearted" in verse 7 has the basic meaning of being strong. It means to do something by exertion of one's strength. In our passage Moses tells the Israelites not to make the heart (the inner person) so tough that it isn't moved by the plight of others.

Moses furthermore forbids closing one's hand to others. Instead, the Hebrews were to open their hands—wide (Deut. 15:8). Their loans to paupers should be such as to offset their shortages.

Because of the sabbatical years, it would be easy in the sixth year to ignore the poor, because the next year land that had been used as collateral for loans would automatically revert to the original owner, and slaves would be freed. Only someone with a "wicked (good-for-nothing) heart" would think that way.

Furthermore, their generosity must itself be benevolent. In other words, its source must be good-heartedness. "Your heart should not be grieved when you give to him" (verse 10, NKJV). The word translated "grieved" in the NKJV can also be translated as "begrudging" (NLT), "ungrudging" (NRSV), "grudging" (NIV), "have no regrets" (Tanakh), "stingy" (Message), and "upset" (NET). This Hebrew word is most often translated as "evil" or "bad." The benevolence must spring from pure motives. And the donors should remember that they were once slaves in Egypt and that God dealt generously with them. It isn't unreasonable, then, to regard this instruction as a variation on the golden rule: Do unto others as God has done to you.

Hebrew slaves—both male and female—not only must be freed during a sabbatical year, but should be let go with perks. "Give . . . a generous farewell gift from your flock, your threshing floor, and your winepress" (verse 14, NLT). The benefactor who helps others for sincere reasons will be blessed by YHWH (verse 10). And there will be no end of opportunities to donate, because "there will always be poor people in the land" (verse 11, NIV).

How do *you* measure up to Moses' counsel? How do *I?* Generosity is an earmark of being under covenant with God.

What Obedience Entails

When you go out to war against your enemies . . . you shall not be afraid of them; for the Lord your God is with you. Deut. 20:1, NRSV.

February 17
Deuteronomy

Taking possession of Canaan wouldn't be easy. However, in the opening verses of Deuteronomy 20, God says: "The Lord your God is with you" and reiterates: "It is the Lord your God who goes with you" (verse 4, NRSV).

That in itself would provide great comfort for any troubled mind, and later in Scripture we encounter the name Immanuel, which means "God [is] with us." It was a term calculated to provide encouragement. But YHWH promised to do more than merely be there with them.

Refusing simply to stand by and play a passive role, He added that He would "fight for you against your enemies, to give you victory" (verse 4, NRSV). YHWH Himself was a warrior, and throughout the Old Testament we read about "the Lord of hosts," military imagery picturing YHWH as a general who leads the heavenly armed forces. The metaphor of warrior gods was not novel in the ancient Near East. The deities of the nations were often depicted as martial heroes. What is novel is that God's Word portrays the Hebrew God as being all-powerful, an attribute not commonly predicated of the Canaanite, Philistine, and Mesopotamian deities.

Despite God's personal presence in battle, Israelite soldiers would become casualties. So it was that YHWH gave "leave" to (1) men who of late had obtained a new house, (2) those who had just planted crops, (3) new grooms, and (4) the young, lily-livered recruits. Why did God exempt these four classes of males? Because they "might die in the battle" (verses 5-7). Oh, and there was one more reason, and it referred to the scaredy-cats—because they "might cause the heart of [their] comrades to melt like [their] own" (verse 8, NRSV).

Doing God's bidding can be perilous. That He is present with us and fighting for us doesn't necessarily mean we're exempt from suffering. The great cosmic conflict has its casualties—and they're not limited to the side of evil. Those who stand for the right can and do fall in battle. Some make the extreme sacrifice. We don't often see religious fatalities in the Western world, but there are cultures in which those who convert to worshipping the true God and Jesus Christ whom He has sent find themselves not only outcasts but also martyrs.

The Feet of Faith
Are Wet Feet

*When those who bore the ark had come to the Jordan,
and the feet of the priests bearing the ark were dipped
in the edge of the water, the waters flowing from
above stood still, rising up in a single heap. Joshua
3:15, 16, NRSV.*

Joshua, Moses' successor, had a job description with two important aspects:
(1) lead the Israelites into the Promised Land and (2) help them to occupy
it.

Joshua quickly acclimated to his new position as Moses' replacement,
and the Israelites obeyed him. Moreover, they told him: "All that you have
commanded us we will do, and wherever you send us we will go" (Joshua
1:16, NRSV).

It had taken 40 years to get this close to Canaan. In just three more days
they would cross the Jordan River and enter the Promised Land. The end was
in sight!

Soon they pitched camp along the banks of the river. Joshua addressed
the people: "Sanctify yourselves; for tomorrow the Lord will do wonders
among you" (Joshua 3:5, NRSV). This must have been a heady time for the
Israelites. About five miles to the west lay the city of Jericho, which had the
distinction of being the oldest walled town in the world as well as the low-
est city in the world, at an elevation of 825 feet below sea level. It would be
the first city taken by the Israelites.

The time had arrived for them to cross the Jordan River. Fortunately,
their location was good, being near the site of al-Maghtas ford.
Unfortunately, the timing was bad, because this occurred, when the river
was still flooded from the winter rains and spring snowmelt in the mountains.

When all were ready to move on, the priests marched ahead of the people, who trailed about 3,000 feet behind. As the priests approached the river,
the water continued swirling by, but as soon as their sandals began slapping
the muddy water, the torrent dammed up. And everyone crossed safely on
the stony riverbed.

When we expect miracles from God, we should act accordingly.
Sometimes the anticipated miracles don't take place . . . until we shift into
gear and behave as though the prayed-for results had already occurred. Yes,
sometimes the feet of faith are wet feet.

Defeat at the Ruins

And they fled before the men of Ai. The men of Ai killed about thirty-six of them. . . . The hearts of the people melted and turned to water.
Joshua 7:4, 5, NRSV.

Jericho sprawled over 10 acres, a good-sized city for the ancient Near East. A rock wall, with a 25-foot tower, surrounded it. The Israelites marched around it once each day but on the seventh day stomped around it seven times. When the seven priests who preceded the ark of the covenant blew their rams' horns seven times and the Hebrew people shouted, the walls crumbled. The warriors overran the city.

The city was torched, and Joshua pronounced a curse upon it: "May the curse of the Lord fall on anyone who tries to rebuild the city of Jericho. At the cost of his firstborn son, he will lay its foundation. At the cost of his youngest son, he will set up its gates" (Joshua 6:26, NLT). Despite this vitriolic hex, the city was later rebuilt, although the Jericho of Jesus' time was not on the same site but nearby.

Exuberant from their success at Jericho, a short time later 3,000 Israelite soldiers marched on Ai, a city not far from Jericho. Ai was another old municipality, and during its heyday covered 27.5 acres—nearly three times the size of Jericho. (Joshua 8:25 reports that 12,000 people lived at Ai.) With much bravado, the 3,000 derring-do Israelite invaders attacked Ai, but were vigorously repulsed and sent fleeing like terrified gophers. Thirty-six Hebrew warriors died in the abortive invasion. Joshua, despondent, learned of Achan's larceny, and we still refer to "an Achan in the camp" when things go wrong.

The story itself is ironical. First, Ai means "ruin(s)." Second, around 2400 B.C. Ai was demolished, lying in ruins for 1,200 years. If the archaeological record is correct, no one was living there at the time of the conquest, or perhaps just a handful of people dwelt in the vicinity. That being the case, the 3,000 Hebrew invaders were whipped by essentially nobody when they attacked a city that was a heap of ruins!

Some students of Scripture figure that archaeologists have misidentified the remains of Ai. That may be true. However, there's another way of understanding this fiasco. Without God's help, the most successful of us end up as failures—even when confronted by mere molehills.

53

An Achan in the Camp

But Israel was unfaithful concerning the things set apart for the Lord. A man named Achan had stolen some of these things, so the Lord was very angry with the Israelites.
Joshua 7:1, NLT.

When the Israelites conquered certain cities, they dedicated the entire plunder to God. These persons, animals, and things were called *chērem*, a Hebrew word meaning consecrated, forbidden, or under the ban. In the context of war, the plunder was dedicated to God and hence destroyed, because it wasn't to be used for secular purposes.

Achan, one of the soldiers who overran Jericho, took some booty for his personal use—a garment from Shinar, nearly six pounds of silver, and more than 1.25 pounds of gold.

After a series of lots had been cast, the last fell upon Achan, who had remained silent throughout the whole procedure. Having been found out, Achan confessed to having coveted some of the booty—robbery against God.

"Joshua and all the Israelites took Achan, the silver, the robe, the bar of gold, his sons, daughters, cattle, donkeys, sheep, tent, and everything he had, and they brought them to the valley of Achor. . . . And all the Israelites stoned Achan and his family and burned their bodies" (Joshua 7:24, 25, NLT). The next raid on Ai succeeded.

For years now we've spoken of the possibility of having "an Achan in the camp" when things have gone dreadfully awry in the church and its institutions. Indeed, this has been the rationale for many a witch hunt, and all too often the "witches" found have been declared guilty despite their actual innocence.

Once the monarchy became firmly established, the practice of *chērem* fell into disuse, so the crime of appropriating for oneself the *chērem* disappeared. Thus, it is a questionable practice to find "an Achan in the camp."

In fact, Jesus taught tolerance rather than witch hunts. The wheat and tares should not be separated until God rendered the judgment (Matt. 13:24-30). Similarly, the "fish" caught in the dragnet of the kingdom were not to be separated until the end of time (verses 47-50). Because we no longer live under a theocracy, as did the ancient Israelites, it seems prudent that Jesus' parables, rather than Achan's story, should be our model.

Cool Heads Prevail

We have not built the altar in rebellion against the Lord. If we have done so, do not spare our lives this day. But the Lord knows, and let all Israel know, too. Joshua 22:22, NLT.

Joshua recounts the wars the Israelites waged against the Canaanites, their miraculous success, and the allotment of the occupied territory to the tribes. Nine and a half of the tribes settled west of the Jordan River. The remaining two and a half tribes lived east of the river. (The tribe of Manasseh moved into territory on both sides of the Jordan.)

"Joshua took control of the entire land. . . . He gave it to the people of Israel as their special possession. . . . So the land finally had rest from war" (Joshua 11:23, NLT). Several more times the book of Joshua repeats that the land had rest.

As the tribes of Reuben and Gad and half the tribe of Manasseh crossed to the eastern side of Jordan, it dawned on them that they wouldn't have ready access to Shiloh, where the Mosaic tabernacle had been situated. So not far from the riverbank they constructed an altar that looked like a twin to the altar of burnt offerings in the sanctuary.

When the nine and a half tribes on the western side of the river learned of the altar, they became distraught. Their "brothers" had established a competing place to offer sacrifices. Not only was this flagrant apostasy, but also it could so anger YHWH that He would react violently against all 12 tribes—and not just the two and a half tribes.

Phinehas, the high priest (a man known for taking decisive action against apostasy), assembled a posse of 10 men. They accused their eastern counterparts of abandoning YHWH: "How could you turn away from the Lord and build an altar in rebellion against him?" (Joshua 22:16, NLT).

To their credit, the two and a half tribes kept their cool, replying that they weren't rebelling and had no intention of offering sacrifices on the duplicate altar. They intended it to serve as a "witness" to their children that they must go to Shiloh with their offerings. "All the Israelites were satisfied . . . and spoke no more of war against Reuben and Gad" (verse 33, NLT).

It's all too easy to jump to conclusions and in "righteous indignation" falsely accuse others who, in fact, may have the best of intentions. Frank discussion helps, but both sides need to explain their actions fairly and squarely. "Blessed are the peacemakers."

The Choice

If you are unwilling to serve the Lord, then choose . . .
whom you will serve. Would you prefer the gods
your ancestors served . . . ? Or will it be the gods
of the Amorites in whose land you now live? But
as for me and my family, we will serve the Lord.
Joshua 24:15, NLT.

Joshua felt concern for the Israelites' future. Despite earlier assertions about "all" the nations they'd defeated and "all" the land they'd occupied, Joshua knew that God's people still had idolatrous neighbors. So he minced no words: "If you turn away from [YHWH] and intermarry with the survivors of these nations remaining among you, then know for certain that the Lord your God will no longer drive them out from your land" (Joshua 23:12, 13, NLT).

God had remained faithful to the covenant. What about them?

It was serious business to be in a covenant relationship with God. As their sovereign He had graciously delivered them from Egypt and had brought them into the Promised Land. As His vassals, it was up to them to hold up their end of the covenant. Through Joshua God reminded them: "I gave you land you had not worked for, and I gave you cities you did not build—the cities in which you are now living. I gave you vineyards and olive groves for food, though you did not plant them" (Joshua 24:13, NLT).

It was up to the Israelites to serve YHWH sincerely and truly. Their Mesopotamian ancestors (as well as their more immediate predecessors in Egypt) may have worshipped other gods, but it was time to repudiate those false deities. The choice was theirs—to serve the Mesopotamian and Egyptian gods their forebears worshipped or the deities of the Amorites among whom they now lived . . . or . . . YHWH, their covenant God.

The people replied, "We would never forsake the Lord and worship other gods" (verse 16, NLT). Archaeology, however, reveals that many of their descendants remained polytheistic.

Joshua, playing the devil's advocate, countered: "You are not able to serve the Lord. . . . He will not forgive your rebellion and sins" (verse 19, NLT), directly contradicting Exodus 34:7.

But the people insisted: "No, we are determined to serve the Lord!" (verse 21, NLT).

Will we let materialism spoil our spirituality? As beneficiaries of the "new covenant" will we keep covenant with our God?

Plucky Woman

Give me a present, for you have given me away
as Negeb-land; give me springs of water.
Judges 1:15, Tanakh.

Before Moses died, God appointed Joshua to serve as his successor. Having received no such divine instructions, Joshua had no one lined up to replace him. For a while Caleb, Joshua's friend, stepped in, but the book of Judges describes various leaders who came and went. It was a time when "the people did whatever seemed right in their own eyes" (Judges 17:6, NLT).

At one point Caleb challenged the soldiers to attack Kiriath-sepher (Debir). He promised to whoever did so "my daughter Achsah as wife" (Judges 1:12, NKJV).

Othniel, Caleb's younger brother (verse 13; Judges 3:9), conquered the city. Caleb gave him Achsah as wife. Othniel seems to have been happy with the reward, but from what happened next, we infer that Achsah wasn't thrilled.

When Othniel came to Achsah, she nagged him to ask her father for land—a far better prize than a woman! Apparently Othniel felt reticent to confront Caleb, so Achsah got on a donkey and trotted off to her father's place. Her actions made Caleb suspect something was amiss.

She bluntly accused, "You have given me away as Negeb-land" and then demanded, "Give me springs of water" (Judges 1:15, Tanakh). The first part of her remark is ambiguous in Hebrew and could mean that Caleb had foisted her off like cheap desert land or that he'd allotted her worthless arid land. Either way, Achsah was not happy. Her own father's actions had demeaned her. He'd treated her like dirt.

Caleb silently accepted her remonstration and gave her a genuinely valuable prize—two springs, which, of course, were absolutely critical in that parched land.

All this was quite strange in a patriarchal society, in which men received inheritances and did the talking, and women were often regarded as the equivalent of material goods, such as farm animals and houses. Achsah was plucky! She chided her father for insensitivity and wasn't put to shame, but was honored for her gutsy character. Women aren't children—to be seen but not heard. God wants women to be highly regarded—and active doers.

57

Two More Plucky Women

Then the Israelites cried out to the Lord for help. . . .
At that time Deborah, a prophetess, wife of
Lappidoth, was judging Israel.
Judges 4:3, 4, NRSV.

For 40 years Othniel served as judge. He was later followed by Ehud, with an interval of 80 years' relative calm. Ehud was followed by Shamgar. Then for 20 years King Jabin tormented the Israelites. So God raised up Deborah, whose name means "bee," to serve as a judge. She's the second female prophet mentioned in Scripture.

Deborah summoned Barak, who elsewhere is identified as judge rather than Deborah. It's unusual for a woman to summon a man, but what women do in this story is extraordinary. Barak complied with his summons, and Deborah told him to lead the armed forces against Jabin's military commander, Sisera. Barak whimpered, "I will go, but only if you go with me!" (Judges 4:8, NLT).

Deborah conceded, but predicted that victory would come not at his hands but from an unnamed woman. So Barak organized the Israelite militia, and Deborah gave the order: "Up!" The battle was enjoined, and it didn't look good for the Israelites, because the enemy had 900 iron chariots. However, a tremendous rainstorm flooded the battlefield, and the chariots got mired in the muck. In disarray, the foe was easy prey for Barak's warriors.

Sisera fled on foot toward the family of Heber, a man who had a peace treaty with Jabin. Jael, Heber's wife, went out to greet Sisera, telling him not to fear and to enter her tent. Sisera was thirsty and asked for water. Instead, Jael gave him goat's milk, which was a soporific, and covered him so he wouldn't easily be seen.

As soon as Sisera fell asleep, Jael grabbed a mallet and spare tent peg and nailed Sisera's head or neck (the Hebrew is ambiguous) to the ground, killing him.

When Barak showed up, he too was invited into Jael's tent, where he saw Sisera's dead body. And "Israel became stronger and stronger" (verse 24, NLT).

In that almost rabid patriarchal society, God used two gutsy women to deliver the Israelites: Deborah, who was so savvy that Israelites came from across the land for her judgment and who provided the gumption Barak needed as a man of war; and wily Jael, who used simple household paraphernalia to slay the enemy general. Exactly where is a woman's place?

Gideon

Israel was reduced to starvation by the Midianites. Then the Israelites cried out to the Lord for help. Judges 6:6, NLT.

While Gideon was threshing wheat in a winepress, a covert operation, the angel of YHWH came, calling him a "mighty hero" (Judges 6:12, NLT). This formulaic military term took Gideon by surprise, because his self-esteem was that of a nobody. Despite his unpretentiousness, Gideon had a sarcastic side. When told that God was with him, he sputtered: "If the Lord is with us, why has all this happened . . . ?" (verse 13, NLT). Nevertheless, Gideon's cynicism didn't deter God from commissioning him.

After twice putting out a fleece before the Lord, Gideon finally decided to lead the Israelite forces against the Midianites, who were "like a swarm of locusts" and "their camels were like grains of sand on the seashore!" (Judges 7:12, NLT). Just 300 torchbearing Hebrews slaughtered 120,000 enemy soldiers! When the residents of Succoth refused to feed his forces, Gideon, at the end of the day, returned and "taught them a lesson, punishing them with thorns and briers" (Judges 8:16, NLT). He was beginning to slide down pride's slippery slope!

"Then the Israelites said to Gideon, 'Be our ruler! You and your son and your grandson . . . , for you have rescued us'" (verse 22, NLT).

What Gideon said and did next are contradictory, but actions speak louder than words! What he *said* was "I will not rule over you. . . . The Lord will rule over you!" (verse 23, NLT). But what he *did* was ask for the jewelry they'd plundered. Gladly they turned over to him about 40 pounds of gold as well as "crescents and . . . purple garments . . . and . . . the collars round their camels' necks" (verse 26, New Jerusalem).

We don't know his motives, but from this booty Gideon constructed an ephod, a priestly vestment, which belies his humility. Despite his demurral to kingship, he was quite willing to grasp the priesthood. "Soon all the Israelites prostituted themselves by worshiping [the ephod], and it became a trap for Gideon and his family" (verse 27, NLT).

Modesty is becoming to spiritual leaders. But too often self-effacing people who receive too much honor and too much responsibility slip into arrogance. It happened to Gideon, and it happens in our church today.

Gideon's Complaint

If the Lord is with us, why has all this happened . . . ? And where are all the miracles our ancestors told us about? Judges 6:13, NLT.

Yesterday we skipped over Gideon's complaint. However, the issue he raised merits further exploration. Notice also a passage from the New Testament. "God will give you whatever you ask of him" (John 11:22, NRSV). Whether answers to prayer or expectations of miracles, the issue is similar because the prayers we're talking about here are supposed to produce miracles. Yet how many of the terminally ill persons for whom you've prayed have miraculously recovered? Just one or two? What about all the others— the "fatalities"?

Maybe God is silent because we don't meet His conditions. However, the promises of John 11:22; 14:13, 14; 15:7; 16:23-27; and Matthew 7:7, 8 state no ifs, ands, or buts. True, sometimes Jesus said that victims' faith had saved them, some of whom weren't even His followers. He also said that faith the size of a mustard seed would move mountains (Matt. 17:20). Do we Christians have less faith than did some of the heathen?

Another rationalization is that God answers every prayer with (1) yes, (2) no, or (3) wait. This is so absurd that it makes a mockery of answered prayer. How do we know God's silence is actually "no" or "wait"? Since we have no empirical contact with God, believing that the lack of fulfillment is an "answer" makes a travesty of what the word "answer" means, pushing us far beyond faith into gullibility. Besides, this rationalization isn't biblical.

Can we reasonably expect miracles? Because God created a cosmos operating via natural laws, should we expect Him, as the sustainer of this cosmos, to disrupt orderliness by miracles? Wouldn't the cosmos crumble into chaos were God to perform miracles? But what about just one miracle each century or year or day? But how would God decide which single miracle to perform once a day . . . or year . . . or century that wouldn't undermine the order upon which our existence depends, let alone not violate human free will?

The best "solution" maybe isn't so much a solution as it is a pacifier. God is afflicted in our afflictions (Isa. 63:9). Jesus weeps over our trials just as He did upon Lazarus' death.

Perhaps the Second Advent is the "final solution" to suffering, and in faith we cling to this blessed hope.

Jephthah's Rash Vow

If you deliver the Ammonites into my grasp, the first thing to come out of the doors of my house to meet me when I return in triumph . . . shall belong to Yahweh, and I shall sacrifice it as a burnt offering. Judges 11:30, 31, New Jerusalem.

February 27
Judges

The Ammonites pitched camp at Gilead, and the Israelites bivouacked at Mizpah. But they had no general to draw up battle plans and stimulate bravery. So they turned to Jephthah. The negotiations went from making him "general" to accepting him as their political "head," and the deal was sealed at Mizpah before YHWH.

Jephthah twice tried to negotiate peace with the Ammonites, but failed. So the battle was joined. For no obvious reason Jephthah impetuously vowed to YHWH: "If you deliver the Ammonites into my grasp, the first thing to come out of the doors of my house to meet me when I return in triumph . . . shall belong to Yahweh, and I shall sacrifice it as a burnt offering."

Jephthah's forces prevailed. Euphoric, he headed for home, and who should come out to greet him with music and dancing but his young daughter—his one and only child! And what did this mighty man of valor do? He told her about his vow and then blamed *her* for running to meet him—her father—as any young woman would do!

After two months of running about in the hills, mourning that she'd never experience marriage, the nameless girl returned home. And Jephthah "did to her as he had vowed" (verse 39, NIV), which means he slit her throat, dismembered her body, and immolated it. And God said not a mumbling word (unlike His response at Mount Moriah).

Jephthah was caught on the horns of a dilemma. Should he break his vow and risk YHWH's wrath, who commanded that vows not be broken (Num. 30:2; Deut. 23:21, 22), or should he carry out his vow, ensuring that although *he* wouldn't die, *she* would?

At one time or another we all find ourselves caught on the horns of a dilemma, with neither alternative being desirable. The process of deciding can be agonizing, especially when we've brought it on ourselves by our thoughtlessness. What should we do? As rational beings, we must pray over the decision, weighing the consequences and then choosing the lesser of two evils—the choice that entails the *least selfishness.*

Jephthah's Successors

Jephthah was Israel's judge for six years. When he died, he was buried in one of the towns of Gilead. Judges 12:7, NLT.

After Jephthah and the Gileadites defeated Ammon, the Ephraimites belligerently told Jephthah that because he hadn't asked for their help they were going to set his house aflame. Jephthah explained that he'd asked for their help but had been turned down. They remained aggressive, so he and his cohorts whipped them in battle and captured the Jordan fords. When the east bank Ephraimites tried to return home, Jephthah's forces intercepted them, asking them to pronounce a word meaning "flood"—*shibboleth*. Those with an eastern accent said "sibboleth," revealing their true identity, and 42,000 Ephraimite soldiers were executed on the spot.

After Jephthah's burial some interesting but obscure characters replaced him. First was Ibzan (his name probably meant "swift") from Bethlehem, a very prolific man. He had 30 sons and 30 daughters (Judges 12:9). As was typical, Ibzan became involved in making arranged marriages—60 of them. From "outside" or "abroad" he found wives for his 30 sons, and he sent "outside" or "abroad" his 30 daughters. The ideal marriage among the Hebrew people was endogamous, meaning the spouses came from within the extended clan. The marriages Ibzan arranged were exogamous, probably with the intent of building a wide circle of peaceful relationships. The spouses may have belonged to other tribes or even to other nations. Scripture doesn't elaborate.

After Ibzan's judgeship, Elon (the name meant "oak"), from the tribe of Zebulon, ruled for 10 years. The only other information we have about him is that he was buried in Aijalon.

Next came Abdon (meaning "service" or "servile"), who was quite fertile also. He had 40 sons and 30 grandsons. We're told that his offspring rode on 70 donkeys. Abdon hailed from the tribe of Ephraim—those hotheaded people who'd threatened Jephthah with mayhem and violence.

From the book of Judges we learn that God presses into His service people of all sorts. They can be of either gender, come from various ethnic backgrounds, have differing skills and tenures of varying lengths, and have distinctive personalities. Some we may like more than others. Regardless, they're all God's servants.

Samson's Escapades

March 1
Judges

Those whom he brought to their death by his death outnumbered those whom he had done to death during his life.
Judges 16:30, New Jerusalem.

Samson found a Philistine lady in Timnath who pleased him well (Judges 14:2). A lion attacked him while he was on his way to the betrothal, but Samson tore it apart. When he returned later for the wedding, he found a beehive in the carcass. He based a riddle on that phenomenon and gave his Philistine guests a week to solve it. They came up with the solution only because his bride wheedled it out of him. The marriage lasted only seven days.

Samson later visited Gaza, or more correctly, a prostitute at Gaza. Intent on nabbing him, a posse hid in the anteroom of the gatehouse. He arose at midnight and hoisted the gate doors, gateposts, and bar onto his shoulders, trundling the whole complex for miles.

He met Delilah in the Valley of Sorek. After three attempts to find the secret of his strength, Delilah finally managed to cajole the truth from him. While he slept with his head in her lap, a barber shaved his head. Samson was captured, and she received 5,500 silver shekels!

His eyes were poked out, and he was sentenced to hard labor, operating a millstone as though he were an ox. But bit by bit his hair began to grow, and when the Philistines held a gala celebration in the temple of Dagon, Samson brought the house down by leveraging the supporting pillars. Among the 3,000 fatalities was Samson himself, his 20-year judgeship over.

Why a cycle of such earthy and titillating stories in the Bible? Samson might make a marvelous hero for secular-minded people, but surely the stories about his antics aren't for converted men and women!

Roman Catholic priest Andrew M. Greeley has written novels about priests—priests who show their moral and ethical "strength" by committing adultery, incest, and sacrilege. The reason he gives for writing such lurid novels, which he calls "religious" books, may be the same reason that the stories about Samson have been preserved in Sacred Writ. Greeley says that his stories "will be successful if the reader" learns that God "draws straight with crooked lines."

God, through His grace, can transform the crooked lines we make with our flawed lives into straight lines—just as He did with Samson's moral ineptitude.

Micah's Shrine

"I know the Lord will bless me now," Micah said, "because I have a Levite serving as my priest."
Judges 17:13, NLT.

A nameless woman, mother of Micah, had 1,100 silver shekels (28 pounds) stolen from her. This large amount reminds us of Delilah, who in the previous story received 1,100 shekels from each of five Philistine lords. Or was it a total of 1,100 shekels? Some scholars speculate that Micah's mother was Delilah (unnamed) and his father, Samson (unnamed).

Mother had cursed the thief, who turned out to be Micah, who confessed his theft. Mother undid her curse with a blessing and dedicated the money to YHWH. She then gave 200 shekels to Micah, telling him to have constructed "a carved image and a cast idol" (Judges 17:3, NIV).

Micah ensconced the two silver statues, an ephod, and some teraphim (other images of deities) in a shrine at his house and ordained one of his sons as priest. At some unspecified future time a young Bethlehemite named Jonathan, a grandson of Moses, wandered into town. When Micah learned that the stranger was a Levite, he hired him to serve as "father" and "priest," saying, "I will give you ten pieces of silver a year, plus a change of clothes and your food" (verse 10, NLT).

The Levite accepted, so Micah fired his son from the priesthood and exclaimed, "I know the Lord will bless me now, because I have a Levite serving as my priest" (verse 13).

Soon five spies from the tribe of Dan arrived. Noting the shrine, they inquired of Jonathan if God would bless their activities. He replied, "Go in peace. . . . The Lord will go ahead of you" (Judges 18:6, NLT). Later 600 Danites, along with the five spies, returned. They stole the contents of the shrine, apparently leaving one idol behind, and employed Jonathan to be their priest. After burning the city of Laish, they renamed it Dan and set up a shrine there, outfitting it with the pillage and priest they'd filched from Micah.

It appears that Micah, his mother (Delilah?), and possibly the marauding Danites were sincere in wanting a holy place for YHWH. However, their methodology smacked of heathenism, including idolatry, a violation of the second commandment. Uninformed ardor typically leads to eccentric behavior. In spiritual matters it is best to compare one's behavior with God's Word. A do-it-yourself religion is deficient, despite one's earnestness.

Good Intentions
Run Amok

*In those days Israel had no king, so the people
did whatever seemed right in their own eyes.
Judges 17:6, NLT.*

A Levite took a girl as a concubine, "but she was unfaithful . . . and returned to her father's home" (Judges 19:2, NLT). After four months
elapsed (by now she'd be "showing" if she were pregnant), the Levite, along
with a servant and two donkeys, went to retrieve her.

After five days of manly conviviality, the Levite, slave, concubine, and
pack animals headed for home. Arriving in Gibeah, a Benjaminite town, the
assemblage hunkered down in the town square, but were ignored by the
local relatives—a baleful omen. Finally an old man returning from the fields
invited them to bunk with him. Soon the neighborhood hellions demanded
the Levite . . . to rape.

Protecting his male guests, the host offered them his own virginal
daughter and the Levite's concubine. Flying into action, the Levite shoved
his concubine out the door. The lascivious ne'er-do-wells "abused her all
night, taking turns raping her" (verse 25, NLT) while the men slept safely inside, ignoring the ruckus outside. "At dawn, they let her go" (verse 25, NLT).
The savaged victim crawled to the front door, "her hands on the threshold"
(verse 27, NLT).

Scripture doesn't say if she was dead or alive, but the Levite tossed her
onto a donkey and headed north. Back at home, she was either DOA or was
killed when the Levite hacked her into 12 pieces and sent one segment to
each tribe.

Righteously indignant, the Israelites cobbled together 400,000 and went
straight to the Levite. After hearing his twisted version of events, they
marched to Gibeah. Civil war ensued, and ultimately just 600 Benjaminites
remained. The Israelites allayed their consciences of ethnic cleansing by providing the 600 with virgins from Jabesh-gilead and Shiloh.

One nightmarishly violated concubine—raped, tortured, murdered, and
dismembered! How many wrongs would it take to right the one wrong?
Statistics: 40,030 dead Israelite soldiers, 50,600 slain Benjaminite warriors, ex-
termination of nearly the entire tribe of Benjamin, and 600 kidnapped virgins. That's what happens when good intentions go wrong—terribly wrong.

The Right Choice

They started weeping loudly all over again;
Orpah then kissed her mother-in-law and went
back to her people. But Ruth stayed with her.
Ruth 1:14, New Jerusalem.

Famine scourged the area around Bethlehem. Elimelech decided he should travel to an area with available food. So he, his wife, Naomi, and their two sons, Mahlon and Chilion, moved to the Moab plateau.

Relations between the Israelites and the Moabites varied from time to time, although many (if not most) of the references in Scripture refer to hostility. Apparently at this point, peace prevailed, allowing the family from Bethlehem to migrate there.

After arriving in Moab, Elimelech died. When Mahlon and Chilion became young adults, they married Moabite girls, which wasn't surprising but was the stated danger against which God warned His people. The girls were Orpah, wife of Chilion, and Ruth, spouse of Mahlon. Alas, in due time both Mahlon and Chilion died also. Naomi was left without husband and sons, and Ruth and Orpah were without husbands.

After 10 years had passed—either the total amount of time the Bethlehemite family stayed in Moab or the time that Orpah and Ruth were widows—Naomi learned that back home the famine was over. So the trio of widows took to the road. Shortly, however, Naomi urged the young women—probably in their mid-20s—to stay in Moab, where they could remarry and worship Chemosh, the Moabite deity.

After more prodding, Orpah kissed Naomi goodbye and turned back. Ruth, however, insisted she would stay with her mother-in-law. Ruth vowed: "Your people will be my people, and your God will be my God. Where you die, I shall die and there I shall be buried" (Ruth 1:16, 17, New Jerusalem). And she accompanied Naomi to Bethlehem.

What do you think? Who did the right thing—Orpah or Ruth? Must we decide? Maybe Orpah did the right thing when she honored her mother-in-law's commands and remained in Moab, receiving Naomi's blessing. And surely Ruth did the right thing by staying with Naomi and putting a curse on herself if she did otherwise. Sometimes our options are such that God can bless any of them. Even if one is less advantageous than the other(s), God is creative enough so that He can still bless!

Woe Is Me!

Do not call me Naomi, call me Mara,
for Shaddai has made my lot bitter.
Ruth 1:20, New Jerusalem.

The lot of widows in the ancient Near East was precarious. Even among God's people, widows found themselves in dire circumstances. Through Isaiah, Jeremiah, Ezekiel, Zechariah, and Malachi, He remonstrated with them about not treating widows fairly.

A dark cloud seems to hover over some people, and Naomi appears to have been one of these unfortunate souls. While living in a foreign land—a place where Israelites weren't always welcome and where false gods such as Chemosh were worshipped—she lost within a 10-year period her husband and her two married sons. Left behind was a trio of widows.

Naomi wasn't one to suffer silently. With sourness in her heart she openly accused God of cruelty. Read her words. "Call me Mara, for Shaddai has made my lot bitter. I departed full, and Yahweh has brought me home empty. . . . Yahweh has pronounced against me and Shaddai has made me wretched" (verses 20, 21, New Jerusalem).

Note her list of accusations: (1) don't call me Naomi ("sweet one"), but call me Mara ("bitter one") instead; (2) the God of breasts (El Shaddai), who should mother His children, "made my lot bitter"; (3) I left Bethlehem full like a pregnant woman, but God made me return empty-handed; (4) YHWH has tried and convicted me (unfairly); and (5) God has been evil, doing me wrong.

Not a pretty picture. And, according to Naomi, it was all God's fault! Instead of treating her as He'd promised to care for His covenant people, God had behaved carelessly—even maliciously—toward this hapless widow! How could He behave like that when elsewhere He insisted that His people should take good care of widows?

What do you think? Was Naomi correct in her grievance? Had God Himself made all those terrible things happen to her? Bad things happen to good people, and I think we're just plain wrong when we blame God for them. That makes a devil out of God!

Affective discourse is expressing emotion or evoking emotion in others. Affective speech isn't a way of expressing fact, an example of informative discourse. God recognizes this and doesn't strike us with a bolt of lightning when we vent our emotions, implicating Him in our heartbreak.

Providence

*Naomi had a kinsman on her husband's side, well-to-do and of Elimelech's clan. His name was Boaz.
Ruth 2:1, New Jerusalem.*

Naomi and Ruth arrived home in April or May. Ruth noticed that clusters of people daily would hike to the fields outside of Bethlehem—site of the grain fields. She decided to join the harvesters as a gleaner. According to Hebrew law, widows, orphans, and foreigners could glean, and Ruth qualified on at least two counts.

"Chance led [Ruth] to a plot of land belonging to Boaz" (Ruth 2:3, New Jerusalem). Man that he was, Boaz noticed her and asked the foreman about her. He explained Ruth's background, calling her a Moabitess (Moabite women seem to have had a "reputation") and pointing out that she'd arrived in Bethlehem with Naomi (not with a man). Boaz, showing more than casual interest in Ruth, instructed her to stay near the group of young women who were harvesting so that the men wouldn't molest her. When she got thirsty, Ruth should help herself to the water jugs. From the chitchat, one begins to suspect that Boaz may have been obliquely wooing Ruth.

Boaz invited Ruth to join the cluster of workers for lunch, although she sat at the edge of the group. He gave her so much bread, parched grain, and wine that she ate until she could eat no more. Furthermore, Boaz gave her heaps of the parched grain to carry home with her. At the end of the day Ruth returned to Naomi with somewhere between 30 and 50 pounds of barley!

Ultimately, as you know, Boaz married Ruth, and they—an Israelite and a Moabite—became King David's great-grandparents.

God doesn't appear as an overt character in the plot, although His name is used in stereotypical fashion in greetings and outbursts of affective discourse. But considerable human initiative is evident in the story line: Ruth, on her own initiative, gleans in Boaz's field; Boaz takes a liking to her; at Naomi's prodding Ruth bathes, dabs on perfume, dons a pretty dress, and slips into Boaz's "bedroom" for an intimate conversation; she gleans for seven weeks—through the wheat harvest; Boaz takes pains to become the "redeemer"; Boaz and Ruth marry; as a result of the consummation of their marriage, Obed is conceived, David's grandfather.

Often we speak of divine providence, making it all one-sided. Maybe we should define it differently: Providence comprises both divine and human activities.

Calling Sin by
Its "Right" Name

Elkanah had two wives, Hannah and Peninnah.
Peninnah had children, while Hannah did not.
1 Sam. 1:2, NLT.

Elkanah lived in Ramathaim-zophim with his two wives, Hannah and Peninnah. Hannah was his favorite, so she's mentioned first (1 Samuel 1:5 confirms this assumption). However, Peninnah had the happy fortune of having given birth, whereas Hannah was barren!

Being childless is hard even for contemporary women, but in the ancient Near East it was an even greater misfortune. Infertility was seen as a woman's flaw, not a husband's defect. She wasn't a receptive garden for the seed planted in her, a constant source of personal shame. Beyond this, childlessness was often seen as God's doing, as indicated in verses 5 and 6.

Elkanah tried to ease Hannah's inner turmoil by giving her twice (NRSV) as much of his annual sacrifice as he apportioned to Peninnah and her children. Nonetheless, Peninnah's taunting only increased Hannah's feelings of self-deprecation, leaving her in tears and with no appetite for her double portion. With typical male insensitivity (despite good intentions), Elkanah soothed, "What's the matter, Hannah? Why aren't you eating? Why be so sad just because you have no children? You have me—isn't that better than having ten sons?" (verse 8, NLT).

One year at Shiloh Hannah cracked under the emotional stress. Falling on her knees at the sanctuary, she cried to God in her desperation: "If you will look down upon my sorrow and answer my prayer and give me a son, then I will give him back to you" (verse 11, NLT).

Priest Eli watched Hannah's emotional outburst but heard no words because she was thinking, not vocalizing, them. Accustomed to denouncing evil, he scolded, "Must you come here drunk? Throw away your wine!" (verse 14, NLT). Although never apologizing, Eli, upon hearing Hannah's clarification, to his credit sent her away with a jolly "Cheer up!" (NLT), along with a blessing.

The practice of calling sin by its right name shouldn't be undertaken lightly. Since in our humanity we're finite, we can easily jump to conclusions about others—making unsound judgments that all too often are erroneous. Perhaps that's why so few of us have been truly called by God to pronounce verdicts on others. Better to let God—the only infinite, all-knowing, and infallible one—do the judging! We aren't cut out to call sin by its right name.

God Doesn't Need Our Defense

The glory has departed from Israel,
for the Ark of God has been captured.
1 Sam. 4:22, NLT.

The Philistines attacked God's people. So the Hebrews encamped at Ebenezer, and the Philistines bivouacked at nearby Aphek. During the first skirmish, the Israelites lost 4,000. To reinforce the soldiers' sagging morale and to assure victory, the leaders fetched the ark of the covenant. When the Philistines learned that "the gods have come into their camp!" (1 Sam. 4:7, NLT), they wailed, "This is a disaster!" (verse 7, NLT), adding, "Who can save us from these mighty gods of Israel?" (verse 8, NLT).

The Philistines reattacked, trouncing the Israelites again, who suffered 30,000 more casualties. Additionally, the Philistines captured the ark and assumed that the Hebrew people were now godless, hence powerless.

The Philistines placed the ark of YHWH in the temple of Dagon, their chief deity. In the morning the image of Dagon was prostrate. He was hoisted back on his pedestal, but the next day he was found again flat on his face and with a mortal wound—headless . . . and handless. Furthermore, the Ashdodites were dying from a plague.

The ark was transferred to Gath, but soon the deadly plague was decimating the population there. So the ark was moved once more, to Ekron, but with the same fatal results.

After seven months of plague, the Philistines decided to return the ark to the Israelites. It was placed, along with some sacrificial gifts, on an unused cart pulled by two cows. After some prodding, the cows began plodding—straight for the Israelite town of Beth-shemesh. Not having a local priest among them, the townspeople petitioned the citizens of Kiriath-jearim to provide for the ark. Eleazar, a priest, tended the ark of YHWH for 20 years.

There's a religious literary type called "apology," in which one's faith is defended against outside naysayers. Additionally, there's a subdivision of theology known as "theodicy," in which God and His very existence are defended in the light of the presence of evil. These religious exercises rarely fulfill their purpose, even though some regard them as worthwhile endeavors. Despite our best efforts and intentions in defending God from the onslaughts of unbelievers, God can—and will—take care of Himself. We might need to be saved by the all-powerful YHWH, but He doesn't need our frail efforts to "save" Him.

Modesty
Becomes Leaders

They consulted Yahweh, "Has [Saul] come here?" Yahweh
replied, "There he is, hiding among the baggage."
1 Sam. 10:22, New Jerusalem.

Some of Kish's donkeys had wandered off—a chance happening, perhaps. So Saul and a servant began a search-and-rescue operation, searching far and wide, but with no success.

Upon reaching Zuph, it just so happened they were near Samuel's home. "Perhaps he will be able to show us the way that we should take" (1 Sam. 9:6, New Jerusalem), the servant suggested. Saul had nothing of monetary value to give to Samuel, but the servant produced from nowhere a quarter of a shekel. As they approached the city, they chanced upon some girls fetching water, who informed the duo that Samuel had just entered town. What a coincidence!

As the two travelers entered the city, they fortuitously met Samuel, who was making his way to a feast. Samuel explained that the donkeys had been found and invited Saul to the feast. The next morning, as Saul turned toward home, Samuel unobtrusively anointed him with oil. Saul was to be the first king of Israel! Samuel further explained that near Rachel's tomb they would meet two men bearing the news that the lost had been found.

Samuel also said that at the Oak of Tabor they'd encounter three men and one of them would give them two loaves of bread. Then when they reached the town of Gibeah, they'd come across a group of ecstatic prophets. "The spirit of Yahweh will then seize on you, and you will go into ecstasy with them" (1 Sam. 10:6, New Jerusalem). From there Saul was to stop at Gilgal, where he needed to wait seven days for Samuel to show up with further instructions.

Later at Mizpah, after these fortuitous events, Samuel cast a series of lots—another succession of chance events—and the final lot pointed to Saul as the newly elected king. But when Samuel was about to proclaim him king, Saul was nowhere to be found, because he was hiding.

Sometimes what at first seems to be a chain of coincidences turns out to be a string of providential events. And when this progression of incidents leads to the appointment of a leader who is not only surprised by the twisting of events but so fearful of the responsibility that he ends up hiding (oh, that all newly nominated leaders were so self-effacing!), we can rest assured that divine providence is at work.

Does God Repent?

The Strength of Israel will not lie nor repent:
for he is not a man, that he should repent.
1 Sam. 15:29.

King Saul, despite his self-effacing start as ruler, soon was ignoring God's directives. For instance, when he fought the Amalekites, Samuel had specifically instructed to place every living thing under the ban, which meant killing all. However, Saul spared King Agag and the best livestock. When Samuel confronted Saul, the king mumbled that it was his soldiers who had disobeyed. Samuel announced that God would transfer the kingship to another.

During the conversation Samuel uttered the words in our text for today, which has become a proof text for theologians who argue that all future events are fixed. Reasons proffered for why the future is inflexible vary.

Those who believe in predestination assure us that the future is set concretely because our sovereign God has decreed it to happen in a specific way. In one way or another, God wills every event—past, present, and future. Where, then, is human free will? It doesn't exist. People behave the way they do because God has declared in advance how they act. Humans may feel as though they have freely chosen their deeds, but that's a mere feeling and doesn't reflect reality.

Those who deny predestination often insist that although God doesn't decree future actions, in His omniscience He knows the future perfectly. So the future is not variable. People do have free will, but God has exact knowledge of how they'll use their freedom of choice.

Free will or not, the future remains certain—either (1) because God ordered it from eternity or (2) because He foresaw it from eternity.

There's a problem, though, with using 1 Samuel 15:29 as a proof text. The same narrative—before and after this verse—avers that God had indeed changed His mind: "It *repenteth* me that I have set up Saul to be king" (verse 11) and "The Lord *repented* that he had made Saul king over Israel" (verse 35).

This isn't an isolated incident. Scripture is replete with clear indications that God is not a prisoner to either His sovereign will or His foreknowledge. He is free to adapt His approach when His creatures use their God-given endowment of free will. His desire to transform and redeem never changes, though.

God's Spirit

An evil spirit from the Lord tormented [Saul].
1 Sam. 16:14, NRSV.

Adventists speak frequently about God's Spirit. We talk about the gift of the Spirit, the third member of the Godhead, bringing every other gift in its train. And so it comes as a shock to read in the Old Testament about some of the workings of the Spirit whom YHWH sends.

True, some passages state what we would expect. "The Spirit of God was moving over the surface of the waters" (Gen. 1:2, NASB). "My Spirit shall not strive with man forever" (Gen. 6:3, NKJV). "I have filled [Bezalel] with the Spirit of God, giving him great wisdom, intelligence, and skill in all kinds of crafts" (Ex. 31:3, NLT).

But other biblical passages leave us quite bewildered. "God sent an evil spirit between Abimelech and the lords of Shechem; and the lords of Shechem dealt treacherously with Abimelech" (Judges 9:23, NRSV). "The Spirit of the Lord came upon [Samson], and he went down to Ashkelon, and slew thirty men of them" (Judges 14:19). "The Spirit of God came upon Saul . . . , and his anger was kindled" (1 Sam. 11:6). "The evil spirit from God came upon Saul, and he prophesied" (1 Sam. 18:10). "The Lord has put a lying spirit in the mouths of your prophets" (2 Chron. 18:22, NLT). We could add other examples.

What should we make of these Bible verses and others like them that attribute what we would regard as strange effects to the presence of YHWH's Spirit? We can't weasel out of the predicament by arguing that in at least some of these verses the word "spirit" isn't capitalized. Uppercase letters aren't in the Hebrew manuscripts. So there must be another explanation. But what is it?

Unfortunately, the Bible writers don't offer insight into what they were thinking and why they wrote the way they did. So any explanations are speculative. But here's a possible explanation: Because idolatry was a constant enticement for ancient Israelites, YHWH and His spokespersons bent over backwards to avoid saying anything that people could construe as proving polytheism. For examples, the Old Testament doesn't emphasize demon possession, and, except for one possible instance, "Satan" isn't presented as a name but as a position or function. To preserve monotheism, therefore, God is said to have done things that in the New Testament would have been ascribed to the devil.

Love Costs

Jonathan made a covenant with David
because he loved him as himself.
1 Sam. 18:3, NIV.

For reasons Scripture doesn't elucidate, Jonathan became David's constant friend. Three times Scripture states that Jonathan "loved" David. We twenty-first-century Westerners don't know what to make of the expression. For us it seems to hint at homosexuality, which apparently wasn't the case, since David and Jonathan were married men with children.

Some biblical scholars note that in some ancient covenant treaties "love" described the political loyalty between a sovereign and his vassals. These scholars suggest that since Jonathan and David had covenanted together, we should understand the expression "Jonathan *loved* David" to mean he had sworn loyalty to David.

Whatever the implication, Jonathan's friendship with David didn't come cheap. First, Jonathan gave his imperial robe, armor, sword, bow, and belt to David (1 Sam. 18:4). Next, when Saul confided to Jonathan his intention to kill David, Jonathan told David about Saul's intention and then interceded with his father on David's behalf. Third, on a festal occasion, Jonathan risked his own life while defending David, who was absent. Saul called Jonathan a son of a "whore" (NLT) or a "slut" (New Jerusalem) and brandished his spear at his own son (1 Sam. 20:30, 33). Fourth, during one of Saul's hunting expeditions against David, Jonathan risked his life to encourage David, telling him, "Don't be afraid," that "you will be king over Israel, and I will be second to you. Even my father Saul knows this" (1 Sam. 23:17, NIV). Unfortunately, Jonathan never got to be David's second in command, because he was killed while fighting the Philistines (1 Sam. 31:2).

Jonathan's friendship with David not only compromised his position as heir apparent but also endangered his life. Nonetheless, Jonathan remained truly loyal to his friend, even though it entailed laying aside his own claim to the throne, along with all the honor that went with such a prestigious position. (Honor was most highly prized in the ancient Near East.)

Friendship is self-effacing. Friendship means laying aside one's own plans to support someone else's. Friendship means letting one's own honor decrease so that another's honor may increase. Friendship rejoices in another's successes. Friendship endures—regardless of what the other says or does. Genuine friendship costs, but it never counts the cost.

A Word From the Prophet

Nathan said to the king, "Go, do all that you have in mind; for the Lord is with you." 2 Sam. 7:3, NRSV.

D avid had become king of Judah, ruling from Hebron. Eshbaal, Saul's son, ascended Israel's throne. After seven and a half years, the divided kingdom was united under David.

David, in an astute political move, captured the city of Jerusalem—a neutral place because it hadn't been part of the territory of either Israel or Judah. It would make an acceptable capital city for all the Hebrews.

After David occupied Jerusalem, Hiram, king of Tyre, sent carpenters, builders, and construction supplies, which included rare cedar paneling from Lebanon, to erect a palace suitable for the king of Israel and Judah. Despite his pleasure in the luxurious bastion, David felt a bit uneasy. He, a mere human, was basking in extravagance, while YHWH, the one and only God, was staying in a tent—a tabernacle housing the ark of the covenant.

David summoned his court seer, Nathan, and said, "See now, I am living in a house of cedar, but the ark of God stays in a tent" (2 Sam. 7:2, NRSV). It just didn't seem right. It was as if the situation were backward. Surely God should have the elaborate dwelling place, not King David. And the prophet agreed, telling David, "Go, do all that you have in mind; for the Lord is with you" (verse 3, NRSV).

Having the prophet's sanction, David was ready to launch into another building project. However, that night God instructed Nathan to tell David, "Thus says the Lord of hosts: I took you from the pasture . . . ; and I have been with you wherever you went. . . . I will raise up your offspring after you. . . . He shall build a house for my name" (verses 8-13, NRSV). So in accordance with God's wishes, David dropped his plans to build a temple.

A word from a prophet isn't necessarily inspired of God. Prophets are people too and say a lot of things during the course of a day. Some of their words may not be about secular, everyday matters, but may have religious content. Even though prophets may speak from a sincere heart, their words are not infallible. Prophets may assume they're speaking for God, because they may presume knowledge of God's mind since He's addressed them so often. But such an assumption may not be valid.

The Movable Deity

*I have not lived in a house since the day I brought
up the people of Israel from Egypt to this day, but I
have been moving about in a tent and a tabernacle.*
2 Sam. 7:6, NRSV.

Despite David's good intentions, God told him through Nathan that He didn't want him to construct a temple. God said that He'd lived in a tent, accompanying His people, since the Exodus. He wasn't interested in settling down into a permanent abode.

Furthermore, God said He'd never complained about these transient quarters. "Wherever I have moved about among all the people of Israel, did I ever speak a word . . . , saying, 'Why have you not built me a house of cedar?'" (2 Sam. 7:7, NRSV). In short, YHWH was content to be a nomadic deity, remaining with His people wherever they wandered.

Evidence indicates that in the ancient Near East the gods were viewed as local deities tied to a particular place—the god of Ekron or the lord of Gath. In certain ancient Greek philosophical thought, God, because He was perceived as perfect, must be unchangeable, hence immovable.

However, YHWH was an immanent (nearby) deity. He behaved like a skilled craftsman at Creation, personally planting a garden, molding a man, and shaping a woman. He personally visited with Abraham, eating the toothsome meal the patriarch prepared. He came to Sodom and Gomorrah so He could see for Himself what was going on. He personally led the Hebrew people throughout their wilderness wanderings from Egypt to Canaan. He thundered the Decalogue from Mount Sinai. When His people suffered, He personally was afflicted also (Isa. 63:9).

Sometimes this personal revelation seemed to be the actual presence of the divine, as happened with Abraham and Moses. At other times God's immanence came via the "angel of YHWH." On occasion the theophany involved a "spirit from, or of, YHWH." Later yet God could speak of someone called "Immanuel," which means "God [is] with us."

As time progressed, however, the concept of divine immanence shifted. It taught the same idea, but in a more abstract way, entailing a philosophical mind-set, which the Hebrew people didn't have. Because they thought in concrete terms, God revealed Himself personally in concrete ways. Later this sense of immanence progressed into the doctrine that God is omnipresent while at the same time transcendent.

Who Dies for Whose Sin?

Since you have outraged Yahweh . . . ,
the child born to you will die.
2 Sam. 12:14, New Jerusalem.

King David strolled across the flat roof of his palace. Scanning the city below, he spotted a beautiful woman ritually bathing. Despite learning that Bathsheba was the wife of Uriah, one of his bravest soldiers, David summoned her to his mansion and violated her. (Women had little say over what men did to them and even less say when the perpetrator was the king.)

Sometime afterward she discovered she was expecting David's child. David had Uriah furloughed, hoping he'd sleep with Bathsheba, but David's soldiers remained ritually "clean" during combat duty. The king then wined and dined him, hoping the intoxicated Uriah would stumble home and into Bathsheba's loving embrace. But Uriah didn't.

David then handed a sealed letter to Uriah, commanding that he personally deliver it to General Joab, and sent Uriah back to the battle. Joab read the imperial orders and saw to it that Uriah became a casualty. After Bathsheba had mourned Uriah's death for seven days, David ordered that she become his wife.

Nine months later Bathsheba gave birth to a son, but according to God's message through the prophet Nathan: "Yahweh . . . forgives your [David's] sin; you are not to die. But . . . the child . . . will die" (2 Sam. 12:13, 14, New Jerusalem). And after a weeklong illness, the innocent newborn—not blameworthy David—died.

In contemporary Christian thought this turn of events was a miscarriage of justice. Indeed, the prophet Jeremiah later wrote that it shouldn't be a matter of fathers eating unripe grapes with the result that their offspring had their own teeth set on edge. Instead, "each will die for his own guilt" (Jer. 31:30, New Jerusalem).

Today we believe we should freely pardon others. Forgiving is a gracious mental act in which we forgo vengeance and psychologically acquit the guilty. However, among ancient Near Easterners, guilt (sin) was something not so "easily" disposed of. If it wasn't to overburden the sinner, it had to be transferred to a third entity—a sacrificial animal, another person, or God Himself. There wasn't any unrequited guilt or evaporating sin.

Thank God you can forgive me without killing my dog or kicking your cat or without your suffering physical and/or mental agony yourself!

Do Trustworthy People Lie?

"Where are Ahimaaz and Jonathan?" The woman said, "They have gone further on. . . ." They searched but, having found nothing, went back to Jerusalem. 2 Sam. 17:20, New Jerusalem.

Despite David's brilliant successes, rebellion was fomenting. Fearing for his life, he and his stalwart militia had to flee. The chief insurgent was none other than his son Absalom.

David left behind Hushai to "defect" to Absalom and thereby infiltrate the mutinous government supplanting his own God-given hegemony. Absalom suspected Hushai's intentions, but mouthing doubletalk and fabricating falsehoods, Hushai convinced Absalom of his support.

Two young men, Ahimaaz and Jonathan, were Hushai's conduits to David. On one occasion as they were en route to inform David of Absalom's plans, they almost got caught by the revolutionaries. "The pair of them, however, made off quickly, reaching the house of a man in Bahurim" (2 Sam. 17:18, New Jerusaslem). A pit was located in the courtyard, so the duo scrambled into it. The woman of the household "took a piece of canvas and, spreading it over the mouth of the storage-well, scattered crushed grain on it so that nothing showed" (verse 19, New Jerusalem).

When Absalom's soldiers arrived, they asked, "Where are Ahimaaz and Jonathan?" (verse 20, New Jerusalem). And this nameless hero lied, "They have gone further on" (verse 20, New Jerusalem). The scouts never located Ahimaaz and Jonathan, and returned to Jerusalem empty-handed. David's two secret agents crawled from their hiding place and reached him with their warning.

Both Hushai and this unnamed woman spoke deceitfully in order to protect David. Should they have been dishonest to save the king's life? These are only two of several instances in Scripture in which individuals were less than straightforward—speaking falsehoods—and sometimes they were actually saying what God told them to!

You've probably heard preachers extol God for being so wise a Creator that He provided some creatures with protective coloration. But isn't lifesaving camouflage yet another species of deception?

Suppose a friend volunteered to conceal you from those seeking your life but wouldn't lie when your enemies showed up at his door and asked him if he knew where you were. I know someone who has often said, "Never entrust your life to someone who won't lie to protect you."

The Prophet's Plot

March 17

1 Kings

Nathan . . . asked her, "Did you realize that Haggith's son, Adonijah, has made himself king and that our lord David doesn't even know about it? If you want to save your own life and the life of . . . Solomon, follow my counsel."
1 Kings 1:11, 12, NLT.

David was 70 years old and feeble. His oldest living son, now that Absalom was dead, was Adonijah. Unlike his half brother Absalom, Adonijah wasn't treasonous. He simply assumed he would ascend the throne upon David's death. Falling short of proclaiming himself king, he told supporters, "I *will* be king" (1 Kings 1:5, NRSV).

Nathan, David's court prophet, decided to remedy the situation. He told Bathsheba about Adonijah's actions, coloring his story with details that may or may not have been perfectly accurate. He urged Bathsheba to inform David of Adonijah's shenanigans, which were going on at that very moment. He even told her the precise words she should use with David in order to rouse the old king's ire. She was also to remind the feeble king of his promise to place Solomon on the throne—a vow that Scripture doesn't attest, making it a dubious claim.

While Bathsheba reported to David, Nathan himself showed up to add force to her story. Choosing his words carefully, the prophet made it sound as though Adonijah had already proclaimed himself king, as Absalom had done. Nathan added that the people had sworn allegiance to Adonijah by saying, "God save king Adonijah" (verse 25). He framed his words in such a way that it sounded as though he assumed that David had sanctioned Adonijah's behavior.

As a result of Bathsheba's and Nathan's accusations, David mustered sufficient energy to order his supporters to proclaim Solomon king that very day—at that very moment. Zadok, the priest, and Nathan, the prophet, were to anoint Solomon as king and proclaim, "God save king Solomon" (verse 34). And when Adonijah and his supporters heard the merriment in Jerusalem, their presumptuous attempt at kingmaking evaporated.

Some people criticize Nathan for getting involved in affairs of state. Prophets and politics, they suggest, don't mix. Perhaps they forget that throughout the duration of the Israelite monarchy God's spokespersons were indeed involved in politics. They reprimanded kings for their lack of justice, taking the side of the politically oppressed. Theirs was, if you please, a kind of social gospel! God is concerned for the marginalized downtrodden.

Getting Rid of Guilt

"Do as he said," the king replied. "Kill him there beside the altar and bury him. This will remove the guilt of his senseless murders from me and from my father's family."
1 Kings 2:31, NLT.

King Solomon was still recently enthroned when he began shoring up his support base. One of David's key military people was Joab, but during Absalom's insurgence Joab ignored David's orders and had been responsible for seditious Absalom's death.

Now King Solomon decided that it was time to set matters right. Joab's bloodguilt must be assuaged. Solomon commanded Benaiah, his right-hand man, to kill Joab, who had fled to the tabernacle for asylum, grabbing the horns of the altar. This maneuver didn't save him. Solomon sent Benaiah into the tent of YHWH, to "remove the guilt of his senseless murders from me and from my father's family. Then the Lord will repay him for the murders of two men who were more righteous and better than he" (1 Kings 2:31, 32, NLT).

In Scripture we meet blood vengeance early on. In Genesis 4 we read about Lamech's vengeance. "One day Lamech said to Adah and Zillah, 'Listen to me, my wives. I have killed a youth who attacked and wounded me. If anyone who kills Cain is to be punished seven times, anyone who takes revenge against me will be punished seventy-seven times!'" (verses 23, 24, NLT).

This way of evening the score continues yet to this day in certain parts of the world. It is seen as the responsibility of members of the aggrieved party to bring about "peace" by avenging the rights of the wounded person upon the perpetrator (and family). That was how wrongs were righted, how atonement was made, how forgiveness was achieved. It is this same principle that serves as the presupposition underlying animal sacrifice. The shedding of blood was seen as bringing about at-one-ment.

In our contemporary Western civilization, personal wrongs can be righted through psychological means. Outside the legal system, for example, we can forgive without extracting vengeance. We've all heard stories about bighearted people finding it within themselves to forgive—despite deep personal hurt—criminals for their heinous behaviors. Just as blood vengeance was costly, so too is forgiveness. It doesn't always come easily. Nonetheless, it has much to commend it.

King Solomon's Wisdom

And the king said, Bring me a sword. And they brought a sword before the king. And the king said, Divide the living child in two, and give half to the one, and half to the other.
1 Kings 3:24, 25.

March 19

1 Kings

Solomon could have been remembered for many reasons—his excessively large harem, the tranquillity that marked his period in office, the extreme opulence of his household, etc. But Solomon has become a legend not because of those and other factors, but because of his wisdom.

Early in his regime, while worshipping at the city of Gibeon, God offered the dreaming king anything his heart desired. Although in a dream state, Solomon had enough presence of mind to ask for wisdom to rule well. God commended the king for his humble yearning, promising to bestow upon him wealth and honor also.

Soon two young women appeared before him. One held an infant in her arms. The first woman accused the second of having kidnapped her baby during the night in order to replace her own child who had just died. The women bickered back and forth in the king's presence.

When it came time for Solomon's ruling, he asked for a sword so that the newborn could be chopped in two, with half going to each of the women. One of the women then countered that rather than kill the infant, it should be given to the other woman. Solomon thereby deduced that the young woman who advocated sparing the baby was indeed the real mother.

We often differentiate between wisdom and knowledge. The latter is something we acquire through intelligence and learning. Wisdom, on the other hand, doesn't necessarily result from a high IQ. We've all known people of extraordinary intelligence who weren't very bright when it came to everyday good judgment. Solomon had both wisdom and knowledge.

According to the biblical account, God is the source of wisdom, which is highly prized. Michael V. Fox in the *Anchor Bible* commentary on Proverbs points out that Hebrew had many words that can be translated "wisdom." The specific word used of Solomon's prudence in these passages is *hokmāh*, which, Fox explains, combines the senses of both theoretical learning and practical skills. He suggests that the best English equivalent is the word "expertise."

Proverbs tells us that awesome reverence of God is the beginning of wisdom. It is something we can attain through devotion to God, the source of all wisdom.

Solomon's Construction Projects

[During] twenty years . . . Solomon built the two houses, the temple of the Lord and the palace of the king.
1 Kings 9:10, NAB.

Among Solomon's building projects was the construction of both the Temple of YHWH and the palace of Solomon. It took him 20 years—half his reign—to complete both projects.

His three-storied Temple took seven years to complete. The Temple itself (assuming that the cubit used was 20.6 inches, as does *The Seventh-day Adventist Bible Commentary*) was 103 feet long, 34 feet wide, and 51.5 feet high. According to Mordechai Cogan, the addition of the Temple "tripled the dimension of the capital city" (*1 Kings, Anchor Bible*, p. 251).

Aside from other costs, Solomon paid Hiram, king of Tyre, 20,000 kors of wheat and 20 kors of pure olive oil every year (1 Kings 5:11). Scholars aren't sure how much a kor would be in modern terms, but Jerome T. Walsh estimates that Solomon annually sent "Hiram between 100,000 and 240,000 bushels of wheat and between 800 and 2,000 gallons of the finest olive oil" (*Berit Olam: 1 Kings*, p. 98).

After the Temple was finished, it took Solomon 13 years to erect his palace, nearly twice the amount of time it had taken to construct the Temple. (He also built yet another edifice for his Egyptian wife and high places for some of his other wives.) The "House of the Forest of Lebanon" was longer and wider than the Temple, and had a square footage more than four times that of the Temple.

It appears that Solomon gave precedence to the construction of the Temple, building it before he commenced work on his palace. However, the longer duration of construction and the much larger area of the latter makes one wonder about Solomon's priorities, because it appears that his palace had more grandeur than the Temple.

Which is more elaborate—my house or my local church? Which is better furnished—your house or your church? Some Christians argue that we shouldn't spend lavish amounts of money on a church edifice, because Jesus is coming soon. Yet what about their houses and other possessions—cars, boats, etc.? I've seen some pretty dilapidated churches, haven't you? If our houses are fancier than our churches, are we really seeking *first* the kingdom of God?

Solomon's Excesses

King Solomon excelled all the kings
of the earth in riches and in wisdom.
1 Kings 10:23, NRSV.

Solomon had legendary wisdom. Not just the queen of Sheba came to ascertain his astuteness, but "the whole earth sought . . . to hear his wisdom" (1 Kings 10:24, NRSV).

Solomon, however, achieved fame for more than good judgment. He became excessively wealthy, dwelling in opulence and drinking from gold vessels. Gold became so ordinary in Jerusalem that "silver [was] as common . . . as stones" (verse 27, NRSV). In one year the gold King Solomon accrued was 666 talents (verse 14). Depending on the weight of the talent, which varied, this equaled between 30 and 85 tons of gold (*Berit Olam: 1 Kings*, p. 129)!

Then there were his horses and cavalry. Solomon "had fourteen hundred chariots and twelve thousand horses" (verse 26, NRSV). Horses had to be imported from other countries, because they weren't native to Canaan.

Additionally, Solomon had the notoriety of amassing one of the largest harems on record—"seven hundred princesses, and three hundred concubines" (1 Kings 11:3, NRSV). As if 700 queens couldn't satisfy him, he enjoyed 300 concubines as well.

Many of these women harked from heathen nations. So Solomon provided for their religious preferences, constructing shrines for Chemosh, the Moabite god, and Milcom, the Ammonite deity. It wasn't enough that his queens worshiped these pagan gods. Solomon himself "worshiped Astarte the goddess of the Sidonians, Chemosh the god of Moab, and Milcom the god of the Ammonites" (verse 33, NRSV).

In retrospect, Solomon ended up doing exactly what Deuteronomy 17:16, 17 proscribed: "He must not . . . acquire more and more horses. . . . Nor must he keep on acquiring more and more wives. . . . Nor must he acquire vast quantities of silver and gold" (New Jerusalem).

Of course, there's nothing wrong with riding a horse, marrying a woman, or owning gold. It's the overindulgence of such goods that can turn into a snare even for someone as dedicated as Solomon was . . . at first. Disproportionate excess of any kind can lead to moral decay. Humble, godly people can become just the opposite when they have too much of anything. "The best is always a hair's breadth from the worst" (William Sloane Coffin, *Credo*, p. 53).

Solomon's Day of Reckoning

Yahweh was angry with Solomon because his heart had turned away from Yahweh, God of Israel.
1 Kings 11:9, New Jerusalem.

Year after year, decade upon decade, King Solomon enjoyed the good life. Wisdom lovers from neighboring nations admired him. The Temple he constructed left everybody in awe. His living quarters were lavishly constructed from the rarest of materials. He sat on a colossal ivory throne decorated with gold. His tables overflowed with delicacies. His personal assets left visitors slack-jawed. His lust was sated, thanks to 1,000 lovers. His warhorses numbered 12,000. His merchant marine armada (it appears that he had two of them) visited far-flung ports and returned with exotic supplies and animals. In his "wisdom" he became so broad-minded that he worshipped Astarte, Milcom, and Chemosh in addition to YHWH.

"King Solomon became richer and wiser than any other king" (1 Kings 10:23, NLT). People who pretty much "have everything" tend to forget to whom they're accountable. Excess acquisition all too often leads to excess loss of common sense and common kindness. Such people become a law unto themselves, forgetting probity and purity and piety. Such people—including Solomon—lose touch with reality, forgetting the simple truth that "to know God is to do justice" (William Sloane Coffin, *Credo*, p. 51). God, however, never forgets that reality. He told this self-sufficient king, "Since you have behaved like this . . . I shall tear the kingdom away from you and give it to one of your servants" (1 Kings 11:11, New Jerusalem).

Furthermore, "Yahweh raised an enemy against Solomon, Hadad" (verse 14, New Jerusalem). Also, "God raised a second enemy against Solomon, Rezon. . . . He was hostile to Israel as long as Solomon lived" (verses 23-25, New Jerusalem). Three times in these three verses the Bible writer refers to a satan (variously translated as "enemy" or "adversary" or "hostile") whom God stirred up against Solomon.

Finally, God told Jeroboam, one of Solomon's high officials, that he would reign over 10 northern Israelite tribes. Rehoboam, Solomon's son, would govern only the tribes making up Judah.

It was a tragic end for the king who had shown such humility and promise at the outset of his reign.

Faithfulness Amid Unfaithfulness

But for the sake of my servant David and the city of Jerusalem, which I have chosen out of all the tribes of Israel, he will have one tribe. 1 Kings 11:32, NIV.

King Solomon had honored God for much of his reign, but, as mentioned earlier, toward the end he added to his worship of YHWH devotion to Astarte, Milcom, and Chemosh, thereby voiding his part of the covenant God had made with his father and had renewed with him.

YHWH confronted Solomon. "I will most certainly tear the kingdom away from you and give it to one of your subordinates" (1 Kings 11:11, NIV). That subordinate turned out to be Jeroboam, who was confronted by Ahijah the prophet. Ahijah took a garment and tore it into a dozen pieces, telling Jeroboam, "Take ten pieces for yourself, for . . . the Lord, the God of Israel, says: 'See, I am going to tear the kingdom out of Solomon's hand and give you ten tribes'" (verse 31, NIV).

What about the remaining two tribes? Ahijah explained that YHWH intended for Solomon's son, Rehoboam, to have just a fraction of the former united monarchy. "He will have one tribe" (verse 32, NIV). (The math here doesn't add up: 12 − 1 = 11, not 10, so this episode is hardly a suitable teaching aid for homeschooling! The answer lies in the fact that the tribe of Joseph consisted of Ephraim and Manasseh.)

God, through Ahijah, explained why He was putting only 10 tribes under Jeroboam. He would leave a small portion to the Davidic hegemony "for the sake of David my servant" (verse 34, NIV). Furthermore, God wouldn't strip Solomon of his kingdom but would wait until his son ascended the throne (verse 35). "I will give one tribe to his son [Rehoboam] so that David . . . may always have a lamp before me in Jerusalem, the city where I chose to put my Name" (verse 36, NIV).

God had covenanted with David, stipulating that David's house would rule in perpetuity. But the covenant wasn't one-sided. David and his descendants must honor and obey God, which Solomon did for most of his reign, but toward the end abandoned loyalty to YHWH alone. However, despite Solomon's breach of covenant, God in His merciful faithfulness would keep covenant with David (and even with Solomon) by allowing Solomon's son to rule over a fraction of the territory—the southern kingdom of Judah. Solomon may have broken covenant, but God hadn't. The continuation of Davidic rule would depend on Rehoboam's allegiance.

Rehoboam's Insolence

*Rehoboam went to Shechem, where all
Israel had gathered to make him king.
1 Kings 12:1, NLT.*

At first it looked as if Ahijah's prophecy wouldn't be fulfilled. "All Israel" had come together to crown Rehoboam. Leaders of the 10 tribes that Ahijah had spoken about sent Jeroboam to Shechem as their spokesperson. Solomon, favoring his own tribal roots, had taxed and pressed into hard labor only the 10 tribes. Now they wanted some relief.

Jeroboam said to Rehoboam, "Your father was a hard master. . . . Lighten the harsh labor demands and heavy taxes that your father imposed on us. Then we will be your loyal subjects" (1 Kings 12:4, NLT). Notice that the 10 tribes weren't asking for the same exemption that the other two tribes had enjoyed. Instead, all they wanted was for the burden to be lightened. Surely this was a sensible appeal.

Rehoboam, as any prudent person would do, I suppose, asked for time. After three days he would announce his decision.

Rehoboam first turned to his father's counselors. "What is your advice? . . . How should I answer these people?" (verse 6, NLT). These seasoned politicians responded with what sounded like good advice. "If you are willing to serve the people today and give them a favorable answer, they will always be your loyal subjects" (verse 7, NLT). Some scholars read between the lines and conclude that the intent was that if Rehoboam acted like a servant now, later his subjects could be pressed into servitude, such as Solomon had required.

Rehoboam then turned to his new set of advisors, young men he'd grown up with. (The Bible writer insults them, labeling them "boys.") These greenhorns replied not only with what can best be called audacity but also with words that were risqué. Omitting their vulgarity, they told him to answer: "My father was harsh on you, but I'll be even harsher! My father used whips on you, but I'll use scorpions!" (verse 11, NLT). The reference to scorpions probably referred not to arthropods with vicious stingers but to a kind of lash with metal tips that shredded the flesh, leaving excruciating wounds. Rehoboam answered Jeroboam by echoing the words of his immature consultants. The 10 tribes reacted to his severity by crowning Jeroboam as their king. Rehoboam learned too late that harshness isn't becoming to a leader.

The Showdown

They . . . called on the name of Baal from morning until noon, crying, "O Baal, answer us!" But there was no voice, and no answer. 1 Kings 18:26, NRSV.

Ahab, king of northern Israel, had succumbed to Baal worship. As an omen of God's displeasure, the land suffered three years of drought. Finally God instructed Elijah, "Go, present yourself to Ahab" (1 Kings 18:1, NRSV). Elijah confronted the king and ordered him to "have all Israel assemble . . . at Mount Carmel, with the four hundred fifty prophets of Baal and the four hundred prophets of Asherah" (verse 19, NRSV) for a showdown between YHWH and Baal.

Elijah proposed to the gathered multitude that the false prophets offer a bull to Baal and he'd sacrifice one to YHWH. Whichever deity answered, by fire, would be the winner. "All the people answered, 'Well spoken!'"(verse 24, NRSV).

All day Baal's prophets prayed and danced around the altar, cutting themselves to induce Baal to action. "But there was no voice, and no answer" (verse 26, NRSV).

When Elijah prayed, after having doused the altar with 12 jars of water, "the fire of the Lord fell and consumed the burnt offering, the wood, the stones, and the dust, and even licked up the water" (verse 38, NRSV).

Popular piety insists that God *always* answers prayers. Sometimes He says no; sometimes, yes; sometimes, wait. By such logic, Baal's silence was an answer—a simple no! (Or maybe Baal said wait, and Elijah was too impatient.) However, in the Mount Carmel story we're told two times that Baal did *not* answer the prayer of his prophets (verses 26 and 29).

If an answer to prayer makes any sense at all, it must clearly correspond with the appeal. Answered prayer means God fulfilled the request. Popular piety is problematical because it makes a verifiable answer to prayer unattainable unless the answer is yes. Then, anything that happens—or doesn't happen, as the case may be—can be twisted into an "answer" to prayer, turning God's response to prayer into a matter of "Tails, I win; heads, you lose."

So maybe we shouldn't be quick to accept the idea that prayers are always answered—with a yes, no, or wait. If we believe prayer genuinely makes a difference, then we should have evidence for that belief, specific and compelling evidence. Otherwise, in the presence of divine silence anything—or nothing—could be construed as an answer to prayer.

A Prophecy Partly Fulfilled

His body was taken to Samaria and buried there. . . .
His chariot was washed beside the pool of Samaria, . . .
and dogs came and licked the king's blood.
1 Kings 22:37, 38, NLT.

Ahab, king of Israel, in alliance with Jehoshaphat, king of Judah, initiated hostilities against Ramoth-gilead. The raid wasn't undertaken lightly. Ahab consulted his 400 prophets, who unanimously assured him—albeit in rather ambiguous terms—that the war effort would succeed. Jehoshaphat wanted a second opinion, so the prophet Micaiah was mustered. Initially he parroted the 400 prophets, but then he explained having seen in vision the soldiers "scattered . . . like sheep without a shepherd. And the Lord said, 'Their master has been killed'" (1 Kings 22:17, NLT).

Ahab and Jehoshaphat led the troops into combat. Ahab fought in disguise but insisted Jehoshaphat wear royal regalia into battle. (Scholars are divided over whether Ahab was protecting himself or Jehoshaphat.)

As it turned out, Ahab's ruse ended up sparing Jehoshaphat's life. However, an anonymous archer shot haphazardly and managed to wound Ahab with an arrow that just happened to find a weak spot in his armor. Ahab bled to death in the chariot. His body was brought to Samaria, and his blood, having been washed from his chariot, was lapped up by undomesticated dogs. Also, "prostitutes washed" (verse 38, New Jerusalem) in his coagulated blood.

Kings tells us Ahab's fate fulfilled two prophecies. One we know of (the dogs lapping his blood), but another is unrecorded (harlots bathing, for whatever reason, in his blood).

Elijah had predicted: "In the place where dogs licked up Naboth's blood, dogs will lick up your blood" (1 Kings 21:19, NIV). Elijah was right . . . but wrong! Although feral dogs lapped up the blood of both Naboth and Ahab, this macabre event didn't happen in the same place as Elijah had predicted. Naboth's body was in Jezreel, whereas Ahab's body was in Samaria.

Neither Elijah nor Micaiah had said anything about prostitutes taking a literal bloodbath, but this enigmatic bathing was apparently the fulfillment of an enigmatic prediction.

This weird turn of events leaves us with an enigma. How could Elijah, Micaiah, and an unnamed prophet be so right about the event while Elijah was so wrong about the place? Prophecies can fail (Paul later admitted that in 1 Corinthians 13:8), most likely because of the element of human free will. That's how much God honors our freedom.

Fire From Heaven

Elijah answered the captain of fifty, "If I am a man of God, let fire come down from heaven and consume you and your fifty." Then fire came down from heaven, and consumed him and his fifty.
2 Kings 1:10, NRSV.

Israel's King Ahaziah suffered an accident in his own palace, falling "through the lattice in his upper chamber" (2 Kings 1:2, NRSV). It's possible he tumbled off the roof of his house. Wondering if he'd survive this mishap, he dispatched messengers to Baal-zebub ("lord of flies"), the god of Ekron, to ask if he would recuperate.

The angel of YHWH visited Elijah and instructed him to intercept Ahaziah's messengers. The prophet wanted to know why they were about to inquire of Baal-zebub. Wasn't there a God in Israel who should be consulted? Then he broke the bad news: "You shall surely die" (verse 4, NRSV). (Sounds like Genesis 2:17, doesn't it? When you eat of the tree, "you shall surely die." The Hebrew is identical in both passages.)

Not happy with Elijah's interference, the king sent "a captain of fifty with his fifty men" (2 Kings 1:9, NRSV) to arrest Elijah. Elijah wasn't intimidated by this show of force and replied, "Let fire come down from heaven and consume you and your fifty" (verse 10, NRSV). And so it happened. Ahaziah commissioned a second military unit of 50 to seize Elijah, but with the same result. He sent yet a third division of 50. Their leader was less foolhardy, pleading with Elijah to spare their lives. Whereupon God told Elijah to accompany the soldiers to Samaria.

Elijah had a reputation for bombast. It was he who staged the showdown between Baal and YHWH on Mount Carmel. It was he who slaughtered the prophets of Baal (1 Kings 18:40). This time he called down fire from heaven, destroying 100 soldiers and their leaders (unlike Jesus, who refused to call down fire to incinerate people). Other prophets were not so flamboyant. Moses was extremely meek. Jonah went AWOL. Jeremiah was prone to spells of weeping. Hosea seems to have been a romantic. Ezekiel appears to have been mentally unhinged. Regardless of our personal idiosyncrasies, God honors our individuality. He appears to shun using cookie-cutter messengers. Men and women of all personality types can serve Him . . . effectively.

The Battle With Moab

"What should we do?" the king of Israel cried out. "The Lord has brought the three of us here to let the king of Moab defeat us." But King Jehoshaphat of Judah asked, "Is there no prophet of the Lord with us? If there is, we can ask the Lord what to do."
2 Kings 3:10, 11, NLT.

Mesha, a Moabite king, had been a vassal to Ahab and then Jehoram, kings of Israel. Annually he had to pay a levy of 100,000 lambs as well as the wool sheared from 100,000 rams (2 Kings 3:4). This amount of tribute certainly must have strained to the max his fiscal interests.

Once Ahab had died and his son Jehoram was ensconced on the throne, Mesha rebelled, breaking the covenant treaty imposed on him. So King Jehoram turned to both Jehoshaphat, king of Judah, and the king of Edom for military support. It was a fragile alliance of three nations that were often at one another's throats.

For seven days the allied troops marched toward Moab, but "water for the men or their pack animals" (verse 9, NLT) ran out. The situation was calamitous; soon the entire militia would consist of corpses shriveling in the sizzling Middle Eastern sun.

Confronted with this dire situation, King Jehoram said, "The Lord has brought the three of us here to let the king of Moab defeat us" (verse 10, NLT). His words sound rather pious, akin to saying, "It is God's will." But such theology is at best Calvinistic, and at worst fatalistic. It implies that all which happens—good, bad, or indifferent—is what God from eternity has willed to occur. But is everything God's will? Does He want 25 to 50 acres of rain forest destroyed every minute? Twenty-five percent of girls to be sexually molested? Hurricanes and tornadoes and tsunamis to devastate our planet? Twenty thousand to 40,000 persons to perish daily from starvation? Ninety-eight thousand to die annually from medical mistakes?

Rather than assuming a given event is God's will, it's better to do as Jehoshaphat did when he took a more positive outlook. He decided it was time to turn to God. "Is there no prophet of the Lord with us? If there is, we can ask the Lord what to do" (verse 11, NLT).

Of course, we don't have access to a prophet living in our area, but we can study for ourselves God's written counsel. And there may be many ways of living within God's will, even if we find no concrete understanding of it.

How to Help the Oppressed

Now sell the olive oil and pay your debts,
and there will be enough money left over
to support you and your sons.
2 Kings 4:7, NLT.

The unnamed man in our story was a husband, father, and one of the sons of the prophets. For some unknown reason he died, leaving his family facing dire straits because of an outstanding debt. Now the creditor was about to make her two children slaves as payment of the amount owed, which was allowed by the Law of Moses.

When the widow explained the situation to Elisha, he responded, "What do you have in the house?" (2 Kings 4:2, NLT). In her poverty she had basically nothing—just a flask of olive oil; but that would suffice. Elisha said, "Borrow as many empty jars as you can from your friends and neighbors. Then go into your house with your sons and shut the door behind you. Pour olive oil from your flask into the jars, setting the jars aside as they are filled" (verses 3, 4, NLT).

That they did, and amazingly the oil in the flask kept filling the jars that her sons kept borrowing from neighbors. When no more jars were available, she asked Elisha what she should do next. He replied, "Now sell the olive oil and pay your debts, and there will be enough money left over to support you and your sons" (verse 7, NLT).

When it comes to helping the needy, we can do three things, none of which are mutually exclusive.

1. We can do the *good* thing by providing financial donations that can sometimes care for the need of the moment. However, many individuals find monetary aid dehumanizing and, despite their poverty, reject such help. Nevertheless, sometimes such generosity, which resolves the immediate effects of unfairness, is all we can do.

2. At other times we can do the *better* thing by enabling the deprived to help themselves, which is what Elisha did in today's story. You've heard the expression: "Give a man a fish, and you have fed him for today. Teach a man to fish, and you have fed him for a lifetime."

3. But we can also do the *best* thing by working to eliminate the causes of oppression, because destitution is often the fault of human beings. We can proactively seek justice for all. "Given human goodness, voluntary contributions are possible, but given human sinfulness, legislation is indispensable. Charity, yes always; but never as a substitute for justice" (William Sloane Coffin).

"Little People"

Naaman went down and plunged into the
Jordan seven times. . . . His flesh became again
like the flesh of a little child, and he was clean.
2 Kings 5:14, NAB.

Naaman commanded the Aramean army when it marched against Israel, subduing God's people. "Highly esteemed and respected" by the king of Aram, he was "valiant" (2 Kings 5:1, NAB). Yet despite his importance, "the man was a leper" (verse 1, NAB).

Naaman brought back Israelite prisoners of war, among whom was an unnamed girl, who became Mrs. Naaman's slave girl. Learning of Naaman's affliction, the girl said, "'If only my master would present himself to the prophet in Samaria' . . . 'he would cure him'" (verse 3, NAB).

Naaman broached the topic with the Aramean king, who wasted no time in sending Naaman back to Israel, but on a different mission this time. For unstated reasons Elisha used his own servant, Gehazi, as an intermediary with Naaman rather than talking to him directly.

The pompous general wasn't thrilled with Elisha's remedy—dipping seven times in the Jordan River. So in a rage he turned toward home, but his own slaves braved his fury and suggested that he should at least give it a try before heading back to Aram. Their good sense prevailed, Naaman took the humiliating treatment . . . and was cured.

With gratitude the important military leader offered Elisha costly gifts, which he declined. However, Gehazi, Elisha's slave, chased after Naaman and made up a lie about some immediate need. When Elisha found out about his slave's newly acquired material goods, he cursed Gehazi, who instantly contracted leprosy and had to leave the prophet (verse 27).

Among the various striking elements of this captivating story is the role that "little people" play in it—for good and for ill. Mrs. Naaman's slave girl and the assemblage of slaves that accompanied the general to Israel would normally have no voice in deference to the big shots they served. But in this story they spoke up bravely with first-rate advice that resulted in good. Gehazi, another slave, also had a voice in the narrative and at first served a beneficent purpose as the intermediary between Elisha and Naaman. Later, however, this "little person" did great harm by lying and taking for himself inappropriate luxuries.

Because most of us are "little people," we often assume that we ourselves don't count for much. Such, of course, is far from the truth.

Jehu the Reformer

*The prophet poured the oil on Jehu's head
and declared, "This is what the Lord, the
God of Israel, says: 'I anoint you king. . . .
You are to destroy the house of Ahab.'"*
2 Kings 9:6, 7, NIV.

March 31
2 Kings

Baal worship had become rampant in Israel, chiefly because of the influence of King Ahab and his wife, Jezebel. The time had come for change—radical change. Elisha sent one of the sons of the prophets to Jehu to inaugurate the reformation.

The apprentice prophet found Jehu fraternizing with some military officers. The young prophet took Jehu into a private room and anointed him there. When Jehu reappeared, he had olive oil dripping from his hair. After a little cajoling from the soldiers, Jehu explained that he'd been anointed king over Israel. With great enthusiasm, his comrades acknowledged his kingship and proclaimed, "Jehu is king!" (2 Kings 9:13, NIV).

Jehu took his prophetic mandate seriously, immediately embarking on rectification. First, he assassinated Jehoram, king of Israel, who was recuperating in Jezreel. Second, it just so happened that Ahaziah, king of Judah, was visiting his convalescing counterpart, so Jehu ordered his servant to kill him also. Next, Jehu saw to the death of Jezebel, whose corpse was subsequently eaten by stray dogs. Then Jehu's henchmen slew Ahab's 70 sons in Samaria. Fifth, Jehu slaughtered all officials who had had anything to do with Ahab's regime. Sixth, he ordered the death of 42 relatives of King Ahaziah. Seventh, Jehu killed the remnant of Ahab's kin living in Samaria. Next, Jehu pretended that he was more devoted to Baal than was Ahab, convening all Baal worshippers to the house of Baal, where his supporters executed all of them.

One wonders if Jehu's thoroughness in putting to death so many people was excessive. Nevertheless, "Jehu destroyed Baal worship in Israel" (2 Kings 10:28, NIV). Despite such zealousness in wiping out the house of Ahab, the relatives of Ahaziah, and Baal worship, "he did not turn away from the sins of Jeroboam . . . , which he had caused Israel to commit—the worship of the golden calves at Bethel and Dan" (verse 29, NIV). Is it possible that Jehu was overzealous in dealing with one or two aspects of reform but was lax in yet another?

Most of us find it very easy to go to extremes. We've all known of someone who was maybe an ardent health reformer—perhaps to the extreme—but who was less than admirable in, say, matters of ethics or morals. Consistency throughout one's life is most commendable.

David's Immediate Family

*All these were sons of David, not
counting the sons of the concubines.*
1 Chron. 3:9, New Jerusalem.

What a strange text for a morning devotional! Yet we find it right here
in Scripture. What do you think? Are some biblical passages unsuitable
for worship time? Perhaps. But maybe we get another snapshot of God here
in addition to the picture we get of David . . . and of others.

It's no secret (although it may surprise some children) that David had
numerous wives, including concubines, but so did other biblical men of
renown. What should we make of such anomalous (to us) data?

Familial customs in Bible times (remember that the cultures of the ancient Near East differed considerably from our Western way of life) often surprise—and even shock—us. Habitually females were regarded more like
personal property than persons. Even in the Decalogue, spoken and then
written by God Himself, a wife is lumped into the same category as a man's
house, ox, donkey, slaves, and whatever else he owned (Ex. 20:17). (There's
even some evidence that in certain cultures women were considered to be a
different species from men!)

Additionally, in ancient Hebrew society (and, for instance, in Egypt) the
most desirable marriages were with close relatives—especially between
cousins, but even with half sisters. And having multiple wives was not extraordinary. Also, female slaves could become a man's sexual partners,
thereby gaining a status superior to the other household maidservants but
with fewer rights than primary wives. These secondary wives were called
concubines. Another strange (to us) custom was that of levirate "marriage,"
which had nothing to do with Levi and his tribe. In this arrangement, which
still prevails in some societies, a brother was supposed to get his sister-in-law
pregnant if she was childless at the time her husband died.

And so David established a family quite different from the nuclear family of
the Western world. Nonetheless, Samuel referred to him as "a man after [God's]
own heart" (1 Sam. 13:14). (Abraham, whose immediate family was also a variant
from ours, was said to be God's friend [Isa. 41:8; James 2:23].) Thankfully, God
accepts who we are, what we are, and where we are. He can use us when we
open ourselves to His guidance and are devoted to Him. God is bigger than any
human culture and can work within it while also converting it.

The Prayer of Jabez

*Oh, that you would bless me and extend my
lands! Please be with me in all that I do,
and keep me from all trouble and pain!*
1 Chron. 4:10, NLT.

The last book of the Hebrew Bible (yes, that's Chronicles) begins with boring genealogies that go on painfully (to us) for page after page. "Abraham
begat Isaac. The sons of Isaac; Esau and Israel. The sons of Esau; Eliphaz. . . .
The sons of Eliphaz . . ." (1 Chron. 1:34-36).

Yet periodically this mind-numbing catalog of "begat" and "sons of" is
punctuated with brief asides that catch us unaware. One of these breaks in
the monotony deals with a man named Jabez, who was "better known than
his brothers" (1 Chron. 4:9, New Jerusalem). Why he was "better known"
back then is something of a mystery, but it's no secret why Jabez today is
"better known" than the rest of his family. Bruce Wilkinson wrote a block-
buster book titled *The Prayer of Jabez*, and it sky-rocketed.

Wilkinson wrote: "I want to teach you how to pray a daring prayer that
God always answers" and urged readers to repeat Jabez' prayer daily so that
they would find their lives unprecedentedly blessed by God through daily
miracles.

What did Jabez pray? His groundbreaking request is today's text. He
prayed for vast landholdings and pleaded for freedom from "all trouble and
pain." While multiple millions of readers now daily parrot the prayer of
Jabez, it's helpful to compare his entreaty with Solomon's: "Give me wisdom
and knowledge to act as leader of this people" (2 Chron. 1:10, New
Jerusalem). The contrast couldn't be more obvious. On the one hand, Jabez'
prayer exudes self-interest—amassing real estate and enjoying total exemption from difficulties and pain. On the other hand, Solomon's prayer expresses self-deprecation—craving wisdom so that he might rule justly.

Perhaps the most surprising thing about the prayer of Jabez is that "God
granted him his request" (1 Chron. 4:10, NLT). Yet haven't most of us experienced something similar in our own lives—even though we often pray more
selfishly than is appropriate? As one pastor used to say, "God is good," and
the congregation would respond, "All the time." Then he'd repeat, "All the
time," and the congregation would intone, "God is good."

Surely, though, Solomon's prayer, which God also answered, is a much
worthier model for us to emulate.

David Becomes King of the United Monarchy

And David became greater and greater,
for the Lord of hosts was with him.
1 Chron. 11:9, NRSV.

David had been a fugitive outlaw, leading a band of 400 to 600 malcontents who were marginalized because either they owed more than they could repay or were resentful and disillusioned for one reason or another. Additionally, during much of this time he and his band of ne'er-do-wells were being hunted down like animals by Saul's imperial troops.

Upon King Saul's death, David, who much earlier had been surreptitiously anointed by Samuel, was proclaimed king at Hebron. For seven years he ruled Judah from this city, while 40-year-old Ish-bosheth ("man of shame"), Saul's only surviving son, was his rival, ruling over Israel. At some point after Ish-bosheth's death at the hands of assassins Rechab and Baanah, leaders from the now-defunct reign of the house of Saul visited David at Hebron. Though the details are minimal, the outcome was that David covenanted with them. In return they anointed him (David's third anointing) as ruler over both Judah and Israel—a united monarchy.

With a stroke of diplomatic genius David decided to transfer the capital to Jerusalem, a city inhabited by the Jebusites and hence neutral territory for both Israelite and Judahite alike, although this was hardly a boon for the locals! After conquering Zion and its environs, David prospered, becoming increasingly powerful because "the Lord of hosts was with him."

It comes as a bit of a shock to read that David "became greater and greater." First, he was the baby of Jesse's family and thus without status. Second, he'd been a renegade and thus on his predecessor's most-wanted list. Third, initially he'd presided over just 600 men and later over a small group of Israelites. Fourth, he'd been subservient to other rulers, such as Achish, Philistine king of Gath.

But it's even more shocking to read that "the Lord . . . was with" David, the newly appointed king of Judah and Israel. God had never wanted His people to subsist under a monarchy. In fact, God had regarded as a slap in the face their earlier demand for a king. Yet despite God's disappointment over this turn of events, He graciously accommodated Himself to the new situation caused by His people's hankering to be like the world and "was with" David—even though the Hebrew king was what we'd term "outside of God's will."

Uzzah's Untimely Demise

Uzzah put out his hand to steady the Ark. Then the Lord's anger blazed out against Uzzah, and he struck him dead because he had laid his hand on the Ark. 1 Chron. 13:9, 10, NLT.

April 4
1 Chronicles

Strewn throughout Scripture are occasional passages that baffle the mind. Fortunately, there aren't lots of them, but we find them in sufficient numbers to challenge our cherished paradigms. The episode about Uzzah is one of those mind-boggling stories.

King Saul had neglected the ark of the covenant, which meant that in essence he had ignored God too much of the time, because the ark represented YHWH's personal presence. Just as the Hebrew people had slapped God in the face by demanding a king, so their very first monarch perpetuated that affront by disregarding the ark. David decided to rectify the situation.

After consulting his followers, David, along with a crowd of supporters, went to Kiriath-jearim, where the ark had been stored in the house of Abinadab. They put it onto an oxcart, and with much enthusiastic singing and dancing began the eight-mile trip back to Jerusalem, where David had erected a tent-shrine to house it.

By the threshing floor owned by Chidon, the oxen stumbled, the cart wobbled, and the ark teetered. Uzzah, son of Abinidab and a driver of the ox-cart, placed his hand on the ark to steady it so that it wouldn't split into pieces by tumbling onto the ground. Unfortunately for Uzzah, this considerate act offended YHWH, who "struck him dead."

The procession got no farther, and the golden object was stashed in the house of one Obed-edom. It was a long time before David tried again. This time he enlisted the Levites to carry the ark by hoisting its poles onto their shoulders per instructions given through Moses. Again amid lively dancing and joyful songs the procession wove its way to Jerusalem, where the ark was placed in a shrine that David had prepared there for it.

David had been sincere in his desire to house the ark of God in the capital city. Uzzah, too, had been sincere in his attempt to keep the ark from falling and breaking. So why did God lash out as He did? In other situations YHWH had been content to adapt to the circumstances. God's response is quite puzzling—almost out of character for Him whose wrath was typically reserved for the rebellious. Perhaps, though, however good one's intentions may be, doing things the right way is best.

Oh, to Be an Issacharite!

From the tribe of Issachar, there were 200 leaders. . . .
All these men understood the temper of the times
and knew the best course for Israel to take.
1 Chron. 12:32, NLT.

A ll of a sudden we find lists of names . . . again. However, this time these catalogs of names aren't technical genealogies as before, but deal with those whom King David appointed to serve at the shrine he'd built to house the ark of the covenant (and later to serve in the Temple Solomon constructed) and to oversee various administrative aspects of government.

In chapter 12 we find lists of soldiers who coalesced around David both before and after he became king. The context for today's verse is given in verse 23: "These are the numbers of armed warriors who joined David at Hebron. They were all eager to see David become king instead of Saul" (NLT). According to this account, the tribe of Zebulun contributed the largest number of warriors—50,000 (verse 33), and the tribe of Issachar sent the fewest number—200.

Although those from Issachar were relatively few in number, the chronicler speaks highly of them: "These men understood the temper of the times and knew the best course for Israel to take." A cluster of four distinct Hebrew words describes the two characteristics of the Issacharites that the chronicler singles out.

First, the men from Issachar discerned the singular time in which they lived. They understood that these times were extraordinary. Some times are relatively routine, pretty much like other times—humdrum. But on occasion the situation is significantly unlike others—a rare opportunity. It's important to be able to differentiate between those times that are ordinary and those that are extraordinary. Not everyone is sharp enough to tell the difference between the two.

Second, the men from Issachar had sufficient savvy to identify the right course of action to take during this special time. They were knowledgeable in how to behave. Singular times require exceptional behavior. It isn't enough to perceive the uniqueness of a situation. A wise person also knows how to use advantageously that exceptional moment in time.

How often we feel at a loss when it comes to knowing the appropriate course of action to take. Oh, to be an Issacharite—to know what to do and when to do it! Surely such insight is a gift from God Himself, the all-wise one.

Temple Music

And he appointed certain of the Levites . . .
to thank and praise the Lord God of Israel: . . .
Jeiel with psalteries and with harps; but Asaph
made a sound with cymbals.
1 Chron. 16:4, 5.

It should come as no surprise that David, "the sweet singer of Israel" (2 Sam. 23:1, NCV), would care deeply about the music used in worshipping God. He was not only an accomplished court instrumentalist (in King Saul's court, of all places!) but also a gifted songwriter. Old Testament scholars attribute to him the establishment of the Temple music guild.

From Old Testament times music has constituted a part of corporate worship services. Hymns sung as well as played on various kinds of instruments have been an integral part of divine worship ever since, praising God and enhancing the adulation of His people.

Ancient Near Eastern music would probably sound somewhat strange to our Western ears because it lacked harmony. However, fairly recent discoveries seem to suggest that the music of the ancient Near East may not have been totally unsavory to Western tastes. (For a sampling, try the following Web sites: www.oeaw.ac.at/kal/mane/ [listen especially to RŠ h. 6] or www.mythinglinks.org/neareast.html [note the Hurrian hymn toward the bottom of this Web page].) The Hebrew people weren't the only ancient Near Easterners who used music to enhance their divine worship rituals. The Egyptians, Mesopotamians, and Canaanites did also. Did you know that the earliest musical excerpt discovered was contemporary with the early beginnings of the alphabet—a song of praise to Nikkal, a moon goddess?

At this time it's close to impossible for archaeomusicologists to know exactly how ancient Near Eastern music actually sounded, but they do know that the instruments used included string, wind, and percussion devices. It's probable that at least some of this religious music had a strong rhythmic beat, which helped devotees reach ecstatic states, such as when David did when his dancing before the ark embarrassed his wife (2 Sam. 6:16), or when Elisha asked for a harpist to help with his inspiration (2 Kings 3:15).

As noted previously, it appears that God can accept our culturally conditioned ways, even that of our musical expressions of worship. So perhaps each of us should be more tolerant of those whose religious musical tastes differ from his or her own.

Whose Kingdom Was It?

*But I will settle him in mine house
and in my kingdom for ever.*
1 Chron. 17:14.

We often talk of the kingdom of Saul or the reign of David over his people. And that isn't a totally erroneous way of speaking. However, there is much more to the picture than Saul, David, Solomon, Joash, or others sitting on their throne, presiding over their kingdom.

Samuel wasn't amused when the Hebrew people clamored for a king (1 Sam. 8:5). But God explained to him that "they have not rejected you, but they have rejected me from being king over them" (verse 7, NRSV). God, however, doesn't give up easily. His people may have rejected Him as their king, but He hadn't rejected them as His people.

Their allegiance to the covenant that God had initiated with Abraham depended on their conformity with God's will, but *His* faithfulness to that same covenant sprang from His unchanging nature of compassion.

Therefore, it shouldn't strike us as strange that God still regarded Himself as their sovereign. He hadn't forgotten His promise: "I will take you to me for a people, and I will be to you a God" (Ex. 6:7). God had also said that they would be His "peculiar treasure" (Ex. 19:5), and elsewhere Moses indicated that God had chosen the Hebrews to be His "peculiar people" (Deut. 14:2). When we use the word "peculiar," we usually think of such synonyms as "odd" or "weird." However, the Hebrew word used in these verses means "personal property" or "valuable possession." (In fact, the Latin word from which we get our English word "peculiar" also meant "private possession.") And so throughout the Bible the Hebrew people were often referred to as "*His* people," and God Himself called them "*My* people."

It was thus not without significance that God told David He would "set [Solomon] over *my* house and *my* kingdom" (1 Chron. 17:14, NIV). The Hebrew people were still God's people. YHWH still ruled over them because they constituted His kingdom. Solomon, in other words, was a vassal king for YHWH. God still reigned; Solomon was second in command. And so it was that Solomon sat on "the throne of the *kingdom of the Lord* over Israel" (1 Chron. 28:5).

We finite, weak humans are powerless to oust the infinite, all-powerful God from His throne. We may exile Him from our hearts, but that doesn't exile Him from us.

Good Leadership

David reigned over all Israel, and executed judgment and justice among all his people.
1 Chron. 18:14.

It isn't uncommon to find the reigns of the Hebrew kings summarized negatively. King Nadab "did evil in the sight of the Lord" (1 Kings 15:26, NKJV); Baasha "did what was evil in the sight of the Lord" (verse 34, NRSV); King Omri "did what was evil in the Lord's sight, even more than any of the kings before him" (1 Kings 16:25, NLT); Jehoram "did evil in the sight of the Lord, but not like his father and mother" (2 Kings 3:2, NKJV). Of even King Solomon it is recorded that he "did evil in the eyes of the Lord" (1 Kings 11:6, NIV).

Yet today's scripture says of King David that (despite his many flaws) he "executed judgment and justice among all his people." Exactly what was it that brought such a glowing summation of his reign? The verse uses the Hebrew verb *'asah*. It is the third most commonly used verb in the Old Testament and can mean "to make," "to create," "to do." In other words, David created something, made something to exist.

So exactly what did David bring about? The verse explains by using the Hebrew nouns *mishpat* (judgment) and *tsedaqah* (justice). David created two conditions—judgment and justice. The two words seem to be synonyms to us, but they had two distinct nuances.

The first noun, *mishpat*, sometimes referred to the act of passing a judicial verdict, but it means more than that. All the kings—good and bad—made legal decisions. So why would David have been praised for doing that? Well, the word also implies that the social order had been broken—two entities had become estranged from each other. So a third party came along—David, in this instance—and restored harmony by establishing *mishpat*.

The second word, *tsedaqah*, has overtones of faithfulness and beneficence. It means that when King David made a legal pronouncement, it was fair and square. The wrongdoers were justly condemned, and the innocent were exonerated. In short, David restored justice.

Now, *that's* good leadership—the only favoritism shown is that which vindicates the innocent! And when the downtrodden are upheld, peace itself is restored—to the whole community. Favoritism destroys relationships; impartiality maintains them. First-rate leaders, including parents, create an atmosphere in which harmonious well-being flourishes.

Whose Fault?

Satan . . . provoked David to number Israel.
1 Chron. 21:1.

Whenever we read this story, questions flood the mind. Clearly, we can't discuss them even superficially here. However, there's one aspect that we can touch on: just who bore responsibility for David's decision to take a census of Israel?

Interestingly, the Bible gives us mixed signals as to who was responsible for this census-taking that caused so much grief to King David and the citizens he governed. That's what I'd like us to think about for a few moments.

Chronicles (in our passage for today) tells us that Satan prompted David to take the census. Everywhere else in Scripture the Hebrew word *satan* takes the definite article—"the satan." In other words, it wasn't so much a proper name as it was a title or an office. Here, though, the article is absent, suggesting that perhaps by the time Chronicles was written the word came to refer to a person. (Compare our usage today of "the pastor" versus "Pastor.") So, according to the chronicler, Satan made David do it.

In 2 Samuel 24:1, which recounts the same story, we're told that YHWH was angry with David and "incited David . . . , saying, 'Go, count the people of Israel and Judah'" (NRSV). So, according to the author of 2 Samuel, God made David do it . . . and then punished him for his conformity to the divine impetus!

But that's not the end of the story. Both 2 Samuel and 1 Chronicles send mixed signals, because in both accounts David admits that it was he himself who decided to take the poll: "Was it not I who commanded the people to be numbered? I am the one who has sinned and done evil indeed" (1 Chron. 21:17, NKJV) and "Lo, I have sinned, and I have done wickedly" (2 Sam. 24:17). It was David who was responsible for the actions that he took (even his right-hand man, Joab, urged him not to take the census), not Satan and not God.

God has given us free will and pays us the painful compliment of calling us to account. That's what the judgment is all about. Like David, we too need to own up to our own culpability. The excuse "The devil made me do it" or "God told me to do it" isn't valid. Because we are blessed with free will, our only legitimate plea is "Guilty." And once we take responsibility for our behavior, then God, our gracious judge, can provide the needed pardon.

God Changed His Mind
. . . Again

He repented him of the evil.
1 Chron. 21:15.

G od became violently upset over David's census-taking, and David quickly acknowledged his own foolish guilt. Noting David's remorse, God sent the king a message through Gad, David's official prophet. Gad (really God) told King David to choose one of three punishment options: (1) three years of famine in the land, (2) three months of fleeing from his enemies, or (3) three days of virulent disease. David opted for what he felt would be the least disastrous of the three alternatives—three days of plague caused by God's destroying angel.

Within hours 70,000 of David's subjects were dead, and the angel of death was hovering over Jerusalem, to pour out the vial of illness there. Soon the city would be destroyed, but God "took note and relented concerning the calamity; he said to the destroying angel, 'Enough! Stay your hand'" (1 Chron. 21:15, NRSV).

The verb in Hebrew describing God's feelings is *nacham*. It means to painfully regret something. Thirty-seven times in the Old Testament this word is used to indicate a change in opinion, and of those 37 times, only seven times are humans said to show regret. Thirty times it is God Himself who is the subject—the one doing the ruing.

The decrees of God (a term Calvinists like to use) are not like the "laws of the Medes and the Persians," exempt from alteration. God is in relationship with His people. Their response to Him can alter His response to them. In this instance, David's initial remorse apparently wasn't sufficient to effect a change in God. However, David's continued penitence ultimately convinced God that He should alter His commission to the death-dealing angel.

This is just one more instance in Scripture in which the dynamic between divinity and humanity and vice versa brings about a change in God's plans. Just as we humans have the freedom to alter our plans and direction in life, so also God has the freedom to act—even to change His plans or course of action. With David's ongoing remorse, a new situation came about, and so God in His merciful flexibility adapted His actions, which in our passage is described as a change of mind. That is why God can speak of the future in unspecific terms, prefacing His words with "perhaps" or "if." In His flexibility God is what Gregory Boyd calls "omniresourceful." God's willingness to adapt is not a flaw. It is a virtue.

The Power of Music

Who should prophesy with harps,
with psalteries, and with cymbals.
1 Chron. 25:1.

M usic has powerful effects on the psyche, something known from ancient times. It can soothe, as in lullabies and love songs. It can stimulate, as in martial music or "eerie" music. (Have you ever muted the sound track of a movie? The overall effect is diminished significantly.) Music has been used to help reduce stress, pain, emotional disturbances, and mental aberrations.

In short, music evokes and expresses emotion, which can itself be a circular effect. Singing of our adoration—whether of humans or of God—can also enhance that emotion. And when the tempo exceeds 100 beats a minute, say, and when the rhythm is prominent, we can experience a state of transcendence in which our thoughts and emotions are heightened. (Sometimes we call this enhanced state "ecstasy.")

It is this latter experience that the Old Testament sometimes links with music, using the noun "prophecy" or the verb "to prophesy" for it. When Saul went to Gibeah, he met a group of prophets with "a harp, a tambourine, a flute, and a lyre" who were "prophesying," and he began prophesying also (1 Sam. 10:5, 6, 10, 11, NLT). (See also 1 Samuel 19:20-24, where he spent an entire night prophesying naked.) And so it was that later David, when he was king, appointed temple musicians to "prophesy with harps, with psalteries, and with cymbals" (1 Chron. 25:1), thereby heightening the worship experience. When Elisha wanted to stimulate his prophetic gift, he called for a musician (2 Kings 3:15).

Pentecostals have no trouble accepting the idea that the spiritual gift of prophecy can be (and has been) manifested in the church, including in Adventism. However, they feel completely mystified that our church services are so insipid. Why should they exchange their emotional ecstasy in corporate worship for our apparent emotional void? Early Adventist gatherings were marked with spiritual enthusiasm as people shouted, wept, and fainted and as women snapped their heads so hard that the combs flew from their hair. I'm not ready for that kind of emotionalism in church (it's just not my cup of tea, as they say), but perhaps we shouldn't fear using music to enhance our ardor for God.

Some complain that certain forms of music are wrong in divine worship, but perhaps we should tone down such criticisms for lack of biblical warrant.

God Deserves
Our Very Best

April 12

2 Chronicles

*This will be a magnificent Temple because our
God is an awesome God, greater than any other.
2 Chron. 2:5, NLT.*

B oth David and Solomon wanted the Temple to stand as a matchless monument to God. The old Mosaic tabernacle was basically a relic by this
time. It had served well as a portable sanctuary, but now that there was a
monarchy with permanent headquarters in Jerusalem, it was time for a more
splendid structure—something in keeping with the majesty of God Himself.

David, having been forbidden by YHWH to build the Temple during his
tenure, began amassing treasure for the edifice that his son would erect.
According to 1 Chronicles 22:14 and 29:1-6, David stockpiled 3,883 tons of gold
and 37, 964 tons of silver for the temple. Additionally, the officers of the
realm donated 188.5 tons of gold, 377 tons of silver, 678.6 tons of bronze, and
3,770 tons of iron, plus many gems and 10,000 darics of gold (1 Chron. 29:7,
8, one talent equaling 75.4 pounds).

King Solomon paid Hiram, king of Tyre, vast amounts for the craftspeople and cedar, cypress, and algum wood from Lebanon needed for the construction: 100,000 bushels of wheat, 100,000 bushels of barley, 110,000
gallons of wine, and 110,000 gallons of olive oil (2 Chron. 2:9, NLT).
Additionally, Solomon enslaved as free laborers the aliens in his realm—
70,000 of whom he made to carry the loads, 80,000 he sent to quarry stone,
and 3,600 he appointed as bosses (verses 17, 18, NLT). The finished edifice
was approximately 100 feet long, 30 feet wide, and 50 feet high.

And we think that our church building projects are costly!

Some Adventists argue that we shouldn't go overboard in our spending
when it comes to constructing a new church, and from the appearance of
many churches these people appear to have won the argument! After all,
they reason, the Lord is coming soon, and we should invest our donations in
other areas, such as missions. Mission projects surely merit our support, but
is that really where we would put our money? The sad fact is that the very
people making this argument often live in sumptuous homes more agree-
ably appointed than is their church home—a situation David found unacceptable. Surely, though, our places of worship ought to reflect our devotion
to God. Oops! Maybe they do . . . and that's the problem.

Unsanctified Workers?

*Huram made the ash containers, the scoops and
the sprinkling bowls. Thus Huram completed all the
work done for King Solomon for the Temple of God.
2 Chron. 4:11, New Jerusalem.*

From time to time the question has arisen in Seventh-day Adventist circles about the appropriateness of utilizing the services of non-Adventists in church work—such as allowing them to print our truth-filled literature ("Do we want the same presses that print *Playboy* to print *Adventist Review*?"); to help underwrite the expenses of church work (use of "tainted money"); or to work physically on the construction of churches, schools, hospitals, and other institutions ("unsanctified hands" touching holy construction supplies). Many early Adventists refused to speak the names of the days of the week but instead referred to day one, day two, day six, etc. Why? Because the days of the week as we know them incorporated the names of pagan deities—the day of the sun, the day of the moon, the day of Thor, etc.

Let's consider the latter Adventist practice first. Should we avoid using terminology that has heathen roots? Should we say "fourth day" rather than Wednesday, which incorporates the name Odin, the supreme Norse god? What kind of biblical precedent can we find, if any, that would help us? Well, 1 Kings 8:2 states that Solomon's Temple was dedicated during the month of Ethanim, a Canaanite term, instead of the Hebrew name for the seventh month—Tishri. The Hebrews called the tenth month of the ritual year (the fourth month of the civil calendar) Tammuz, the name of a deity as well as the name for a month—a Mesopotamian term they learned during the Babylonian exile.

Now we can turn to the former problem. It may come as a surprise to some that it was not just Hebrews who worked on various aspects of construction for Solomon's Temple. As our scripture for today points out, Huram, who had a Danite mother but a Tyrian father, crafted some of the implements used in the offering of sacrifices to YHWH. Hiram, king of Tyre, provided this man as well as other craftspeople to help with the project. Additionally, Solomon employed (a euphemism for "enslaved") more than 100,000 resident aliens to work on various aspects of the project (2 Chron. 2:2, 17, 18).

Just maybe, then, we should not let our consciences become overly sensitive. It's possible to become spiritually neurotic in our standards and in our tastes.

Temple Versus Synagogue

*The temple . . . filled with a cloud, and the
priests could not perform their service because
. . . the glory of the Lord filled the temple of God.*
2 Chron. 5:13, 14, NIV.

At the dedication of Solomon's Temple, two times God's glorious presence blessed the new edifice, making it a holy place. One of the crucial pieces of equipment in Solomon's Temple was the altar of burnt offerings. It was here the Hebrews brought their sin offerings and where the priests went about their sacred work of administering the sacrifices, thereby approaching God for the people. (Access to God was, however, limited: men were allowed just inside the courtyard, where they brought their sacrificial animals; regular priests slaughtered the animal and ministered its blood in the holy place; and the high priest once yearly—on Yom Kippur—was allowed entrance into the Most Holy Place, before the Shekinah presence.)

After Nebuchadnezzar destroyed this magnificent Temple, the Judahites in captivity came up with a substitute—synagogues. No sacrifices were offered, so no priests were needed. "Run" by the laity, the Torah scroll replaced the bronze altar as the core of worship. The synagogues also replaced God's presence with His Word. By the time of Jesus (and after), synagogues existed (sometimes in houses) in towns where small groups of Jews had settled.

Although early Christians were not reluctant to visit the Temple in Jerusalem, their weekly worship services were patterned largely after synagogue services. God's Word, not a sacrifice, was the center of attention, and laypersons, not priests, officiated. The Christian church and its order of service had little in common with the Temple but a lot in common with the synagogue, having no altar and no priesthood. (The Roman Catholic version of Christianity more closely mimicked the Temple, and each week their priests offered—and still do—the sacrifice of the Mass.)

It's a bit puzzling, therefore, to hear people speak of "altar calls," because there are no altars in our churches. The exposition of Scripture, not an animal sacrifice, is the focal point of services. Also, the emphasis on maintaining silence in God's presence at church is a bit off target because churches are not temples that enshrine the manifestation of God's presence. So voices raised in divine adoration of God and even of greeting fellow worshippers can be appropriate.

The Immensity of God

Will God indeed reside with mortals on earth?
Even heaven and the highest heaven cannot contain
you, how much less this house that I have built!
2 Chron. 6:18, NRSV.

The dedication of Solomon's Temple was an extravagant occurrence. Scripture tells us that he slaughtered as sacrifices an awesome number of animals—22,000 oxen and 120,000 sheep (2 Chron. 7:5). Blood must have flowed like streams of water, and the sacrificial actions must have exhausted the officiates who had spent seven days of bloodletting. This was followed by yet another seven days of feasting, after which Solomon "sent the people away into their tents, glad and merry in heart" (verse 10). Surely this extraordinary celebration would remain in the memories of all the observers to their dying day.

Equally as memorable, I suppose, was something else that happened during the dedicatory ceremonies. While music filled the air, a cloud indicating God's presence filled the Temple. Then the king forgot all about his royal highness and fell on his knees and offered a lengthy prayer, which was followed by fire from heaven that consumed the sacrificial animal on the altar of burnt offerings.

His prayer has great content—ideas that could be commented on for many pages. One of those concepts that Solomon put forward is found in our passage for today. Solomon and the throng of participants had already seen the cloud of God's glory that had so filled the Temple that the priests had to cease their ministrations and leave. Nonetheless, despite that great show of God's presence, Solomon said that God really doesn't "reside with mortals on earth." How could even an edifice as glorious as Solomon's Temple "contain" God when "even heaven and the highest heaven cannot contain" Him?

Solomon's admission was way ahead of its time! This was a giant theological step forward during a time that people were clearly superstitious. (Remember, the ancient Near East wasn't America or any other Western culture.)

Theologians stress a certain paradox (sometimes called an "antinomy"). In His immanency God is here with us—by our side as a compatriot would be. However, that's not all that must be said about God. He is also transcendent—way "above," "outside," and "beyond" His creation and beyond our knowledge. Overemphasis on either one leads to heresy.

Cheap Look-alikes

*King Shishak of Egypt came to Jerusalem
and took away all the treasures . . . , including
all of Solomon's gold shields. King Rehoboam
later replaced them with bronze shields.*
2 Chron. 12:9, 10, NLT.

Judah was suffering bad times. Rehoboam, Solomon's son who took the throne about 931 B.C., wasn't wise as was his father. Refusing to heed the advice of his father's counselors, he oppressed his own subjects, which split the monarchy into the northern kingdom of Israel and the southern kingdom of Judah.

Scripture adds that he "abandoned the Law of Yahweh" (2 Chron. 12:1, New Jerusalem), and soon things went from bad to worse. In 926 B.C. Shishak, pharaoh of Egypt, marched northward with 1,200 chariots and 60,000 cavalry (verse 3). According to Jacob M. Myers, he "was the first strong king of the twenty-second dynasty" of Egypt (2 *Chronicles, Anchor Bible*, p. 74). Although he didn't destroy Jerusalem, Shishak returned home with much booty, including the 200 large shields made of 15 pounds of gold apiece and the 300 smaller shields made of seven and a half pounds of gold each that Solomon had hung on the walls of his "House of the Forest of Lebanon."

It didn't speak well of Rehoboam that those expensive shields were gone. So he replaced them with shields made of bronze, cheap replicas. "Whenever the king went to the Temple of Yahweh, the guards would come out carrying them, returning them to the guardroom afterwards" (verse 11, New Jerusalem). Thus Rehoboam satisfied himself with these inferior look-alikes.

If you've ever watched the *Antiques Roadshow* on television, you're well aware that reproductions typically have little value in contrast to the originals. Most of us, though, like King Rehoboam, have become used to imitations of the genuine. People settle for "paste" rather than genuine gems. We place artificial flowers up front in church. Some foods we devour contain more artificial ingredients than real food! Some oriental rugs are made not of wool but from synthetic fibers. Indeed, we live in an age of plastic this, that, and the other thing. Some Christians have even replaced true doctrines (golden shields of faith) with false doctrines (tawdry bronze shields).

But when it comes to truth, we should accept no substitutes.

Simultaneity, Correlation, or Causation?

Although the Aramean army had come with only a few men, the Lord delivered into their hands a much larger army. Because Judah had forsaken the Lord, the God of their fathers, judgment was executed on Joash. 2 Chron. 24:24, NIV.

O ur passage typifies many written by the chronicler. The key word for our purposes is "because." *Because* God's people sinned, something bad happened to them. A corollary of this logic is that good things happen to good people and bad things happen to bad people. On this theology, if someone is suffering, one can presume that this person is evil. Similarly, if someone is living the good life, one can deduce that this person is virtuous. But is this line of reasoning too simplistic? What is the relationship between peace and well-being (*shalom* is the Hebrew term) and the ups and downs of life? There are three possibilities.

First, there may be no connection between disaster, disease, and death and a person's morality. A "bad" event may take place while a person is sinning or has sinned, but that indicates only simultaneity. A boy walking home one evening thwacked a utility pole with the stick he was carrying. Instantly a large part of the northeast was plunged into darkness. Was that the reason for the power failure?

Second, there may be a correlation between disaster, disease, and death and a person's morality. A correlative relationship is much weaker than a cause-and-effect relationship. For instance, blue eyes and blond hair tend to occur together, but one doesn't cause the other.

Third, a person's bad morality may cause disaster, disease, and death. However, it's difficult to demonstrate an inflexible cause-and-effect connection. The scientific method helps to control variables that might skew or hide a relationship of cause and effect. If one event inevitably follows another, if all other variables have been controlled, and if the other two possible relationships have been ruled out, then there is probably a cause-and-effect link. We can comfortably call this "knowledge," because there's sufficient warrant to back such a conclusion.

In the realm of ethics and religion, we deal not with knowledge but with belief, and rely on prophetic authority to help us understand connections. We refrain from passing judgment on victims, because too much evidence shows that the innocent do indeed suffer evil.

The Rest of the Story

And [Manasseh] prayed to Him; and He . . .
brought him back to Jerusalem into his kingdom.
Then Manasseh knew that the Lord was God.
2 Chron. 33:13, NKJV.

In 687 B.C. Manasseh, who was 12 years old at the time, became king of Judah, replacing his deceased father Hezekiah. For 55 years Manasseh ruled, and for most of that time "he did evil in the sight of the Lord" (2 Chron. 33:2, NKJV).

Hezekiah had worked hard to bring about a religious reformation in the kingdom. Not all was rosy during his reign, but good came even from the military threats. For example, Hezekiah secured the water sources for Jerusalem and had a long tunnel cut into the rock to transport water to Jerusalem, a blessing wrought from a near disaster. Scripture indicates that "he put his trust in Yahweh, God of Israel. No king of Judah after him could be compared with him—nor any of those before him" (2 Kings 18:5, New Jerusalem).

All Hezekiah's reforms were undermined by Manasseh. His list of sins included: (1) rebuilding pagan high places, (2) establishing altars to Baal, (3) making Asherahs (sacred poles for the worship of a heathen goddess), (4) worshipping the planets, (5) passing his male children through fire, (6) allowing soothsaying, (7) engaging in divination, (8) dealing in spiritualism, (9) setting up a strange statue in the Temple, and (10) killing rather than defending innocent victims.

In 2 Kings the account of Manasseh's reign ends on a low note. "Now the rest of the acts of Manasseh—all that he did, and the sin that he committed—are they not written in the book of the chronicles of the kings of Judah? So Manasseh . . . was buried in the garden of his own house, in the garden of Uzza." (2 Kings 21:17, 18, NKJV). He went to his grave in disgrace—as one of the worst kings Judah endured. He wasn't even buried in the royal cemetery.

End of story—at least in 2 Kings. But there's more—the rest of the story. The chronicler tells us that Manasseh repented, an event about which 2 Kings is silent. "He implored the Lord . . . and humbled himself greatly before the God of his fathers. . . . Manasseh knew that the Lord was God" (2 Chron. 33:12, 13, NKJV).

Thankfully, the chronicler provides us with the rest of the story. Even someone as wicked as Manasseh isn't inevitably beyond repentance. Bad people don't have to be irredeemable. If we allow Him, God can draw straight with our crooked lines. It's called grace.

The Right Man at the Right Time

*In the first year of Cyrus king of Persia, in order
to fulfill the word of the Lord spoken by Jeremiah,
the Lord moved the heart of Cyrus king of Persia.
Ezra 1:1, NIV.*

Jeremiah had prophesied that the Babylonian exile would last for 70 years (Jer. 25:11, 12; 29:10). Isaiah had predicted that a king named Cyrus would sanction a return from that captivity, even referring to this heathen ruler as His anointed shepherd (Isa. 44:28; 45:1, 13). Apparently these forecasts were common knowledge, at least among some of the Judahites. Daniel, the most famous exile, knew about Jeremiah's statements (Dan. 9:2). The chronicler was aware of them (2 Chron. 36:22). And Ezra also knew of them (Ezra 1:1, 2).

Seventy years, of course, is a long time, and many of those original captives whom Nebuchadnezzar had taken to Babylon as prisoners of war would have died during that period. Those still alive would have been very elderly. A whole new generation, people whose only environment had been that of Babylon, would be on the scene. And yet a third generation—of young people—would also have been among the exiles.

Cyrus decreed: "Let the temple be rebuilt as a place to present sacrifices, and let its foundations be laid. . . . The costs are to be paid by the royal treasury. Also, the gold and silver articles of the house of God, which Nebuchadnezzar took from the temple in Jerusalem and brought to Babylon, are to be returned to their places in the temple in Jerusalem; they are to be deposited in the house of God" (Ezra 6:3-5, NIV).

King Cyrus was indeed the right man in the right place at the right time. But one man cannot be everything to everyone or be responsible for everything needing to be done. So others were also involved: Sheshbazzar, Zerubbabel, Joshua, Ezra, Nehemiah, Haggai, Zechariah, among others. These too appear to have been the right men in the right place at the right time.

Perhaps you've known people, as have I, who seem to have been the right people in the right place at the right time. Oh, that may not have seemed to have been true at first. Sometimes the things these people did weren't popular—maybe were even disadvantageous. But in retrospect, as we look back on what they accomplished, it becomes clear to the eye of faith that these people—despite their flaws—did the work God appointed. In other words, they truly were the right people in the right place at the right time. And you and I can be also.

Biblical Accuracy?

The singers of the family of Asaph: 128.
Ezra 2:41, NLT.

April 20
Ezra

What sort of passage is this for a devotional reading? What kind of food for thought does one snippet of a directory of religious personnel offer—especially to us living in the twenty-first century?

Good questions, but let me complicate the matter even further. Our verse says that there were 128 singers descended from Asaph. But . . . Nehemiah 7:44 indicates that the number of people was 148. A clear contradiction. Maybe not a significant one, but an inconsistency nonetheless. Now, if this were the only discrepancy in Scripture, it probably wouldn't matter much. But—and I almost hesitate to say it—there are many more. And this may upset many readers of this book. I have a growing list of such irregularities, and it's just a partial list.

What was the name of Kish's father—Abiel or Ner (1 Sam. 9:1; 1 Chron. 8:33; 9:39)? Second Samuel 24:9 says that in Israel there were 800,000 swordsmen, but 1 Chronicles 21:5 gives the number as 1,100,000. Second Kings 25:8 talks about an event that took place on the seventh day of the month, but Jeremiah 52:12 says that the same event occurred on the tenth day of the month. Did Jesus heal Bartimaeus on the way *into* Jericho or on the way *out* of the city? The list could go on . . . and on.

Various explanations have been given by scholars both conservative and liberal to harmonize these (and other) contradictions in Scripture. None of these rationalizations are entirely satisfactory. The fact is that inspired people can get their facts wrong, even contradicting one another.

You've probably heard that Ellen White at times contradicted a Bible author (sometimes even disagreeing with herself) and also on occasion got her data wrong. Well, from the evidence inherent in Scripture, factual accuracy isn't a foolproof indicator of inspiration. If that were the case, then the *Encyclopaedia Britannica* would be inspired. If those Adventist scholars who try to uphold the inspiration of the Bible by eliminating such inconsistencies are correct in their efforts, then in so doing they inadvertently undermine the inspiration of Ellen White. It would be wiser to concede that inspired writers can contradict one another (as Ellen White herself acknowledged).

Divorce Your Wives

*Now make confession. . . . Separate yourselves
. . . from your foreign wives. . . . (They all gave
their hands in pledge to put away their wives. . . .)*
Ezra 10:11-19, NIV.

People in the ancient Near East were not individualistic as we Westerners are. We pride ourselves on being independent, distinctive, and unique persons. We think in terms of each person having a distinctive self-image. Not so in the ancient world (and in most cultures today). These people had what anthropologists call "dyadic personalities," which means that their identity originated not so much from inside their psyches but from the evaluations of their friends and neighbors. "I am who I am because of how you (and others) perceive and assess me."

Additionally, one's ancestors and kinfolk helped contribute to and maintain one's sense of self, which led to the practice of endogamy: marriage within the clan—matrimony with close relatives. In Egypt the pharaohs often married a sister or another close relative. Abraham sent his servant to the "motherland" to find a wife for Isaac among the cousins. Isaac and Rebekah sent Jacob off to Uncle Laban's house to find a suitable wife. That's one reason the marriage of Israelites with Canaanites, people who spoke the same language and had many of the same customs as the Israelites, was severely frowned upon. Matrimony with individuals outside the clan jeopardized the solidarity of the kinship system. Such a practice also brought with it the adoration of other deities, which could have (and did have) the effect of watering down the Israelite religion and putting at risk the covenant that YHWH had made with the Hebrew people.

The Babylonian captivity had already gutted the Jewish identity, isolated as these exiles were from the Promised Land and the Temple with its rituals. Now, after Ezra visited Jerusalem, he was informed that some of the Jews there had married non-Hebrew women. And some of these "mixed" marriages had produced children. The cultural uniqueness, which included religious distinctiveness, was thereby at risk, an unthinkable state of affairs.

Little wonder, then, that Ezra was appalled at this situation. There was only one suitable cure—putting away the non-Israelite wives along with their boys and girls. This radical treatment of breaking up families seems barbaric to us. How can two wrongs (marrying a heathen and then divorcing her and expelling her children) make a right? But for dyadic personalities, this radical surgery was "just what the doctor ordered."

The Role of Laity

At the time I was cupbearer to the king.
Neh. 1:11, New Jerusalem.

For some unstated reason, a delegation from Jerusalem showed up at Susa, where the Persian king's summer palace was located. Among this group was Hanani, Nehemiah's brother. To his request for news from the "homeland," Nehemiah was told: "The survivors remaining there in the province since the captivity are in a very bad and demoralised condition: the walls of Jerusalem are in ruins and its gates have been burnt down" (Neh. 1:3, New Jerusalem).

Nehemiah served as King Artaxerxes' cupbearer, which meant that it was his responsibility to provide the king with nonhazardous wine. (Yes, there was always the danger that someone might try to assassinate the ruler, perhaps with poisoned wine.) Nehemiah, therefore, would drink some of the beverage first, and if he survived without illness (or worse), then he would serve the rest to the king. His was a position of high honor and enormous responsibility. How and why Artaxerxes, a Persian, decided to trust a POW Jew with this weighty position remains unknown. Oh, and because Nehemiah had access to the king's most intimate chambers, he probably had been castrated, as such servants habitually were—just in case he might find the queen or a member of the royal harem too alluring.

This bad news from his kinfolk plunged Nehemiah into deep melancholy, and he spent much time praying and fasting—to the point that Artaxerxes noticed a drastic change in Nehemiah's demeanor. When the king inquired about his state, he replied, choosing his words carefully, "How can I not look depressed when the city where the tombs of my ancestors are lies in ruins and its gates have been burnt down?" (Neh. 2:3, New Jerusalem).

Sensing that his cupbearer would like to visit Jerusalem and rectify the problem, Artaxerxes asked how long Nehemiah thought it would take for him to help remedy the situation. Hearing Nehemiah's time estimate, the king sent his trusted servant to Jerusalem, where he served as governor for 12 years (Neh. 5:14).

There at Jerusalem Nehemiah, the layperson, and Ezra, the priest and scribe, joined forces in the prodigious endeavor of rebuilding the Temple and the city walls. It took the united leadership of the clergy and the laity to get the restoration moving, which shouldn't surprise any of us. It's the reciprocal collaboration of both that forwards God's work on earth.

Who Was Right?

The king also sent with me army officers and cavalry.
Neh. 2:9, NAB.

Nehemiah's report that King Artaxerxes provided him with a military escort sounds inoffensive enough. Travel in the ancient world could be quite hazardous. Oh, the dangers weren't with flat tires, though if a chariot was involved it just might end up with a broken wheel or axle. Neither were the hazards from vehicle crashes. No, the perils lay elsewhere—in the personal harm one might encounter from assaults by robbers. By law in Mesopotamia, merchants were required to provide restitution for property stolen in transit during business trips. That's why most travelers didn't go solo but formed caravans. Even then raids from unscrupulous people occurred, but usually there was safety in numbers.

It was thoughtful (and prudent) of the king, therefore, to supply Nehemiah with armed guards for the long trip from Susa to Jerusalem. It also, of course, cost the king to provide soldiers, even cavalry—wages and meals for the troops and fodder for the horses. But, then, it was in Artaxerxes' best interests to do so, for this could assure that Nehemiah would return to his old job as cupbearer back in Persia.

So far, so good. King Artaxerxes generously provided for Nehemiah's safety en route, and Nehemiah accepted that liberal gesture of goodwill. But . . .

When Ezra had petitioned the same king for support to rebuild in the homeland, he refused a military escort, even though he was carrying 24.5 tons of gold, 3.75 tons of silver, plus costly temple vessels of copper, silver, and gold (*Ezra, Anchor Bible*, pp. 67, 68). Why? "I would have been ashamed to ask the king for troops and horsemen to protect us . . . since we had said to the king, 'The favoring hand of our God is upon all who seek him, but his mighty wrath is against all who forsake him.' So we fasted, and prayed to our God'" (Ezra 8:22, 23, NAB).

What should we make of this? On the one hand, Ezra, the man of God, refused a military escort from Artaxerxes to provide safety for the trek to Jerusalem. He reasoned that such a safeguard would show a lack of faith on his part. On the other hand, Nehemiah, the man of God, accepted a military escort from the very same king. Apparently he didn't regard acceptance of armed soldiers as a lack of faith. Was Ezra right and Nehemiah wrong? Was Ezra's faith presumption? Was Nehemiah more prudent? Maybe it isn't for us to judge.

Pray for What?

Make their sneers fall back on their own heads! Send them as booty to a land of captivity! Do not pardon their wickedness, may their sin never be erased before you! Neh. 3:36, 37, New Jerusalem.

The reconstruction of Jerusalem and its Temple didn't progress without a hitch. In fact, there were several instances of ups and downs in the progress. Sometimes the obstacles resulted from the actions of the "people of the land," and sometimes the impediments came from the behavior of the Jews themselves. Whatever the source of the holdups, they frustrated the leadership, as well they might.

But Nehemiah's prayer of vengeance stuns us. He prayed that bad things would happen to his opponents. He even instructed God not to provide pardon. Doesn't sound like "love your enemies," does it? How can such a vituperative prayer be justified? Well, in light of Jesus' life and admonition, it can't be defended. Nonetheless, there's something we need to understand.

We use communication—be it oral or written—in five different ways. And each type of "speech" has its own special purpose. *Informative* communication provides names and information. Encyclopedias and almanacs are examples of informative language. *Cognitive* communication shares thoughts. Theology books and editorials utilize cognitive language. *Affective* communication shares and evokes emotions. Greeting cards, expletives, and sweet nothings are forms of affective language. *Performative* communication produces action. Laws and requests are kinds of performative language. And *phatic* communication eases tension and builds solidarity. Salutations, farewells, and icebreakers are phatic language. None of these kinds of speech acts is bad; each is appropriate at the right time and under the proper circumstances. We need to identify the kind of language in order to understand the communication.

Just as in poems and hymns, so in prayer we often use affective language. Now we can return to Nehemiah and his prayer for revenge. He was frustrated and was venting his spleen to God. It seems to me that God takes our affective language seriously (as when we rant and rave to Him). But He doesn't take such speech literally. He knows that we use affective speech to express our joys when we're ecstatic as well as our anger when we're irritated. And careful students of Scripture don't construct theology from what is said in affective communication.

Social Justice

*The men and their wives raised a great outcry against
their Jewish brothers. . . . 'We are mortgaging our fields,
our vineyards and our homes to get grain during the
famine.' . . . 'Although we are of the same flesh and
blood as our countrymen . . . , yet we have to subject our
sons and daughters to slavery. Some of our daughters
have already been enslaved.'" Neh. 5:1-5, NIV.*

The situation in Judea had reached the boiling point. Financial demands
were driving people to the brink of despair. Maybe some of them had already fallen over that brink!

Apparently there had been a famine, and just to survive they'd had to
mortgage property—the land that God had given them—so that they could
buy food. Then to add insult to injury they had to pay to Persia taxes on the
property that had liens on it. "We have had to borrow money to pay the
king's tax on our fields and vineyards" (Neh. 5:4, NIV). In order to scrape by,
they had to sell some of their chilren into slavery. "We are powerless," they
complained to Nehemiah (verse 5, NIV).

And if that weren't enough, the moneylenders and lienholders were
their own countrymen—Jews, not the "people of the land" and not the
Persians. "Although we are of the same flesh and blood as our countrymen
and though our sons are as good as theirs," they protested, "yet we have to
subject our sons and daughters to slavery" (verse 5, NIV). For most people in
the ancient Near East economic assets were comprised solely of those two
items.

The appalling predicament of these people whom he governed shocked
Nehemiah. He called the "nobles and officials" together and scolded, "You
are exacting usury from your own countrymen!" (verse 7, NIV).

Their rejoinder? Silence. Nothing. They didn't even plead "no contest."
"They kept quiet, because they could find nothing to say" (verse 8, NIV).

Nehemiah continued, "Give back to them immediately their fields, vineyards, olive groves and houses, and also the usury you are charging them"
(verse 11, NIV).

Most of us have heard of businesspeople (some of whom are Seventh-day
Adventists) who have achieved their riches by running roughshod over their
employees. But people are not to be used and abused. We wouldn't do that
to God, would we? Then we shouldn't do that to those who bear God's
image. Right?

Slippery Slope

The queen's conduct will soon become known
to all the women, who will adopt a contemptuous
attitude towards their own husbands.
Esther 1:17, New Jerusalem.

I n the third year of [King Ahasuerus'] reign, he gave a banquet at his court for all his officers-of-state and ministers, Persian and Median army commanders, nobles and provincial governors. . . . The festivities went on for . . . a hundred and eighty days" (Esther 1:3, 4, New Jerusalem). If that weren't sufficient, as soon as that bash ended, he threw another one, including among the guests the citizens of Susa. This one continued for only a week. Queen Vashti simultaneously hosted a banquet for the women of the realm.

By the last day of these extravaganzas the Persian king was quite inebriated. He ordered his closest servants to "bring Queen Vashti before the king, crowned with her royal diadem, in order to display her beauty to the people and the officers-of-state" (verse 11, New Jerusalem).

For some unstated reason the queen refused the invitation. Perhaps she was too engrossed with the banquet she was hosting for the women. Maybe she had a headache. A rabbinic tradition has it that the king wanted her to appear wearing *only* the royal crown. Nevertheless, her refusal was an unthinkable thing to do in a patriarchal culture, where women didn't count for much and where wives were their husband's property and were expected to kowtow to their husbands, whom they addressed deferentially as "lord." Thankfully the word "obey" has dropped out of modern wedding vows. Happily, in enlightened Western society women are not "things," and are regarded as men's peers.

King Ahasuerus flew into a rage at this humiliating public affront. Clearly the queen was shaming him—badly. In order to replenish his savings account of honor, he consulted his closest advisors, one of whom replied, "Queen Vashti has wronged not only the king but also all the officers-of-state and all the peoples inhabiting the provinces of King Ahasuerus" (verse 16, New Jerusalem). Invoking the slippery-slope argument, Memucan urged the king to decree that "Vashti is never to appear again before King Ahasuerus, and let the king confer her royal dignity on a worthier woman" (verse 19, New Jerusalem). And so the king ruled, fortunately sparing Vashti's life.

Although commonly invoked even today, it's most prudent to think twice about slippery-slope reasoning, because it tends to exaggerate the consequences, needlessly alarming us.

Deferred Award

Mordecai heard about the plot and passed the information on to Queen Esther. She then told the king about it and gave Mordecai credit for the report. . . . Mordecai's story was found to be true, [and] the two men were hanged on a gallows.
Esther 2:22, 23, NLT.

Mordecai held an important post in the Persian regime, spending his days at the royal gate. In such a public place, one would hear much gossip as well as legitimate news. "One day as Mordecai was on duty at the palace, two of the king's eunuchs, Bigthana and Teresh—who were guards at the door of the king's private quarters—became angry at King Xerxes [Ahasuerus] and plotted to assassinate him" (Esther 2:21, NLT). Mordecai reported the plot, saving the king's life, but received no official token of gratitude. So he continued with his usual duties as an unsung hero. Until . . .

We don't know how much time elapsed, but one night King Xerxes tossed and turned on his bed, unable to sleep. So he finally asked for a soporific—readings from *The Book of the History of King Xerxes' Reign*.

One of the recitations reported the courage of Mordecai. The king asked, "What reward or recognition did we ever give Mordecai for this?" (Esther 6:3, NLT). He was told, "Nothing has been done." Just then Haman, whom the king had recently promoted and who had already used the king's signet ring to issue a royal edict that authorized the genocide of the Jews, arrived at the palace. Haman's mission? To get royal authorization to hang Mordecai on the 75-foot gallows he'd erected.

Before Haman could present his request, the king asked him what should be done for the man whom Xerxes wished to honor. Assuming that the honoree was he, Haman, he urged the king to dress the man in a robe worn by the sovereign himself, place a royal insignia on his head, mount him on a horse that the king had ridden, and have some poor sucker parade the hero through the streets. King Xerxes thought this a wonderful idea and placed Haman in charge of doing this for Mordecai! Talk about poetic justice!

Since we all have egos—some of a greater size than others—we crave recognition. However, it isn't for us to applaud ourselves, even when praise is due but not forthcoming. Our task is to fulfill our responsibilities, even if that means anonymously.

The Unseen Hand of Providence

These letters established the Festival of Purim— . . . decreed by both Mordecai the Jew and Queen Esther. Esther 9:31, NLT.

The Jewish Festival of Purim is a biblical celebration not sanctioned by God's direct command. The weekly Sabbath, the monthly celebration of Rosh Chodesh (the new moon), and the annual festivals (such as Passover) were celebrated because God explicitly authorized them. Not so with the Festival of Purim, which was established by Mordecai and Esther.

Esther is one of two books in the Bible that doesn't mention God. (The other is Song of Solomon.) Additionally, it doesn't refer to prayer or any other explicitly religious practice. The closest it comes to talking about a religious exercise is the fasting Esther initiated, which was so spiritually inoffensive that even her Zoroastrian attendants could observe it without compromise or complaint. (Fasting among Jews can connote mourning or gratitude, rather secular attitudes.)

This book of Scripture is so overtly secular that some scholars have questioned its place in the Bible. Indeed, the court conspiracies with their various twists and turns make the book of Esther read like a short story: drunken King Ahasuerus demands that the queen publicly display her charms before a crowd of inebriated men; Esther, a Jewish girl, spends the night with the king, greatly pleasing this lecherous man; two of the king's bodyguards plot to assassinate him; Haman, one of the king's most trusted aides, plots genocide; Esther risks her life to invite the king to a banquet—actually two banquets; the anti-Semitic Haman is also invited to the feasts, at which time Esther fingers him as the man with the final solution; the enraged king finds Haman falling all over the gorgeous queen while pleading for his life; Ahasuerus accuses Haman of rape and has him hanged on the 75-foot gallows that he (Haman) had erected for Mordecai's destruction; an edict goes out, authorizing the Jews to kill their enemies and to loot their property; and Mordecai and Esther initiate a feast that continues to this day as a merry annual celebration.

It is only with the eye of faith that readers detect divine providence stealthily at work behind the machinations of both Persian and Jew alike, which is pretty much the way things are today. God's benevolent hand remains hidden from view and is detected only by the eye of faith . . . after the fact. The hand of providence typically remains hidden, but there nonetheless.

The Lord's Fault?

The Lord gave, and the Lord hath taken away;
blessed be the name of the Lord.
Job 1:21.

The words in today's passage sound so devout, don't they? But was Job correct? Job, a God-fearing man, prayed daily for his large family. In addition to his seven sons and three daughters, personal assets for sure, Job also had 7,000 sheep, 3,000 camels, 500 yoke of oxen, 500 donkeys, "and a very great household," which meant servants (Job 1:3). He "was the greatest of all the men of the east" (verse 3). He enjoyed the good life.

Though a godly man, Job wasn't immune from disaster, disease, and death, and became legendary because of his ill fortune. In a single day he lost all his oxen and asses to the Sabeans; his entire flock of sheep, along with the shepherds, were incinerated by lightning; three bands of Chaldeans rustled his entire herd of camels; and, despite his prayers to God on behalf of his children, a windstorm splintered the house where all his children had been partying. And if that weren't enough, a short time later Job himself broke out "with sore boils from the sole of his foot unto his crown" (Job 2:7).

Disease, disaster, and death scourge Planet Earth every day. Some of it we hear about; most takes place without our notice. Worldwide tens of thousands of people die daily from starvation. Tens of millions, including innocent boys and girls, have AIDS, and it kills several million people every year. In the United States alone many hundreds of thousands annually die from heart disease, and hundreds of thousands more die from cancer. About 100 tropical storms—hurricanes and cyclones—lash the world each year, and annually the United States alone gets scoured by some 1,200 tornadoes. Around the world, lightning bolts strike about 100 times each second. And these statistics are only the tip of the proverbial iceberg.

One aspect of chaos theory puts the responsibility for some tornadoes on butterflies—the "butterfly effect." (Theoretically, a butterfly flapping its wings in France could generate a series of effects that ultimately cause a tornado in Oklahoma.) Insurance companies like to categorize some of these disasters as "acts of God." However, we learn from the introduction to the book of Job that the cause of Job's multiple disasters wasn't God but "the satan" (later Satan, without the definite article). So whenever we talk about God being the cause of disaster, disease, and death, we're making a devil out of God.

Job's Friends

Then they sat on the ground with him for seven
days and seven nights. No one said a word to him,
because they saw how great his suffering was.
Job 2:13, NIV.

In his profound grief Job sat in ashes, probably the local dump. Job literally was down in the dumps. Not only did he suffer from emotional and mental anguish, but also he was in great physical pain. No one knows the precise disease he was suffering from, although some have suggested boils or savage fire. The discharge from his oozing skin and the resultant scabs had to be scraped away, flies laid eggs in the skin eruptions and maggots appeared, his body stank, he developed halitosis, and his bones ached so severely that he couldn't stand up.

His wife didn't help much. She blurted out, "Curse God and die!" (Job 2:9, NIV). And Job snapped back, "You are talking like a foolish woman" (verse 10, NIV).

Later, when Eliphaz, Bildad, and Zophar arrived to "sympathize with him and comfort him" (verse 11, NIV), they didn't even recognize him and burst into tears. When they joined him on the garbage heap, they tore their robes and tossed dirt into the air above their heads—both ancient Near Eastern customs to show one's anguish.

What his friends did next awes me, and I admire them for it. For a week they sat out there next to Job—night and day on the rubbish. And *"no one said a word to him, because they saw how great his suffering was"* (verse 13, NIV). When we're suffering, we don't want or need admonition. The words from well-meaning well-wishers often sound corny . . . or worse.

When my father died from congestive heart failure just a couple of weeks before Christmas, I phoned my son from the airport while I was waiting to board the plane for California. "Ron," I blurted out, "my dad just died."

And Ron said . . . nothing. For several long minutes I heard nothing but silence before he spoke. Ron's silence meant more to me than all the consoling words from others combined, and I contemplated his response as the Boeing 747 whisked me away to California.

Most of us (including me) rush in where even angels fear to tread, as the old expression goes. Without much reflective thought, we spew out words that when analyzed really make little sense. We fail to appreciate that no speech—just a simple hush—can communicate more than a deluge of verbiage. That's solace at its best.

There's a Reason

Stop and think! Does the innocent person perish?
When has the upright person been destroyed?
Job 4:7, NLT.

Job himself broke the silence at the end of a week, doing so by sputtering, "Cursed be the day of my birth, and cursed be the night when I was conceived" (Job 3:3, NLT).

Shocked by Job's eruption, Job's friends found their tongues, and thus began a lengthy and rather vituperative conversation between Job and his friends. How long the argumentation continued, we don't know. But certainly no one was at a lack for words as had originally been the case. Point and counterpoint flew back and forth, with each man giving a piece of his mind.

Eliphaz admonished, "Stop and think! Does the innocent person perish? When has the upright person been destroyed?" (Job 4:7, NLT). In his lengthy oration Eliphaz argued that there was a reason for Job's suffering. Disaster, disease, and death don't come haphazardly. "Can a mortal be just and upright before God? Can a person be pure before the Creator?" (verse 17, NLT). The implication, of course, is that Job was suffering because he was not the righteous man everyone thought he was. And he gave Job a little brotherly counsel: "My advice to you is this: Go to God and present your case to him" (Job 5:8, NLT).

Next Bildad felt constrained to speak, referring to what history teaches. "Does God twist justice? . . . Your children obviously sinned against him, so their punishment was well deserved" (Job 8:3, 4, NLT). He told Job, "If you . . . seek the favor of the Almighty, if you are pure and live with complete integrity, he will rise up and restore your happy home" (verses 5, 6, NLT).

Zophar chimed in with variations on the same theme. "You claim . . . 'I am clean in the sight of God.' If only God would speak; if only he would tell you what he thinks!" (Job 11:4, 5, NLT).

Finally Elihu—a younger fourth friend who suddenly appears without introduction—adds his comments, indicating that God had sent the suffering to purify Job. "God disciplines people with sickness and pain, with ceaseless aching in their bones" (Job 33:19, NLT). In fact, God will chastise as many as three times in order to rescue the person whom He is purifying (Job 33:29, 30, NIV).

We've all heard similar explanations for disaster, disease, and death: "There's a reason." But God told Job's friends, "You have not been right in what you said about me" (Job 42:8, NLT).

God's Turn to Talk

Get ready for a difficult task like a man;
I will question you and you will inform me!
Job 38:3, NET.

May 2
Job

After Job's four friends had pretty much talked themselves out and Job had responded to their multiple speeches with lengthy rebuttals, God decided that it was His turn to speak. The problem with God's explanation is that it isn't a clarification because it doesn't appear to address the problem at hand. Job had accused God of treating him, an innocent man, unfairly. Job's friends had argued (1) that Job was righteous only in his own eyes; (2) that he was simply feasting on his own just desserts; and (3) that God was really benevolent despite Job's misfortunes. Therefore, he should submit to God's discipline, which was intended to improve his character.

Whether or not we agree with their basic premises, their line of reasoning appears to be pertinent. But God's responses to Job seem hardly relevant at all. Didn't God "get it"?

Instead of providing clarification for the disaster, disease, and death that had plagued Job, God merely boasted about the cosmos He'd made. Additionally, God was sarcastic. "Where were you when I laid the foundation of the earth? Tell me, if you possess understanding! . . . You know, for you were born before them; and the number of your days is great!" (Job 38:4-21, NET).

First God bragged about shutting the doors of the sea, making the thunderheads, and forming the earth. Next His discourse meandered to the animals. He talked about providing food for the lions, watching the mountain goats give birth, freeing the wild donkey, subduing the undomesticated ox, and giving the horse its vigor. Job admitted his inadequacy, and God continued His recitation of creative prowess. He boasted about creating the mythical Behemoth, with its bones of bronze, and hooking the fabled Leviathan, which spews smoke from its nostrils.

Duly mortified, Job had to admit that he'd spoken "without understanding" (Job 42:3, NET). He confessed, "I repent in dust and ashes!" (verse 6, NET).

Biblical scholars have tried to make sense out of God's ramblings, but solutions are hard to come by. Perhaps, though, the implication boils down to this: If God is so personally involved in creating the cosmos and totally committed to its awesome creatures, He must take even more interest in those whom He'd made in His image. That means Job . . . and you . . . and me.

God's Preference

*How well God must like you—you don't hang out at
Sin Saloon . . . you don't go to Smart-Mouth College.
Ps. 1:1, Message.*

Before we talk about Psalm 1, we need to remind ourselves that this lengthy book of Scripture is made up totally of poetry. Furthermore, we need to remember something we talked about in the reading for April 24, when we discussed Nehemiah's strange prayer for vengeance. In that devotional we met what is called "affective discourse." In case you've forgotten, affective speech intends to either (1) evoke emotion or (2) express emotion. Indeed, when it comes to the goal of affective communication, it may not be an issue of either/or but perhaps a matter of both/and. Affective speech can not only give vent to feelings but also elicit feelings.

And, if you recall, poems afford a prime example of affective discourse. Poets not only intend to give voice to their own feelings but also hope to produce similar sentiments in the readers of their poetry. And because these are poems, we shouldn't press too much theological cider from them. We need to keep this in mind whenever we read from the book of Psalms.

The first psalm, with its vivid language, contrasts righteous people with evildoers. We're citing from *The Message* because despite his free paraphrase, Eugene Peterson captures the graphic language of the psalmists. (Yes, several people—not just David—composed the poems in the book of Psalms.)

The good people "thrill to God's Word" and "chew on Scripture day and night" (Ps. 1:2, Message). As a result of feeding on God's Word, they become like flourishing trees "bearing fresh fruit . . . never dropping a leaf, always in blossom" (verse 3, Message). The security relished by the righteous is in stark contrast to the fortunes of the wicked. They're "mere windblown dust" and are "without defense in [God's] court" (verses 4, 5, Message). Addressing those who love God and His Word, the psalmist concludes: "God charts the road you take. The road *they* take is Skid Row" (verse 6, Message).

The fact is, of course, that the poet here overstates the case. Bad things do, indeed, happen to good people, and many bad people flourish. Nonetheless, the purpose of this sacred song is to encourage the righteous to feast on Scripture and to discourage the unrighteous from their wicked ways. All are reminded that God does observe . . . and does judge.

The Image of God

We've so narrowly missed being gods.
Ps. 8:5, Message.

Psalm 8 extols God for His masterful creativity. Why, even "nursing infants gurgle choruses about" Him (Ps. 8:2, Message). The poet continues: "I look up at your macro-skies . . . your handmade sky-jewelry. Moon and stars mounted in their settings" (verse 3, Message). Their splendor, especially now in light of our knowledge of astronomy, is awesome.

Then the psalmist turns introspective, looking at himself: "I look at my micro-self and wonder, Why do you bother with us? Why take a second look our way?" (verse 4, Message). Fair questions, don't you think? What is our value in comparison with the vast universe? And the answer is . . . "We've so narrowly missed being gods" (verse 5, Message).

The King James Version indicates that we humans were made a little lower than the angels. That in itself would make us of great value, don't you think? But the Hebrew here doesn't use the word for angels. Rather the psalmist says that we humans were made just a little lower than God. (The Hebrew word is *elohim*, which is plural; hence *The Message* version uses the term "gods"—with a lowercase "g." However, throughout the Old Testament, the plural *elohim* is regularly used of God—the one divine being with a capital G. Thus, the New Revised Standard Version renders the Hebrew: "You have made them a little lower than God.") This heightened importance of humanity is consonant with the startling emphasis in the Old Testament that the Creator made human beings in His own image.

The image of God in us invests us with value. That *you* bear God's image and I bear His image has ramifications for ethical behavior. That's why God prohibited murder—because we're made in His image (Gen. 9:6).

This rationale for moral behavior goes far beyond banning murder. When I look at you, I see God's image. Surely, then, I should treat you in the same deferential manner that I would treat God. No, you aren't God, of course, but you do bear His image. So I should treat you with affectionate respect. And because I bear God's image, my actions toward you should mirror the loving way that God would deal with you. If the image of God latent in human beings would inform our behavior toward one another, as I've just outlined, wouldn't this world be almost heaven on earth?

God's Silence

God, are you avoiding me?
Where are you when I need you?
Ps. 10:1, Message.

One of the most serious challenges to faith is God's silence when troubles beset those of us who trust in Him. We know the various biblical promises indicating God answers prayers—especially when we're down and out. Both testaments emphasize God's regard for the oppressed. We're led to believe that God begins answering our petitions even before we verbalize them.

Yet people who serve God faithfully often find themselves in dire circumstances. They teeter on the brink of bankruptcy. The cupboard is like Mother Hubbard's—bare. The children are crying for want of food. The house bursts into flames, and there's no time to save anything. A tornado picks up the car and crashes it into the ground a mile distant. Burglars break into the home and steal family treasures. Mother contracts melanoma and dies, leaving an infant, a toddler, and a teenager motherless. The business falls upon difficult times and must lay off a dozen people, including father, the sole breadwinner. The chief church gossiper spreads untrue rumors about the local elder. And this is the short, short list!

The psalmist found himself in the same situation and bemoaned the impudence of evildoers. "The wicked are windbags. . . . Their graffiti are scrawled on the walls: 'Catch us if you can!' 'God is dead'" (Ps. 10:2, 3, Message). Evildoers "mark the luckless, then wait like a hunter in a blind" (verse 8, Message).

Little wonder that he scolded YHWH. "God, are you avoiding me? Where are you when I need you?" (verse 1, Message). "Time to get up, God—get moving" (verse 12, Message). Most of us have uttered similar cries at one time or another. Exactly where *is* God when we need Him? The divine silence begins to suck the verve from our faith.

Despite his frustration, the psalmist ended up confident that someday, somehow God would respond positively. "I dare to believe that the luckless will get lucky someday in you. You won't let them down: orphans won't be orphans forever" (verse 14, Message). "God's grace and order wins; godlessness loses" (verse 16, Message). But when?

It takes pretty bold faith to admit that things will get better because God cares. Theodicies, logical though they may be, can sound intolerably hollow, failing to quell our raucous emotions. Nevertheless, God sees . . . and cares, even when we don't feel Him with us!

The Shepherd's Psalm

God, my shepherd! I don't need a thing.
Ps. 23:1, Message.

I f there is a more familiar biblical passage than Psalm 23, it would probably be John 3:16. However, the shepherd's psalm undoubtedly wins the distinction of having provided more solace. As an extended metaphor, the vivid language captivates the imagination yet today—even though most Westerners know precious little about sheep and their care. Despite our ignorance of matters ovine, it's difficult to envision a psalm that more graphically exudes more confidence and trust than does this one. That's why we recite these verses by deathbeds and at funerals. The familiar wording of the King James Version soothes our frayed nerves and devastated emotions. Psalm 23 is affective language at its best!

The imagery of God as shepherd wasn't an alien concept in the ancient Near East. The term *shepherd* was used for a number of ancient Near Eastern kings. The Hyksos pharaohs of Egypt were known as the "shepherd kings." They have the distinction of introducing the horse-drawn chariot and composite bow to Egypt. In Mesopotamia the kings often called themselves "shepherd." Gilgamesh was known as the shepherd of Uruk. Also in Sumeria the god Tammuz or Dumuzi was known as the shepherd of Uruk. The Greeks later saw the function of good leadership as being that of a shepherd. During the rabbinic period, however, shepherds were no longer universally admired. Indeed, the rabbis regarded them with suspicion as being unprincipled and unclean.

So it came as no shock to the ancient Hebrews to learn that YHWH could also be called a shepherd, a figure of speech that connoted tender and patient oversight of the people. God provided sleep for His flock. He gave them water and food. The author of the poem felt that he lacked for nothing because of the thoughtful tending provided by Shepherd YHWH.

We assume that the psalmist is addressing life in the here and now, which means the poem focuses on God's present care for His people. However, the late Mitchell Dahood in his three-volume *Anchor Bible* commentary on the Psalms proposes that the verbs be translated with the future tense. He suggests that the terminology of Psalm 23 comes from language about the coming world of bliss, which makes the poem a description of how "Yahweh . . . will guide him through the vicissitudes of this life to the eternal bliss of Paradise" (*Psalms I*, p. 145).

Another Imprecatory Psalm

I've got more enemies than hairs on my head. . . .
Strike their names from the list of the living;
No rock-carved honor for them.
Ps. 69:4-28, Message.

What's that big word in today's title—"imprecatory"? The dictionary tells us that the verb *imprecate* means to call down curses—to invoke evil upon someone. And there are quite a few such poems in the biblical Psalter. In their emotional turmoil the psalmists vent their feelings, wishing not the best but the worst upon their enemies. Indeed, we've all probably experienced such feelings.

Uttering blessings or cursings in the ancient Near East was a serious matter, because it was assumed that the outcome wished for would indeed take place. This means that blessings and cursings were examples of performative language. The assumption was that there was power in the words—utter them and sit back while the blessed or cursed events actually took place. Cursing was serious in biblical times—far more serious than when a carpenter hits his thumb with a hammer and verbally consigns that tool to utter damnation. He knows deep down that it won't really happen.

The writer of Psalm 69 was frustrated. Things weren't going his way. His enemies seemed to have gotten the upper hand. "Drunks and gluttons make up drinking songs about me" (verse 12, Message). Just where was God? "Don't look the other way. . . . I'm in trouble. Answer right now!" (verse 17, Message). "Strike their names from the list of the living; no rock-carved honor for them" (verse 28, Message).

But . . . how does the psalmist's wish compare with Jesus' words on the cross: "Father, forgive them; for they know not what they do" (Luke 23:34)?

This contrast is especially striking because many people regard Psalm 69 as messianic because of verse 21: "In my thirst they gave me vinegar to drink," which happened at Calvary. But throughout the context of Psalm 69 the wording just doesn't sound like Jesus speaking. The narrator even refers to his own wickedness: "My sins are not hid from thee" (verse 5).

The psalmist's venting is understandable, but it flies in the face of Jesus' instruction and example—more easily said than done, but also the Christian's goal.

Evildoers Prosper

*I was . . . looking up to the people at the top,
envying the wicked who have it made.*
Ps. 73:3, Message.

The book of Psalms opens with descriptions of the righteous as well as of the wicked. On the one hand, the righteous are like trees transplanted next to an ever-flowing river. They perpetually blossom and bear fruit, season after season. On the other hand, the wicked are like worthless hulls of chaff that the wind sifts from the grain and blows away during winnowing.

The theology presented in Psalm 1 is what we might call "Deuteronomic," because that very same philosophy is presented in graphic detail throughout the book of Deuteronomy. Good people flourish under the blessing of God, whereas bad people shrivel and dry up under His curse. The fact is that this perspective makes a lot of sense . . . even today . . . until . . .

It's no secret that sometimes (maybe more often than not?) there's a startling role reversal. (Rabbi Harold Kushner wrote a best-seller titled *When Bad Things Happen to Good People*.) This was the major theme debated in the book of Job. Job couldn't understand why such an innocent fellow as he was had undergone so many afflictions. (Even the introduction to Job tells us that he was righteous. God boasted of him: "He is the finest man in all the earth—a man of complete integrity. He fears God and will have nothing to do with evil" (Job 1:8, NLT). But Job's friends argued loud and long that there had to be a reason for Job's hardships. He must have done something appalling and so should repent. Then God would forgive him and transpose his woes into benefits.

In today's passage the inspired poet grapples with *cognitive dissonance*, which is the mental, emotional, and spiritual turmoil a person struggles with when theological suppositions and life experiences don't correspond. The theory predicts one thing, but the living experiment falsifies the theory's validity. We can choose one of several responses to cognitive dissonance. We can repeat the theory with stentorian tones, ignoring the lack of correspondence between the postulate and the result. We can give up on the theory, losing our confidence entirely. Or we can reassess the evidence and modify the theory while maintaining our faith.

The psalmist ultimately chose the latter option. He was able to maintain a trust in God while admitting that the theory lacked verity—at least in the short run. What's your response?

God's Self-control

And God? Compassionate! Forgave the sin!
Didn't destroy! Over and over he reined
in his anger, restrained his considerable wrath.
Ps. 78:38, Message.

The psalmist reviews three things in Psalm 78—what God did for the Israelites, what they did in return, and God's counterresponse. It's a lengthy poem because God's activities for His people and their feeble responses were many. We don't have room to review all of them. Throughout all there was "God's fame and fortune, the marvelous things he has done" (verse 4, Message) and the Israelites, that "fickle and faithless bunch who never stayed true to God" (verse 8, Message). Finally, there was His fury followed by His gracious clemency.

God's actions—God's care for the Israelites, His people, was memorable. "He performed miracles in . . . Egypt. . . . He split the Sea and they walked right through it" (verses 12, 13, Message). God "led his people . . . like sheep . . . safely through the wilderness" (verse 52, Message). "He rained down showers of manna to eat . . . the Bread of Heaven" (verse 24, Message). "He chose David, his servant. . . . His good heart made him a good shepherd" (verses 70-72, Message).

Israel's actions—Despite God's beneficence toward His people, "they kept on giving him a hard time, rebelled against God, the High God, refused to do anything he told them" (verse 56, Message). "They were cowards to God's Covenant" (verse 10, Message). "All they did was sin even more" (verse 17, Message). "Their greed knew no bounds" (verse 30, Message). "They kept right on sinning, all those wonders and they still wouldn't believe" (verse 32, Message).

God's reactions—Sometimes God punished their unfaithfulness. "Their pagan orgies provoked God's anger" (verse 58, Message). But again and again He pardoned them. "God helped them anyway" (verse 21, Message). "Over and over he reined in his anger, restrained his considerable wrath" (verse 38, Message).

What obstinate people those Israelites were! Despite God's blessings and His rebukes, they persisted in sinning again and yet again. Nevertheless, God forgave them again and again!

But we shouldn't come down too hard on them. It seems that we do the same . . . and get the same gracious treatment from the same merciful God. Why? The psalmist explains: "He knew what they were made of; he knew there wasn't much to them" (verse 3, Message).

God Did That?

You've dropped me into a bottomless pit,
sunk me in a pitch-black abyss.
Ps. 88:6, Message.

We all have our ups and downs, and apparently it had been a bad day—maybe even a bad year—for the psalmist, who spewed out his guts to God. We just don't know. What we do know is that the poet was feeling about as low as a person can get when he penned Psalm 88.

"God, you're my last chance of the day" (Ps. 88:1, Message). "Take notes on the trouble I'm in. I've had my fill of trouble" (verses 2, 3, Message). "I'm written off as a lost cause, one more statistic, a hopeless case" (verse 4, Message).

Where did his troubles come from? He makes it quite clear in our verse for today. "*You've* dropped me into a bottomless pit, sunk me in a pitch-black abyss" (verse 6, Message). Remember, he's addressing God. He's blaming God, of all people, for his personal woes. "I'm battered senseless by your rage, relentlessly pounded by your waves of anger" (verse 7, Message). Furthermore, because of God, the psalmist's friends had also abandoned him. "You turned my friends against me" (verse 8, Message). Really?

Did the psalmist have his theology right? Were his afflictions coming directly from God? Did God have it in for him? Was God irate with him? Is God the source of human misery? There are, of course, scriptural passages that make God the cause of every effect, even nasty, mean-spirited effects—disasters, diseases, and deaths. But because of other biblical verses about God's perfect, holy love, we may infer that perhaps the inspired writers were attempting to maintain the integrity of monotheism by attributing all good and bad effects to the one and only God.

If the psalmist had been using cognitive discourse when he wrote his poems, we'd have to accept his blame-God theology at face value. You see, we use cognitive language when we're communicating ideas—philosophy, theology. But the psalms are poems, and poetry isn't an example of cognitive speech. Poems utilize affective discourse, in which one shares (and evokes) emotion. And God graciously allows us—even His inspired communicators—to vent our frustrations without condemning us, without striking us dead, despite how blasphemous our use of affective speech may be. However, when using cognitive discourse, we should beware lest we make a devil out of God. That's mischievous theology.

133

Broken Promises?

Blessed be God forever and always! Yes. Oh, yes.
Ps. 89:52, Message.

We hear a lot about God's eagerness to keep His promises, but sometimes the promises seem empty—with no follow-up . . . on God's part. Psalm 89 just might provide a model for us when we're upset and scold God.

Ethan, son of Kushaiah, had been appointed by David as one of the singers in the cultus, along with Heman and Asaph. They not only sang but also played the brass cymbals (1 Chron. 15:19). Ethan was renowned for his wisdom, but King Solomon was even more astute (1 Kings 4:30, 31). Apparently it was this man who penned this psalm.

The psalm begins by praising God for His love. "Your love, God, is my song, and I'll sing it!" (Ps. 89:1, Message). Immediately the psalmist turns to God's creative power, which the poet sees as a demonstration of God's love. "You own the cosmos—you made everything in it. . . . You positioned the North and South Poles" (verses 11, 12, Message). God is not only the loving Creator but also trustworthy. "Right and Justice are the roots of your rule; Love and Truth are its fruits" (verse 14, Message).

Next the psalmist lauds YHWH's choice of David for king. "You spoke to your faithful beloved: 'I've crowned a hero, I chose the best I could find; I found David, my servant, poured holy oil on his head'" (verses 19, 20, Message). In other words, God made King David a messiah—an anointed one. Furthermore, God pledged: "I'll preserve him eternally . . . , I'll faithfully do all I so solemnly promised. I'll guarantee his family tree" (verses 28, 29, Message). But . . . the divine promise evaporated. God, "you tore up the promise you made to your servant" (verse 39, Message). "What happened to your promise to David?" (verse 49, Message).

The Davidides were gone. The golden age was long ago. The kingdom lay in ruins. God's chosen people were exiles—prisoners of war. What had happened? This truly was a crisis of faith, and Psalm 89 provides no answer, no word from the God who'd promised so much—an eternal rule for the hegemony of the house of David.

Then the psalm ends . . . with God's silence. But it ends as it began, with praise. "Blessed be God forever and always! Yes. Oh, yes" (verse 52, Message). Yes, it's a model prayer.

Proper Worship Decorum

On your feet now—applaud God! Bring a gift
of laughter, sing yourselves into his presence.
Ps. 100:1, 2, Message.

The hundredth psalm is a brief hymn of worship in which the psalmist tells us how God's people should deport themselves in the Temple. The entire poem is upbeat in tone and emphasis.

Ancient places of worship, whether they were Egyptian, Mesopotamian, Canaanite, or Israelite, weren't places where the worshippers sat down for services. Sitting would have been too passive. Devotees stood during their religious rites. The Hebrew text really doesn't say anything about standing erect while praising God, but Eugene Peterson assumes, surely correctly, that standing was the usual posture in the Temple.

Literally, the text tells us to come before God shouting. The Hebrew word behind our English word "applaud" means to raise a loud noise and could refer to the sound of the ram's horn (*shofar*), as well as to a person's loud voice, and was often used as an indication of victory and/or joy. In our Western culture we assume that reverence entails silence, but the ancient Near Eastern Hebrews regarded loud vocalizations as part of a reverential attitude.

Additionally, God's people were to express their adoration with merriment. "Bring a gift of laughter" (verse 2, Message). They were also instructed in this psalm to "serve" Him. The verb comes from the Hebrew noun *ebed*, which means "slave" or "servant." The way to show one's service to YHWH is through one's gleefulness—joy. "Serve Yahweh with gladness, come into his presence with songs of joy!" (verse 2, New Jerusalem). Service and worship entail the same behavior—jubilation.

God is worthy of joyful worship because "he made us; we didn't make him. We're . . . his well-tended sheep" (verse 3, Message). YHWH is not only the Creator but also the Sustainer. As a result, gratitude should be added to ecstasy while worshipping "God," who "is sheer beauty, all-generous in love, loyal always and ever" (verse 5, Message).

Although the context of Psalm 100 is thoroughly Israelite—God's name is YHWH, He has made a people, He keeps covenant with the people He made and sustains, namely, Abraham's physical descendants—perhaps we don't do it injustice to apply its words to ourselves. New Testament writers talk about the new (or renewed) covenant, which we're under.

God's Forgetfulness

If you, God, kept records on wrongdoings,
who would stand a chance?
Ps. 130:3, Message.

The people in the ancient Near East had long memories. Because dyadic personalities constituted the society and because honor was a fundamental requisite for individuals (especially the males), blood vengeance was commonly practiced to maintain the honor of one's family. Such feuds could lap over from one generation to another. Even today in many cultures people harbor resentment for wrongs done in previous centuries. Forgiveness in dyadic cultures doesn't come easily.

The author of Psalm 130 portrays YHWH, who is just the opposite. Although certain passages lead us to believe that God knows everything, there are some things He doesn't remember. For example, He doesn't remember the sins that He says He forgets. And in today's scripture, we learn that "if . . . God kept records on wrongdoings, who would stand a chance?" The language used here implies that YHWH *doesn't* preserve for posterity one's perversely twisted ways—assuming, of course, that one has confessed. God may, as indicated elsewhere in Scripture, keep a record of misdeeds, but that record need not be permanent. According to the Psalms, although God preserves Israel (Ps. 121:4), He doesn't preserve their iniquities.

As a result of God's ever-present merciful attitude of forgiveness—not watching over sins in scrutiny—we worship Him. "Forgiveness is your habit, and that's why you're worshiped" (Ps. 130:4, Message). Psalm 86:5 describes YHWH as the God who "is well-known as good and forgiving" (Message). (The verb meaning "to forgive" [*sallach*], is infrequent in the Bible, and interestingly enough, the Old Testament reserves the word for God's activity. It is always *He* who does the forgiving, not human beings.)

And so Psalm 130 ends on a high note. "O Israel, wait and watch for God—with God's arrival comes love, with God's arrival comes generous redemption. No doubt about it—he'll redeem Israel, buy back Israel from captivity to sin" (verses 7, 8, Message).

To people in a culture that valued keeping in mind offenses and perpetuating reprisal, the psalmist's depiction of God here must have come as a pleasant disclosure. And from Jesus' later instruction, it should also have been behavior worthy of emulation.

Parental Guidance

Listen, my son, to your father's instruction and do not forsake your mother's teaching. They will be a garland to grace your head and a chain to adorn your neck. Prov. 1:8, 9, NIV.

May 14
Proverbs

Perhaps every culture has its own collection of folk sayings. We often call them "proverbs"—pithy sayings that are easily remembered and encapsulate a truth. In Afghanistan they say: "Don't show me the palm tree, show me the dates." In China it's said that "a clever person turns great troubles into little ones and little ones into none at all." Egyptians say: "Learn politeness from the impolite." In Vietnam it is said that "the higher you climb, the heavier you fall." And in Zimbabwe people like to say: "A coward has no scar."

The trouble with such adages is that although they sum up a truth, it's only one facet of truth. Indeed, proverbs, true though they may be, can contradict each other. Perhaps you heard your mother admonish that "many hands make light work." And did your father say, "Too many cooks spoil the broth"? Both sayings are right, but . . . We find the same thing in the biblical collection of proverbs. Proverbs 26:4 instructs: "Answer not a fool according to his folly, lest thou also be like unto him." Good advice, don't you think? But the very next verse admonishes precisely the opposite: "Answer a fool according to his folly, lest he be wise in his own conceit" (verse 5).

Throughout the biblical book of Proverbs we read good parental advice: "Listen, my son, to your father's instruction and do not forsake your mother's teaching" (Prov. 1:8, NIV; cf. Prov. 2:1; 3:1; 4:10; 5:1; 6:1, 2; 7:1; etc.). The identity of the person speaking—a parent or a figure in authority—hardly matters. Here we find distilled the wisdom that is handed down from one generation to the next. Fools might ignore these bons mots, but wise people—regardless of their age—will cherish them.

The Hebrew word translated "proverb" comes from the noun *mashal*, which refers to a comparison or a likeness. We would probably refer to these as similes or metaphors. For example: "A merry heart doeth good *like* a medicine: but a broken spirit drieth the bones" (Prov. 17:22).

Dealing with traditional wisdom, the book of Proverbs has a major theme that is emphasized: "The fear of the Lord is the beginning of knowledge" (Prov. 1:7; cf. Prov. 9:10). God-fearing is what the wise do but what the foolish avoid. It's the proper attitude, though, that makes one wise.

The Self-destructiveness of Sin

These men lie in wait for their own blood;
they waylay only themselves!
Prov. 1:18, NIV.

A major theme in the book of Proverbs is that wise people choose to live righteously, but foolish people opt for wrongdoing. According to the received wisdom, right living has its own rewards, whereas evildoing is inherently self-destructive. This motif appears in the very first chapter.

The "son" is warned about joining a group of ne'er-do-wells. "My son, if sinners entice you, do not give in to them" (Prov. 1:10, NIV). The Hebrew noun translated here as "sinners" is *hatta'im*, which denotes those who habitually do wrong. It can easily be rendered into English as "criminals." These people are inveterate reprobates who relish doing that which is wicked.

The spicy, hush-hush whispering of these people might serve as an attractive enticement to a young person. It can feed one's ego to be invited to join a gang of misdirected souls. In this biblical example they wish to dupe this adolescent into joining them in a nefarious enterprise. "Let's waylay some harmless soul" (verse 11, NIV), they urge. They even intend to bump off the victim (verse 12). After attacking this unwary person, they'll divvy up their ill-gotten loot. They suggest that they'll be able to "fill our houses with plunder" (verse 13, NIV). Quick riches, that's what it is—but gained illegally and through violence.

The youngster has been forewarned. "My son, do not go along with them, do not set foot on their paths; for their feet rush into sin" (verses 15, 16, NIV). This is not the pathway that young people should take. Even if no murder were involved, the proposed activity violates the selfhood of the injured party. If you've ever had anything stolen from you, you know how violated you felt—even if you weren't physically harmed. Aggressive crime breaches the selfhood of the quarry.

What's more, the trap these hoodlums plan to set—even if they might succeed in carrying out the nefarious scheme—is self-defeating. "These men lie in wait for their own blood; they waylay only themselves! . . . [Ill-gotten gain] takes away the lives of those who get it" (verses 18, 19, NIV). The boomeranging consequences of evil may not appear as instantaneously as this passage implies. Nonetheless, "evildoers destroy themselves by means of the evil that they themselves create" (Michael V. Fox, *Proverbs 1-9, Anchor Bible*, pp. 89, 90).

God's Pet Peeves

There are six things the Lord hates.
There are seven things he cannot stand.
Prov. 6:16, NCV.

Most people have pet peeves. Sometimes the irritating behavior may be quite innocent yet nonetheless bothersome. Other times the behaviors described as pet peeves could be more serious offenses. However, because peeves tend to be minor aggravations, it is probably more accurate in this devotional to speak of behaviors that God finds morally offensive.

Here are the seven behaviors God finds especially offensive. The first five in the list involve parts of the body (beginning from the head and working downward) that stand for a way of acting.

1. "A proud look" (Prov. 6:17, NCV). Literally, the verse speaks of high (haughty) eyes. In Isaiah 10:12 God uses the same terminology of Sargon II, king of Assyria, who had invaded the land.

2. "A lying tongue" (verse 17, NCV). Elsewhere in Scripture the same expression describes the messages of false prophets (Jer. 14:14) and the behavior of those who betray others (Ps. 109:2). Their actions speak more loudly than their words.

3. "Hands that kill innocent people" (Prov. 6:17, NCV). Often murder involves the use of the hands. Taking human life is a serious matter because we bear the image of God.

4. "A mind that thinks up evil plans" (verse 18, NCV). The author refers to the heart that devises wickedness. The Hebrews considered the heart as the source of volition, not emotion.

5. "Feet that are quick to do evil" (verse 18, NCV). Some people rush into actions that are meant to harm others. It's not a matter of inadvertently hurting others, because the verse previously spoke of the heart conjuring up such hurtful behavior—willful troublemaking.

6. "A witness who lies" (verse 19, NCV). Perjury is still regarded as particularly offensive and was forbidden in the Ten Commandments (Ex. 20:16).

7. "Someone who starts arguments among families" (Prov. 6:19, NCV). Some people earn the title "troublemaker" by always stirring up dissension—even within their own family or social group. In their presence mischief—and worse—is inevitable.

The common denominator underlying these seven behaviors that God finds detestable is that they all undermine social relationships, tearing apart the fabric of society.

Corporal Punishment

Spare the rod and spoil the child.

M ore times than I care to admit, I've gone to a concordance or to the Internet to locate that saying in Scripture. Each time I failed to find the biblical reference. Well, searching the World Wide Web wasn't a total loss. The adage is there, but the tie to Scripture is tentative. Proverbs 13:24 does say (in the King James Version): "He that spareth his rod hateth his son; but he that loveth him chasteneth him betimes." Close enough, I guess.

As a child I heard stories from adults about their receiving parental punishment. One pastor told about his father whipping him severely for his childish infractions. It was rumored that the conference education superintendent, while visiting church schools, would take an unruly child into the hallway and administer a sound spanking. Today, of course, such behavior would draw lawsuits the way a night-light attracts moths.

A growing consensus denies the value of physical punishment, labeling it a form of child abuse. When adults hit children, their actions teach that "might makes right" and that violence is an acceptable form of behavior. Some studies have found that corporal punishment might actually have the opposite of the intended effect—producing more aggressiveness (antisocial behavior) in children, not less.

In the ancient Near East severe corporal punishment was considered beneficial. Many children (mostly boys) were beaten so severely that their bodies had lifelong scars. "The beating of a boy is like manure to the garden," opined an Egyptian proverb (*Aramaic Proverbs of Ahiqar* [Syriac Version]). "You beat my back; your teaching entered my ear" (*Papyrus Lansing*).

Perhaps it would be helpful if we differentiated among (1) consequence, the natural result of cause and effect (lung cancer from smoking); (2) discipline, the loving inculcation of lessons by positive and sometimes negative reinforcement (a time-out in the bathroom); and (3) punishment, the penal retribution for evil behavior (incarceration for lawbreaking).

The wisdom teacher said, "If thou beatest [a child] with the rod, he shall not die" (Prov. 23:13), but he was wrong. Children *have* died from being shaken or from other forms of corporal punishment administered by well-intentioned people. Child abuse must never be whitewashed as discipline.

Hurtful Remarks

Like one who takes away a garment in
cold weather, and like vinegar on soda,
is one who sings songs to a heavy heart.
Prov. 25:20, NKJV.

Few of us want to be cruel when we talk to people who have aching hearts—whether their mind is burdened by perplexity or sorrow. Yet sometimes, despite our best intentions, our comments hurt rather than help. Maybe the problem is that we fail to think before we open our mouth and speak. Regardless of the reason for our inappropriate words and irrespective of our well-meaning intent, what we say can do more harm than good.

On one occasion I was troubled over some issue at work, and so I spouted off to my dad. After I ended my complaint, Dad, who was normally a sensitive person, proffered me advice. The truth was, however, that I didn't want counsel; I was only venting. But Dad's words felt very much "like one who takes away a garment in cold weather" and seemed to me to be "like vinegar on soda" (NKJV)—the foaming that occurs when one pours acetic acid on sodium carbonate.

The pastor at the funeral of a 4-year-old boy comforted the parents, saying, "It was God's will." All the way home those words spun through my mind—"It was God's will" that an innocent child should drown? Others at the same funeral found those words as unhelpful as I did. And the parents . . . did they take comfort in the concept that God wanted their only child to die? Once again, words proffered to aching hearts and troubled minds left the mourners cold, because the preacher was "like one who takes away a garment in cold weather, and like vinegar on soda."

One might try to ameliorate such talk by interpreting it as affective speech (expressing emotion) rather than cognitive speech (proclaiming theology). And such an understanding can be helpful. Nonetheless, even such affective communication fails to work, and so can be classified as "idle words," which Jesus warned against. Sound theology (accurate cognitive speech) ought to produce good condolences (effectual affective speech). Proverbs 16:24 is right on target when it says that suitable (the Hebrew is often translated "pleasant") words are like a honeycomb.

When we see others hurting emotionally or mentally, we naturally want to say something helpful. However, too often what we spew from our mouth makes us "like one who takes away a garment in cold weather, and like vinegar on soda." And so it is that "a truly wise person uses few words" (Prov. 17:27, NLT).

Egotists

*There are three things that make the
earth tremble—no, four it cannot endure.
Prov. 30:21, NLT.*

During the nineteenth century Horatio Alger wrote 135 novels. One plot that has become almost synonymous with his name is that in which a poor boy, because of his honesty and work ethic, "makes good." Such tales leave readers satisfied with the assurance that honest "losers" can rise above their abject circumstances.

If such happens—and it sometimes does—there's a flip side to such "rags-to-riches" experiences. Not everyone handles success with aplomb, and that's what the author of Proverbs 30:21-23 addressed when he penned: "There are three things that make the earth tremble—no, four it cannot endure." The biblical writer may be guilty of overgeneralization, or maybe he was speaking somewhat with tongue in cheek. Nevertheless, most of us have probably encountered at least one of the three—no, four—examples given.

The first example is "a slave who becomes a king" (verse 22, NLT). People who've had to grovel because of their lowly position but who suddenly, through a twist of ironic fate, end up with a position of dominance can seem to have a change in personality.

The second case in point is "a fool when glutted with food" (verse 22, NRS). The saying describes someone who has customarily gone without but who all of a sudden is sated. One expression that describes such people is "nouveau riche."

The third illustration is that of "an unloved woman when she gets a husband" (verse 23, RSV). The proverbial old maid gets married! Why she'd been a spinster for so long, we aren't told, but the woman who had been so undesirable now has found favor.

The fourth example speaks of "a maid when she succeeds her mistress" (verse 23, RSV). The biblical story of Hagar, Sarah's slave girl, immediately springs to mind.

Unfortunately, a sudden reversal of circumstances doesn't always end up with rejoicing—at least not for those who remain in the lower echelons. Too many new achievers become arrogant. We sometimes assume that they've become too high and mighty in their own eyes. Yet the truth may be that their intolerable arrogance springs from a persistent lack of self-esteem, which means they are candidates more for our sympathy than for our antipathy.

All Is Futile

Sheer futility. . . . Sheer futility: everything is futile!
Eccl. 1:2, New Jerusalem.

Ecclesiastes wasn't a shoe-in for the canon of Scripture. As late as A.D. 90, the rabbis kept arguing over whether or not it "defiled the hands," which meant that it was divinely inspired. The House of Shammai reasoned that it was uninspired, whereas the House of Hillel argued that it was indeed inspired by God. The rabbinic consensus at a meeting in Jamnia was that the book should be deemed canonical.

The juxtaposition of Ecclesiastes and Proverbs didn't help support its inspiration. On the one hand, the collection of Proverbs supported the conservative wisdom position that fearing God was the foundation for true wisdom and that inherent in evildoing were the seeds of its own annihilation. On the other hand, the book of Ecclesiastes preached the far more liberal position that the same fate awaited both the righteous and the unrighteous, so "all is vanity" (Eccl. 1:2).

The idea that the teachings of these two biblical books is contradictory continues among biblical scholars. Some may exaggerate the disagreements, but that shouldn't undermine the scholarly accord that the authors of both biblical books hardly saw eye to eye. Some Bible students have tried to argue that the author of Ecclesiastes wrote with tongue firmly in his cheek, but that seems to be a position of desperation. Besides, it's nearly impossible to detect literary irony unless authors tip their hand. But we find no emoticons in Ecclesiastes! Perhaps the author was depressed, and we need not assume that the gift of divine inspiration overrides an inspired writer's personality or disposition. The concept of inspiration refers to the miracle of divine influence, not to a miracle of modifying someone's genetic makeup or neurochemistry.

The difference between Proverbs and Ecclesiastes is not without precedent in Scripture. We find it in the Deuteronomist's claim that God punishes descendants for their forebears' sins versus Ezekiel's insistence that only the guilty parties, not their blameless offspring, die for their evildoing.

Our text for today sets forth the major premise of Ecclesiastes: "Sheer futility. . . . Sheer futility: everything is futile!" (verse 2, New Jerusalem). Not only does the book begin that way, but it also concludes that way: "Sheer futility, . . . everything is futile" (12:8, New Jerusalem). Sometimes we need a hefty dose of sophisticated pessimism as an antidote for naive optimism—even in theology.

What of the Future?

Time and chance happen to them all.
Eccl. 9:11, NIV.

What are we to make of life's events—all its ups and downs? We can't modify the past, because what was done is beyond our control. But what about the future? Is it determined? Is it outside our control also? Then there's the present, which lasts only momentarily. Is what is taking place this very moment cut-and-dried? Can we affect the present to the same degree that we can change past events or bring about future events?

The first verse of Ecclesiastes 3 is familiar to all of us: "There is an appointed time for everything. And there is a time for every event under heaven" (NASB). The verses that follow have even been put to music: "A time to be born, and a time to die; a time to plant, and a time to pluck up that which is planted; a time to kill, and a time to heal; a time to break down, and a time to build up; a time to weep, and a time to laugh; a time to mourn, and a time to dance; a time to cast away stones, and a time to gather stones together; a time to embrace, and a time to refrain from embracing; a time to get, and a time to lose; a time to keep, and a time to cast away; a time to rend, and a time to sew; a time to keep silence, and a time to speak; a time to love, and a time to hate; a time of war, and a time of peace" (verses 2-8).

The language and context appear to support predestination—everything that occurs was appointed ahead of time. John Calvin taught that in eternity past God with His inscrutable will preordained every event. Our job is to understand the predetermined events and behave appropriately. But is that really the whole story? It seems that there is more. Even Qoheleth, as the author of Ecclesiastes is known in scholarly circles, admits as much. Today's biblical passage indicates that some things just happen by chance, and these random events happen to all of us.

Long before Ecclesiastes was written, Joshua challenged: "Choose for yourselves today whom you will serve" (Joshua 24:15, NASB). A considerable amount of our behavior may be determined by our genetic makeup, our instincts, and our upbringing. But we are not solely at the mercy of DNA or fate. Our power to choose can counterbalance that which we have no control over, and thus can indeed influence the future. As human beings who bear God's image, we have the "power to think and to do" (*Education*, p. 17). It's ours to exercise . . . today.

With Old Age in View

May 22

Ecclesiastes

Don't let the excitement of youth cause you to forget your Creator. Honor him in your youth before you grow old and no longer enjoy living. Eccl. 12:1, NLT.

The Preacher combined multiple metaphors of old age, each image graphically portraying the physical deterioration that accompanies what we euphemistically call the "golden years."

Solomon speaks about the approaching time "when the light of the sun and moon and stars [becomes] dim" (Eccl. 12:2, NLT). Clearly, the sun and moon really don't wane as we age, but anyone who has had cataracts knows how they obscure one's vision. He further writes about the time when "the keepers of the house tremble, and the strong men stoop" (verse 3, NIV)—a reference either to the tremors that often accompany advancing age or the apprehension that besets the elderly. Furthermore, the time will come "when the grinders cease because they are few" (verse 3, NKJV). On the literal level, the words refer to the women who daily ground grain but who, because of physical weakness, could no longer fulfill the task. On the figurative level, the wording seems to point to fewer and crumbling teeth. (In the ancient Near East, the teeth gradually wore down to stubs because of grit in the food.)

"One rises up at the sound of a bird" (verse 4, NRSV). How often the elderly suffer from lack of sleep! The least little noise that penetrates their muffled hearing causes them to stir. Additionally, "men are afraid of heights and of dangers in the streets" (verse 5, NIV). That which never bothered brash young people becomes in old age almost an obsession. Now "the almond tree is in flower" (verse 5, New Jerusalem), the white blossoms of which hint at white hair. "The caper berry is without effect" (verse 5, NAB). Ancient Near Easterners regarded the fruit of *Capparis spinosa* to be an aphrodisiac, but as old age advanced even aphrodisiacs failed to have the desired effect.

With such imminent geriatric symptoms, it behooved young people to be contemplative. The object of reflection may be a double or even triple entendre. Depending on which vowels one places between the consonants (biblical Hebrew used no vowels), young people should keep in mind (a) their Maker (*bôrĕ'ēkā*), honoring Him in and with the vigor of youth; (b) their well (*bĕ'ērêkā*), an analogy for wife as a sexual object whose erotic lure would fade; or (c) their pit (*bôrᵉkā*), another term for grave, their "eternal home" (verse 5, NIV). Grave and practical advice.

The Conclusion of the Matter

To sum up the whole matter: fear God and keep
his commandments, for that is the duty of everyone.
For God will call all our deeds to judgment,
all that is hidden, be it good or bad.
Eccl. 12:13, 14, New Jerusalem.

A s we earlier noted, much of the emphasis in Ecclesiastes seems to fly in the face of the more conservative biblical wisdom tradition found in the book of Proverbs. However, the closing instruction in the epilogue certainly complies with the traditionalist sages.

The closing statement "to sum up the whole matter" is a conventional ancient Near Eastern literary device at the end of an essay. It's a fitting capstone, and because of the conservative nature of the advice that follows, some scholars assume that these closing words may have tipped the scale in favor of including Ecclesiastes in the canon.

This literary abstract of all that has gone before is said to encompass "the duty of everyone" (Eccl. 12:13, New Jerusalem). The Hebrew wording is a bit elliptical and thus can be rendered in several ways, although all translations are pretty much variations on a single theme: "for this is the whole duty of man" (KJV, NIV, RSV), "this is the duty of every person" (NLT), "this applies to every person" (NASB), "that is the whole duty of everyone" (NRSV), "there is no more to man than this" (NEB), and "this is the most important thing people can do" (ICB).

Two elements make up the summation. Both are worthy of emphasis, and both are performative language, which means that the instruction is expected to produce a result.

First, "fear God." The Hebrews had reason to hold God in awe because of His austerity, but the idea of fear includes more than mere trepidation. Wrapped up in the command is the sense of honoring God. The word "fear" could properly be translated by the verbs "respect" or "revere."

Second, "keep his commandments" (verse 13, New Jerusalem). Whereas the first injunction admonishes an attitude, the second urges action. Honoring YHWH entails obeying Him. In fact, to the Hebrew mind, thought and action went hand in hand. The one entailed the other.

The author of Ecclesiastes also provides motivation for the attitude of fearing God and the behavior of complying with His will. YHWH sees all and reviews our behavior, calling us to account for what we do, whether that be overt or covert, good or bad.

For the Love of . . .

Let him kiss me with the kisses of his mouth,
for your love-making is sweeter than wine.
S. of Sol. 1:2, New Jerusalem.

What kind of devotional readings does one write on the Song of Solomon? If you're like me, you can't recall the last time you heard a sermon based on this enigmatic book of the Bible. The book probably should be rated R, if not X! Let's face it, reading this book even to oneself is a bit embarrassing, let alone reading it aloud . . . whether at home or at church.

Why such erotic poetry is part of the sacred canon has puzzled students of Scripture for centuries. Although about half of the Old Testament books are cited by New Testament writers, we find no quotations from it or even allusions to it in the Christian Scriptures. Furthermore, the rabbis at Jamnia argued over the appropriateness of its being part of Sacred Writ. In order to defend its inclusion in the Holy Bible, some interpreters—both Jewish and Christian—have resorted to calling it an allegory. Jewish allegorists have understood it to describe Yahweh's relationship with Israel, His chosen people, His bride. Certain Christian interpreters (the first of whom was Hippolytus [circa A.D. 200]) have regarded it as a depiction of Jesus Christ's relationship to the church, His bride. While it is true that the imagery of God's marriage to His people can be found in both the Hebrew and Christian Scriptures, that this is what the Song of Solomon depicts is implausible.

One of the problems with the allegorical approach is the book's inconsistency with the details. For example, Jesus is supposed to be the male lover and the church His sexual partner. The woman's breasts ("My lover is to me a sachet of myrrh resting between my breasts" [S. of Sol. 1:13, NIV]) are alleged to be the Old and New Testaments, but if that's the case, wouldn't it be more appropriate to postulate those as organs of Christ, the one who inspired the Scriptures? It strains one's credulity to think of the church having the Old and New Testaments and Christ lying between them, sucking them for nourishment, which some allegorists assert.

The best approach to this strange book of the Bible is that it affords yet another instance of explicit ancient Near Eastern love songs, such as were common in Egypt. This poetry, with its earthy imagery, may be off-putting to Western readers, but it celebrated the joys of lovemaking and found wide acceptance among those in the biblical world.

Celebrate Lovemaking

*His left arm is under my head,
and his right arm embraces me.*
S. of Sol. 2:6, NIV.

S ome evangelical Christian authors have urged that the Song of Songs is a manual about lovemaking. Any erotic practice alluded to in this biblical book can, therefore, be freely engaged in by conservative Christian couples. That the Song of Solomon is an erotic how-to manual can be debated. Nonetheless, those who uphold this viewpoint are probably not far from the truth, because they forthrightly admit the sexual nature of the book. In fact, there are three levels of erotic imagery in this canonical book: (1) some of the imagery is unquestionably overtly sexual, (2) other references are a bit obscure but can be understood after a little reflection, and finally (3) some of the metaphors are opaque to modern readers but were nevertheless explicit to the ancient audience.

Overtly explicit imagery—Readers need not be particularly perceptive to pick up on some of the graphic language found in Canticles. Our verse for today offers a good example: "His left arm is under my head, and his right arm embraces me." Clearly these words refer to more than a hug of greeting. "Your two breasts are like two fawns, twins of a gazelle, that feed among the lilies" (S. of Sol. 4:5, RSV). This "adult" description requires no explanation.

Ambiguously subtle imagery—Consider this verse: "You are tall and slim like a palm tree, and your breasts are like its clusters of dates. I said, 'I will climb up into the palm tree and take hold of its branches'" (S. of Sol. 7:7, 8, NLT). It requires a second thought to understand the implication of the imagery.

Opaquely obscure imagery—"My beloved thrust his hand into the opening, and my inmost being yearned for him. I arose to open to my beloved, and my hands dripped with myrrh . . . upon the handles of the bolt" (S. of Sol. 5:4, 5, NRSV). At first reading, the language seems to refer to the keyhole of an ancient door, an opening indeed large enough for a man's hand because keys often were very large. But when one learns that in Hebrew the word "hand" could be interpreted as the male sex organ, then the language in this context appears to refer to the moist readiness of both partners for coitus.

Perhaps the explicit frankness in God's Word should encourage those of us with Victorian hang-ups to surmount our prudish inhibitions and celebrate our God-given sexuality.

Is There Hope for Those With Asinine Behavior?

Even the animals—the donkey and the ox—know their owner and appreciate his care, but not my people. Isa. 1:3, NLT.

I t's hard to believe, but the long-suffering YHWH declared that He'd had it! His children had spurned Him. Why, even dumb animals such as donkeys and oxen appreciated the care bestowed upon them by their owners. But not Israel! They were behaving worse than jackasses! They were idolatrous. They pursued evil and ignored justice, adding to the woes of the oppressed. They abused orphans, took advantage of widows. Yet they had the audacity to offer sacrificial animals at the Temple, assuming that this delighted God. But God scolded: "'I am sick of your sacrifices.' . . . 'Don't bring me any more burnt offerings'" (Isa. 1:11, NLT).

Now, ancient Near Eastern fathers weren't known for coddling their children. Joseph Blenkinsopp in his *Anchor Bible* commentary on Isaiah 1-39 speaks of the severity of the beating that YHWH was meting out to His rebellious children, which was "dangerously abusive, even by the draconian standards . . . of the ancient Near East" (p. 183). God described their condition after the whipping He inflicted. "Your head is injured. . . . You are . . . covered with bruises, welts, and infected wounds—without any ointments or bandages" (Isa. 1:5, 6, NLT). Putting words into the mouths of his insubordinate brood, God had them moaning, "If the Lord Almighty had not spared a few of us, we would have been wiped out as completely as Sodom and Gomorrah" (verse 9, NLT).

God even said He'd turn a deaf ear to them. "When you lift up your hands in prayer, I will refuse to look. Even though you offer many prayers, I will not listen" (verse 15, NLT). Pretty hopeless!

But YHWH's strident tones softened a bit. "Come now, let us argue this out" (verse 18, NLT). Blenkinsopp understands this to mean that God wanted them to settle out of court to avert more pain (p. 185). "I can make you as clean as freshly fallen snow. Even if you are stained as red as crimson, I can make you as white as wool" (verse 18, NLT). God offers hope for those of us who act like donkeys! When we abandon our wicked ways (verse 16) and support the marginalized, God—if we let Him help us (verse 19)—works His miracle of grace, eradicating the scarlet stain of our sinfulness and making us as white as snow or wool.

Immanuel

Look, this young woman is about to conceive and will give birth to a son. You, young woman, will name him Immanuel.
Isa. 7:14, NET.

Twenty-one-year-old Ahaz, king of Judah, feared for his very life—and rightfully so. Rezin, king of Syria, and Pekah, king of Israel, had forged a formidable juggernaut to oppose Assyria. Unfortunately (for them and later for Judah), King Ahaz refused to join their mutual defense coalition and had turned to Assyria's king Tiglath-pileser III for help. In return, kings Rezin and Pekah had ransacked parts of the kingdom of Judah and had even erected siege works at Jerusalem, Ahaz's capital city. Their objective was to kill Ahaz, thereby ending the Davidic dynasty, and set up their own puppet king, the son of Tabeal (Isa. 7:6).

Enter the prophet Isaiah. His name (which meant "YHWH will save") and the names of his sons, Shear-jashub ("a remnant will return") and later Maher-shalal-hash-baz ("speed the spoil, hasten the plunder"), functioned as divinely inspired "reminders and object lessons" (Isa. 8:18, NET). Despite Ahaz's apostasy, God sent Isaiah and little Shear-jashub (and possibly Isaiah's wife also) to encourage the king.

Despite the imminent threat posed by kings Rezin and Pekah, God reassured King Ahaz that the House of David would not become extinct as a result of their nefarious machinations. Isaiah pointed to the young wife standing there and said, "Look, this young woman is about to conceive and will give birth to a son." And then addressing her, he commanded, "You, young woman, will name him Immanuel" (Isa. 7:14, NET). Like Isaiah's name and that of his firstborn son, this name was also what scholars call a "sentence name." It meant "God [is] with us." Furthermore, by the time this "sign child" would turn 2 years old, both King Rezin and King Pekah would no longer threaten, because they'd be dead and gone.

In chapter 8, which syntactically continues chapter 7, Isaiah explains how the "omen baby" came to be. He spent a loving night with his wife. Nine months later she gave birth to "speed the spoil, hasten the plunder," a.k.a. "God is with us." It was a name later applied to Jesus, another "sign child," who assured a troubled people that God is, indeed, with us.

It's easy to forget, while we suffer through crises, that we aren't alone. When times get tough, we too need to recall this endearing and enduring message: God is with us—Immanuel!

Brokenhearted God

My heart throbs like a harp for Moab.
Isa. 16:11, NRSV.

The people of the land of Moab traced their ancestry all the way back to Lot, Abraham's nephew. After the destruction of Sodom, you will recall, Lot and his two daughters ended up living in a cave overlooking the Dead Sea. With no eligible bachelors in that isolated area, the daughters got their father intoxicated and became pregnant by him. The older girl named her baby boy Moab, the forebear of the Moabites, who settled in that same remote area.

These cousins to the Hebrew people were not always amicable. Moses wanted the Israelites during the exodus to trek through Moabite territory, but the Moabite ruler denied the request. Later Balak, a Moabite king, hired Balaam to curse the Hebrews. Ultimately the Moabites enticed their cousins to apostasy. (The chief Moabite deity was Chemosh.) Relations between the Moabites and the Israelites continued to have ups and downs. Friendliness didn't always characterize the relationships between the two peoples.

God gave Isaiah an oracle of doom for arrogant and overconfident Moab (Isa. 16:6). The Moabites had fallen upon difficult times. "The grass is withered . . . the verdure is no more (Isa. 15:6, NRSV). The people themselves became escapees, wailing as they fled their native land (verses 5, 8). "Like scattered nestlings, so are the daughters of Moab" (Isa. 16:2, NRSV).

Although the people of Judah would have considered that their cousins were reaping their just deserts, God instructed them to do what the Moabites had refused to do for them so many centuries earlier—provide them with safe passage and/or succor. "Hide the outcasts, do not betray the fugitive; let the outcasts of Moab settle among you; be a refuge to them from the destroyer" (verses 3, 4, NRSV).

The judgment upon Moab must not be a cause for exultation. "Let Moab wail, let everyone wail for Moab" (verse 7, NRSV). During this terror-filled time, "the loins of Moab [quivered]" (Isa. 15:4, NRSV), but they weren't alone in their trembling. It pained God to see their suffering, and with them He trembled, even though they weren't His chosen people. "My heart cries out for Moab" (verse 5, NRSV). "My heart throbs like a harp for Moab" (Isa. 16:11, NRSV).

That's how God relates to human miseries. "In all their affliction he was afflicted" (Isa. 63:9). Regardless of the reason for our pain, God suffers with us. He hurts when we hurt.

God Is Redeemer

Do not be afraid, Jacob, you worm! You little handful of Israel! I shall help you, declares Yahweh; your redeemer is the Holy One of Israel. Isa. 41:14, New Jerusalem.

Way back in the time of Moses, the Hebrew noun *gō'ēl* came into vogue. It derives from the verb that means "to buy back." The personal economic atmosphere of the ancient Near East was not always very stable. Based not on money but on agricultural pursuits that included gardening and husbandry, individual financial well-being was precarious. Starvation was often just the absence of one or two rainstorms away. Borrowing was common, and many people were always in hock. Peasants often had to put their clothing or land as security against a loan. If borrowers couldn't repay their debts, the lender could confiscate their land and/or put the debtors into prison, where they'd be abused until payment of what they owed. Some desperate peasants even sold their children or themselves into slavery in order to cover their financial obligations.

Widows found themselves trapped in circumstances that were even worse, especially if their husband left them childless. With no children to help with household chores, farming, or herding, widows were pretty much trapped in poverty. Unfortunately, there were always lurking unscrupulous people who readily took advantage of such destitute widows.

Relief, however, came via the nearest male relative, who was called *gō'ēl*, typically translated into English as "redeemer," "revenger," "kinsman," or "avenger." The role of the *gō'ēl* was to rescue the oppressed and destitute relative. This deliverance could come in one of several ways: (1) avenge the blood (death) of the murdered relative by fulfilling the *lex talionis*, which sanctioned "life for life, eye for eye, tooth for tooth, hand for hand, foot for foot" (Ex. 21:23, 24); (2) repurchase the lost real estate and restore it to the original owner (Lev. 25:25); (3) buy back the destitute relative who had been forced to sell himself into slavery (verse 48); or (4) become a levir, impregnating his widowed childless sister-in-law, thereby raising up a child for his deceased brother (Deut. 25:5ff.).

In the book of Ruth, Boaz, Naomi's nearest kin, performed two of the functions of a *gō'ēl*. He bought back land that had been sold, and married the childless Ruth (Ruth 4). Jeremiah also functioned as *gō'ēl*. But most amazing of all is that in today's scripture, God is said to be the *gō'ēl* of His people. And He's our Redeemer (*gō'ēl*), too.

God Is Creator

This is what the Lord says—he who created you, O Jacob, he who formed you, O Israel: "Fear not . . . ; you are mine." Isa. 43:1, NIV.

O ne of the dominant themes throughout Scripture is the concept of creation. Starting from the very first verse of the Hebrew Bible, God is described as the Creator, something granted even by liberal theologians. The emphasis hasn't changed by the time of Isaiah. Embedded within the messages of the prophet are repeated assertions about God's creative power.

Here's just a sampling. "O Lord Almighty, you alone are God. . . . You have made heaven and earth" (Isa. 37:16, NIV). "The Lord is . . . the Creator of the ends of the earth" (Isa. 40:28, NIV). "I am the Lord, . . . Israel's Creator" (Isa. 43:15, NIV). "I have made you" (Isa. 44:21, NIV). "I am the Lord, who has made all things, who alone stretched out the heavens, who spread out the earth by myself" (verse 24, NIV). "This is what the Lord says—the Holy One of Israel, and its Maker. . . . It is I who made the earth and created mankind upon it. My own hands stretched out the heavens; I marshaled their starry hosts" (Isa. 45:11, 12, NIV). "For this is what the Lord says—he who created the heavens, he is God; he who fashioned and made the earth, he founded it; he did not create it to be empty, but formed it to be inhabited" (verse 18, NIV).

Notice that God's creative power is revealed in two ways: (1) by His creation of this earth and (2) by His creation of a people, Israel. Isaiah's message refers to these two aspects of divine creation almost interchangeably. The two creation events come from the hand of one and the same God—YHWH. It's almost as though both events were in reality a single exhibit of God's creativity. YHWH created Planet Earth, and His intent was that it be inhabited. To do that, He formed Israel, entrusting to them the land, the Promised Land. The Hebrew people served as His tenant farmers. He owned their land, and when they sold it to survive, He would be the *gō'ēl* and redeem the land for them, as we noted in yesterday's reading.

Today we Westerners tend to read the biblical passages about Creation as if Scripture were a geology textbook. We press the descriptions for clues to earth's age. We try to extract information about how and when it was formed. The main point of all this, though, seems to be an assertion of God's creative powers toward one chief end—the formation of a people. For this reason He could legitimately call them "My people." And the Sabbath memorialized it.

God Is Mother

Can a woman forget her nursing child, or show no compassion for the child of her womb? Even these may forget, yet I will not forget you.
Isa. 49:15, NRSV.

For centuries God's people had plenty of occasions to surmise that YHWH had forgotten them. During their stay in Egypt—at Joseph's behest—they suffered as slave laborers for Pharaoh. During the time of the judges, periodically the Philistines oppressed them. During the monarchy, troubles came from various fronts—from their Canaanite neighbors, from the Egyptians, from the Assyrians, from the Babylonians. Furthermore, some of God's harsh reprimands helped shore up the thought that God had abandoned them.

Little wonder that "Zion said, 'The Lord has forsaken me, my Lord has forgotten me'" (Isa. 49:14, NRSV).

God responded to their negativism by comparing Himself to a mother. "Can a woman forget her nursing child, or show no compassion for the child of her womb? Even these may forget, yet I will not forget you" (verse 15, NRSV).

Each May people in many nations celebrate a mother's love. More than 150 million Mother's Day cards are purchased annually in the United States. These greeting cards contain lovely, even flattering sentiments about the height and depth and breadth of a mother's devotion. It's a privilege to highlight their enduring love. However, God says that the unthinkable is possible—a mother might reject her baby. But despite that unnerving prospect, His love endures forever.

There's more to this picture of God as a fond mother. Moses learned that God has compassion (Deut. 30:3). And the psalmist wrote that God "is . . . compassionate" (Ps. 111:4, NIV). We take such assertions for granted; of course YHWH has compassion on His people. What most of us fail to realize is that the Hebrew word from which we get our words "compassion" and "mercy" means "womb." It's the same root behind the word "compassion" as shown by a mother in today's passage. Just as a mother carrying her unborn child for nine months forms a deep emotional attachment to that baby, so God is "wombish" to His people. His insides yearn for His "children."

Yes, God's love is deeper than even the love we commemorate on Mother's Day.

The Sabbath Sign

Blessed is anyone who does this, anyone who clings to it, observing the Sabbath, not profaning it. Isa. 56:2, New Jerusalem.

Throughout Scripture we encounter numerous beatitudes, passages that are typically translated into English as "Blessed are . . ." Our scriptural passage for today is one of them—a blessing on those who keep the Sabbath.

Of course, one would expect the Hebrew people to keep the Sabbath, because they saw it as a memorial of God's creative and redeeming power. But the book of Isaiah envisions other Sabbathkeepers. Isaiah 56 anticipates that "foreigners" (often translated as "strangers") would "bind themselves to the Lord to serve him . . . and . . . keep the Sabbath without desecrating it and who hold fast to my covenant" (verse 6, NIV). From what other Old Testament passages say about non-Israelites, it would be easy for them to perceive of themselves as outsiders "beyond the pale." Here, however, the door is opened to them to serve YHWH and celebrate the Sabbath along with the Judahites. Additionally, verse 6 says that these (former) outsiders would be His servants, a term that had come to refer to members of the priesthood. Indeed, God asserts that He would appoint some of these people "from all the nations" "to be priests" (Isa. 66:20, 21, NIV).

Similarly, God says that eunuchs, who obviously had no chance of having descendants and hence could not be blessed, would "keep my Sabbaths . . . and hold fast to my covenant" (Isa. 56:4, NIV). God says of these unfortunate souls, who in the Pentateuch were discriminated against, "To them I will give within my temple and its walls a memorial and a name better than sons and daughters; I will give them an everlasting name that will not be cut off" (verse 5, NIV).

It becomes clear in these passages of Scripture that something had changed—drastically. Whereas in the Pentateuch the sign par excellence of being a member of the covenant community was circumcision, now it had become Sabbathkeeping. The covenant privilege had become expansive. Covenant had become inclusive rather than exclusive.

YHWH intended to "gather all nations and tongues" (Isa. 66:18, NIV) from Tarshish, Libya, Lydia, Tubal, and Greece. They would arrive at Jerusalem "on horses, in chariots and wagons, and on mules and camels" (verse 20, NIV). "Their burnt offerings and sacrifices will be accepted on my altar; for my house will be called a house of prayer for all nations" (Isa. 56:7, NIV).

God's New Creation

Look! I am creating new heavens and a new earth—so wonderful that no one will even think about the old ones anymore.
Isa. 65:17, NLT.

An aspect of the expansive, inclusive covenant that YHWH would make was the creation of a new world order. (No, not the one that presidents Gerald Ford and George H. W. Bush spoke about.) We find a description—with some detailed specifics—in Isaiah 65 and 66.

"I will create Jerusalem," God says. But wait! Wasn't it already in existence? But *this* Jerusalem will be "a place of happiness" (Isa. 65:18, NLT). Surely this isn't the Jerusalem during the apostate monarchy or the one during the Babylonian exile or the one reconstructed under Ezra and Nehemiah or the one we hear about on the evening news. In *this* Jerusalem "the sound of weeping and crying will be heard in it no more" (verse 19, NIV). No Wailing Wall here!

Oh, people *will* die in this new creation, but . . . "no longer will babies die when only a few days old" (verse 20, NLT). The infant mortality rate was appalling in the ancient Near East. As late as the first century, nearly one third of babies died at birth. Then about a third of those who reached their first birthday died before they turned 6. "No longer will adults die before they have lived a full life" (verse 20, NLT). Again, during the first century only a small percentage of live births reached age 60. "No longer will people be considered old at one hundred! Only sinners will die that young!" (verse 20, NLT). Members of the inclusive covenant would take weekly and monthly tours of "the dead bodies of those who have rebelled" (Isa. 66:24, NLT).

"People will live in the houses they build and eat the fruit of their own vineyards" (Isa. 65:21, NLT)—an encouraging picture when so many tenant farmers went into bankruptcy, losing possessions and property because they couldn't pay the exorbitant interest. Furthermore, life would be blissful, because God said He'd "answer them before they even call" (verse 24, NLT).

Even the dumb animals would enjoy the tranquillity of God's new creation. "The wolf and lamb will feed together. The lion will eat straw like the ox. . . . No one will be hurt . . . on my holy mountain" (verse 25, NLT).

Clearly, the new world order depicted here never happened. However, many Christians have recycled the prophecy, although in doing so they've overlooked certain details (such as the references to death), and applied that which remains to what they read in Revelation 21 and 22.

Prophet *and* Priest

The words of Jeremiah son of Hilkiah,
of the priests who were in Anathoth . . . ,
to whom the word of the Lord came.
Jer. 1:1, 2, NRSV.

June 3
Jeremiah

It's not often that a Bible personage is both a priest and prophet. It appears that Samuel was, and clearly Jeremiah also was. Typically, priests tended to preserve the religious status quo, and prophets tended to criticize it. Perhaps we could say that priests by and large were conservative, whereas prophets were progressives, maybe even radicals! Priests emphasized the importance of offering animal sacrifices, but prophets criticized them as meaningless . . . unless they were accompanied by a lifestyle of fairness and justice. But then, if one had been living righteously, why would he or she need to offer a sacrifice?

On the one hand, the priestly function consisted chiefly of approaching God for the people—serving as their intercessor as they ministered the blood of the sacrifices. (Some scholars argue that later priests took on the role of praying for the people—another intercessory function.) On the other hand, the prophetic function consisted chiefly of approaching the people for God—serving as His go-between or messenger. That's why we often find the prophets introducing their messages with words such as "Thus says YHWH . . ."

Jeremiah embodied both aspects in his ministry. His communications were two-way streets, speaking to YHWH on behalf of the people and to the people on behalf of YHWH.

As pointed out in our reading for January 30, Protestant pastors function not as priests but as prophets. No, they don't go around predicting the future, but that's only one meaning of prophecy. Prophecy can also—and most often does—refer to messages from God delivered by His spokespersons. Preachers approach the people on God's behalf by explaining His Word.

In Roman Catholicism, of course, the clergy function as priests—men (not women) offer the sacrifice of the Mass. Catholic churches function as temples, where the supposed transubstantiated flesh and blood of Jesus are central. But in Protestant churches there is no altar upon which the sacrifice of the Mass is offered. Rather the Scriptures are the focus of attention, as preachers—both male and female—explain and apply the Bible in their sermons.

The role of priest versus prophet makes a difference in the perception and conduct of worship services.

The Honeymoon Is Over

Go and proclaim in the hearing of Jerusalem:
"I remember the devotion of your youth, how
as a bride you loved me and followed me through
the desert, through a land not sown."
Jer. 2:2, NIV.

God had a troubled marriage—to the Hebrew people. It had been an exciting union they'd entered, but now there was a problem that was clearly one-sided. God as the groom was blameless. But now . . . all God could cling to were memories of the past. "I remember . . . how as a bride you loved me and followed me through the desert." Yes, the Sinai desert was a rather strange place for a honeymoon, but God looked back on it with wistfulness. (One wonders how God could have such fond memories of the Exodus since His new bride's behavior at that time had caused Moses to exclaim, "You have been rebelling against the Lord as long as I have known you" [Deut. 9:24, NLT]. Apparently YHWH had a selective memory.)

As God remembered it, the marriage degenerated pretty much as soon as He'd brought His bride into the Promised Land. "I brought you into a fertile land to eat its fruit and rich produce. But you . . . defiled my land and made my inheritance detestable" (Jer. 2:7, NIV). You can almost see the tears in God's eyes as He queried with heartache, "What did your ancestors find wrong in me for them to have deserted me?" (verse 5, New Jerusalem).

For several chapters God indicts Israel, sometimes with colorful language. His spouse had been two-timing Him. "They have turned their backs to me" (verse 27, NIV). "You have lived as a prostitute with many lovers" (Jer. 3:1, NIV). "You have the brazen look of a prostitute; you refuse to blush with shame" (verse 3, NIV). "Have I been a desert to Israel?" (Jer. 2:31, NIV), He mused. The situation deteriorated to the point that He "gave faithless Israel her certificate of divorce" (Jer. 3:8, NIV). Divorces were supposed to be final, with no remarriage of the original partners. Nevertheless, God was willing to take His unfaithful wife back. "'Return, faithless Israel.' . . . 'I will not be angry forever'" (verse 12, NIV). YHWH opined, "I thought that after . . . all this she would return to me but she did not" (verse 7, NIV). What God expected didn't happen.

Our choices make a difference. When we exercise the freedom that God has given us, a new element is added to the picture, one that God chooses to respond to.

The Boast

If someone wants to brag, let him brag that
he understands and knows me.
Jer. 9:24, NCV.

It's rather incongruous that much of the time braggarts really don't have all that much to gloat over. Of course, some people actually do have a basis for bragging. Nevertheless, their boasting isn't proper. "The wise must not brag about their wisdom. The strong must not brag about their strength. The rich must not brag about their money" (Jer. 9:23, NCV).

The world has seen plenty of smart people. Most of us, when we think of geniuses, think of Albert Einstein, who was truly brilliant. More recently there's been Stephen Hawking, who, despite the scourge of Lou Gehrig's disease, is a great genius. Mensa International has allegedly proclaimed Michael Tienken to be the smartest person in the world.

The world has also seen many brawny individuals. Some think that the late Louis Cyr has been the strongest man ever. On one occasion he reportedly lifted 1,000 pounds with just one finger. In 1895 he lifted 4,337 pounds. In 2006 American Phil Pfister won the Met-RX World's Strongest Man contest.

Forbes magazine has consistently proclaimed college dropout Bill Gates, founder of the Microsoft Company, to be the richest man in the world. On March 9, 2007, he was worth $56 billion. At one point in 1999 his worth soared to $100 billion. For many years Warren Buffett of Omaha, Nebraska, was deemed the second-richest person in the world. In 2008 Buffett edged out Bill Gates to become the richest, only to be replaced by Gates in 2009. Mexican entrepreneur Carlos Helú currently holds third place.

Wisdom, strength, and monetary assets, however, give no legitimacy to boasting. God says, "If someone wants to brag, let him brag that he understands and knows me." Why is knowing God so extraordinary? Because of who God is: "Let him brag that . . . I am kind and fair, and that I do things that are right on earth" (verse 24, NCV). God says, "This kind of bragging pleases me" (verse 24, NCV).

Furthermore, it's the privilege of God's people to emulate Him—to be kind, fair, and just in all that they do. Ironically, when we actually become Godlike by being loving and impartial and honest, we'll also be self-effacing.

The Bona Fides of a Prophet

"So be it!" the prophet Jeremiah said. "May Yahweh do so! May he fulfil the words that you have prophesied and bring . . . all the exiles back . . . from Babylon."
Jer. 28:6, New Jerusalem.

Scripture refers to the prophets of Baal. By definition they were false prophets, and Elijah dealt with them severely. However, the Bible also speaks about prophets of YHWH, some of whom were authentic (Jeremiah) and others who weren't (Hananiah). How can one differentiate (because all claim to speak on God's behalf)?

One way to determine legitimacy is the accuracy of the predictions. "When a prophet speaks in the name of Yahweh and the thing does not happen . . . , then it has not been said by Yahweh. The prophet has spoken presumptuously" (Deut. 18:22, New Jerusalem). This "test" of a prophet, of course, requires waiting to see whether or not the predicted event will occur. But what if the prophetic message calls for immediate decisive action?

Furthermore, the appearance of the predicted event doesn't necessarily demonstrate a prophet's integrity. Elsewhere in Deuteronomy we read: "If a prophet . . . [offers] you some sign or wonder, and the sign or wonder comes about; and if he then says to you, 'Let us follow other gods . . . and serve them,' you must not listen to that prophet's words" (Deut. 13:1-4, New Jerusalem).

Jeremiah found himself in an analogous quandary. He had predicted that the Babylonian army would carry off much of the population as prisoners of war and that this exile would last 70 years. But Hananiah, another prophet of YHWH, predicted: "Yahweh . . . says this, 'I have broken the yoke of the king of Babylon. In exactly two years' time I shall bring back all the vessels of the Temple. . . . And I shall also bring back . . . all the exiles of Judah who have gone to Babylon'" (Jer. 28:2-4, New Jerusalem).

Who was right? Jeremiah? Hananiah? Jeremiah himself appears to have been flummoxed, at least for the moment. Was Hananiah right? Hence his wishful rejoinder in today's passage: "May [Yahweh] fulfil the words that you have prophesied." Nonetheless, Jeremiah had the authentic message, and within two months Hananiah was dead and buried!

There's no easy procedure for testing a prophet's bona fides. However, the apostle Paul, much later, taught that one of the gifts of the Spirit is that of "distinguishing spirits" (1 Cor. 12:10, New Jerusalem). It requires a spiritual gift in order to differentiate among prophetic claimants.

Rachel's Weeping

A cry of anguish is heard in Ramah—mourning and weeping unrestrained. Rachel weeps for her children, refusing to be comforted—for her children are dead. Jer. 31:15, NLT.

B iblical scholars talk about "intertextuality." The expression refers to one biblical author's quoting of another, finding "new" meaning in the passage cited and applying it to a scenario quite different from what the original author had in mind. Another way of saying the same thing is that one author quotes another out of context, a practice that academics in training learn is taboo because it misconstrues the original author's meaning.

Because authors in the ancient Near East didn't understand modern theories of interpreting biblical passages (the word "exegesis" is commonly used of the science and art of scriptural interpretation), they felt free to extract meaning from isolated verses.

YHWH in today's passage speaks of long-dead Rachel, who perished during childbirth, as still alive and still mourning her tragic loss.

Historically, Rachel was the ancestor of the northern kingdom of Israel, the tribes who had seceded from the kingdom of Judah. However, her descendants had been carried into captivity by Shalmaneser V, king of Assyria, in 721 B.C. Later, after Assyria had fallen to the Neo-Babylonian Empire, the southern kingdom of Judah would meet a similar fate. But there was hope— for both sets of evacuees. Thus YHWH admonished: "Do not weep any longer, for I will reward you. Your children will come back to you from the distant land of the enemy. . . . Your children will come again to their own land" (Jer. 31:16, 17, NLT).

Matthew quoted verse 15 (Matt. 2:17, 18) to describe the wailing mothers when Herod the Great slaughtered their toddler sons in an abortive attempt to eliminate Baby Jesus. Clearly, God through Jeremiah referred to a very different event. Nonetheless, inspired Matthew's out-of-context usage preserved Jeremiah's original message of hope amid grief-stricken despair.

Perhaps modern students of Scripture should leave the practice of out-of-context intertextuality to inspired writers and concentrate on conventional exegetical methodology so as to rightly divide the word of truth (2 Tim. 2:15).

God's Gut-wrenching Love

Indeed, the people of Israel are my dear children. They are the children I take delight in. For even though I must often speak against them, I still remember them with fondness. So I am deeply moved with pity for them and will surely have compassion on them.
Jer. 31:20, NET.

Here in one verse we find an extraordinary word picture of YHWH. The imagery that God used of Himself is so striking that when we understand the nuances of His words, we're taken aback! Unfortunately, no one English translation captures the charm of God's self-analogy.

In referring to the people of the break-away northern kingdom of Israel as His son, YHWH admitted that He'd spoken some strongly harsh words against His own child. The fact is that, like a headstrong adolescent, the Israelites had rebelled against their Father. But they had come to their senses (verse 19), admitting that they'd been "like a calf untrained to the yoke" (verse 18, NET). As a result of God's discipline they'd "repented" (verse 19, NET).

God described these wayward people with amazing terms of endearment. They were *yaqqîr,* "dear." The idea is that they were extremely precious—even valuable—to God. The word can also be translated "costly." In other words, they cost God something—the heartache of parental love! Furthermore, God insisted that He took "delight in" them. The Hebrew word here, *ša'ǎšū'îm,* has a sense of keen delight—an object of amusement. In short, God viewed His people as His enjoyable playmate. The Jewish commentator Kimchi said that God described Himself as a father playing with His child.

Despite His harsh discipline, God said they'd preyed on His mind all the while. He may have acted severely in disciplining His rebellious child (as ancient Near Eastern fathers were wont to do), but that didn't mean He'd forgotten them. Not at all! As He observed them take a punishment at the hands of the Assyrians, God "was moved with pity for them." The Hebrew means that YHWH's guts churned. His gastrointestinal tract roared and rumbled in sympathy—no, in agony—for them. The Assyrian onslaught may have terrified the Israelites, but it also upset God to the point that His gut quavered! And so God would have "compassion" on them. Once again we meet the Hebrew word that came from the root meaning "womb." Like a mother, YHWH had gut-wrenching feelings of adoration for the Israelites.

That's right, God takes no delight when His creatures hurt; He hurts with them.

The New Covenant

The days are surely coming, says the Lord, when I will make a new covenant with the house of Israel and the house of Judah. It will not be like the covenant that I made with their ancestors when I took them by the hand to bring them out of the land of Egypt. Jer. 31:31, 32, NRSV.

June 9
Jeremiah

Wherein lies the dissimilarity that makes the new covenant of Jeremiah 31 vary from the Sinai covenant?

The new covenant stipulated, "They shall be my people" (verse 33, NRSV). But that wasn't different. Moses averred that God had established them "as his people" (Deut. 29:13, NRSV). In the new covenant God said, "I will be their God" (Jer. 31:33, NRSV). Again, this was hardly novel, for in Deuteronomy 29:13 (and other places) God said the same thing.

H'mmm. In Jeremiah 31 we learn something further. God promised, "I will put my law within them, and I will write it on their hearts" (verse 33, NRSV). Maybe *that* is what's dissimilar—the Sinai covenant was, in contrast, written on tables of stone. Sorry, but of the Sinai covenant God had said, "This commandment [the Ten Commandments were called the "covenant" in Exodus 34:28] that I am commanding you today is not too hard for you, nor is it too far away. . . . No, the word is very near to you; it is in . . . your heart for you to observe" (Deut. 30:11-14, NRSV).

But here's something additional to consider: "I will forgive their iniquity, and remember their sin no more" (Jer. 31:34, NRSV). Aha! Here's where we find a distinction. But no, not the case! Forgiveness was readily available under the Sinai covenant also. Again and again we read statements such as "they shall be forgiven" (Lev. 4:20, NRSV).

So what is new in the new covenant? The chief difference seems to be this: "No longer shall they teach one another, or say to each other, 'Know the Lord,' for they shall all know me, from the least of them to the greatest" (Jer. 31:34, NRSV).

Whatever the novelty of the new covenant may have been, its content, as well as the Sinai covenant, was the Decalogue. Ellen White wrote: "The covenant that God made with His people at Sinai is to be our refuge and defense" (*The SDA Bible Commentary,* Ellen G. White Comments, vol. 1, p. 1103). So maybe the new covenant is an extension of the old. Obedience doesn't produce the covenant relationship, but it is its effect—a grateful response to God's gracious act(s) of salvation, which is a far cry from legalism.

In _____ We Trust

For I will surely save you, and you shall not fall by the sword; but you shall have your life as a prize of war, because you have trusted in me, says the Lord. Jer. 39:18, NRSV.

E bed-melech, a man from heathen Ethiopia who served in King Zedekiah's palace, came to Jeremiah's rescue. This was a gutsy thing to do, because such boldness flew in the face of the wishes of the king's princes, who had confined the prophet in an empty cistern—empty, that is, of water but with a thick layer of muck at the bottom into which Jeremiah sank. Ebed-melech took exception to such treatment of God's prophet, and when the opportunity arose, he accosted King Zedekiah: "My lord king, these men have acted wickedly in all they did to the prophet Jeremiah by throwing him into the cistern" (Jer. 38:9, NRSV).

With the king's blessing, Ebed-melech along with 30 helpers headed off to rescue Jeremiah. Finding long ropes and a bunch of rags, Ebed-melech instructed the prophet to put the rags under his armpits so that the ropes wouldn't injure him when they extracted him from the cistern. And with a loud sucking sound Jeremiah's feet were pulled from inches of mud.

God then gave Jeremiah a reassuring message for Ebed-melech. Despite the Babylonian invasion of Jerusalem, Ebed-melech would escape from the dreaded hand of Nebuchadnezzar. YHWH promised, "I will surely save you, and you shall not fall by the sword" (Jer. 39:18, NRSV). And exactly why would Ebed-melech not go into captivity or lose his life? Because he rescued Jeremiah? That would have been a good reason, don't you think? But that would be salvation by works! God explained why Ebed-melech would be saved: "Because you have trusted in me" (verse 18, NRSV).

According to Jeremiah, God's people had placed trust in various objects. They'd trusted deceptions (Jer. 13:25). They'd put trust in walled cities (Jer. 5:17). They'd trusted human beings (Jer. 17:5). They'd put their trust in military allies such as Egypt (Jer. 2:36, 37). They'd trusted God's earthly dwelling, the Temple (Jer. 7:4). This was misplaced trust, but Ebed-melech had trusted in YHWH. Today it's easy to put our trust in bank accounts, in our employer, in church leaders, in our housing, in insurance, in the government, in physical prowess, when our trust should be put in God. He alone is ultimately trustworthy.

Barometer of God's Blessing

We will burn incense to the Queen of Heaven and will pour out drink offerings to her just as we and our fathers . . . did in the towns of Judah and in the streets of Jerusalem. At that time we had plenty of food and were well off and suffered no harm. Jer. 44:17, NIV.

Jeremiah's recent lot had been horrible. Three times he'd been imprisoned, and at one point he'd despaired of his life. Fortunately, Nebuchadnezzar treated him more respectfully and kindly than did his own Hebrew king, giving him carte blanche to settle wherever he desired. Now the prophet was in the company of a band of assassins heading south toward Egypt. It was at this point that an assemblage of leaders approached him, urging him to "pray that the Lord your God will tell us where we should go and what we should do" (Jer. 42:3, NIV). They promised, "Whether it is favorable or unfavorable, we will obey the Lord" (verse 6, NIV).

But they didn't like Jeremiah's counsel not to settle in Egypt and were hell-bent to go there anyway, in unswerving disobedience to God's advice. They settled in the city of Tahpanhes, where again they confronted Jeremiah with their insurgence against God's express will. This time they cheekily affirmed their intent to worship the Mesopotamian goddess Ishtar, also known as "Queen of Heaven." (That this Assyrian-Babylonian goddess had become a darling in Judah is supported by the more than 800 figurines that archaeologists have unearthed in Judah, with nearly half of them found in Jerusalem itself.)

Their rationale for Ishtar worship is remarkable: things had gone well for them—food and affluence—when they worshipped her, but they encountered misfortune when they reformed their ways and worshipped YHWH. This raises the interesting question of how one can measure divine pleasure.

Today we hear something similar when popular clerics preach a gospel of prosperity: Good things happen to those devoted to God because riches constitute a barometer of God's smile. (The flip side is assumed to be true also: Hard times signify God's frown.) So is God happier with Bill Gates and his charitable foundation (worth $33.4 billion) than with the widow who donated only two mites (worth $.00176)?

Is having a brimming pantry and humongous bank account the best way to measure God's love? Hardly. Here's the best barometer of God's smile—Jesus Christ.

A Theological Whodunit

He is like a bear lying in wait for me, like a hidden lion stalking its prey. He . . . tore me to pieces.
Lam. 3:10, 11, NET.

The book of Lamentations is full of explicit depictions of YHWH as the enemy of His people. Other Old Testament books contain similar references to God as the author of disaster, disease, and death, but Lamentations seems to have a high concentration of such references.

Nebuchadnezzar, king of Babylon, had ruined Jerusalem three times: in 605 B.C., in 597 B.C., and (with more overwhelming effects) in 586 B.C. In some ways, this ancient destruction ranks right up there in Jewish memory with the Holocaust under Hitler more than 2,500 years later. It is this ruination that the book of Lamentations bewails.

Surely such suffering requires justification, and we find it throughout Lamentations. "The Lord afflicted her" (Lam. 1:5, NET). "The Lord . . . burned with anger" (verse 12, NET). "He made me desolate" (verse 13, NET). "The Lord has destroyed . . . ; and he has shown no mercy" (Jer. 2:2, NET). "The Lord was like an enemy; he has devastated Israel" (verse 5, NET). "The Lord was determined to tear down the walls around the city of Zion" (verse 8, NET). "You killed them when you were angry; you slaughtered them" (verse 21, NET). "He repeatedly attacked me" (Lam. 3:3, NET). "He shot his arrows into my heart" (verse 13, NET). "The Lord has fully vented his wrath" (Lam. 4:11, NET). And there's this: "Is it not from . . . the Most High that everything comes—both calamity and blessings?" (Lam. 3:38, NET).

What should we make of this theology—that when it comes to disaster, disease, and death, God is the answer to the question "whodunit?" Is it true that He is the source of human misery—even the suffering of His own people? Especially since the Holocaust, most theologians would answer with a resounding no. But why, then, these scriptural assertions?

Several reasons may be postulated. Perhaps people in the ancient Near East didn't understand cause-and-effect relationships as we do. Maybe in the face of rampant polytheism—even among His chosen people—YHWH felt He must claim responsibility for all that happened in order to preserve monotheism. Most often such statements are embedded in affective language, which expresses and evokes emotion. Cognitive language is that which we use to share ideas theological and philosophical. So it's not wise to extract theology from affective speech, because that's beyond its function. Rather, we should read it and grieve with the victims.

A Glimmer of Hope

Yahweh's mercy is surely not at an end,
nor is his pity exhausted. It is new every
morning. Great is your faithfulness!
Lam. 3:22, 23, Anchor.

One of the most eloquent gospel songs is titled "Great Is Thy Faithfulness." In 1923 Thomas O. Chisholm penned the lyrics, and a few years later William N. Runyan composed the accompanying music. The first stanza, familiar to nearly all of us, actually paraphrases Lamentations 3:22, 23 in a paean of praise, of trust. The words and melody are hard to forget.

The attacks by the Babylonian armies of King Nebuchadnezzar were dreadfully lethal. If it wasn't the siege, on the one hand, that gave cause for bereavement, then it was the removal of most survivors to Babylon, on the other hand, that produced yet an added reason for mourning. Indeed, the book of Lamentations is almost unrelenting in its descriptions of the devastation.

"The people of Zion, once so precious, . . . are now treated like cheap crockery" (Lam. 4:2, Anchor). "The tongue of the sucking child, from thirst, sticks to its palate" (verse 4, Anchor). "Those brought up in scarlet clothing pick through garbage" (verse 5, Anchor). "Those killed by the sword had it better than those killed by famine" (verse 9, Anchor). "With their own hands the kindly women cooked their children" (verse 10, Anchor). "We have become orphans, fatherless; our mothers are like widows. We pay money to drink our own water" (Lam. 5:3, 4, Anchor). "They raped women in Zion; virgins in the cities of Judah" (verse 11, Anchor).

The calamity that befell Judah could hardly have been any worse! And so the book winds up with these ominous words: "You have completely rejected us" (verse 22, Anchor). Nonetheless, here in the middle chapter (chapter 3) we find a glimmer of hope. Despite those bleak days, maybe—just maybe—better times would return. (In the book of Jeremiah we learn that it would take 70 years—two generations—before the good times would roll once more.) "Yet one thing I will keep in mind which will give me hope" (Lam. 3:21, Anchor).

But where could a basis for hope be found? Not in Nebuchadnezzar. Not in Jeremiah. Not in the Temple. That one thing that constituted the basis for hope was God's character. God couldn't help Himself! Because of His attributes, or character traits, hope could be imagined. "Yahweh's mercy is surely not at an end, nor is his pity exhausted. It is new every morning. Great is your faithfulness!" And He's the same even today!

Strange Ezekiel

The word of the Lord came to Ezekiel the priest, the son of Buzi, by the Kebar River in the land of the Babylonians. There the hand of the Lord was upon him.
Eze. 1:3, NIV.

Both the prophet Ezekiel and the book he wrote are rather enigmatic. So much so that finding at least some of the contents of Ezekiel troubling, various rabbis (mainly of the School of Shammai) debated its rightful place in the canon. What's so enigmatic—if not downright strange—about Ezekiel?

First, his personality seems rather peculiar. Ecstatic trance prophets were at this time a thing of the past, pretty much having died out with Elijah and Elisha. Yet Ezekiel was more in line with them than he was with Joel, Amos, Isaiah, Jeremiah, etc. He spoke of being infused with the Spirit (Eze. 2:2). He talked in terms of being grabbed by the hand of God (Eze. 3:14), which on one occasion clutched him by the hair and took him some 500 miles to Jerusalem (Eze. 8:3). He was dumb for extended periods of time (Eze. 3:26; 24:27). Some scholars have speculated that he may have been mentally ill.

Second, his prophetic behavior was a bit bizarre. He lay on his left side for 390 days and then on his right side for 40 more days (Eze. 4:4-6). He cut off his hair and divided it into three parts, burning one third, striking at one third with a sword, and throwing a third into the wind (Eze. 5:1-4). He destroyed part of his house by digging through the wall with his bare hands (Eze. 12:7). When his wife died suddenly, he didn't mourn her death (Eze. 24:16-18) because of God's command.

Third, his writings contain peculiar—even vulgar—elements. In chapter 16 God is depicted as having an incestuous relationship, and chapter 23 uses graphically erotic language. Some of his imagery is quite convoluted and difficult to unravel (Eze. 1 and 10). His book even contains elements that seem to contradict other inspired writings (Eze. 18:20).

Fourth, his prophetic batting average was off—yes, low. (More about this later. For instance, his lengthy descriptions of the rebuilt Temple and its services never came to pass.)

Nevertheless, God pressed this strange, maybe abnormal, man into divine service as a prophet. You see, God can use all of us, despite our foibles and eccentricities.

Soul Food

He said to me, "Son of man, feed your stomach and fill your body with this scroll which I am giving you." Then I ate it, and it was sweet as honey in my mouth.
Eze. 3:3, NASB.

E zekiel was a priest. But now that he was among the 10,000 prisoners of war whom Nebuchadnezzar marched off to Babylon after his 597 B.C. attack on Jerusalem, Ezekiel could no longer approach God for the people. So, during July of 593 B.C., God changed Ezekiel's vocation from priest to prophet. Now he would speak to the people for God.

After receiving an astounding vision of bizarre creatures with four heads and four wings and wheels within wheels, Ezekiel heard God say, "Open your mouth and eat what I am giving you" (Eze. 2:8, NASB). And he saw in God's hand "a scroll. . . . It was written on the front and back" (verses 9, 10, NASB). God repeated His initial command two more times: "Eat what you find; eat this scroll, and go, speak to the house of Israel" (Eze. 3:1, NASB).

An interesting meal, this scroll. Papyrus was made from strips of pith cut from the papyrus sedge. These strips were placed crisscross, sloshed with water and/or glue, hammered together, dried in a press, and then rubbed smooth with a rock. So tough was the resulting "paper" that pieces of it have survived for thousands of years. Even shoes were constructed from it. Ezekiel was to chew this long piece of papyrus and swallow it, which he did. And it tasted like dessert—sweet as honey. God then instructed Ezekiel to relate His words to the people.

One can understand this graphic imagery of revelation and inspiration in one of two ways. On the one hand, one can deduce verbal inspiration. God provides the exact words. Then the prophets swallow them, only to spit them back out to the people—same words in, same words out. On the other hand, one can deduce thought inspiration. God provides the revelation, which the prophets ingest so that it becomes part of their being. They then share this modified (digested and absorbed) message in their own words and literary style. The latter is the official Seventh-day Adventist understanding of the dynamics of revelation and inspiration.

"The Bible is written by inspired men, but it is not God's mode of thought and expression. It is that of humanity. God, as a writer, is not represented. . . . God has not put Himself in words, in logic, in rhetoric, on trial in the Bible. . . . It is not the words of the Bible that are inspired, but the men that were inspired" (*Selected Messages*, book 1, p. 21).

God Told Me to Do It

*Each day prepare your bread as you would
barley cakes. While all the people are watching,
bake it over a fire using dried human dung
as fuel and then eat the bread.*
Eze. 4:12, NLT.

"God said it; I believe it." "God told me to do it; I did it." Ever heard such statements? Is the sentiment they express right? Is it virtuous to blindly obey . . . even God? What do you think?

While Ezekiel was to lie on his left side for 390 days and on his right side for 40 more days, he was to eat a prescribed daily diet of eight ounces of wheat, barley, beans, lentils, millet, and spelt along with about a pint and a half of water (Eze. 4:9-11). God also told him to eat his meager rations publicly, where all could see him. God instructed, "Bake it over a fire using dried human dung as fuel and then eat the bread."

God's gross command repulsed Ezekiel, because using human feces for fuel was considered unclean, so he had the audacity to complain, "Must I be defiled by using human dung? For I have never been defiled before" (verse 14, NLT). As a priest, Ezekiel scrupulously kept himself from defilement, as God's law demanded. YHWH then had second thoughts and conceded that Ezekiel could use cow dung instead. Just because God said to do it, Ezekiel didn't blindly conform.

One wonders what would have happened had Abraham (another person willing to quarrel with God) argued once again when God had told him to offer Isaac as a sacrifice on Mount Moriah. Would God have given in as He had previously? Did Abraham (and Isaac) needlessly suffer through that ordeal without protest?

Between Abraham and Ezekiel's time God again gave a clear command, this time to Moses, who refused to comply unquestioningly. Instead, he also tried to reason with God—and won the argument (Ex. 32:7-14)!

Three times in Scripture we find three separate individuals who refused to roll over and play dead, who instead put up an argument despite YHWH's explicit words—twice a direct order. Each time what YHWH had said was morally and spiritually offensive. God doesn't seem to mind losing arguments with His faithful followers. Could it be that contrary to popular opinion God doesn't value mindless compliance with His unambiguous word? Just maybe God sends His revelations not to bring an end to our thinking but rather to spur us into thoughtful action.

Who Dies for Whom?

The soul that sinneth, it shall die.
Eze. 18:4.

E zekiel 18:4 has been a favorite verse of Seventh-day Adventist evangelists who want to make the point that the soul isn't immortal. It dies. Surely none of us would argue with that theology, although most Christians believe in the immortality of the soul. However, does Ezekiel 18:4 (and its counterpart, verse 20) refer to the state of the dead? No. This passage makes another important point, one that countered a common assumption of the ancient Hebrews, as well as one of modern Christians.

A common saying back then was: "The fathers have eaten sour grapes, and the children's teeth are set on edge" (verse 2). The point of this adage was that God held innocent people responsible for their ancestors' wrongdoing and would punish them for it.

The concept had an honored past. It was even mentioned in the Ten Commandments: "I the Lord thy God am a jealous God, visiting the iniquity of the fathers upon the children unto the third and fourth generation" (Ex. 20:5). It wasn't just the next generation that would be punished for their forebears' sins—the punishment could extend to the grandchildren, to the great-grandchildren, even to the great-great-grandchildren. And in Numbers 14:18 Moses echoed the concept that guilt and punishment could be passed from one generation to the next.

Not so, God informed Ezekiel. That isn't good theology. The innocent won't suffer divine retribution in lieu of the party in the wrong. A good man "shall not die for the iniquity of his father, he shall surely live" (Eze. 18:17). In fact, the rest of chapter 18 turns that well-used proverb on its head. "The soul that sinneth, it shall die. The son shall not bear the iniquity of the father, neither shall the father bear the iniquity of the son" (verse 20).

Ezekiel's words must have seemed scandalous to his audience. Who was he to argue with the Decalogue and with Moses? Nevertheless, it was time for God to clarify matters. He does indeed hold us responsible for our actions, but any punishment the heavenly Judge metes out will be individualistic—limited to the perpetrator.

However, if we will, we can be exempt from even our own just deserts. All we need do is accept His gracious atonement.

A Flat Tyre?

*They shall destroy the walls of Tyre . . . ; I will
. . . make her like the top of a rock. It shall be a
place for spreading nets in the midst of the sea.*
Eze. 26:4, 5, NKJV.

Tyre had been an ally of God's people for many years. King Hiram I had aided Solomon's Temple-building efforts by providing materials, work-force, and transportation. But when Nebuchadnezzar's armed forces sacked Jerusalem (586 B.C.), Tyre rejoiced. That same year God instructed Ezekiel to prophesy against Tyre.

Ezekiel's words are unambiguous. "They shall destroy the walls of Tyre and break down her towers; I will also scrape her dust from her, and make her like the top of a rock" (Eze. 26:4, NKJV). The divine agent who would do all this was specified by name: "Nebuchadnezzar . . . with horses, with char-iots, and with horsemen, and an army with many people" (verse 7, NKJV). Nebuchadnezzar's militia would besiege the city (verse 8). "With the hooves of his horses he will trample all your streets; he will slay your people by the sword. . . . They will plunder your riches and pillage your merchandise . . . they will lay your stones, your timber, and your soil in the midst of the water" (verses 11, 12, NKJV). Tyre would be so thoroughly destroyed that it would never be rebuilt—gone forever (verse 14; 27:36; 28:19).

For 13 years Nebuchadnezzar's soldiers besieged the island fortress, and although the Tyrians suffered greatly, the destruction Ezekiel foretold never happened—at least not because of Nebuchadnezzar's invasion. In fact, Tyre remained strong, although subject to Babylon. Some 200 years went by be-fore Alexander the Great built a causeway from the mainland to the island and destroyed the city. What about Tyre now, in the twenty-first century? Despite Ezekiel's (read God's) insistence that Tyre would disappear forever, today Tyre is one of Lebanon's largest cities.

Oops! Prophecy failed. Even God acknowledged the failure and promised to give Egypt to Nebuchadnezzar as a consolation prize (Eze. 29:17-20).

Prophecy isn't cut-and-dried. Because the Creator has given human beings free will, His own omniscience has become partial, oxymoron that it may be. God doesn't know our future choices, because we've not yet made them. How people respond—both positively and negatively—can modify a divinely pre-dicted outcome. God may act decisively so that a prophesied event occurs, but He doesn't necessarily or always do so.

What God Really Wants

June 19

Ezekiel

"As I live!" declares the Lord God, "I take no pleasure in the death of the wicked, but rather that the wicked turn from his way and live.... Why then will you die...?"
Eze. 33:11, NASB.

Through His prophets God predicted a woefully bleak future for His own people—predictions of horrendous disaster. He'd become sick at heart because of their trust in heathen allies and because of their idolatry, both of which He considered marital infidelity on their part. "They have committed adultery with their idols" (Eze. 23:37, NASB). Worse than that, the sacrifices they offered weren't just sheep or goats. They "even caused their sons, whom they bore to Me, to pass through the fire" (verse 37, NASB)—human sacrifice.

YHWH, the faithful husband, had had enough! He ordered, "Bring up a company against them and give them over to terror and plunder. The company will stone them with stones and cut them down with their swords; they will slay their sons and their daughters and burn their houses with fire" (verses 46, 47, NASB). He vented His frustration with them, saying: "Because I would have cleansed you, yet you are not clean, you will not be cleansed from your filthiness again, until I have spent My wrath on you.... I shall not relent, and I shall not pity and I shall not be sorry" (Eze. 24:13, 14, NASB).

YHWH sounded *very* serious! Because His people were intent on snubbing Him, He was intent on destroying them. Yet despite His grim intentions, God began to sound as though He didn't mean what He'd been saying. Was YHWH making empty threats? Hardly. He meant every word, but God's basic intention wasn't to destroy but to save. "I take no pleasure in the death of the wicked, but rather that the wicked turn from his way and live."

Although God's predictions of doom weren't usually prefaced with "if," He would have gladly abandoned His plans had His people repented. All they needed to do was ask for forgiveness—and mean it. God's prophesied destruction of Judah expressed His minor intention to destroy, not His major objective to preserve life. God's love, not His anger, is immutable. He threatens with the elevated purpose of eliciting reformation. He really wants His words of doom to fail. He really wants the annulment of His verdict of capital punishment. Predictions are an interface between God and man. Action (and reaction) can take place on both sides of prophecies.

Prisoners of War

Among them were the Judaeans Daniel,
Hananiah, Mishael and Azariah.
Dan. 1:6, New Jerusalem.

I n ancient Mesopotamia local kingdoms, fighting with one another, rose and fell on a regular basis. Some of them achieved legendary status. Sumer, Akkad, Assyria, Babylon, Hatti Land, Neo-Assyria, and Neo-Babylon are among the more well known. The Neo-Babylon Empire began with King Nabopolassar, "the King of Justice, the Shepherd called by Marduk" (Nabopolassar Cylinder, col. 1), who led an uprising against the Assyrians. He died unexpectedly on August 15, 605 B.C., and his son Nebuchadnezzar, on a military campaign against Egypt, raced back home and ascended the throne on September 7, 605 B.C.

It was in this year, 605 B.C., during a long military foray into Egypt and Palestine, that General Nebuchadnezzar had taken as prisoners of war a select group of Judeans, mostly from the royal family. Among them were Daniel and his three friends, Hananiah, Mishael, and Azariah. As Nebuchadnezzar tried to consolidate his domain, again and again he scoured the kingdom of Judah. Finally Jerusalem fell, after a prolonged siege, in 586 B.C., and the Babylonian armed forces destroyed Solomon's Temple.

Daniel spent the rest of his life in Babylon, more than 65 years. He kept memoirs, which ended up being incorporated into the book of Daniel, although liberal biblical scholarship doubts that this Daniel wrote the book that now bears his name.

Although we typically think of Daniel's book as prophecy, the ancient Jewish canon included it not among the prophets but rather among the "writings," which included the Psalms and Proverbs. (Josephus, Jewish historian and contemporary of Jesus, and the Essenes at Qumran, however, included the book of Daniel with the other prophetic books.)

Scholars today generally regard the book as apocalyptic rather than prophetic. In contrast to prophetic writing, apocalyptic literature tends to be more dualistic—speaking of contrasts between light and darkness. It also tends to be more future-oriented and utilizes graphic imagery—conglomerate beasts, birds, seraphim, cherubim, etc. One interesting factor is the reason given for the suffering of God's people. Typically in the prophetic writings God's people suffer because they're bad. However, generally in apocalyptic literature God's people suffer because they're good. Ultimately God's faithful but suffering people are vindicated.

Daniel's Diet

Daniel resolved that he would not defile himself with the royal rations of food and wine; so he asked the palace master to allow him not to defile himself.
Dan. 1:8, NRSV.

June 21

Daniel

King Nebuchadnezzar wanted the Judean royalty prisoners of war to adopt Babylonian culture (acculturation). To accomplish his purpose, he provided them with special training in Chaldean literature (a three-year course of study) and language as well as a special diet—food and wine directly from the king's own table.

Daniel, however, rejected the dietary regimen, and Hananiah, Mishael, and Azariah followed suit. When Daniel appealed to the palace master for exemption from the king's food and drink, the officer wanted nothing to do with it. If he complied with Daniel's request, he'd be disobeying a direct order from King Nebuchadnezzar. What if Daniel's health (and that of his three buddies) failed? Daniel next went to the warden and negotiated a 10-day trial of just vegetables and water. At the end of the 10-day experiment Daniel and his three pals were "better and fatter than all the young men who had been eating the royal rations" (Dan. 1:15, NRSV).

Daniel's nutritional scruples remain a mystery, and numerous rationales have been postulated for his behavior. Maybe the food had been offered to idols. Paul, however, didn't think eating food offered to idols was harmful, because idols are nothing (1 Cor. 8:4). Perhaps Daniel was a teetotaler. However, in Daniel 10:3 we learn that Daniel drank wine but drank none during a three-week fast. Maybe Daniel was resisting the king's efforts to acculturate him to a Chaldean lifestyle. However, the attempt to acculturate him included two elements—diet as well as schooling. Why refuse the former but accept the latter? Perhaps the meat wasn't kosher. However, why did he also reject the wine? Maybe eating the king's food entailed showing allegiance to Nebuchadnezzar. However, Daniel later called him "king of kings," a title elsewhere given to God (Rev. 17:14), and he said that YHWH had given Nebuchadnezzar sovereignty (Dan. 2:37).

So the enigma remains and indeed intensifies when we consider Esther, another Jewish hero in Mesopotamia, who accepted acculturation without a whimper, whereas Daniel seems to have resisted it. God blessed both heroes, despite their different approaches. Maybe He's more flexible than we're willing to think. At any rate, it's not our place to scrutinize motives.

Four Plus Two

There is a God in heaven who reveals secrets, and
He has made known to King Nebuchadnezzar
what will be in the latter days.
Dan. 2:28, NKJV.

Nebuchadnezzar's dream as related in Daniel 2 and Daniel's explanation of its significance is arguably the easiest of Daniel's prophecies to understand.

Modern presentations of Daniel 2 overstate the case, though. We hear that Babylon, Medo-Persia, Greece (Macedonia), and Rome ruled the world. Well, that's not really the case. Each successive domain encompassed larger and larger areas, but even the Roman Empire didn't rule the world. Despite the vast number of square miles under Roman domination, large portions of the planet lay outside the empire. And it doesn't help to tone down the claim that these four successive kingdoms ruled the then-known world. That also stretches the truth. Also, we focus on the western portion of the Roman Empire, forgetting its significant eastern sector.

Simply put, the four kingdoms symbolized by body parts were those ancient empires that had the greatest impact on God's people. Babylon, represented by the head of gold, annihilated the Davidic hegemony, devastated Jerusalem, carted off thousands of POWs to Mesopotamia, unsettled and resettled others, and razed Solomon's Temple. The Persian rulers enacted several edicts authorizing Jews to return to their ancestral homeland and rebuild their ruined place of worship. The Macedonians under Alexander the Great and his successors revolutionized society wherever they marched, Hellenizing cultures everywhere. It spread Koine Greek, which was an ideal language for the New Testament authors. The Roman Empire allowed a certain amount of autonomy for the Jews, although its long arm of influence was keenly felt in Judea and Galilee. Pax Romana, the "peace" maintained by Rome, established a good environment for Jesus Christ's ministry and later for the expansion of the early church.

What is truly significant, though, in Nebuchadnezzar's dream was the stone that "was cut out without hands, which struck the image on its feet of iron and clay, and broke them in pieces" (Dan. 2:34, NKJV). It then "became a great mountain and filled the whole earth" (verse 35, NKJV). This was a "kingdom which shall never be destroyed; . . . it shall stand forever" (verse 44, NKJV). Jesus announced the immediate establishment of that kingdom of grace, which one day shall morph into the kingdom of glory when He returns.

Grandstanding

There is a God in heaven who reveals mysteries.
Dan. 2:28, NIV.

When Nebuchadnezzar's own "magicians, enchanters, sorcerers and astrologers" (Dan. 2:2, NIV) couldn't interpret his forgotten dream of the multielement image, he flew into a rage, ordering that all his wise men be executed. Daniel and his three friends were among this group, although they hadn't been summoned with their Babylonian colleagues to the king's throne room. It fell to Arioch's lot to inform all the wise men of their impending demise.

Upon hearing this unsettling news, Daniel asked, "Why did the king issue such a harsh decree?" (verse 15, NIV) and asked for a temporary reprieve, during which time he and his three companions asked God for insight. God consented, revealing to Daniel the dream that Nebuchadnezzar had seen along with its meaning.

When Daniel got back in touch with Arioch, he said, "Do not execute the wise men of Babylon. Take me to the king, and I will interpret his dream for him" (verse 24, NIV).

Arioch wasted no time in getting an audience for Daniel, telling the king, "I have found a man among the exiles from Judah who can tell the king what his dream means" (verse 25, NIV). Notice Arioch's grandstanding. He took credit for ferreting out Daniel, the answer man, when in reality Arioch hadn't investigated anything but had merely informed Daniel of the death decree.

In contrast, Daniel denied having any special insight at all and showed no self-aggrandizement when he addressed the king: "There is a God in heaven who reveals mysteries." And throughout his explanation of the king's dream, Daniel continued to speak self-effacingly.

King Nebuchadnezzar wasn't beyond grandstanding as well. Like Arioch, he spoke in glowing terms of himself: "Is not this the great Babylon I have built as the royal residence, by my mighty power and for the glory of my majesty?" (Dan. 4:30, NIV). (In their written chronicles, ancient Near Eastern monarchs spoke of themselves in pretentious terms.)

Probably we should expect egotistical grandstanding from pagans, but surely it's inappropriate for God's people. Sadly, though, most of us have met Christians who habitually toot their own horn. Don't you agree, though, that Daniel's example is truly worth copying?

Three Inflammable Men

If we are thrown into the blazing furnace, the God whom we serve is able to save us. He will rescue us from your power, Your Majesty. But even if he doesn't, Your Majesty can be sure that we will never serve your gods or worship the gold statue you have set up.
Dan. 3:17, 18, NLT.

King Nebuchadnezzar decided to erect a statue that was all gold, not just its head. So he constructed an all-gold image—90 feet high. And if that weren't sufficient, he also summoned the "princes, prefects, governors, advisers, counselors, judges, magistrates, and all the provincial officials to come to the dedication of the statue he had set up" (Dan. 3:2, NLT).

Yes, Nebuchadnezzar was grandstanding . . . again! Furthermore, this vast throng of leaders were supposed to "bow to the ground to worship . . . [the] gold statue" (verse 5, NLT) when the royal orchestra began playing. Anyone who failed to comply would "immediately be thrown into a blazing furnace" (verse 7, NLT)—most likely a brick kiln shaped like a beehive.

When the orchestra started to play, everyone on the Plain of Dura fell prostrate before the golden statue—all, that is, except Shadrach, Meshach, and Abednego. (Daniel, for some reason, isn't mentioned.) Immediately "some of the astrologers went to the king and informed on the Jews" (verse 8, NLT). The Hebrew translated "informed on" literally means "ate their pieces." Nebuchadnezzar angrily demanded an accounting from these three fractious Jews and offered them a second chance, which they refused. Shadrach, Meshach, and Abednego were ready to take the punishment because they had no intention of compromising.

Before "the strongest men of his army" (verse 20, NLT) threw the three worthies into the brick kiln, Nebuchadnezzar ordered more chaff and crude oil to be added so that the fire could be made seven times hotter. These "strongest men" dutifully tossed the three Jews into the kiln. When the king peered through the flames, he was astounded to see not three but four persons inside the oven, and the fourth looked like "a divine being" (verse 25, NLT), whom the king identified as an angel (verse 28). As sizzling as it was, the fire didn't incinerate even their clothing—just the ropes that had bound them (and the "strongest men" who'd tossed them in).

Although this was a remarkable miracle, even the three Jews recognized that God doesn't always extraordinarily deliver His faithful people. Martyrdom is the rule; deliverance is the exception. However, it isn't the outcome that matters, but the fidelity of God's people.

God's Graffiti

Immediately the fingers of a human hand appeared and began writing on the plaster of the wall of the royal palace.
Dan. 5:5, NRSV.

It was October 11, 539 B.C. Belshazzar, coregent with his father, Nabonidus, sponsored a gala banquet while Persian soldiers occupied a base camp outside the city. He felt smug because two double walls fortified the city of Babylon, making a total thickness of 84 feet. At the height of the merriment, Belshazzar and guests, having quaffed wine and beer from the holy vessels that Nebuchadnezzar had looted from Solomon's Temple, lauded their heathen deities, including the mood god Sin. However, everyone's attention abruptly focused on a severed hand that wrote indecipherable graffiti on the white plastered wall of the banquet hall.

The eerie phenomenon made Belshazzar's composure disintegrate, and "his knees knocked together" (Dan. 5:6, NRSV). As usual, the Babylonian wise men afforded no help and couldn't decode the words, which had neither vowels nor word spacing. So Daniel, now in his 80s, was summoned. He read: MN, MN, TKL, and PRSN (see verse 25).

Daniel understood the words to be a double entendre, depending on the vowels he supplied. As words serving as *nouns*, they described three kinds of money: the mina; the tekel, which was Aramaic for shekel and worth 1/60 of a mina; and two peres, each worth half a mina. Freely rendered into English, it meant: "A half dollar, a half dollar, a penny, and two bits" (W. Sibley Towner, *Daniel*, p. 75). As words serving as *verbs*, the meaning would be: counted, numbered, or assigned; weighed, divided, or found wanting; and broken up, shattered. Because four terms were used, it's possible that each monetary unit also symbolized one of the four Neo-Babylonian kings who had succeeded Nebuchadnezzar: mina—Amel-Marduk (562-560 B.C.); mina—Neriglissar (560-556 B.C.); tekel—Labashi-Marduk (556 B.C.); peres in its dual form—Nabonidus and Belshazzar (556-539 B.C.).

In other words, God had found the Neo-Babylonian kings defective and had put them on a clearance sale—to be "bought" by the king of Persia. As the Supreme Inspector, God weighs the evidence, pronounces His finding(s), and executes the verdict. On October 12, 539 B.C., the Neo-Babylonian Empire crumbled, replaced by the Medo-Persian Empire.

Immutable Decrees

*My God sent His angel and shut the lions' mouths,
and they have not harmed me, inasmuch as I was
found innocent before Him; and also toward you,
O king, I have committed no crime.*
Dan. 6:22, NASB.

The Medo-Persian conquerors of Babylon found a religious crisis in the newly conquered empire. Nabonidus, the last Neo-Babylonian king, had tried to acquire security by removing the statues of gods from the various cities of the kingdom and enshrining them within the metropolis of Babylon. Surely such a concentration of deities would entail that they would keep Babylon from falling to the Medo-Persian armed forces. The importation of the gods produced empty temples and shrines throughout the land, leaving the local citizens with no idols to pray to. Upon the Medo-Persian occupation, measures were taken to transport the gods back to their original locales, but that would take months to accomplish.

Daniel, of course, had no such problem, because YHWH was not manufactured into an idol. So he continued praying as usual. It was during this time of religious turmoil that Daniel's invidious peers approached Darius and suggested that for 30 days he should be the only object of prayer. In effect, this made King Darius the one and only god worthy of worship for a month.

Daniel didn't change his habits, and ended up in the lions' lair. Purportedly, the laws of the Medes and Persians couldn't be changed. Once Daniel survived this ordeal, theoretically the decree had run its course, allowing the lions to dine instead on his enemies.

What about unchangeable decrees? Are they ever really immutable? YHWH made decrees that He was willing to annul. "When I say to the wicked, 'You will surely die,' and he turns from his sin . . . he will surely live; he shall not die" (Eze. 33:14, 15, NASB). Even though God's decree said that the wicked person would "surely" die, He would rescind that edict when the sinner repented. Clearly, in His compassion God can alter His decrees.

God Himself may be immutable, but not so His decrees. He isn't ensnared by His own unchanging character. So why should the edicts of a mere human who has been supposedly deified be any different? The concept of unchangeable decrees—Medo-Persian or otherwise—is based on a flawed assumption. The precedent set by YHWH undermines the idea of ironclad decrees. Humans mustn't arrogate to themselves that which even God refuses to do.

Prophecy Without Math

*For two thousand and three hundred evenings
and mornings; then the sanctuary shall be
restored to its rightful state.
Dan. 8:14, RSV.*

The prophecy found in Daniel 8:14 has been widely cherished by Seventh-day Adventists. However, because of the arithmetic involved in unraveling this prediction, average members in the pew find themselves at a loss to interpret the prophecy adequately. There is a way, however, of reading Daniel 8:14 without getting mired in mathematical calculations.

When Nebuchadnezzar's soldiers were finished with Jerusalem in 586 B.C., Solomon's Temple, which had been an object of Hebrew pride for about 400 years, lay in ruins. The ark of the covenant was nowhere to be found, and the sacrificial system God through Moses had instituted more than 800 years earlier had come to a screeching halt. The Temple had been desecrated.

Why? God's people had broken covenant with God. They had constructed deities from wood and precious metals and worshipped these human-made idols. The women treasured little figurines of the goddess Ishtar. Some offered their children as burnt offerings to Moloch.

Now that the "sanctuary was overthrown" (Dan. 8:11, RSV), the question was: "For how long is the vision concerning the continual burnt offering, the transgression that makes desolate, and the giving over of the sanctuary and host to be trampled under foot?" (verse 13, RSV). And the reply was: "For two thousand and three hundred evenings and mornings; then the sanctuary shall be restored to its rightful state" (verse 14, RSV).

Nebuchadnezzar's invasion of the Temple wasn't the only time such sacrilege took place. In 167 B.C. the restored Temple was ravaged by Antiochus Epiphanes, who rededicated it to Zeus. Then in A.D. 70, history repeated itself when the Romans incinerated Herod's Temple. Another 65 years later Hadrian set about building a temple to Jupiter, Minerva, and Juno on the very site where the Jewish Temple had stood. Today a mosque sits on that ancient site.

Without recourse to arithmetic formulas, we can understand that again and again non-Jewish rulers insulted God by violating the place of His sanctuary. But God can't be snubbed with impunity. His holy place would be "restored to its rightful state" (verse 14, RSV). Despite the appearance of utter devastation, God and right ultimately win. Always.

A Not-So-Minor Prophet

The word of the Lord that came to Hosea son of Beeri during the reigns of Uzziah, Jotham, Ahaz and Hezekiah, kings of Judah, and during the reign of Jeroboam son of Jehoash king of Israel. Hosea 1:1, NIV.

When we turn the last page of Daniel, we enter a time machine that takes us back more than 150 years. Assyria, like a boa constrictor, was tightening its coils around various parts of the ancient Near East. Hosea, who apparently lived in the northern kingdom of Israel, called its rulers to account for their political dalliance with Assyria by which they hoped to gain security and maintain their own hegemony. Assyrian forces hadn't yet crushed Samaria, the capital city, into submission, abolishing the already-unstable northern kingdom of Israel in 722 B.C.

Kingship in northern Israel had become a revolving door. Jeroboam II had remained king for 41 years. His son Zechariah (not the prophet) inherited the throne as heir apparent, but after six months he was assassinated by Shallum, who ruled for only a month before dying at the hands of Menahem. Menahem's reign lasted 10 years, during which time he paid a steep tribute to Assyrian king Tiglath-pileser. He raised the money by taxing 60,000 of the richest men in his realm. Menahem was a cruel king. His son Pekahiah, a chip off the old block, ascended the throne, but remained king for just two years until Pekah killed him and usurped the throne. Pekah's reign was cut short when Hoshea (not the prophet) stole the throne by assassination.

It was during this time of political unrest that God called Hosea to the prophetic office, giving him a puzzling order: "Go, take to yourself an adulterous wife" (Hosea 1:2, NIV). Scholars debate whether or not Gomer, his bride, was a "professional" prostitute and whether or not she was that at the time of the marriage. What becomes clear is that later she proved unfaithful, and at least two of her three children (Lo-Ruhama, a girl, and Lo-Ammi, a boy) were illegitimate—"children of unfaithfulness" (verse 2, NIV). Lo-Ruhama's name meant "not pitied." Lo-Ammi's name meant "not my people." The firstborn, Jezreel, appears to have been legitimate.

God encouraged Hosea into committing himself to a dysfunctional family life so that Gomer's marital unfaithfulness would parallel the situation in Israel: "The land is guilty of the vilest adultery in departing from the Lord" (verse 2, NIV). And Hosea's unwavering love illustrated God's undying care for His people.

Never Again, But . . .

I shall show no more pity for the House of Israel, I shall never forgive them again.
Hosea 1:6, New Jerusalem.

Worship of Baal, a Canaanite god, spread like the bubonic plague throughout the ancient Near East. As the god responsible for storms and fertility, he was called "He Who Rides on the Clouds" and "Lord of the Earth." Although Baal was commonly known to God's people (the book of Judges shows they worshipped him early on), notorious Queen Jezebel is usually given credit for officially introducing Baal worship among the Hebrew people. Both biblical and extrabiblical (archaeological) evidence indicate that Baal worship flourished in both the northern kingdom of Israel and the southern kingdom of Judah.

Baal had at least two consorts, the goddesses Anath—his beautiful yet violent virgin sister, goddess of bloodshed—and Astarte (Asherah). There may have been only one Baal, but he was called by other names that identified him with local areas: Baal-Peor, Baal-Hermon, Baal-Hazor, Baal-Shamen, Baal of Sidon, etc.

Although archaeologists have found and deciphered ancient documents about him, details about what Baal worship involved remain meager. Apparently his idols were kissed (1 Kings 19:18). Also, Hebrew Baal worshippers burned their children to him (Jer. 19:5). Because the worship of fertility deities typically entailed erotic rituals, it's often assumed that such orgies accompanied Baal worship also. If that's so, it's possible that Gomer, Hosea's ne'er-do-well wife, participated in these orgiastic rites in an attempt to foster fruitful marriages.

With all this Baal worship, God had had it up to here! He wanted nothing to do with Baal. The devotion His chosen people gave to Baal offended Him. He regarded their actions as spiritual adultery. Hence YHWH's insistence that He'd no longer pity (have wombish feelings for) them. In fact, He'd never forgive them . . . again. But God's fury subsided quickly, and He said, "I shall take pity on Lo-Ruhamah, I shall tell Lo-Ammi, 'You are my people'" (Hosea 2:23, New Jerusalem).

Why is YHWH so wishy-washy? He hardly conforms to the proposed theological model of divine immutability and impassibility. His vacillation, however, isn't a symptom of weakness but a sign of His profound benevolence. Scripture says that God is love, not that He is wrath. Love is what and who He is, and God's deep-seated love moves Him to show mercy, to forgive.

Whatever Works

I will punish her. . . . I will allure her.
Hosea 2:13, 14, NKJV.

The story line becomes a bit difficult to unravel because sometimes it appears that Hosea is doing the talking, whereas at other times it seems that God is the one speaking. The interweaving of the stories about the two jilted lovers—Hosea and God—is probably no accident. Hosea's troubled marriage symbolized God's troubled relationship with Israel. So in essence it hardly matters who is doing the talking.

The proposed actions Hosea/God will take are negative and positive. Whatever works!

Negatively, certain behaviors spring from ire. Gomer/Israel will be caged in so that she'll have no access to her illegitimate lovers (Hosea 2:6, 7), the hope being that she'll conclude, "I will go and return to my first husband, for then it was better for me than now" (verse 7, NKJV). Furthermore, her clothing and food will be withheld (verse 9). And her husband will rip off her dress, publicly shaming her by exposing her nudity (verse 10). All her "mirth" will cease (verse 11, NKJV), including annual feast days, monthly festivals, and weekly Sabbath celebrations.

Positively, certain other behaviors spring from love. Negative sanctions can work, at least temporarily, but positive reinforcements just might work even better. "I will allure her" (verse 14, NKJV). The verb means to entice and in sexual contexts can be translated "seduce" or "woo." Her husband will take her back to the wilderness, where their romance came to fruition, and speak to her heart (verse 14). He will restore her fortunes and transform the valley of trouble into a gateway or opportunity of hope (verse 15). Surely then she will sing (verse 15) and will coo "My husband" rather than "My master" (verse 16). He will then make a covenant of peace and safety with her (verse 18). Let the good times roll!

"I will betroth you to Me in faithfulness" (verse 20, NKJV). And they will live happily ever after. "I will sow her for Myself in the earth, and I will have mercy on her who had not obtained mercy; then I will say to those who were not My people, 'You are My people!' And they shall say, 'You are my God!'" (verse 23, NKJV).

God uses whatever works—both negative and positive reinforcements— and pays whatever it costs to win back His people's affection. Lost love is tragic, but it need not be permanent. God does all that He can do, but it's up to us either to accept or to spurn His love.

Double-Whammy Nightmare

Solemnize a fast, proclaim an assembly;
gather the elders—all the inhabitants of
the land—in the House of the Lord.
Joel 1:14, Tanakh.

No one had ever seen anything like it, and no one would ever see anything like it again (Joel 1:2; 2:2)—two decimating plagues!

The first plague was a huge horde of locusts. Teeming locusts were relatively common in the ancient Near East. As many as 80 million individual insects can constitute a single swarm and can fly more than 80 miles a day. They can eat their own weight every day, and one ton of locusts can daily devour as much as 10 elephants or 2,500 people would eat.

However, this particular scourge of flying insects seemed more devastating than any previous locust swarm. So numerous were the marauders that they resembled YHWH's armies (Joel 2:11)! The hungry critters ate everything in sight—even the bark on trees (Joel 1:7). "The new grain is ravaged, the new wine is dried up, the new oil has failed. . . . The fig tree withers, pomegranate, palm, and apple" trees were stripped naked (verses 10-12, Tanakh). Domesticated animals starved to death because of the lack of vegetation. "How the beasts groan! The herds of cattle are bewildered . . . and the flocks of sheep are dazed" (verse 18, Tanakh). "Offering and libation have ceased" (verse 9, Tanakh) because herds and flocks and crops were in short supply.

The second devastating scourge was a drought. The predictable and anticipated early (autumn) and latter (spring) rains hadn't fallen. Any flora that had escaped the jaws of the locusts couldn't renew its growth for lack of moisture. "Fire has consumed the pastures . . . and flame has devoured all the trees. . . . The watercourses are dried up, and fire has consumed the pastures" (verses 19, 20, Tanakh).

Surely God must have been irate, but why? Joel (or YHWH through Joel) remained silent on the specific sins that might merit such divine reprisal. The land, which had resembled the Garden of Eden prior to the two plagues, now looked like "a desolate waste" (Joel 2:3, Tanakh).

The time had come for an eleventh-hour effort—for fasting, gathering for prayer at the Temple, and offering sacrifices costly because of the scarcity of plants and animals. Their picture of YHWH's character precluded the catastrophic locusts and ruinous drought having the last word. "He is gracious and compassionate, slow to anger, abounding in kindness" (verse 13, Tanakh).

A Reversal of Fortunes

July 2

Joel

The Mountains shall drip with wine, the hills shall flow with milk, and all the watercourses of Judah shall flow with water.
Joel 3:18, Tanakh.

The tragedy of the two plagues left a faint glimmer of hope as the last viable option. It appeared that the great day of YHWH had arrived. To what would the languishing people pin their hope? God, of course. Nevertheless, hope contains more wishful thinking than it does certainty. "Who knows but He may turn and relent, and leave a blessing behind" (Joel 2:14, Tanakh).

Their wagered hope, though, was based on more than mere speculation. At the height of the destruction God Himself had said, "'Yet even now' . . . 'turn back to Me with all your hearts'" (verse 12, Tanakh). Even at this remove, we can sense the yearning—not so much in the people's voices—but in God's voice.

It may have seemed as though General YHWH was commander in chief of the locust armies that had been scaling the walls, dashing through the city, scrambling into homes, and crawling through windows (see verses 7-9, Tanakh). But no matter how late the hour, no matter how bleak the situation, no matter how intense YHWH's wrath, the future hadn't been immutably predetermined. Divine unchangeableness doesn't entail rigidity.

God urged, "Turn back to Me with all your hearts, and with fasting, weeping, and lamenting" (verse 12, Tanakh). No superficial contrition would do. "Rend your hearts rather than your garments" (verse 13, Tanakh). Their internal state of mind mattered far more than their external trappings of goat's-hair sackcloth, sniffling noses, and growling stomachs. And no one must be excluded. All—golden-agers, nursing infants, newlyweds, priests, laity—must evidence genuine penitence. "Between the portico and the altar" the priests implored God, "Oh, spare Your people, Lord!" (verse 17, Tanakh).

It shouldn't shock us to learn that God regarded their repentance as authentic. "The Lord was roused on behalf of His land and had compassion upon His people. . . . The Lord declared: 'I will grant you the new grain, the new wine, and the new oil'" (verses 18, 19, Tanakh). Furthermore, He pledged, "I will repay you for the years consumed by swarms and hoppers, by grubs and locusts" (verse 25, Tanakh). Not only that, but He promised: "I will pour out My spirit upon all flesh" (Joel 3:1, Tanakh). He would treat His people as innocent (verse 21). Amazing grace!

Amos, a Nobody

[Amos] was one of the herdsmen from Tekoa.
Amos 1:1, NET.

July 3
Amos

A mos was a nobody.

Most of the time biblical characters were introduced by genealogical data, even when limited to one generation: "So-and-so, the son of . . ." The Hebrews considered this essential information providing insight into the personality of the individual. But no father is mentioned for Amos. As to his origins, all we know is that he'd lived in Tekoa, which may have been his hometown or may simply have been where he hailed from when he received his prophetic call.

Amos appears to have had at least three jobs—shepherd, cowboy, migrant agricultural worker. The book bearing his name calls him a *nōqēd*, a term not clearly understood, but likely a shepherd or perhaps a sheep owner (cf. Amos 7:15, where he's a follower of sheep and goats). In verse 14 Amos says he'd been a *boqer*, a cowboy. The same passage tells us that he'd been a *bâlac*, a nipper of sycamore trees. (At least two kinds of figs grew in Palestine. Sycamore figs were the less desirable and were eaten mainly by poor people. Each piece of fruit had to be pinched or nicked prior to ripening, or else they'd rot on the tree.) The climate in Tekoa wasn't suitable for growing sycamore figs, so Amos had to "nip" them elsewhere—as an itinerant worker.

Additionally, Amos claimed that he wasn't a prophet or a son of a prophet (verse 14). Sons of the prophets were professionals trained to be seers in schools established by Elijah—seminaries. Prophet, like priest, was a profession. Amos, however, claimed no such thing. He was a simple farmer.

Finally, Amos prophesied as a "foreigner." Tekoa, his residence, was in Judah. Amos was a Judean, but he prophesied at Bethel, located in the northern kingdom of Israel. The Israelite high priest Amaziah, *the* religious authority figure there, didn't appreciate Amos' meddling and told this persona non grata to go back home and prophesy *there* to his own kind (verses 12, 13).

God, however, is no "respecter of persons" (Acts 10:34). Privileged birth, Ivy League education, or professional certification doesn't make one eligible for God's service. Those characteristics can be truly useful—even desirable— but they aren't prerequisites for doing God's work. God wants loving hearts and willing minds and then compensates for our deficiencies. We may look down upon those in lower social strata, but YHWH doesn't. Another reassuring snapshot.

God's Verdict

Because Damascus has committed three crimes—make that four!—I will not revoke my decree of judgment. . . . So I will set Hazael's house on fire.
Amos 1:3, 4, NET.

A mos begins with messages of doom against Israel's and Judah's neighbors. The oracles follow a somewhat specific pattern: (1) the name of the country, (2) the accusation of "three crimes—make that four," (3) the enumeration of misdeeds, (4) the threat of conflagration, and (5) the name of the Judge who has issued the verdict—YHWH.

The city-states under divine judgment included Damascus, Gaza, Tyre, Edom, Ammon, and Moab. These verdicts of condemnation must have sounded like music to the ears of the Israelites and Judahites. Their foes would finally get their comeuppance! But God, through Amos, left little time for exultation. His list of oracles of doom ends with similar verdicts pronounced against the larger northern kingdom of Israel and the smaller kingdom of Judah. God singles out His elect precisely because of that—He'd elected them to be His special people, private property, who would live in the land He'd promised them.

That YHWH sat as judge over His unfaithful people comes as no surprise. But that He also pronounced judgment on their heathen neighbors may raise eyebrows. He didn't claim that He was their God and that they were His people, terms He reserved for the Hebrews. Nonetheless, as Creator and Sustainer of all, He legitimately could call the world to account also. Furthermore, He also claimed to have "brought the Philistines from Caphtor [Crete?] and the Arameans from Kir" (Amos 9:7, NET). He probably could have made the same claim for the other six nations. Note what He later said through Isaiah: "Blessed be my people, Egypt, and the work of my hands, Assyria, and my special possession, Israel" (Isa. 19:25, NET). He claimed them all!

God's indictments, however, varied. Whereas He accused the nations of civil or ethical misdeeds—crimes against humanity—He accused Israel and Judah, His special people, of religious offenses: disloyalty to YHWH, idolatry. And of the divided monarchy, Israel received the much lengthier condemnation. Indeed, much of the rest of the collection of Amos' prophecies deals with the situation in northern Israel.

The snapshot of God that Amos provides is that of Universal Sovereign. No one is exempt from His inspection. No one.

No Animal Sacrifices?

*Even though you offer up to Me burnt offerings and
your grain offerings, I will not accept them; and I will
not even look at the peace offerings of your fatlings.
Amos 5:22, NASB.*

One thing is certain—the Hebrew people offered animal sacrifices to YHWH. Primitive though such a religious practice may be, both the Old and New Testaments refer to them. Indeed, we read about them as early as Cain and Abel. Noah and Abraham also offered them. In the books of Exodus and Leviticus we find specific commands about what should be sacrificed, when, why, and by whom. The judges offered animal sacrifices, including a human sacrifice by Jephthah (his only child, a daughter).

During the monarchy sacrificial offerings remained in vogue, sometimes excessively so. At the dedication of Solomon's Temple, blood of sacrificial animals flowed like water as 22,000 cows and 120,000 sheep were slaughtered (2 Chron. 7:5)—that's 17,750 animals slaughtered during each of the eight days of dedication, which is 739 an hour or more than 12 a minute!

Now God, through Amos, announced that He was fed up with their animal offerings. "Even though you offer up to Me burnt offerings and your grain offerings, I will not accept them; and I will not even look at the peace offerings of your fatlings." Not only that, but God said He'd never wanted them! "Did you present Me with sacrifices and grain offerings in the wilderness for forty years, O house of Israel?" (Amos 5:25, NASB). The answer to this rhetorical question is an expected "No."

YHWH's assertion has troubled expositors. Were all the previous historical records that talked about offering animal sacrifices, specifically those in Exodus, Leviticus, Numbers, and Deuteronomy, wrong? Interestingly, even many biblical scholars whom we'd regard as liberal reject such an idea. The dissonance caused by Amos 5 can be resolved when we recognize that the issue at stake here wasn't the Temple in Jerusalem but the competing temple in Bethel, which was tainted by idolatry. So the religious rites under divine criticism were those alternate ones.

Even more important to the discussion is God's emphasis that religious rites cannot and must not substitute for obeying God. It's a travesty to sing hymns and offer sacrifices when at the same time we oppress others. It's justice and mercy that God wants (verses 15, 24).

When we lack inner decency and integrity, our religious trappings insult God.

Stop It, God!

Oh, Lord God, refrain! How will
Jacob survive? He is so small.
Amos 7:5, Tanakh.

Amos had a series of four visions, each a graphic visual aid about what was about to take place. Amos prefaced each account with a statement indicating that God had shown him something: "This is what my Lord God showed me . . ." (verse 1, Tanakh; see also verse 7; 8:1) and "I saw my Lord standing . . ." (Amos 9:1, Tanakh).

In the first vision Amos saw pretty much the same thing that Joel had described—a locust plague. The ravenous little beasties devoured everything in sight at the very time "when the late-sown crops were beginning to sprout" Amos 7:1, Tanakh). Amos pleaded with God to halt the scourge: "O Lord God, pray forgive. How will Jacob survive? He is so small" (verse 2, Tanakh).

Amos didn't need to intercede for the people, because that was part of the job description for priests, not for prophets. But by pointing out how little Jacob was, he tugged at God's heartstrings, and "the Lord relented" (verse 3, Tanakh). The locust swarm that Amos saw in advance never happened, because He prayed and God changed His mind.

Our passage for today's reading comes from the second vision that God gave to Amos. According to his report, "my Lord God was summoning to contend by fire which consumed the Great Deep and was consuming the fields" (verse 4, Tanakh). The conflagration was no ordinary blaze. Having destroyed the Great Deep, the fire also consumed the Promised Land with its fertile fields.

Amos was appalled and repeated his earlier prayer in hopes that he could trigger a change in God's plans: "Oh, Lord God, refrain! How will Jacob survive? He is so small." Again the idea that Jacob was such a little guy moved God so profoundly that once again He abandoned His plans and said, "That shall not come to pass, either" (verse 6, Tanakh).

As we've turned the pages of the biblical photo album, we've noted numerous times God repented, changed His mind. That God does this should come as good news to all of us. However, His repentance can be just as temporary as His original intent that He'd been talked out of doing. God's repentance lasts only if we follow up with our own repentance. Nonetheless, the divine capacity to change is an unchanging component of Bible-based theology.

Literary Dependency

Vision of Obadiah: . . . I have received a message from Yahweh, a herald has been sent throughout the nations: "Up! Let us march against this people. Into battle!" Obadiah 1, New Jerusalem.

The book of Obadiah is the shortest in Old Testament Scripture, with only 21 verses. However, the book could be even shorter. At least eight of the passages in Obadiah are almost verbatim from what Jeremiah had written. Deduct those verses from the total of 21, and Obadiah becomes a very short book indeed.

Why do we think Obadiah borrowed from Jeremiah rather than the other way around? Simple. Jeremiah's ministry preceded Obadiah's. So any literary dependency surely indicates that Obadiah copied from Jeremiah, not vice versa. This is even more amazing because this borrowing took place during a time when illiteracy was rampant (maybe as high as 80 percent or more) and when written documents were at a premium (rare because of the expense involved).

Here are some examples.

"Vision of Obadiah: . . . I have received a message from Yahweh, a herald has been sent throughout the nations: 'Up! Let us march against this people. Into battle!'" (Obadiah 1, New Jerusalem).

"I have received a message from Yahweh, a herald has been sent throughout the nations, 'Muster! March against this people! Prepare for battle!'" (Jer. 49:14, New Jerusalem).

"If thieves were to come to you (or robbers during the night) surely they would steal only as much as they wanted?" (Obadiah 5, New Jerusalem).

"If robbers came during the night, would they not steal only as much as they wanted?" (Jer. 49:9, New Jerusalem).

"If grape-pickers were to come to you, surely they would leave a few gleanings?" (Obadiah 5, New Jerusalem).

"If grape-pickers were to come to you, would they not leave a few gleanings?" (Jer. 49:9, New Jerusalem).

Why talk about literary borrowing in a daily devotional book? Because in recent decades a lot of ink has been spilled criticizing Ellen White because of her alleged plagiarism. The argument reasons that an inspired writer wouldn't copy what other authors have written without giving credit. As we've just seen, this "problem" has parallels in Scripture itself. (Obadiah isn't the only example of literary borrowing in Scripture.) Other "problems" have also been found in her writings. However, these very same issues also crop up in the Bible. If Ellen White's inspiration is jeopardized by these "problems," then the inspiration of the Bible writers should also be jeopardized. Ellen White is in the same boat as Obadiah, Isaiah, etc. Inspiration doesn't prevent "problems." The human element, never perfect, is always present.

High and Mighty

July 8
Obadiah

*Though you soar like an eagle, though you
set your nest among the stars, I shall bring
you down from there!—declares Yahweh.
Obadiah 4, New Jerusalem.*

E dom was another name for Esau, who lived in the high country of Seir. The Edomites were distant relatives of the Hebrew people. The relationships between Edom and Judah were marked by the same sort of stormy controversy that had existed between the twins Esau and Jacob. The hostilities weren't one-sided and had roots in the favoritism shown by the parents. Isaac favored Esau, whereas Rebekah favored Jacob.

When Moses led Jacob's descendants out of Egypt on their trek to the Promised Land, he asked the progeny of Esau for permission to cross their territory. Moses assured the Edomites, "'We shall not go through the fields or vineyards; we shall not drink the water from the wells; we shall keep to the king's highway without turning to right or left.' . . . 'We shall keep to the high road; if I and my flocks drink any of your water, I·am willing to pay for it'" (Num. 20:17-19, New Jerusalem). The Edomites refused to allow them safe passage and actually mustered their army against them. As a result, the Israelites had to take a longer, more circuitous route.

Ancient Near Easterners had long memories, and King David evened the score by routing the Edomites and annexing Edom to his kingdom (2 Sam. 8:13, 14). Around 845 B.C. the Edomites rebelled and regained their autonomy. Jehoram, king of Judah, tried to reclaim the territory but failed.

According to Obadiah, when the Babylonians sacked Jerusalem, the Edomites not only gloated over Judah's misfortunes but took advantage of its troubles and joined in the looting (Obadiah 12, 13). In fact, as Judahites fled to the hills, the Edomites attacked them (verse 14)!

The Edomites assumed that they were so high and mighty that their future was secure. Like an eagle, they'd made their home in the mountains— among the stars (verse 4)! They chortled, "Who can bring me down to earth?" (verse 3, New Jerusalem). But despite its high-ground advantage, Edom wasn't as secure as it assumed. God said, "I have reduced you to the smallest of nations, you are now beneath contempt. . . . The people of Mount Esau will be massacred to the last one" (verses 2-9, New Jerusalem).

Just as we can't abide arrogance, neither can God.

Runaway Prophet

Arise, go to Nineveh, that great city, and cry against it; for their wickedness has come up before me.
Jonah 1:2, RSV.

Jonah is known in Scripture for two predictions. Second Kings 14:25 mentions his first prophecy—that the kingdom of Israel would flourish, expanding its boundaries. During the reign of Jeroboam II that's exactly what happened. "He restored the border of Israel from the entrance of Hamath as far as the Sea of the Arabah" (RSV). The only time more territory was ruled was under the united monarch when kings David and Solomon reigned. This helps us date Jonah's ministry to sometime during the late 800s or early 700s B.C.

The Assyrian kings during this period were Adad-nirari III, Shalmaneser IV, Ashur-dan III, and Ashur-nirari V. These rulers struggled to keep the empire intact and dispatched their armed forces in attempts to solidify their territory. Despite the political distractions of a weakened empire, King Adad-nirari III managed to initiate several building projects, including construction in the city of Nineveh. Eventually several strong kings acceded to the throne and transformed Assyria into an awesome military power known for its cruelty. During its future heyday Assyria would attack the northern kingdom of Israel, annihilating it.

We find Jonah's second prophecy in the book bearing his name. God had another mission for Jonah, whose bona fides as a prophet had solidified because his prediction of an expanded Israelite kingdom had proven correct. God commissioned Jonah to speak for Him again. This time, however, the prediction that he was to pronounce wasn't as glamorous. He must trek over to Nineveh and announce its immediate destruction.

Jonah sprang into action, but instead of heading for Nineveh, he traveled to the seaport of Joppa. He must have been a man of means, because at Joppa he hired a ship and its crew to sail to Tarshish. (It appears that the ancient world didn't have terminology for "fare" or "buying a ticket" for individual passage until the Roman Empire.) The location of Tarshish remains a matter of debate, but many think it was a city in Spain—the opposite direction from Nineveh.

Sometimes doing God's work is more congenial than at other times. The quality of our faithfulness in His service is measured not so much by our behavior when God's work is fun but rather by our compliance when our duty is onerous.

SOG-7

The Fish With a Tummyache

Yahweh spoke to the fish, which then vomited Jonah onto the dry land.
Jonah 2:11, New Jerusalem.

Jonah, the dove, flew off toward Tarshish. But things didn't go his way. Suddenly a huge storm blew up, and the ship feared that it would break apart (that's the way the Hebrew puts it). The panicked crew screamed to their gods, tossed as much stuff as was prudent overboard, and dug the oars into the water in a futile attempt to get nearer to shore.

Jonah, however, had gone downstairs beneath deck, where he fell into a deep sleep or trance. Here the boatswain found him and said, "What do you mean by sleeping? Get up! Call on your god! Perhaps he will spare us a thought and not leave us to die" (Jonah 1:6, New Jerusalem).

The sailors decided to cast lots, and the lot pointed to Jonah. He explained that he'd run away from a divine assignment and suggested that if they threw him overboard, the storm would cease. The crew hesitated to murder Jonah, but all their efforts to combat the wind and waves failed. So they prayed to YHWH for forgiveness and threw him overboard. Calm seas returned. They offered YHWH a sacrifice and made vows.

A gigantic fish, specially prepared by God, gobbled the delinquent prophet. And after three days and nights of dyspepsia, the fish found relief by vomiting Jonah onto dry land.

Jonah, the dove, now flitted straight for Nineveh after again receiving the same orders from God. The citizens of Nineveh must have found Jonah an amusing if not downright creepy sight as he walked up and down the city's streets. His oration wasn't wordy: "Only forty days more and Nineveh will be overthrown" (Jonah 3:4, New Jerusalem).

Despite hearing no conditions, the inhabitants of Nineveh, including its king and livestock, put on sackcloth and fasted. "Perhaps God will change his mind and relent and renounce his burning wrath, so that we shall not perish," the king said (verse 9, New Jerusalem).

And the result? The immutable God (some today even claim that He's impassible—incapable of any kind of change or emotion) repented (verse 10, RSV), or changed His mind (NRSV). Nineveh survived until 612 B.C.

It's the same picture of God we've seen again and again. He predicts doom but with the hope that the situation will change.

Flora Versus Fauna

You were upset about this little plant, something for which you have not worked nor did you do anything to make it grow. . . . Should I not be even more concerned about Nineveh. . . ? There are more than one hundred twenty thousand people in it . . . , as well as many animals! Jonah 4:10, 11, NET.

After his great bravado in announcing Nineveh's pending doom, Jonah "sat down east of the city, made a shelter for himself there, and sat down under it . . . to see what would happen" (Jonah 4:5, NET). Would YHWH rain fire upon it? Would an earthquake crumble its sturdy walls? Would a devastating illness decimate the populace? Would a powerful army appear out of nowhere? The Hebrew word Jonah used in his pronouncement was a general term that could denote being overthrown, tumbled down, inundated, drained, etc. But, as Jonah deep down had surmised, nothing happened . . . because the people had repented.

Jonah wasn't happy with God, to put it mildly. He grumbled, "I knew that you are gracious and compassionate, slow to anger and abounding in mercy, and one who relents concerning threatened judgment" (verse 2, NET). You'd think that God's benevolence would be good news. It certainly was good news for the Ninevites! And Jonah, of all people, should have rejoiced that God is "gracious and compassionate, slow to anger and abounding in mercy." That's why he was still alive after his ordeal with a violent ocean gale and a ravenous fish.

Because Jonah's hastily thrown together hovel failed to provide him with the shade needed in the sweltering Mesopotamian weather, "God appointed a little plant and caused it to grow up . . . to be a shade over [Jonah's] head to rescue him from his misery" (verse 6, NET). Jonah felt elated . . . until the next morning when a voracious little worm devoured the fast-growing weed. Then an east wind blew up, but it was so hot (temperatures as high as 123 degrees Fahrenheit have been recorded in the region) that it provided no relief, and Jonah fainted. Despairing of life, he sputtered, "I would rather die than live!" (verse 8, NET).

God's response contrasts Jonah's pity for a here-today-gone-tomorrow weed with His own compassion for human beings and their animals (verse 11). Which has the most inherent moral value? God opted for sentient fauna, whereas Jonah opted for insentient flora. While plant life is essential, it cannot respond to God. Animal life is surely more responsive and thus to be more cherished. Whose priorities were straight—God's or Jonah's?

Blessed Are Those Who Mourn

Because of this I will weep and wail; I will go about barefoot and naked. I will howl like a jackal and moan like an owl.
Micah 1:8, NIV.

Aristotle insisted that because God is perfect, He never changes. All change is illogical for the only perfect Being. Physically God doesn't change; He is immutable. That's why He creates solely by thinking. Mentally and emotionally God doesn't change; He is impassible. That's why He thinks only of Himself, the only Perfect Thought. Today many Christians— Protestant and Catholic alike—regard these theological concepts as orthodox. But . . .

Micah had received bad news from God. "Because of the sins of the house of Israel" (Micah 1:5, NIV), "the Lord is coming from his dwelling place" (verse 3, NIV). Samaria would regress from its status as national headquarters to what it originally had been—a vineyard. "Because of this I will weep and wail; I will go about barefoot and naked. I will howl like a jackal and moan like an owl. For her wound is incurable" (verses 8, 9, NIV).

Precisely who would weep and wail, bay like a wild dog, and groan like a bird? Who would walk around unshod and unclothed? Who is speaking here? The embedded clues are scanty at best, but they seem to point in just one direction.

First, the context helps. In verse 6 it's clear that YHWH is doing the talking. Similarly, in verse 15 God speaks. Although Micah may have interjected his own feelings at verse 8, that's not an inescapable conclusion. It's just as logical to assume that the original voice—the voice of YHWH—continues. But this evidence just barely tilts us toward thinking God is the speaker.

Second, there's perhaps an even stronger clue in verse 9. Here the person talking refers to "my people." That term Scripture typically places on God's lips, not on a prophet's. The Israelites and Judahites were YHWH's people, and He was their God. Again and again He refers to them by His pet term of "my people."

It seems possible, therefore, even probable, that we find here another snapshot of a God who is emotionally torn up—a basket case—because of what He must announce will soon happen to the very people whom He cherished.

From other biblical evidence we've noted, impassibility is hardly a divine virtue. As the living God, He changes; only dead or inanimate objects don't change on their own.

When Good Ideas Turn Sour

When they cry to the Lord, he shall not answer them; rather shall he hide his face from them at that time, because of the evil they have done.
Micah 3:4, NAB.

A little more than a century before Micah, Jehoshaphat, king of the southern kingdom of Judah, adjusted the legal system (see 2 Chron. 19:4-11). The reformation meant a boon for those who had suffered at the hands of their greedy neighbors. The king admonished the newly installed judges—two priests, nine Levites, and five princes—that they weren't making decisions for humans (although they were the complainants) but for YHWH (verse 6). He reminded them: "Act carefully, for with the Lord, our God there is no injustice, no partiality, no bribe-taking. . . . Act faithfully and wholeheartedly in the fear of the Lord" (verses 7-9, NAB).

But as Lord Acton observed: "Power tends to corrupt, and absolute power corrupts absolutely." The decades elapsed, and the edge of the reformed jurisprudence system became blunted . . . again. If indeed people in the same positions—priests, Levites, and princes—continued as arbiters of justice, King Jehoshaphat's good idea had turned sour.

Once again the plight of the disadvantaged evoked a response from YHWH, who castigated the administrators of justice. Micah described these perverters of justice as having turned justice inside out, hating that which is good and loving that which is evil (Micah 3:2).

But the language turned even more graphic when he addressed them as "you who tear their skin from them, and their flesh from their bones!" (verse 2, NAB). The unjust judges were cannibals! "They eat the flesh of my people, and flay their skin from them, and break their bones. They chop them in pieces like flesh in a kettle, and like meat in a caldron" (verse 3, NAB).

We mustn't take Micah's indictment literally. Rather, he was describing in repulsive language the rapacious judges who worsened the condition of the oppressed. And when these purveyors of unjust justice prayed, YHWH would "hide his face from them" (verse 4, NAB). More about this in our next reading.

It's true, of course, that situations change. And prudent leaders acclimatize to shifting circumstances. Altered situations, though, don't necessarily entail the abandonment of the principles behind reformations. It takes constant fervor to maintain the goals of the original alterations that had been so badly needed, lest we lose sight of the intended purpose.

The Flip Side of God's Love

They lean upon the Lord and say, "Surely the Lord is with us! No harm shall come upon us."
Micah 3:11, NRSV.

Many of the candid photos of God in our album have focused on His steadfast love, which includes His determined (maybe even stubborn) faithfulness to the covenant He made with His people. The covenant relationship began with Abraham, Isaac, and Jacob. God renewed it at Mount Sinai. It metamorphosed into a covenant with David and his successors. Throughout, we've stressed God's compassion and His eagerness to forgive. And all this is true and terribly important. That's the kind of deity YHWH is. His very nature is love, and not just some theoretical attribute of love. His love is transitive, concretized in His dealings with His people.

However, there's a flip side to God's love for His specially chosen people, those whom He claims as His personal property. When the people whom He adored were injured, especially by their compatriots, it was like jabbing one's finger into God's eye. It got His attention! He wanted to preserve not only His covenant people but also justice for them. When we love people, we also love their inalienable rights. Injustice is intolerable.

The situation in Jerusalem, which symbolized the entire southern kingdom of Judah, had degenerated. Through Micah God addressed those who were "building Jerusalem on a foundation of murder and corruption" and those "rulers [who] govern for the bribes . . . [and] priests [who] teach God's laws only for a price . . . [and those] prophets [who] won't prophesy unless [they] are paid" (Micah 3:10, 11, NLT). God scolded the corrupt leaders of His people: "You . . . hate good and love evil. You skin my people alive and tear the flesh off their bones. You eat my people's flesh, cut away their skin, and break their bones. You chop them up like meat for the cooking pot" (verses 2, 3, NLT).

Nonetheless, because God's Temple, hence His presence, was situated in Jerusalem, the leaders felt smug. They knew that God is inherently compassionate and avidly forgives, so they kept on brazenly mistreating their fellow Judahites, those whom God called "My people."

It would be a defect in God if He turned a blind eye to those treated unfairly and a deaf ear to their cries for help. The very fact that YHWH is merciful means that He cannot and will not tolerate it when those He loves are abused. Such divine love gets irate and flies into action.

What God Requires

This is what [God] requires: to do what is right, to love mercy, and to walk humbly with your God. Micah 6:8, NLT.

Despite all that God had done throughout the history of His people, especially in view of His gracious act of emancipating them from slavery in Egypt, they had turned their backs on Him. God felt deeply hurt, and His emotions overflowed (you can almost hear Him sobbing) when He asked, "O my people, what have I done to make you turn from me?" (Micah 6:3, NLT).

Apparently God got through to His people—at least on some level—and they decided they must return to Him. But how? Through the Temple, of course. That was a given, because it was in the Temple that God's presence had been manifested. It was in the Temple that His people, through the priestly ministrations, approached Him.

But exactly what sacrificial offerings should they bring when they returned to God? Note the increasing value of the offerings that they suggest. "Should we bow before God with offerings of yearling calves? Should we offer him thousands of rams and tens of thousands of rivers of olive oil? Would that please the Lord? Should we sacrifice our firstborn children to pay for the sins of our souls? Would that make him glad?" (verses 6, 7, NLT).

Year-old animals were specified not only for the daily burnt offerings but also for the guilt offerings, sin offerings, and festival offerings. Thousands of animals sacrificed at a single gathering was not unheard-of, as when Solomon dedicated the Temple. Oil was a constituent of sacrificial offerings. Would "tens of thousands of rivers of olive oil" do the job? As far as scholars can determine, ten thousand was the highest number in the Hebrew vocabulary. Maybe they should offer the ultimate sacrifice—their children—as burnt offerings.

But none of that was what YHWH wanted. He desired just three things: that they (1) do, (2) love, and (3) walk. They should *do* justice, preserve fairness. It wasn't enough, though, merely to *do* justice. God wanted them to *love* mercy or kindness. The Hebrew word here, *chesed*, often referred to the way God treated His people, anticipating the gracious behavior being reflected back from them. Finally, He desired them to *walk* humbly and attentively (the Hebrew is somewhat ambiguous) with Him—without cockiness, perhaps—willing to listen and learn.

Surely God looks for the same behavior on our part today.

What God Scuttles

You will cast all our sins into the depths of the sea.
Micah 7:19, NRSV.

M icah's oracles end with reassuring words after some very scouring accusations, such as: "You are the very ones who hate good and love evil. You
skin my people alive and tear the flesh off their bones" (Micah 3:2, NLT). And
there was a lot more for which God through Micah castigated His people.

Fortunately, God counterbalanced those harsh, condemnatory words
with assurances of restoration that culminated in some of the most encouraging passages in the Old Testament. Micah described God as incomparable
because He is "pardoning iniquity and passing over the transgression of the
remnant. . . . He does not retain his anger forever, because he delights in
showing clemency. He . . . will tread our iniquities under foot." Then, addressing YHWH, Micah says, "You will cast all our sins into the depths of the
sea" (Micah 7:18, 19, NRSV).

Some Christians are such sensitive souls that they languish under feelings
of guilt. Now, make no mistake about it, guilt is appropriate. Some people
have become so hardened in sin that they can engage in all sorts of dastardly
behavior without even a twinge of conscience. We call these people so-
ciopaths. They can torture pets and molest small children and take pleasure
from it. But many of us go to the opposite extreme and torture ourselves by
replaying again and again the videotape of actions that we've confessed.

Those of us in that latter category need to read and reread the biblical
passages that provide assurance that God eagerly forgives. And when we confess our sins, our omniscient God not only forgives them but cannot even remember them. What a paradox! Micah says that God scuttles our sins to the
bottom of the ocean. Now, as far as we know, the deepest part of the ocean
is the Marianas Trench, which is 36,201 feet deep. Is that where God dumps
our confessed (and forgiven) sins?

In one of my Bibles, Micah 7:18, 19 is just across the page from Nahum
1:3, which asserts that YHWH "is slow to anger" (NRSV). Aristotle, who lived
some 300 years after Nahum, taught that God is static—doesn't move.
Nahum, however, offered a different perspective. YHWH wasn't immobile,
He was slow—slow to get angry.

Is this snapshot of God how you picture Him?

Slow, But . . .

The Lord is slow to get angry.
Nahum 1:3, NLT.

Nahum's confidence that God doesn't have a short fuse is embedded in an interesting context. In Nahum 1:2 we read that YHWH is "filled with vengeance and wrath. He takes revenge on all who oppose him and furiously destroys his enemies!" (NLT). And in the last part of verse 3 we read that "he never lets the guilty go unpunished" (NLT). Indeed, "who can stand before his fierce anger? Who can survive his burning fury?" (verse 6, NLT).

What kind of picture does Nahum portray of God? Is this a double exposure? Not really. Maybe Nahum presents us with a hologram that shows two dimensions of God—two sides of YHWH.

God's chosen people had again and again broken covenant with Him, and His protection ceased. Not only were they harassed by their neighbors, but they suffered most under the onslaughts of Assyria and then Babylon. Should they repent, though, God would forget their sins, scuttling them to the bottom of the sea. "The Lord is good. When trouble comes, he is a strong refuge. And he knows everyone who trusts in him" (verse 7, NLT). After 70 years in Babylonian captivity, His contrite people could return to their homeland—actually, God's land, which He'd promised to share with them.

Assyria had ravaged both Israel and Judah. It had effectively destroyed Israel and placed Judah under a heavy burden of taxation. Now, Assyrian armies had a reputation for cruelty. King Assurbanipal II wrote: "I burnt many captives. . . . I cut off of some their arms [and] hands; I cut off of others their noses, ears, [and] extremities. I gouged out the eyes of many troops. I made one pile . . . of heads. I hung their heads on trees. . . . I burnt their adolescent boys [and] girls" (in Albert Kirk Grayson, *The Royal Inscriptions of Mesopotamia*, vol. 2, p. 201).

Nineveh, the last capital city of the Assyrian Empire, sprawled over 1,800 acres. Its citizens felt invincible, but the nation that had terrorized much of the ancient Near East made its final boast in 612 B.C., when the city was sacked, ending Assyrian domination.

To those who hope and trust in Him, YHWH is a gracious, forgiving God who has amnesia when it comes to remembering their sins. But to those who love injustice and perpetrate atrocities of varying kinds, His "rage blazes forth like fire" (verse 6, NLT).

Why Does Prophecy Fail?

*Never again shall scoundrels invade you,
they have totally vanished.
Nahum 2:1, Tanakh.*

H ouston, we have a problem!" This prophecy failed. (If the Tanakh's translation is correct.) Within a few short years Judah fell to Babylon, later was under Persian domination, then suffered under Syrian oppression, and after that chafed under Roman rule. This failure—and other biblical predictions that likewise never happened—shouldn't bother us. Here's why.

Language is a tool that we use in several ways.

Through *informative discourse* we offer factual data, as in encyclopedias, almanacs, and maps. A biblical example is: "Against him came up Nebuchadnezzar king of Babylon" (2 Chron. 36:6). Informative communication must be *accurate*. Through *cognitive discourse* we share ideas, as in philosophy and theology. A biblical example is: "God is love" (1 John 4:8). Cognitive communication must be *rational*. Through *affective discourse* we express our own feelings and elicit emotions in others, as in greeting cards or love letters. A biblical example is: "Let every thing that hath breath praise the Lord" (Ps. 150:6). Affective communication must be *sincere*. Through *performative discourse* we produce or modify volition and behavior. A biblical example is: "Let there be light" (Gen. 1:3). Performative communication must be *effective*. Through *phatic discourse* we express sociability, as when we utter relatively nonsensical things such as "Great weather, huh?" or "Glad to meet you." A biblical example is: "Beloved, I wish above all things that thou mayest prosper and be in health" (3 John 2). Phatic communication must be *friendly*.

If prophecies were informative discourse, then we'd expect them to map out the future with pinpoint accuracy. We'd be justifiably upset if the predictions failed to "come true"—just as people have become upset with the online *Wikipedia* "encyclopedia" because it has contained inaccuracies (some might even call them falsehoods).

However, if prophecies exemplify any of the other four forms of communication, if the predictions fail to come to pass, it wouldn't trouble us a whole lot. Biblical prophecies are instances of performative speech, with overtones of affective speech. Through prophecy God expressed His emotions so as to evoke feelings among His people, thereby eliciting altered behavior on their part. If changed behavior didn't follow, then the prediction(s) became capable of failure.

Habakkuk Rebukes God

How long, O Lord, must I call for help? . . .
Why do you tolerate wrong?
Hab. 1:2, 3, NIV.

Why does evil (moral, physical, mental, and natural) exist? Why do the innocent suffer if God wants fairness? If God is omnipotent, He must have the power to avert evil; if He is inherently morally good, then He must want to forestall evil. We find ourselves on the horns of a dilemma: Since evil exists, God is either (1) not omnipotent or (2) not inherently morally good.

Habakkuk wanted a theodicy, a defense of God's existence and behavior (or lack thereof) in the face of evil. Various explanations have been proffered, among them: (1) God doesn't exist; (2) evil doesn't exist; (3) what appears to us to be bad is really good incognito; (4) there are no innocent sufferers; (5) God isn't all-good but has a shadowy dark side; (6) God isn't all-powerful; (7) God doesn't want evil but has limited Himself by granting us free will; (8) God wills the existence of evilness as well as of goodness; (9) the cosmos is the best possible universe and operates under natural law, which God cannot violate without destroying order, and so God behaves like an absentee landlord; (10) personal spiritual maturation requires the presence of evil as something to be resisted; (11) a cosmic conflict rages in which God's goodness and omnipotence ultimately receive vindication; and (12) two powerful persons manipulate the cosmos—one benevolent, the other malevolent.

Each argument crumbles under scrutiny. Atheism is unacceptable. Experience shows that evil isn't an illusion. That evilness is really goodness plays havoc with meaning. That all victims deserve their suffering is mean-spirited. The supposed existence of God's dark side flies in the face of abundant scriptural assertions. If God isn't all-powerful, is He God? God's allowing free will is self-defeating. Predestination of all evil as well as all good contradicts our experience of free will. The idea that the best possible universe must operate under inviolable natural law eliminates the possibility of miracles. That God made us imperfect but perfectible contradicts the biblical doctrine of a perfect creation. The great controversy theme assumes that the end (the vindication of God) justifies the means (the existence of disaster, disease, and death); besides, how much evil does it take to prove His goodness? Monotheism must not be compromised.

Habakkuk reminded God, "Your eyes are too pure to look on evil. . . . Why then . . . ?" (verse 13, NIV). Good question.

Wait and See

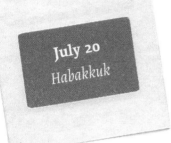

I will stand on my watch . . . and wait to see what He will say to me, what He will reply to my complaint. Hab. 2:1, Tanakh.

When Habakkuk saw all the evilness around him, he wanted a clarification. So he complained . . . to YHWH . . . and demanded an explanation.

Most of us have probably felt the same way at one time or another. We're diagnosed with incurable cancer. A little granddaughter is molested by a trusted adult in her life. A brother contracts Lou Gehrig's disease. A sister, mother to three precious children, is killed when a drunken driver crashes into her minivan. A house is blown to smithereens by a tornado. A son steps on a land mine in a military hot spot. A cousin is felled by a stray bullet in the inner city. A 23-year-old neighbor is raped, tortured, and murdered.

All too often God remains silent, despite our frenetic efforts to understand why such bad things happen to such good people. And with Habakkuk we cry, "How long, O Lord, shall I cry out and You not listen. . . . Why do you make me see iniquity . . . ? . . . Violence [is] before me" (Hab. 1:2, 3, Tanakh). Habakkuk, in voicing his complaint, sat in stunned silence as he waited for God to give an account of Himself. And, surprisingly, YHWH replied, although His response lacks the clarity that we crave.

First, God retorted, "Observe well and be utterly astounded; for a work is being wrought in your days which you would not believe if it were told. . . . I am raising up the Chaldeans . . . to seize homes not their own" (verses 5-7, Tanakh). *That* kind of theodicy only exacerbated the situation. Better for God to have remained silent. Two wrongs hardly make a right.

Next, after describing the Chaldeans' invasion of the Promised Land, God explained that turnabout is indeed fair play. He predicted that "all surviving peoples shall plunder you [the Chaldeans]—for crimes against men and wrongs against lands" (Hab. 2:8, Tanakh).

Habakkuk then looked at the flip side of this coin, understanding that God in this backhanded way was predicting ultimate restitution for His people. He rejoiced that "You have come forth to deliver Your people" (Hab. 3:13, Tanakh).

Good will one day triumph over evil, but we must leave the details to God. For now, in our suffering, God hurts—and weeps—with us. Maybe that's the only theodicy we need.

Judge of All the Earth

I shall sweep away everything off the face of the earth, declares Yahweh. I shall sweep away humans and animals, the birds of the air and the fish of the sea. Zeph. 1:2, 3, New Jerusalem.

God's creation of Planet Earth culminated with His creation of a people— the Hebrew people. "Yahweh . . . created you, Jacob . . . formed you, Israel. . . . You are mine. . . . Everyone who bears my name, whom I have created for my glory, whom I have formed, whom I have made" (Isa. 43:1-7, New Jerusalem). His selection of Abraham and his descendants through Isaac rather than anyone else was quite arbitrary. "Yahweh set his heart on you and chose you not because you were the most numerous of all peoples—for indeed you were the smallest of all—but because he loved" (Deut. 7:7, 8, New Jerusalem).

That the Israelites and Judahites constituted God's specially chosen people ("My people") doesn't mean that He ignored all other nations and ethnic groups. God involved Himself with their existence also. "When the Most High gave the nations each their heritage, when he partitioned out the human race, he assigned the boundaries of nations" (Deut. 32:8, New Jerusalem). "From one . . . he not only created the whole human race so that they could occupy the entire earth, but he decreed the times and limits of their habitation" (Acts 17:26, New Jerusalem).

Because YHWH, by virtue of being Creator, exercises Lordship over all the cosmos, His prophets addressed not only the Hebrew people but also other nations. Scholars count between 40 or 50 oracles addressed to nations other than Israel and Judah. These prophecies to alien peoples can be found in Isaiah, Jeremiah, Ezekiel, Amos, Joel, Jonah . . . and Zephaniah.

Through Zephaniah God specifically took note of the cities of Gaza, Ashkelon, Ashdod, Ekron, and the nations made up of the Assyrians, Moabites, Ammonites, Cherethites, Canaanites, and Cushites. Undoubtedly God took umbrage with them for various reasons, among them their harsh attitude shown toward His chosen people—their insults and jeers (Zeph. 2:8). Whatever His rationale, God threatened, "I shall subdue. . . . I shall destroy . . . till there are no inhabitants left" (verse 5, New Jerusalem). Indeed, with typical Near Eastern hyperbole, He said, "I shall sweep away everything off the face of the earth" (Zeph. 1:2, New Jerusalem).

It's a temptation for us to assume that God is interested only in us. Not the case! His "eyes watch over the world" (Ps. 11:4, New Jerusalem).

Power Tends to Corrupt

July 22

Zephaniah

Her prophets have the audacity to lie; they are deceitful men. Her priests defile what is holy; they break God's laws.
Zeph. 3:4, NET.

L ord Acton (1834-1902) was a well-respected English historian. Although most of us know nothing about him, we're aware of his observation that "power tends to corrupt; absolute power corrupts absolutely."

Typically, the more power people have, the less attention they pay to the fine points of fairness and personal responsibility. Zephaniah mentions particularly the Hebrew officials, judges, prophets, and priests—the ruling class at that time other than the king himself, Josiah, who was regarded as a righteous monarch.

The officials (princes or captains), Zephaniah says, were "roaring lions" (Zeph. 3:3, NET). Whoever these leaders were, they roared like lions about to pounce on their prey.

The judges were "as hungry as wolves in the desert, who completely devour their prey by morning" (verse 3, NET). When these wolves had finished gnawing, they left nothing but bones. The concept of judging in the Old Testament includes the idea of helping—helping the oppressed by defending them with fair verdicts.

The prophets were "deceitful men" (verse 4, NET). Zephaniah wasn't referring to the prophets of Baal. He spoke here of prophets who claimed to pronounce messages from YHWH. It required audacity to claim to speak for God when one was really speaking for oneself.

And the priests "[defiled] what [was] holy; they [broke] God's laws" (verse 4, NET). The priests treated profanely that which was holy. Their explanations of God's instructions actually flew in the face of the divine will.

Unfortunately, the same thing happens today. Good people can become perverted when they hold too much power. Administrators can become autocratic. Stewardship and Trust Services directors can amass material goods—fancy houses, luxury automobiles, boats, etc.—while they encourage widows to go without and donate more than they can afford to the church. Preachers can become arrogant, becoming engorged on the compliments from parishioners.

It doesn't have to be this way, but human nature being what it is, such happens.

"Surely They Will Listen"

I thought, "Surely they will have reverence
for me now! Surely they will listen to my
warnings, so I won't need to strike again."
Zeph. 3:7, NLT.

Once again we find ourselves confronted with one of the more than 100 biblical passages that affirm or imply that God does not have exhaustive knowledge of the future. Many Christians find these passages from both Testaments disquieting. They argue that God knows perfectly every event (good or bad, infinitesimal or momentous) that will ever take place.

Their reasoning runs: God knows the future in absolute detail either (1) because He decreed or predestined it to happen or (2) because He exists outside of time and so has all-inclusive knowledge of past, present, and future. Such theologians buttress their philosophy by a smattering of scriptural passages from which they deduce that God's attributes include omniscience, omnipotence, eternity, infinity, transcendence, immutability, and impassibility. Most of these concepts originated with the Greek philosophers and got baptized when given Latin names.

Here in Zephaniah YHWH asserts that in His dealings with His chosen people, "I thought, 'Surely they will have reverence for me now! Surely they will listen to my warnings, so I won't need to strike again.'" He'd hoped that through relatively minor disciplinary measures His people would learn obedience. When that didn't happen, He expressed His surprise: "However much I punish them, they continue their evil practices from dawn till dusk and dusk till dawn" (Zeph. 3:7, NLT). His people's obstinacy in evil startled Him.

Zephaniah 3:7 indicates that God "is open to new experiences, has a capacity for novelty and is open to reality, which itself is open to change" (Clark H. Pinnock, *The Most Moved Mover*, p. 41). "God is open to the changing realities of history . . . God cares about us and lets what we do impact him. Our lives make a difference to God" (Clark H. Pinnock, *The Openness of God*, p. 104). Contrary to its critics, "openness of God" theology is not the same as "process theology."

These 100+ scriptural references provide us with a significantly meaningful snapshot of a God who has given us free will. Regardless of the choices we make, He is always seeking to show His love and to redeem us.

A Homeless God

Is it a time for you yourselves to be living in your paneled houses, while this house remains a ruin? Haggai 1:4, NIV.

Cyrus conquered Babylon in 539 B.C. Shortly thereafter he issued an edict giving the exiled Jews the freedom to return to Jerusalem and rebuild what Nebuchadnezzar had destroyed. A group of hopefuls under the leadership of Sheshbazzar headed for the homeland.

The repatriation attempt of 538 B.C. didn't succeed very well. King Cyrus died nine years after defeating Babylon and was succeeded by Cambyses, who himself suddenly died the same amount of time into his reign. After a seven-month interim in which Gaumata sat on his usurped throne, Darius became king. Early in his reign Darius authorized Zerubbabel to serve as governor of Yehud (Judah).

Zerubbabel, the governor whom God called "my signet ring" (Haggai 3:23, NIV), and Joshua, the high priest, tried to motivate the newly returned Jews in Jerusalem to reconstruct the Temple, but the people invested their endeavors in constructing their own houses, in which they lounged and thus left YHWH homeless!

Despite their lolling around in leisure, things didn't go all that well for them. The grain crops were only 50 percent of what they should have been, and the grape crop was 60 percent below normal.

Enter Haggai the prophet, through whom God said: "You have planted much, but have harvested little. You eat, but never have enough. You drink, but never have your fill. You put on clothes, but are not warm. You earn wages, only to put them in a purse with holes in it. . . . Build the [Temple], so that I may take pleasure in it and be honored" (Haggai 1:6-8, NIV).

"Then Zerubbabel . . . Joshua . . . and the whole remnant of the people obeyed the voice of the Lord their God" (verse 12, NIV). And within just 24 days "they . . . began to work on the house of the Lord Almighty, their God" (verse 14, NIV).

The repatriated Jews basked in their new or newly rebuilt houses while the Temple remained a heap of debris. They thought more of themselves than they did of God. They watched out for number one! They focused their energies on themselves and not on God. Are *you* that way? Am I? Do we devote more time and money and energy to ourselves than to our God?

Which Is More Contagious?

*If one of you is carrying a holy sacrifice in his robes
and happens to brush against some bread or stew . . . ,
will it also become holy? The priests replied, "No."
Haggai 2:12, NLT.*

God told Haggai to ask the priests for a pronouncement regarding two theoretical situations dealing with holiness and uncleanness. Although hypothetical, both situations were possible, even probable.

Hypothetical situation 1—After the priest had ministered the blood of a sin offering and burned its fat on the altar, he ate the meat of the sacrificial animal, which was considered holy. With this understanding as background, Haggai wanted to know what would happen if the priest wrapped part of his robe around the meat but then by chance brushed up against some other food items with his robe. Would the holiness of the meat transfer to the other food?

The priestly pronouncement: No.

Hypothetical situation 2—Human corpses were deemed unclean, and those who came in contact with a dead body inside a house or outside in an open field became unclean for seven days. On the third and on the seventh day of defilement, those so defiled had to go through a special purification ritual. Haggai wanted to know what would happen if a person who was thus defiled touched some food items. Would their uncleanness transfer to the food?

The priestly pronouncement: Yes. (Actually, they repeated the word "unclean," because although Hebrew had a word for no, it didn't have a word for yes.)

Uncleanness was more transmittable than was holiness. "Then Haggai said, 'That is how it is with this people and this nation'" (Haggai 2:14, NLT). Because of their self-centeredness, they had neglected YHWH, and as a result, "'everything they do and everything they offer is defiled'" (verse 14, NLT). That's why they lacked the blessing of fruitfulness. Their bad attitude tainted everything. They'd neglected God, so He would neglect them.

Since nowadays we don't concern ourselves with matters of ritual holiness and uncleanness, perhaps Haggai would ask, "Can one good apple restore a bushel of rotten apples? Can one rotten apple spoil a bushel of good apples?"

What do you think? Can disobedience—even in just one area of life—contaminate everything else we do? Experience shows that goodness is far less "contagious" than badness.

God's People—Again

I shall bring them back to live in the heart
of Jerusalem, and they will be my people
and I shall be their God, faithful and just.
Zech. 8:8, New Jerusalem.

The Babylonian exile came as a tremendous blow to God's people. Oh, attacks by Mesopotamian armies were hardly unique. It was the enormity of the event—two raids by Nebuchadnezzar, the collapse of Jerusalem's fortifications, people carried off as prisoners of war, the king having to watch his own children slaughtered, the king himself marched off in chains to Babylon. But even worse, the razing of YHWH's glorious Temple, which Solomon had constructed.

The 70 years of exile predicted by Jeremiah had pretty much elapsed. Nebuchadnezzar and his successors lay in their graves. A new regime under the Medes and Persians had been ushered in. Already Persian edicts had provided the Jews opportunity to return to the homeland, a place that many of them had only heard about. Indeed, 16 years had passed since the first wave of repatriated Jews had made the long trek back to Jerusalem. Now God had called Zechariah, a priest, to the prophetic office as a colleague of Haggai. Their mission: to encourage Zerubbabel's and Joshua's efforts to reconstruct the Temple.

In the ancient Near East one of the major responsibilities of the gods was to maintain justice. Similarly, YHWH upheld justice (unlike other gods, He Himself was just and/or righteous) and expected His chosen people to follow suit. The Babylonian captivity had taken place because the people had forsaken YHWH, breaking covenant with Him. YHWH had told them to "apply the law fairly, and show faithful love and compassion towards one another. Do not oppress the widow and the orphan, the foreigner and the poor, and do not secretly plan evil against one another" (Zech. 7:9, 10, New Jerusalem). However, they'd ignored YHWH's admonition.

Now God was appealing to His people to "return to me . . . and I will return to you" (Zech. 1:3, New Jerusalem). He said that He'd been angry with them, but for only a short time (verse 15). God envisioned a rosy future for His people. He spoke with "kind and comforting words" (verse 13, New Jerusalem). However, they must "administer fair judgement conducive to peace" (Zech. 8:16, New Jerusalem). God said, "Do not secretly plot evil against one another; do not love perjury" (verse 17, New Jerusalem).

It may be true that life isn't fair, but God's people must embody fairness.

Who Causes Storms?

It is the Lord who makes storm clouds.
And sends men the pouring rain.
Zech. 10:1, NAB.

Ancient Near Eastern peoples knew storm gods, such as Enlil, Ishtar, Hadad, Teshub, Tarhun, and Baal, who was known as the "Rider of the Clouds." Did you know that our word "hurricane" comes from the Taino/Carib storm god Hurakán?

Sometimes Scripture tells us that God sends the early and latter rains, which were essential to fertility. Without them, crops failed. Indeed, people were a drought away from starvation. On average, there was one drought per decade, and the typical dry spell lasted three years. When we think of nice weather, we mean sunny skies. In Canaan when they thought about good weather, they envisioned rain! Little wonder, then, that YHWH was seen as sending the rain showers.

However, Scripture also contains passages that posit YHWH as responsible for frightful tempests. Not gentle showers these. "Fire and hail . . . storm winds . . . fulfill his word" (Ps. 148:8, NAB). YHWH visits "with thunder . . . whirlwind, storm" (Isa. 29:6, NAB). "His arm descends in . . . driving storm and hail" (Isa. 30:30, NAB). "He makes the lightning flash in the rain, and releases stormwinds from their chambers" (Jer. 10:13, NAB). God says, "I will bring down a flooding rain; hailstones shall fall, and a stormwind shall break out" (Eze. 13:11, NAB). "In hurricane and tempest is his path" (Nahum 1:3, NAB).

What about killer hail? On June 22, 2003, seven-inch-diameter hail fell in Aurora, Nebraska, the largest hailstones on record. In late August of 2005, Hurricane Katrina killed more than 1,800 people and left behind $81.2 billion of damage. During the first half of 2007, the world experienced unique weather extremes: appalling floods in Asia; drenching downpours in northern Europe, Sudan, Mozambique, and Uruguay; scorching heat waves in southeastern Europe and Russia; and snowstorms in South Africa and South America. Texas nearly drowned under unprecedented amounts of rain.

Were these phenomena God's handiwork? If the nightly news meteorologists were responsible for the bad weather they predicted, we'd not only fire them but also prosecute them for crimes against humanity. John Greenleaf Whittier wrote: "Nothing can be good in Him which evil is in me." Perhaps we should be more careful about what we attribute to God.

The Embarrassed Prophets

July 28
Zechariah

*And if anyone asks them, "What are these wounds
on your chest?" the answer will be "The wounds
I received in the house of my friends."
Zech. 13:6, NRSV.*

The Hebrew people had their share of prophets—good and bad. We're all familiar with the hundreds of prophets of Baal whom Queen Jezebel imported. Clearly they were false prophets. But not all false prophets were aligned with pagan deities. Among God's people arose prophets who claimed to speak for YHWH but were impostors. And it wasn't always easy to decide which prophets spoke in God's behalf and which didn't. Jeremiah seems to have been a bit bewildered when confronted by Hananiah, who turned out to be a counterfeit prophet.

YHWH didn't value such pretenders. "I am against those who prophesy lying dreams . . . , and who lead my people astray by their lies and their recklessness, when I did not send them or appoint them" (Jer. 23:32, NRSV). "I did not send them, nor did I command them or speak to them. They are prophesying . . . a lying vision . . . and the deceit of their own minds" (Jer. 14:14, NRSV). The bogus prophets were especially pernicious because they had "not exposed your iniquity," and that's why their oracles were "false and misleading (Lam. 2:14, NRSV)." Genuine prophecies had an important goal—"to restore [the] fortunes" of God's people (verse 14, NRSV).

According to Zechariah, in the heyday to come "a fountain shall be opened for the house of David and the inhabitants of Jerusalem, to cleanse them from sin and impurity" (Zech. 13:1, NRSV). Furthermore, God promised, "I will remove from the land the prophets and the unclean spirit" (verse 2, NRSV).

As a result, the false prophets would be persona non grata. Their own parents would disown them . . . and worse. "Their fathers and their mothers who bore them shall pierce them through when they prophesy" (verse 3, NRSV).

Even the prophets, bearing their obvious scars, would feel so ashamed that they'd deny their careers. They'd shed their hairy mantles (verse 4, NRSV), which they wore in imitation of Elijah. And when people pointed to their scars, clear indications of their claiming to be prophets, they'd claim that they were really farmers (verse 5) and that they'd gotten the scars in the house of their friends (verse 6).

One lie inevitably leads to another, which saddens God, because He is a God of truth.

Lame Offerings

When you offer the lame and sick, is it not evil?
Mal 1:8, NKJV.

D uring the time of Jesus, the priests rigorously examined the animals brought as sacrifices. They wanted to be sure that the animal offerings were as perfect as possible. For instance, the rabbis said that if the sacrifice was a red heifer, the priests would look for a single white hair among the red hairs, which would exclude the animal for the altar.

That's one of the reasons sheep were sold in the Temple court. These animals were especially bred to be without blemish. The priests wouldn't have to scrutinize these sacrifices, because they were certified as perfect. (Another reason for selling sacrificial animals was that Jewish pilgrims wouldn't have been able to bring animals along with them. So it was convenient for them when prequalified animals were readily available—despite the premium cost.)

But it wasn't always such. After the Jews had rebuilt the Temple, some began to bring to the altar blind, lame, or otherwise sick animals. This livestock wasn't very valuable and wouldn't bring a decent profit in the marketplace, so why not sacrifice them at the Temple and receive a double blessing—eliminating worthless animals and worshiping God at the same time?

God wasn't pleased. "Offer it then to your governor! Would he be pleased with you? Would he accept you favorably?" (Mal. 1:8, NKJV). If Zerubbabel wouldn't regard such gifts as pleasing, why would God? Indeed, isn't God far superior to an earthly ruler? If so, then shouldn't the gifts brought to Him exceed in quality the gifts given to someone such as Zerubbabel?

We wouldn't think of cheating God that way today, would we? Or might we? Remember the Sabbath school projects called Investment? It was another way to raise funds for missions without putting an additional burden on one's budget. It was a great idea: Invest a certain amount of money into a project and at the end give the net profit to God.

Some people thought that "dedicating" an unfruitful peach tree, for example, to the Investment offering was clever. And we used to hear stories of how suddenly that tree bore more peaches than expected. The profit from selling these "miracle" peaches went to Investment for foreign missions.

Wasn't that, though, just another example of giving lame (inferior) offerings to God? Why should we assume that such a practice pleases Him?

God's Opinion on Divorce

I hate divorce, says the Lord.
Mal. 2:16, NRSV.

In today's passage, God through Malachi addressed the priests. We don't know much about the circumstances that elicited these comments from God. It appears, though, that at least some of the priests—how many, we don't know—had divorced their wives. And it got God's attention. "The Lord was a witness between you and the wife of your youth, to whom you have been faithless, though she is your companion and your wife by covenant. Did not one God make her?" (Mal. 2:14, 15, NRSV).

YHWH also gave a reason He detested divorce. "What does the one God desire? Godly offspring" (verse 15, NRSV). In the Old Testament, children were viewed as a divine gift. The Israelites gained a kind of immortality through their offspring, who perpetuated the father's name. Also, once the young people got old enough, they helped shoulder the burdens of keeping the family safe and fed and clothed—an important job in a subsistence society. "So," God cautioned, "look to yourselves, and do not let anyone be faithless to the wife of his youth" (verse 15, NRSV).

Scholars puzzle over exactly who the "wife of his youth" was that the priests had divorced. On the one hand, she might be a Jewess. Marriage among kinfolk was regarded not only as normal but as preferable. On the other hand, she might have been a non-Israelite. After all, Hebrew women may well have been in scarce supply in Babylon or later in Palestine after the return from exile. We know from Ezra 10 and Nehemiah 13:23-30 that a number of Jewish leaders had taken foreign wives, and they were ordered to get rid of them.

How could the Israelite men, including some priests, be told that God wanted them to divorce their heathen wives when in Malachi 2:16 God puts Himself on record as hating divorce? Well, the fact is that although God said He hated divorce, nowhere in the Old Testament did He proscribe it. In fact, in Deuteronomy 24:1-3 God through Moses legislated a "certificate of divorce." God was realistic enough to know that despite His loathing for divorce, sometimes it just might be an option. Because in marriage the husband and wife become "one flesh" (Gen. 2:24), perhaps divorce can be compared to major surgery. Having any organ excised is sometimes the lesser of two evils. It seems that divorce is a fruit of faithlessness.

God Doesn't Change?

I the Lord do not change.
Mal. 3:6, RSV.

Several of our devotional readings have dealt with biblical passages that indicated that YHWH had repented. These readings explained that God interacts with His creatures who have free will, adapting Himself to their varying behaviors. The position advocated in this book is sometimes known as "presentism," or more popularly, "openness of God theology."

But Malachi 3:6 seems to support the opposite concept—that God is immutable and impassible. (Both of those attributes means that He doesn't change because He cannot change.)

Aristotle, one of the most brilliant of Greek philosophers, reasoned that God must be perfect. Perfection entailed changelessness because to change for the worse meant losing perfection and to change for the better implied not having perfection originally. God was the only perfect being, which necessitated being static. (Note that the word "being" is extremely significant in Aristotle's argument. It was the opposite of the word "becoming." God never was becoming but always was being—motionless.) Aristotle concluded his tight-knit logic that it would be irrational for a perfect God to think upon anything that wasn't perfect. Therefore, God's thought focused only on Himself, because He was the only perfect being.

This line of thinking ultimately found its way into Christian theology because of the backgrounds of certain influential Church Fathers. Now, just because an idea has its roots firmly planted in pagan Greek philosophy doesn't necessarily make it erroneous. Nevertheless, the origin of the "orthodox" Christian doctrines of divine immutability and impassibility should give us pause.

One of the proof texts used by those who disagree with presentism is our verse for today, which affirms that God doesn't change. But does Malachi 3:6 demolish openness of God theology? Not necessarily. God Himself explains His changelessness. Because He didn't change, "therefore you, O sons of Jacob, are not consumed" (RSV). God is referring to His covenant love, His faithfulness. His chosen people may have broken covenant, but not God. He might have chastised His unfaithful people—even in anger—but He didn't break covenant with them. And proof of that was their continuing existence.

The point in Malachi 3:6 is God's merciful faithfulness or steadfastness.

Jesus-Messiah

*An account of the genealogy of Jesus
the Messiah, the son of David.
Matt. 1:1, NRSV.*

M essiah. What comes to mind when you hear that word? Handel's famous oratorio, with its spine-tingling "Hallelujah Chorus"? Jesus
Himself, the centerpiece of Handel's *Messiah*? Most of us realize that the word
"Christ" is simply the Greek equivalent of the Hebrew word "messiah." Both
terms mean "anointed one."

The concept has old and deep roots. In the first five books of the Bible,
namely, Leviticus, the Hebrew word *mâshîach* first appears as a description of
the high priest (Lev. 4:3). Literally, the term designated someone who had
been set apart for special service by having olive oil poured on him. Less literally, it referred to someone who had been commissioned. And whether
the term was used literally or metaphorically, the act of setting apart or commissioning was done by God or at His request.

The Old Testament refers to various messiahs, in addition to the high
priest. Abraham, Isaac, and Jacob were said to have been anointed (Ps. 105:15;
cf. 1 Chron. 16:22). The term also applied to the Hebrew kings, such as King
Saul and King David (1 Sam. 24:6; Ps. 18:50). What is especially surprising is
that God called the heathen king Cyrus His anointed or messiah (Isa. 45:1).

Between the close of the Old Testament and the beginning of the New
Testament the term continued to be used by the Jewish people. And the
people who wrote the scrolls found at Qumram (the Dead Sea scrolls) talked
about a coming messiah. Actually, they referred to two messiahs—one a
king, and the other a priest.

With the ministry of Jesus, the term quickly was applied to Him because
He Himself had quoted Isaiah 61:1 as a description of His own mission. "The
Spirit of the Lord is upon me, because he has anointed me to bring good
news to the poor" (Luke 4:18, NRSV).

It shouldn't disturb our faith in Jesus that in these uses the term did not
imply that the anointed person was divine. It said nothing about Jesus' inner
nature but referred to His status of having been sent by God, specially commissioned by Him. There are other ways of upholding the divinity of Jesus
Christ. That He was *the* Messiah expresses the belief that God stood behind
Jesus, specially commissioning Him for His lifework.

Detour to Nazareth

*When he heard that Archelaus was reigning
over Judea instead of his father Herod,
he was afraid to go there.*
Matt. 2:22, NKJV.

We all know the story of Jesus' birth in Bethlehem, His dedication in Jerusalem, the visit of the Magi, and the family's flight to Egypt. We don't know Jesus' age when Joseph returned to Palestine, but we can come up with a rough estimate. Herod died in 4 B.C., and not until after that would they have returned to their homeland. If Jesus was between His first and second birthdays when they fled to Egypt, He would have probably been about 3 years old when they left the relative safety of Egypt, assuming that He'd been born around 6 B.C.

Joseph may have received the news of Herod's death before others in Egypt because "when Herod was dead . . . an angel of the Lord appeared in a dream to Joseph in Egypt" (Matt. 2:19, NKJV). The angel said, "Arise, take the young Child and His mother, and go to the land of Israel, for those who sought the young Child's life are dead" (verse 20, NKJV).

Joseph, ever a man of action, left Egypt as promptly as he'd fled there. "He arose, took the young Child and His mother, and came into the land of Israel" (verse 21, NKJV). Once the little family got back to their homeland, they learned disconcerting news—Archelaus ruled. Although he originally promised to rule with more kindness than did his father, Archelaus ended up outdoing Herod the Great's brutality. (Finally, in A.D. 6, Emperor Augustus banished him to Gaul.)

Matthew tells us that Joseph "was afraid to go [to Judea]" (verse 22, NKJV). In his quandary, Joseph was relieved when again he was "warned by God in a dream" (verse 22, NKJV). Joseph then "turned aside into the region of Galilee" (verse 22, NKJV).

Joseph relied on divine guidance and on human common sense. His own good sense made him uneasy, and another dream validated his anxiety. Further, Matthew seems to assume it was Joseph's decision to relocate in Nazareth of Galilee.

Direct divine guidance is no substitute for common sense. God expects us to use both. We're blessed with Scripture and Ellen White's writings, but they should complement, not replace, our kingly power of reason in our decision-making processes.

Tempted and Tried

Jesus was led out into the wilderness by the Holy Spirit to be tempted there by the Devil.
Matt. 4:1, NLT

After His baptism, Jesus roamed the desert, with the voice from heaven still ringing in His ears: "This is my beloved Son, and I am fully pleased with him" (Matt. 3:17, NLT). But temptation dogged His steps. The devil worded each temptation with what is known as the "simple condition." Simple condition statements highlight the truth or reality of the assumption, and rather than use the word "if," it's clearer to use the word "since." So it would be helpful to translate Satan's introductions to the temptations as "Since You are the Son of God . . ."

First temptation—Since "you are the Son of God, change these stones into loaves of bread" (Matt. 4:3, NLT). Surely there's nothing wrong with eating, especially to break a 40-day period of fasting. In His weakened condition Jesus needed nourishment. Were He not to take nourishment soon, He'd die, and His mission would be over before He could heal the sick, cast out demons, raise the dead, and proclaim the good news that the kingdom of heaven had arrived.

Second temptation—Since "you are the Son of God, jump off!" (verse 6, NLT). The devil had transported Jesus to Jerusalem and "to the highest point of the Temple" (verse 5, NLT). A rabbinic tradition held that when the Messiah came, He'd jump from a Temple pinnacle and survive without harm. Why not demonstrate His Messiahship? Most any PR rep would love such a publicity stunt. Instantaneous fame; instantaneous recognition; instantaneous acceptance.

Third temptation—"'I will give it all to you,' he said, 'if you will only kneel down and worship me'" (verse 9, NLT). From a high mountain the devil showed Jesus "the nations of the world and all their glory" (verse 8, NLT). What a shortcut! Jesus could be Lord of the nations—the anticipated Davidic Messiah—if He'd simply do homage to Satan. No agony in Gethsemane, no scourging to within an inch of His life, no excruciating crucifixion.

Why not? Because (1) the "benefits" came from the wrong source; (2) Jesus didn't come to meet His own physical needs; (3) He wasn't born to be a show-off; and (4) the end doesn't justify the means.

The latter is perhaps our biggest temptation, but we need not cave in to expediency.

For Jesus' Sake

Blessed are you when people abuse you and persecute you and speak all kinds of calumny against you.
Matt. 5:11, New Jerusalem.

Suffering is nearly always a great mystery. Nonsmokers get cancer of the lung or tongue. Infants are born with cerebral palsy, Tay-Sachs syndrome, Niemann-Pick disease, and other dreadful disorders. Mothers, whose children need their love, die in horrifying accidents. A tornado bypasses non-Adventist neighbors but turns an Adventist's house into toothpicks. These and billions of other cases boggle the mind, causing us to ask, "Why?"

Sometimes we're tempted to soothe such sufferers' troubled emotions with the observation that God calls His children to suffer and that they are "blessed" when that happens. But those are not the sort of afflictions to which Scripture writers refer when they speak of the privilege of suffering and the great reward that such suffering will bring.

These afflictions are of a different class, and the cause is not baffling. Before the Western Roman Empire collapsed, there were 10 forays of persecution of early Christians, beginning with Nero and ending with Diocletian. When Emperor Constantine converted to Christianity, persecution of Christians for their beliefs ended. Later, though, during the Inquisitions, thousands were killed for being "heretics." (Some estimates run as high as 50 million, but these statistics are currently regarded as exaggerations.) In some areas of Europe, Protestants later persecuted Roman Catholics.

In more recent times, various groups of Christians have been persecuted under Communist regimes, such as the People's Republic of China, the U.S.S.R., and several Eastern European countries. Estimates indicate that some 1.5 million Christians have been killed by the Janjaweed Muslim militia that emerged in Africa's Sudan and Chad in 1988.

Jesus' statement contains two terms that qualify the type of persecution: "falsely" and "on my account." The afflictions the biblical writers addressed arose from false charges. (Early Christians, for example, were accused of being cannibals and/or atheists.) The suffering discussed in the New Testament wasn't the product of drunk drivers, bacterial or viral infections, or genetic defects. It was the direct result of being a faithful Christian.

These are the people who are blessed and who will have great reward.

This Little Light of Mine

*Let your light shine before men in such a
way that they may see your good works,
and glorify your Father who is in heaven.*
Matt. 5:16, NASB.

Thanks to Thomas Edison, we enjoy well-lit homes. We not only have many lights inside our houses—usually several lamps or bulbs in a room—but also utilize floodlights to illuminate our front and back yards. In recent years we've been encouraged to purchase fluorescent bulbs that provide illumination equal to traditional incandescent light bulbs but use a fraction of the electricity, thereby saving us money and helping to "green" America as good stewards. And our neighborhoods have streetlights, which provide additional illumination.

Being accustomed as we are to well-lighted living areas, we often find it difficult to understand what life in Bible times was like. Once the sun set, towns were plunged into intense darkness, darkness that was almost palpable. If you've ever been in a cave when the lights were turned off, you know how intense darkness can get. Ancient Near Easterners regarded the darkness not as the absence of light but as a "thing," just as they considered light to be a "thing."

To illuminate the interior of their houses (many were small one-room quarters), people in Bible times lit clay lamps. These relatively flat containers were small enough to fit in the palm of the hand. They contained olive oil, and a small wick made from flax or a tiny piece of rag fed the weak flame produced by these utensils. The light produced, when the lamp was set on a stand or a shelf, was barely sufficient to enable the family to move around the small inner space without bumping into one another. In fact, these lamps produced less illumination than do wax candles. Because of their meager capacity, lamps in New Testament times would burn for only four or five hours. In order to keep the room from filling with too much smoke and fumes, householders put the extinguished lamps under a "bushel."

Small and dim though they were, these lamps were a boon to their owners. The light they produced may have been only a few lumens, but nonetheless they made darkness tolerable.

In verse 14 Jesus said that His followers were lights in this world wrapped in the darkness of sin. Their presence made living here tolerable. Despite their saving presence, the deeds they performed were to bring honor not to themselves but to their God, who created His people for His glory (Isa. 43:7). Does your light reflect your God?

Eye for an Eye

The law of Moses says, "If an eye is injured, injure the eye of the person who did it. If a tooth gets knocked out, knock out the tooth of the person who did it."
Matt. 5:38, NLT.

Jesus cited here one of the Mosaic laws (Ex. 21:24; Lev. 24:20; Deut. 19:21), which scholars call *lex talionis*. Today this legislation sounds barbaric. However, when first introduced, the concept of *lex talionis* was a giant step forward in jurisprudence.

In Genesis 4:23, 24, we read about Lamech's boast to his wives: "I have killed a youth who attacked and wounded me. If anyone who kills Cain is to be punished seven times, anyone who takes revenge against me will be punished seventy-seven times!" (NLT).

Lamech apparently had received some sort of injury—an attack by a youngster, not an adult. Obviously Lamech hadn't received a mortal wound, otherwise he'd not have made this boast! Nevertheless, he took revenge by killing the lad. Furthermore, Lamech assured his wives with braggadocio tones that he felt prepared to take reprisal to the nth degree. He'd punish any assailant 77 times! (Do you think his wives were impressed?)

Ancient Near Eastern males felt duty-bound to avenge any attacks leading to a diminution of their honor. They simply couldn't endure any shame, any losing face. This mind-set led to blood feuds. The problem with blood feuds is that rather than evening the score, they often escalated the violence, perpetuating it in a vicious circle of payback.

So the *lex talionis* commanded in the Pentateuch was intended to ratchet down the excessiveness of avenging one's honor through blood feuds. Retribution had to be equivalent and in kind: If someone pokes out your eye, then you're entitled to poke out one of his eyes—not both of them. If someone knocks out one of your teeth, then you mustn't cripple him or kill him, but you could knock out *one* of his teeth.

But Jesus taught an even better way—a behavior far superior to that proposed by *lex talionis*. "Don't resist an evil person! If you are slapped on the right cheek, turn the other, too" (Matt. 5:39, NLT). The Greek word translated "resist" means to "set yourself against" or "stand your ground against."

If only Lamech could have heard such words of wisdom! Oh, and what about us? Are we Christlike enough to lay aside any attempts to settle the score?

When You Pray

August 7

Matthew

When you pray, do not imitate the hypocrites:
they love to say their prayers standing up in the
synagogues and at the street corners for people to see
them. In truth I tell you, they have had their reward.
Matt. 6:5, New Jerusalem.

I f you've ever attended a General Conference world session, you know that
praying takes a central place. Prayers are spoken in Swahili or Chinese or
Russian or Spanish or French, etc., etc. During Sabbath worship service (not
counting the Sabbath school program) one can almost lose count of the number of prayers uttered. A person might give the invocation in Danish; another
might ask in Tagalog God's blessing on the offering; someone else might offer
the pastoral prayer in Tamil; the preacher might begin with a prayer in
English; and yet another person might offer in Mandarin the benediction.

Although the congregation attending these meetings is widely diverse,
not all language groups are represented with an equal number of persons.
Some of the prayers are understood by only a handful; others are compre-
hensible to maybe 15 or 20 people; some are intelligible to several hundred
delegates; and other prayers are comprehended by literally thousands. It
seems to me that the fewer who understand the language, the shorter the
prayer. The length of prayers seems to increase in direct proportion to the
number of people who understand that particular language. And when peti-
tioners pray in English or Spanish, the languages spoken by most of the at-
tendees, the supplications become flowery and verbose and long—even
tedious.

In today's verse Jesus takes aim at public prayer, which is quite shocking
since popular piety increasingly favors public praying. What's even more
shocking is that He targets praying in the synagogue. Jesus calls those who
habitually pray in public "hypocrites."

What Jesus commands is also equally surprising. "When you pray, go to
your private room, shut yourself in" (verse 6, New Jerusalem). He refers to
the innermost room of a house, one without windows, where the valuables
were stored. Additionally, He says to shut the door, which assured even more
solitude and privacy. These prayers—said in total isolation—are the prayers,
Jesus says, that God hears and answers.

Strangely, Jesus never commanded praying in public, but He *did* command praying in utmost privacy. Where do you do most of your talking to
God? Where do I?

Prayer Warriors

If you then, who are evil, know how to give good gifts to your children, how much more will your Father who is in heaven give good things to those who ask him!
Matt. 7:11, RSV.

August 8
Matthew

The expression "prayer warrior" has become rather popular in recent years. As I understand the term, it refers to men and women who "specialize" in intercessory prayer. There's an organization called Prayer Warriors of the World, which consists of "a group of people who believe in the power of prayer and have come together to form a world wide prayer chain." Another group calls itself Spiritual Warfare Prayer Warriors.

Also on the Web, I came across an article by Victor M. Parachin titled "Are You a Prayer Warrior or a Prayer Wimp?" Surely, that's an interesting question, because it appears that Christians are either prayer warriors or prayer wimps. Take your choice.

Somehow, though, the terminology is bothersome. Why must one be a prayer *warrior*? Does God need to be battered into submission before He answers prayer? Is God reluctant to respond to our requests? Do we need to battle with God before He hears us? The 450 prophets of Baal and 400 prophets of Asherah were certainly prayer "warriors." They spent all morning long—five hours—atop Mount Carmel praying (1 Kings 18:26-29). Elijah, on the contrary, spent just a few seconds in prayer. (It took me 17 seconds to repeat Elijah's petition. Maybe it took longer in the Hebrew language, so let's double the time—34 seconds. That's 850 people praying for 18,000 seconds versus 1 person praying for 34 seconds!) And whose prayer received an answer? Not the prayer "warriors" of Baal and Asherah.

If you have children, you know how pleasurable it is to comply with their requests. As parents we recognize that we shouldn't spoil our little ones by catering to their every whim. Nonetheless, we don't find it onerous to provide them with good things—food, clothing, and even toys. Most of us don't even wait until birthdays or Christmas to buy things for them. According to our passage for today, God is *even more* eager than that to give His children good gifts. All they need to do is make the request. Elsewhere Matthew quotes Jesus as saying, "Ask, and it will be given you; seek, and you will find; knock, and it will be opened to you" (Matt. 7:7, RSV). That doesn't sound like it's necessary to gang up on God and beat Him into submission!

Maybe we should be known as prayer *children* rather than prayer warriors.

Forgiven

Peter came to Jesus and asked, "Lord, how many times shall I forgive my brother when he sins against me? Up to seven times?"
Matt. 18:21, NIV.

Jesus broached the important topic of forgiveness several times. He even included the concept of forgiveness in the prayer that He taught His disciples: "Forgive us our sins, for we also forgive everyone who sins against us" (Luke 11:4, NIV). Jesus clearly taught that if we expect forgiveness, we must show mercy: "Forgive, and you will be forgiven" (Luke 6:37, NIV).

Jesus' teachings about forgiveness weren't all that innovative. Judaism taught the same thing. "If [anyone] confesses and repents, forgive him" (Testament of Gad, 6:4). "Forgive your neighbor's injustice; then when you pray, your own sins will be forgiven" (Sirach 28:2, NAB). Nonetheless, such a vital topic was worth reiterating . . . again and again.

Amos 1:6 states: "For three sins of Gaza, even for four, I will not turn back my wrath" (NIV). Allegedly certain rabbis deduced from this passage that we need forgive others only three times. If that is indeed the case, then Peter may have assumed that forgiving a "brother" (a fellow Christian) seven times was being truly magnanimous. After all, seven was a "perfect" number! It connoted completion. After that, the well of clemency went dry.

Jesus' response must have set Peter back on his heels! "Not seven times, but seventy-seven times" (Matt. 18:22, NIV). The Greek wording here is ambiguous. It can be translated as 70 times 7, which equals 490, or it can be rendered 77. The better translation well may be the latter, because it is the exact wording found in Genesis 4:24, in which Lamech boasted about avenging 77 times. In other words, Jesus taught the exact opposite of what Lamech said he practiced. Whatever the number—77 or 490—the idea is that we should forgive to the nth degree.

Forgiveness isn't usually easy to do, but psychologically it frees us from the tyranny of someone who did us harm. It begins with a set of the will and ends with an effect on the heart. Forgiveness paves the way for personal healing, and when it is totally successful, it recaptures the heart of the person whom we've forgiven. That's how to maintain peace within the community of faith. It's also how we preserve our own sanity despite the affronts of others.

Jesus practiced what He preached. He not only talked about the importance of forgiveness; but also demonstrated it—on the cross.

The Audit

The kingdom of heaven is like a king who wanted to settle accounts with his slaves.
Matt. 18:23, NET.

Jesus' poignant story has three scenes.

Scene 1—In the opening scene we meet Lord-King and Defaulter A. Lord-King ordered an audit, which revealed that Defaulter A owed Lord-King 10,000 talents, or more than 60 million denarii if these were silver talents. To put this amount of money in perspective, know that Judea, Idumaea, and Samaria paid an annual tax of only 200 talents. Galilee and Peraea each paid annual taxes of 100 talents (Josephus *Antiquities of the Jews* 17. 11. 4).

Lord-King demanded that Defaulter A repay the debt then and there. Of course, the servant couldn't possibly comply, so Lord-King ordered that he and his family, along with all their possessions, be sold. The slave pleaded for time, promising that he'd pay the IOU in full, a ridiculous promise because it would take a day laborer more than 160,000 years, if he worked 365 days each year, to earn that much—if these were *silver* talents. If they were *gold* talents, it would take a day laborer nearly 5 million years to earn that much!

Lord-King did more than grant Defaulter A time—he completely canceled the debt.

Scene 2—This scene opens with a lighthearted Defaulter A heading home a free man. He met Defaulter B, who owed him (Defaulter A) 100 denarii—1/600,000 of the amount that he himself had owed Lord-King! It would take a day laborer only 100 days to earn that much money.

Alas! Defaulter A failed to emulate Lord-King, but grabbed his fellow slave by the throat and "threw [Defaulter B] in prison until he repaid the debt" (Matt. 18:30, NET).

Scene 3—The story closes on a depressing note. When Defaulter A's fellow slaves saw what had taken place, they wasted no time in reporting the incident to Lord-King, who scolded Defaulter A: "Should you not have shown mercy to your fellow slave, just as I showed it to you?" (verse 33, NET). And Defaulter A ended up in prison with Defaulter B, for "the prison guards to torture . . . until he repaid all he owed" (verse 34, NET).

Jesus left no doubt about the moral of the story: "So also my heavenly Father will do to you, if each of you does not forgive your brother from your heart" (verse 35, NET).

SOG-8

It's Not Fair!

August 11

Matthew

Is it against the law for me to do what I want with my money? Should you be angry because I am kind?
Matt. 20:15, NLT.

When we read the story behind today's devotional reading, it rankles us because it outrages our sense of fair play. Indeed, it advocates an illegal practice. We believe in equal pay for equal work.

Jesus' story revolves around three actors or groups of actors: (1) an estate owner, (2) temporary employees who worked all day, and (3) temps who didn't put in a full day's work. Bright and early the estate owner (boss) found some hired hands. He offered to pay them a denarius for a day's work, which was the going rate. Then at 9:00 a.m., while in the marketplace, he found some more people needing jobs, so he hired them, assuring them that he'd pay them "whatever was right" (Matt. 20:4, NLT). "At noon and again around three o'clock he did the same thing" (verse 5, NLT). Finally, around "five o'clock that evening he was in town again and saw some more people standing around. . . . The owner of the estate told them . . . 'Go on out and join the others in my vineyard'" (verses 6, 7, NLT). He must have had a bumper crop of grapes to be picked.

Soon it would turn dark, so he told the foreman to blow the quitting-time whistle and pay each worker, beginning with the last hires and ending with the first. "When those hired at five o'clock were paid, each received a full day's wage" (verse 9, NLT)—one denarius. That in itself raises eyebrows, but that's not the end of the story. If those who worked such a short time received a denarius, what about those who'd toiled from sunup to sunset? "They, too, were paid a day's wage" (verse 10, NLT)—a single denarius.

The all-day workers complained, of course. Who'd blame them? But the workers who were last in didn't complain! The landowner merely countered with "Is it against the law for me to do what I want with my money? Should you be angry because I am kind?"

On the one hand, I identify with the complainers. But on the other hand, I secretly wish I had been among those hired last. What fortune—a day's pay for a few hours' work! Since the landowner stood for God, we learn that God doesn't treat us fairly. We don't earn our way into the kingdom. We don't merit our eternal reward. Our good works don't obligate God. All is of grace. It isn't fairness but goodness—God's goodness—that gets us into heaven.

Lord or Servant?

But among you it should be quite different. Whoever wants to be a leader among you must be your servant. Matt. 20:26, NLT.

The ancient Near East was an honor-shame culture. Honor was an especially male foundational value—a "virtue" underpinning society. Honor included one's standing both horizontally and vertically within society. It also took into account one's material wealth. But especially, it consisted of the value placed on others within society.

There were two ways to get honor: (a) by being born with it—"ascribed honor"; (b) by acquiring it—"achieved honor." One had *ascribed honor* by virtue of the family into which one was born. No one earned ascribed honor. It was something of a birthright. One got *achieved honor* by one's behavior and by the opinions of others. A soldier could gain honor by his brave feats in warfare. Someone could achieve honor by being appointed to a prestigious position.

Having honor was like owning a bank account of status. It could be added to and subtracted from. When one's bank account of repute received deposits, the person enjoyed more honor. When one's bank account of repute received withdrawals, the person suffered shame. Because this was a patriarchal society, most of the honor was held in deposit for the males, who strove to maintain a bank account of ever-increasing honor—being honor-full.

Middle Eastern mothers, like all mothers, I suppose, wanted their sons to add achieved honor to the ascribed honor that they already possessed. So it was that the mother of John and James came to Jesus and pleaded, "In your Kingdom, will you let my two sons sit in places of honor next to you, one at your right and the other at your left?" (verse 21, NLT).

Jesus had two responses to her request. First, He indicated that these two privileged positions were not His to give (verse 23) and that achieving such honor would entail suffering. Were they prepared for that? Second, Jesus redefined honor. Governmental rulers, with their honorable positions, took full advantage of their status by lording it over their subjects and demanding their esteem. In the kingdom of God, however, the most honorable positions would be filled by slaves, those viewed as having the least honor and the most shame.

Jesus Himself exemplified this upside-down sense of honor by coming "not to be served but to serve others" (verse 28, NLT). That's the way it is with God.

Get Ready or Be Ready?

*You also must be ready, for the Son of Man
is coming at an unexpected hour.*
Matt. 24:44, NRSV.

W e're all familiar with the omens that Jesus predicted in Matthew 24 that would precede (1) the destruction of Jerusalem and (2) the second coming of Jesus, the Son of man. Jesus assured the disciples that "this generation will not pass away until all these things have taken place" (Matt. 24:34, NRSV). Despite sharing this inside information with His disciples, He proceeded to warn them that "about that day and hour no one knows" (verse 36, NRSV). The event would be soon, but would nevertheless come as a surprise.

Although His return didn't take place within the time frame Jesus expected, the biblical consensus that it is imminent still informs Seventh-day Adventist preaching. Our fellow church members often express the sentiment that "it won't be much longer now." And we've all heard Adventist preachers urge people both inside and outside the church to get ready.

However, the really big question that faces those of us living in the twenty-first century is quite simple: How shall we live in face of the imminence of the Second Advent despite the time that has elapsed since Jesus first talked about it?

First, we need to recognize our ignorance concerning the future, specifically about the time Jesus will return. Yet, in spite of our lack of knowledge, we hold on in faith to the belief that He *will* come back.

Second, we need to admit that the delay might continue. The delay is a reality, but it isn't indefinite. If Jesus returns shortly, fine; if He tarries, OK.

Third, we need to live in the present. We don't live in the past, although we can learn from it. We don't live for or in the future, because we have no idea what tomorrow will bring. We lead our lives today, doing our present tasks.

Finally, we should avoid the panic syndrome. As faithful servants, we live every day doing the work our Lord has assigned. We must avoid espousing emergency lifestyles. We must steer clear of crash programs to "get ready" for Jesus to come. Rather, by living as faithful Christians in the present, we "are ready" for His return. That way the timing of the Advent doesn't matter nearly as much, and the delay isn't nearly as bothersome.

Inasmuch

Whatever you did for one of the least of these brothers of mine, you did for me.
Matt. 25:40, NIV.

It's possible to look forward to the Second Advent yet lack the indispensable readiness for it. To illustrate the point, Jesus spoke of a shepherd separating the sheep from the goats, something shepherds did every night because during the day the sheep and goats intermingled in the flock. Indeed, it's possible that goats were seen as savvier than sheep and allowed to help lead a herd of silly, headstrong sheep, which are prone to wander off on their own if there were no goats for them to tag along behind.

When the shepherd divided the sheep from the goats, the sheep went to his right while the goats went to his left. It's this act of differentiation that Jesus used to illustrate that the Second Coming will reveal the true character of His flock. Will the right-hand Christians look different from the left-hand ones? Today sheep look quite distinctive from goats, but in biblical times that wasn't necessarily so. How does the shepherd differentiate between the two groups? Do the sheep say "ba-a-a" and the goats say "ma-a-a"? No.

Those on the right hand will have behaved uniquely. They'll have eased the way of others by having fed the hungry, given water to the thirsty, welcomed those they didn't know personally, clothed the garmentless, and visited the ailing and incarcerated. Those on the left hand will have ignored the starving, thirsty, itinerating, unclothed, unwell, and imprisoned.

The "King's" verdict surprised both groups. When had they performed or not performed these charitable activities? What was even more unanticipated was that they had or had not done these things to the King Himself! How or when had they seen their King ravenous, parched, itinerating, nude, ailing, or jailed?

The King's answer? "Whatever you did for one of the least of these brothers of mine, you did for me." And the King consigned the sheep to eternal bliss and the goats to eternal damnation (verse 40, NIV).

"A person's spirituality is measured in terms of humanitarian relief efforts and societal reform" (Brad H. Young, *The Parables*, p. 296). Makes one think of Mother Teresa or Albert Schweitzer before her. What about us? Are we sheep or goats?

Two Turncoats

Judas came straight to Jesus. "Greetings, Teacher!" he exclaimed and gave him the kiss. Matt. 26:49, NLT.

But Peter denied it in front of everyone. "I don't know what you are talking about," he said. Matt. 26:70, NLT.

Judas and Peter were among Jesus' 12 friends. On the one hand, Judas, according to the gospel records, served as Jesus' treasurer and rarely received a rebuke from Him. On the other hand, Peter, who didn't have such a weighty position but was among the inner circle of Jesus' three closest friends, received more rebukes than did Judas.

Judas connived with the priests to hand Jesus over to them. Many have speculated on his motives, some suggesting that he felt that he could "help" Jesus assert His kingship and claim His kingdom by forcing His hand. Irrespective of the immediate rationale behind his actions, Judas has been remembered for betraying Jesus Christ . . . with a kiss of greeting at that!

Peter did something similar, though instead of identifying with Jesus as His disciple, he denied knowing Jesus. What made his behavior so reprehensible was that he didn't deny Jesus just once, or twice, but three times. Furthermore, according to the Greek of Mark 14:71, two speech acts accompanied his denial, both of which are closely related. Peter swore, meaning that he took an oath, which is the same denotation of his second speech act—cursing. In short, Peter's words meant: "May I drop dead if I'm not telling the truth; I don't know the man."

Both turncoats rued what they'd done. Judas frankly admitted that he'd betrayed an innocent person and returned the 30 pieces of silver to the priests. Peter fled from the courtyard and wept (bitterly, according to Mark 14:72). One lived; the other didn't. God never followed through on Peter's curse, in which he'd asked that God strike him dead if he truly did know Jesus. Judas took matters into his own hand and hanged himself.

Was Judas' sin more heinous than Peter's? Not necessarily. Both men had behaved atrociously. Jesus forgives . . . if we let Him. However, Judas didn't give Jesus an opportunity to forgive him. Peter did, and Jesus commissioned him to feed His sheep and lambs, thereby answering His own prayer on the cross: "Father, forgive these people, because they don't know what they are doing" (Luke 23:34, NLT).

Despite our deficiencies, we aren't hopeless . . . unless we make ourselves so.

The Gospel Commission

Go therefore and make disciples of all the nations,
baptizing them in the name of the Father and
the Son and the Holy Spirit, teaching them
to observe all that I commanded you.
Matt. 28:19, 20, NASB.

Before His ascension, Jesus had sent the disciples to Galilee, promising to meet them at a prearranged place in the hill country. It was there on this hillside that He gave what we now call the Great Commission. Jesus used four verbal forms in His instruction—three participles and one imperative. However, Greek participles could also function as imperatives, so basically Jesus' commission included four separate commands.

First command—"Go." Jesus' point was that they must travel about. He'd been itinerant Himself, and He expected them to move about as they fulfilled the Great Commission. What He wanted them to do was not a sedentary job. They must be men on the go.

Second command—"Make disciples." As they roamed about, the apostles must teach (KJV), but Jesus envisioned something more than intellectual learning. The word He used means to make disciples. Now, it's true that disciples are students, but they study more than facts. They learn how to live. The word entailed personal attachment to the leader. Jesus wanted His disciples to make clones of themselves, so to speak—to persuade others to follow Jesus.

Third command—"Baptizing." Lustrations of various kinds were performed in the ancient Near East, including cleansings at Qumran (source of the Dead Sea scrolls) and ablutions for converts to Judaism. But evidence indicates that these rites were performed by the person undergoing the washing. From John the Baptist onward, it seems that baptism was a passive ritual in which an authority figure baptized the recipient. Baptism became the initiatory rite for becoming a disciple of Jesus and later of joining the church.

Fourth command—"Teaching." Once individuals had become Jesus' followers, they would learn what Jesus Himself had taught. In other words, the intellectual aspect followed, rather than preceded, the decision to follow Jesus. Becoming a disciple was a sociological experience followed by an intellectual process. In other words, commitment preceded learning.

These four steps—and in that order—constitute the biblical procedure for enlarging the kingdom of God.

The Good News

*The beginning of the gospel of
Jesus Christ, the Son of God.
Mark 1:1, NKJV.*

We've become so accustomed to speaking about the four Gospels that we sometimes forget the significance of the word "gospel." First, it meant "good news." In secular Greek the term was used, among other ways, in reference to the birth of an emperor, his reaching his majority, and his accession to leadership. For instance, of Emperor Augustus it was written on a calendar at the Greek city of Priene: "The birthday of the god [Augustus] was for the world the beginning of good news" (line 40). Second, because of Christianity "gospel" came to refer to a kind of writing—semibiographical accounts of Jesus. Both the inscription at Priene and the Gospels referred to Augustus and Jesus as divine (who/what they were) and as savior (what they did). Prior to Christianity there were no literary Gospels.

It's one thing, of course, to assert the humanity of someone, but it's altogether another matter to claim divinity for a human being. Grammatically, the following sentences are identical: (1) "Jesus is human" and (2) "Jesus is divine." Each consists of three words: (1) noun [Jesus], (2) verb [is], and (3) adjective [human; divine]. Despite the close similarity of those two sentences, they are quite distinct from each other when it comes to language usage.

"Jesus is human" is an example of *informative* discourse. It makes a statement of fact that is theoretically demonstrable. We know what human beings are like, being ourselves human. The statement that Jesus belonged to the species *Homo sapiens* can be independently verified through empirical methods—sight, hearing, touch, smell, taste (a more theoretical possibility). "Jesus is human" is a statement of knowledge akin to saying that "Rin Tin Tin is a dog."

"Jesus is divine" is an example of *cognitive* discourse. It makes a statement of truth (ideas—theoretical constructs) that cannot be empirically proven. We don't even know what species God belongs to, or if that's even an appropriate term. We've never physically encountered God. We cannot see, hear, feel, smell, or taste God. "Jesus is divine" is a statement of faith akin to saying that "Gabriel is an angel."

Both types of discourse are legitimate; neither is inferior to the other. But when we confuse one with the other, we end up not making ourselves clear and appear to be silly to those who think critically. Knowledge and faith are two ways of expressing ourselves.

Jesus' Family Comes to Get Him

When his family heard it, they went out to restrain him, for people were saying, "He has gone out of his mind."
Mark 3:21, NRSV.

Jesus faced much opposition during the few years of His public ministry. In some ways this shouldn't come as a surprise, because the society of the ancient Near East was an agonistic society. In agonistic societies, honor and shame were of utmost importance. Because "goods" (such as honor or money) were regarded as being in limited supply, ancient Near Easterners—especially men—were in constant competition with one another. Peers, those with essentially comparable honor, felt the compunction to maintain their honor (how other people regarded them) at nearly any cost, and this defense of honor had to be done publicly. Males in such an agonistic society confronted one another with what sociologists call "challenge and riposte," verbal skirmishing. So a lot of social tension pervaded Jesus' world.

No wonder, then, that the scribes, Pharisees, Sadducees, Herodians, and others were constantly confronting Jesus, initiating verbal duels. Unfortunately for them, Jesus' ripostes (responses) were so cogent that He ended up gaining honor while His challengers lost honor and gained shame. Touché!

What comes as a shock, though, is that Jesus' immediate family tried to shame Him because His behavior was detracting from their honor, their good name. While He was teaching a crowd, "his family . . . went out to restrain him, for people were saying, 'He has gone out of his mind.'" And exactly who were these family members? Mark 3:31 tells us: "his mother and his brothers" (NRSV).

Also in the crowd were some scribes from Jerusalem, who accused Jesus of being demon-possessed. "He has Beelzebul, and by the ruler of the demons he casts out demons" (verse 22, NRSV). The name Beelzebul had a long history, going back all the way to the documents found at ancient Ugarit, where Baal was known as *zbl ba'al*, Exalted Baal. The reverse would be *ba'al zbl*, Baal Exalted. By New Testament times the term had become a synonym for Satan.

Jesus' riposte to the scribes was to show how illogical it would be for Satan to cast out himself! And His riposte to His family was to insist that His *real* mother and brothers were "whoever does the will of God" (verse 35, NRSV). Do we honor or dishonor Him today?

It's No Picnic

He answered and said to them,
"You give them something to eat!"
Mark 6:37, NASB.

A large crowd had gathered around Jesus and His disciples at a time that He very much wanted a little peace and quiet alone with the twelve. Jesus, who always put people first, modified His plans and began teaching the throng. Now it was late afternoon. The disciples, thinking of the crowd (who must have been hungry), urged Him to send the people home.

Jesus had a different idea. "You give them something to eat!" Sarcastically they retorted, "Shall we go and spend two hundred denarii on bread and give them something to eat?" (Mark 6:37, NASB). (Two hundred denarii was the equivalent of eight months' wages.) "He said to them, 'How many loaves do you have? Go look!' And when they found out, they said, 'Five, and two fish'" (verse 38, NASB).

Jesus "commanded them all to recline by groups on the green grass" (verse 39, NASB). People usually ate sitting up, but at banquets they reclined, which is what Jesus had them do on this occasion—our first clue that this was no ordinary picnic.

After uttering a prayer over the loaves of flatbread and salted fish, He had the disciples act like servants, distributing the food. Five thousand men (there were probably some women and children present also) ate their fill, after which there were 12 baskets of leftovers.

The entire scenario was strange. Not all invitees to formal feasts sat at the same table, drank the same beverages, ate the same foods, or enjoyed the same amount of food. It was gauche of Jesus to offer the same menu to not only men, women, and children, but also elites, peasants, and paupers. Additionally, it was religiously careless of Him to throw a party in a field outside of town. No one would have been able to perform their ritual washings. And had the food been properly tithed by the family that prepared it? Had the salt that preserved the fish been tithed? Had the spices in the bread been tithed? What about the woman who had baked the bread? Had she been ritually unclean when she made it?

Jesus hosted a meal at which cultural boundaries didn't matter. He disregarded those social and religious niceties that served to keep people apart. You see, the kingdom of heaven is for everyone. In Christ there is no Jew or Gentile, no free or slave, no male or female. God's grace is freely dispensed to all.

Puppies and Crumbs

She answered and said to Him, "Yes, Lord, yet even the little dogs under the table eat from the children's crumbs."
Mark 7:28, NKJV.

Jesus, ever on the move, made a stopover at Tyre for some privacy. Although not Jewish territory, a number of Jews lived there, and the house in which He stayed was most likely owned by Jews. Relations between Tyrians and Jews were often amicable, but not always. At this time much of the produce grown in Galilee ended up in the markets of Tyre, while numerous Galileans had barely enough on which to survive.

Suddenly a Gentile mother interrupted Jesus' serenity. She needed His intervention because her little girl "had an unclean spirit" (Mark 7:25, NKJV), and this unnamed mother had heard about Jesus' reputation as an exorcist. (Casting out demons was a primary piece of evidence that Jesus had inaugurated the kingdom of God.)

Surprisingly Jesus turned a cold shoulder. Worse than that, He insulted her by derogatorily remarking, "It is not good to take the children's bread and throw it to the little dogs" (verse 27, NKJV). Generally speaking, at that time dogs weren't seen as beloved pets. So when Jesus implied that she and her daughter were dogs, it could have sent her reeling. But Jesus dropped two hints that could lead to optimism. First, His retort intimated that once the children were fed, the dogs could also eat. Second, He implied that while puppies getting the children's bread was an exception, it was not impossible.

So the frantic mother refused to cringe. Instead, she flung Jesus' words back at Him, like a good dyadic personality would do in a situation of challenge and riposte. She also showed a sense of humor when she replied, "Yet even the little dogs under the table eat from the children's crumbs." Even puppies enjoy food—although it might consist of table scraps slipped to them surreptitiously by the children. (Yes, kids will be kids!)

Jews might be children and Gentiles dogs, but both could benefit from beneficence through even the meager kindness of good-hearted Jews. Since Jesus Himself was good-hearted, He could hardly refuse her request, so He healed the little daughter, by long distance.

Although the Jews had been specially blessed by God, that didn't mean He couldn't deal kindly with those outside His covenant—a lesson that took the disciples quite a while to learn.

Cross-bearing

They enlisted a passer-by, Simon of Cyrene . . . to carry his cross.
Mark 15:21, New Jerusalem.

Jesus had gained great honor in the eyes of the public—far more than the typical person belonging to the artisan class; He had acquired so much honor that the religious authorities postponed arresting Him because "they were afraid of the crowds" (Mark 12:12, New Jerusalem).

Finally the leaders made their move, subjecting Jesus to a series of humiliations that anthropologists call a "status degradation ritual." They arrested Him as they would a common criminal; they tried Him at the home of the high priest; they blindfolded Him and hit Him and mocked Him; Pilate had Him flogged; soldiers scrunched a crown of thorns on His head, placed a make-believe scepter in His hand, and mocked Him; the rabble demanded the release of Barabbas and the execution of Jesus; the soldiers stripped off His clothing and nailed Him to a cross between two brigands; they affixed to His cross a notice identifying Him as the king of the Judeans; etc. All these activities were calculated to strip away His honor and demean Him with shame, the worst thing that could happen to a Middle Eastern male.

Another part of the status degradation ritual consisted of making Him shuffle through the streets while carrying the *patibulum,* or crosspiece, which weighed between 75 and 125 pounds, to Golgotha, the place of execution. Jesus, who had been the darling of the masses and a famous healer and exorcist, now looked like a piece of chopped meat, a pitiful specimen of humanity. He was so weakened by the mistreatment (it wasn't unusual for a person being scourged to die from the beating) that He kept stumbling along the Via Dolorosa.

The shame that Jesus endured in the public eye is unimaginable to Westerners, and in the midst of this incredible humiliation, He couldn't take another step. When the Roman soldiers noticed passerby Simon from Cyrene— a famous city in Libya—they drafted him to carry the *patibulum* for Jesus.

Although in retrospect we think it was a great honor for Simon to carry Jesus' cross, at that particular moment he must have regarded it as a most onerous task. Perhaps in the years to come, Simon finally understood he'd done something honorable . . . for Jesus. Today it's ironic that the heaviest cross-bearing most Christians do is to wear a crucifix around the neck! But thanks to Jesus, that in itself is a privilege. In His divinity He transformed the shame to honor.

The Inspired Researcher

It seemed good to me also, having followed
all things closely for some time past, to
write an orderly account for you.
Luke 1:3, RSV.

When we think about the biblical writers, we typically assume that they all were prophets. In other words, we presume that (1) God revealed data to them and that (2) what they wrote accurately related that revealed truth. Theologians call the first activity "revelation" and the second, "inspiration." However, our usual supposition isn't always accurate.

Before we pursue the matter further, we should consider a simple transmission model of communication. The Shannon-Weaver model proposes that all communication consists of (1) an information source, which originates the communication process; (2) an encoder, which puts the message in a transmittal form; (3) a channel, through which the message is sent; (4) a decoder, which reconstructs or interprets the message being communicated; (5) a receiver, which is the destination for the message; and (6) noise, which at any step of the process makes the message less clear.

During revelation (1) God was the source; (2) He encoded the message into human terms; (3) visions and/or auditions were the channel; (4) the prophet's mind decoded the message; (5) the prophet was the receiver; and (6) the prophet's perceptive faculties, including worldview, culture, and language, added noise that might have made the message less clear. The same steps occurred during inspiration, when the prophet spoke or wrote or acted out the message received.

Luke, along with Moses and the authors of Samuel and Chronicles, didn't need divine revelations. He and they utilized research instead. They considered the testimony of eyewitnesses and/or written documents such as royal annals or, in Luke's case, other Gospels. They then constructed their own account(s) of what had taken place. It's a matter of faith that God (through His Spirit) guided them as they reconstructed the events they were communicating.

Their use of the Hebrew, Aramaic, and Greek languages, their grammatical and syntactical mistakes, their faulty memory or use of inadequate sources, their other idiosyncrasies, the slipups of copyists—all contributed noise, making it possible for us today to misconstrue what they wrote. So in addition to revelation and inspiration, theologians speak of illumination, which is the work that the Holy Spirit performs for the readers of Scripture—you and me.

Son of God

The holy one to be born will be called the Son of God.
Luke 1:35, NIV.

Gabriel told Mary that the Baby she'd give birth to would be "called the Son of God." Most of us take for granted that "Son of God" means that Jesus was divine—a God/man. But is such an assumption proper? Now, let's be clear. The issue here is not the nature of Jesus Christ. Other passages of Scripture either hint at His divine nature or clearly support that concept. How do we understand the expression "Son of God"?

Here are the facts. In the Gospel of Matthew we find eight verses using "Son of God." Satan used the expression twice; demoniacs, once; overawed disciples, once; skeptical priests and leaders, twice; the unbelieving crowds, once; and a pagan centurion, once. In Mark we find the expression just three times: the author of the Gospel refers to Jesus as "Son of God" once; a demoniac, once; and the centurion, once. In Luke we come across the expression seven times: Gabriel called Jesus "Son of God" one time; the devil called Him that twice; demoniacs, twice; the leaders and priests, once. With the Gospel of John, things change. The author applies "Son of God" to Jesus two times; Nathanael calls Jesus that once; Martha, once; Jesus calls Himself "Son of God" five times, though the best manuscripts substitute "son of man" for "Son of God" once; and the unbelieving Jews, once.

Oh, in Luke 3:38 we learn in Jesus' genealogy that Adam was also the "son of God." Should it surprise us that the same expression exactly is used of a human being? Not really. According to Ellen White, in Genesis "sons of God" referred to devout men. Six times in the New Testament the expression "sons of God" describes Christians. In Job "sons of God" refers either to angels or (in Adventist tradition) inhabitants of unfallen planets.

"Son of God" and "sons of God" point to various referents. However, in the earliest Christian records, the term was typically used of Jesus by nonbelievers—Satan/devil, demoniacs, religious leaders, the rabble, and a Roman centurion. Later authors of the New Testament used the term in the singular in reference to Jesus and in the plural to refer to Jesus' followers.

"Son of . . ." was a Hebrew idiom that didn't necessarily refer to birth origin or to a species. For example, son(s) of Belial described someone who behaved like the devil. Jesus, then, behaved like God, focusing God for us so we could know what God is like.

Mercy!

Be merciful, just as your Father is merciful.
Luke 6:36, NRSV.

L uke's version of Matthew's Sermon on the Mount took place on a plain or level place. And the instruction Jesus gave has been a source of both praise and perplexity ever since—praise because it presents a lofty ethic and perplexity because that lofty ethic seems unattainable. His blessings are counterbalanced with woes. "Blessed are you who are hungry now. . . . Blessed are you who weep now. . . . Blessed are you when people hate you. . . . But woe to you who are rich. . . . Woe to you who are full now. . . . Woe to you who are laughing now. . . . Woe to you when all speak well of you" (Luke 6:21-26, NRSV).

But Jesus' instruction gets even more troublesome. "Love your enemies, do good to those who hate you, bless those who curse you, pray for those who abuse you" (verses 27, 28, NRSV). It's one thing to pray for people who mistreat us. Most of us could probably do that, albeit with some reluctance. But what about loving those who are our enemies? Or treating kindly those who hate us? Or uttering a blessing over those who put a hex on us? (Blessings and curses were treated as performative speech acts, meaning that the one doing the blessing or cursing expected the good or evil result to follow. In other words, you expect good things to happen to the person who expects bad things to happen to you.)

What Jesus said next makes sense but remains nevertheless a genuine challenge. There's nothing special about loving those who love us. After all, "even sinners love those who love them" (verse 32, NRSV). And there's nothing unusual about doing good things to those who do good things to us. After all, one good turn deserves another, and "even sinners do the same" (verse 33, NRSV). And why should Jesus' disciples behave in this unusual manner? Because Jesus urged them, "Do to others as you would have them do to you" (verse 31, NRSV).

Jesus challenged His disciples to behave the way God does. "Be merciful, just as your Father is merciful" (verse 36, NRSV). Matthew says that we should be perfect, as God is. The concept behind Christian perfection, then, isn't sinlessness but mercifulness. Yet I've met Christians who've claimed they'd not sinned for years but didn't seem to be all that merciful! Instead they came across as being harsh, demanding. If that's what perfection entails, then I'll have none of it. But if showing kindness is what perfection is all about, then . . .

The Quality of Mercy

When the Lord saw her, He had compassion on her.
Luke 7:13, NKJV.

Jesus left Capernaum, where He lived, for the city of Nain, a walled city that was about 20 to 25 miles distant. (On the east side of the city, archaeologists have discovered a cemetery with tombs cut into the rock.)

The name meant "lovely," but it wasn't a lovely place the day Jesus stopped by. "When He came near the gate of the city, behold, a dead man was being carried out" (Luke 7:12, NKJV). Funerals are never much fun, and this one was no exception. Indeed, this one was even sadder than most. The mother of the deceased was a widow, which was not out of the ordinary, because mortality rates were high. However, widows often found themselves taken advantage of, and in both the Old and New Testaments God took a special interest in them. The deceased was an only son. (John 3:16 uses the same word of Jesus—"only begotten Son.") Scripture doesn't mention daughters, and most likely the widow of Nain had none. Her closest support system—her only son—was gone. A large crowd accompanied the grieving widow, probably wailing, as was customary in the ancient Near East.

"When the Lord saw her, He had compassion on her" (verse 13, NKJV). Luke doesn't often refer to Jesus' emotional state, but here Luke shows Jesus' emotional side: "He had compassion on her." The word translated "compassion" comes from a Greek term that refers to entrails—guts. The concept here is that Jesus' insides writhed for the poor widow. It was a gut-wrenching sight for Him. The sense of the term is active—pity overwhelmed Jesus. A synonym for the word is translated "mercy."

Jesus tried to console the grieving mother: "Do not weep" (verse 13, NKJV). Jesus then approached the bier and touched it, rendering Himself ritually unclean. But that hardly mattered to Him. Next Jesus did something strange. He spoke to the corpse! "Young man, I say to you, arise" (verse 14, NKJV). And the corpse sat up and spoke. And Jesus "presented him to his mother" (verse 15, NKJV).

This is the kind of God we serve. Our plight moves Him . . . to act in our behalf. Sometimes the result is obvious, and we call it a miracle. Most of the time, though, we must view things through the eyes of faith, believing that He hurts when we hurt and cries when we cry.

Mutual Admiration Society

Among those born of women no one is greater than John.
Luke 7:28, NET.

John the Baptist grew up away from the milling crowds. Urban life with its attendant evils and nerve-wracking pace was foreign to him. Instead, he thrived in the quietness of the wide-open spaces of the desert. His diet consisted of simple, natural foods—that which was most accessible. He slaked his thirst with that which lay nearest—cool, pure water. Similarly, his clothing was simple—suitable to the rugged environment in which he dwelt. He set up his pulpit in the wilderness, and if people wanted to hear him, they had to seek him out.

Jesus grew up in a city known for its corruption. ("Can anything good come out of Nazareth?" [John 1:46, NKJV]). City ways marked His daily environment. As He grew older, His lifestyle reflected His urban upbringing. He kept "bad company." He was a ladies' man, and wherever He went they flitted about Him. Indeed, one of His closest female friends, Mary, had something of a reputation. Men who lacked a decent standing (publicans) also accompanied Him. Because of His eating habits, some nicknamed Him "pig," and because of His drinking habits, some called Him "lush." Unlike the situation of His country cousin, crowds didn't need to seek out Jesus in some out-of-the-way place, because He found them.

What do you think? Which of these two cousins offered the world a proper witness—the country bumpkin with his simplicity and asceticism, or the city boy with His sophistication and partygoing? "John the Baptist has come eating no bread and drinking no wine, and you say, 'He has a demon!' The Son of Man has come eating and drinking, and you say, 'Look at him, a glutton and a drunk, a friend of tax collectors and sinners!'" (Luke 7:33, 34, NET).

And what did these cousins say about each other? Did they criticize each other? John said of Jesus, "He must become more important while I become less important" (John 3:30, NET). Jesus said, "Among those born of women no one is greater than John" (Luke 7:28, NET).

"Historic Adventists" often come down pretty hard on the rest of us. And "average Adventists" hardly approve of those from Wildwood or Hartland. Conservative SDAs take jabs at liberal SDAs and vice versa. That's not how Jesus and John behaved. And tolerance is hardly the key word here; it's respect. God has plenty of room in His kingdom for all of us.

The Prodigal Father

"This son of mine was dead and has now returned to life. He was lost, but now he is found." So the party began. Luke 15:24 , NLT.

It was an elite family—in the top 10 percent of society. But despite their comfortable circumstances, the younger son decided he'd had enough of home and asked his father for his share of the inheritance—one third of the estate. His request must have shocked the father, for it was tantamount to saying, "Dad, I can't wait for you to die. Give me my inheritance now."

The father acceded, and quickly the young man turned his inheritance into cash and left home for "a distant land" (Luke 15:13, NLT). Things went well for the foolhardy son . . . at first. Jesus says that the son "wasted all his money on wild living" (verse 13, NKJV). The word translated "wild" means "unsavedness"—in other words, he didn't put aside any money.

Soon all his cash was gone! And if that weren't bad enough, "a great famine swept over the land" (verse 14, NLT). With no more money to waste, the boy "began to starve" (verse 14, NLT). The word translated "starve" actually means that the boy lived like a pig!

Desperate to keep alive, the lad glued (that's the Greek term) himself to one of the natives, who in turn dispatched the kid out to the farm to feed slop to the swine. From having been reduced to living like a pig he was sent out to feed the pigs, as though he were one of them! The young man became so hungry that "even the pods he was feeding the pigs looked good to him" (verse 16, NLT). However, no one was inclined to let the starving lad eat pig food.

The ne'er-do-well son swallowed his pride and returned home, where his father saw him "a long distance away" (verse 20, NLT). And the father, "filled with love and compassion . . . ran to his son, embraced him, and kissed him" (verse 20, NLT). He then dressed the lad in the finest robe, gave him the family signet ring (today it would be the credit card or checkbook), and threw a lavish party for his wayward son—a party that included a live band and a fatted calf.

Although we refer to Jesus' story as the parable of the prodigal son, it was actually the father who was prodigal. And he provides us with a snapshot of God, who pampers His children, allowing us to exercise our free will—whether or not it's in our best interests (or in His best interests). And should we lose our way but later return to Him, He's there watching for us! He treats us like royalty, leaving others to shake their heads in bewilderment.

Humility Becomes Us

This man . . . went home again justified; the other did not.
For everyone who raises himself up will be humbled, but
anyone who humbles himself will be raised up.
Luke 18:14, New Jerusalem.

The times Jews set aside for public prayer were 9:00 a.m. and 3:00 p.m. Among those gathered at the Temple were two men who caught Jesus' eye—a Pharisee and a farmer of taxes.

Pharisees were highly regarded by their fellow citizens. They tried to live in meticulous conformity to both the written laws (the Mosaic law) and the oral laws (the traditions of the fathers). They especially concerned themselves with maintaining ritual purity, appropriate Sabbathkeeping (if God's people kept one Sabbath properly, the Messiah would come), and exactitude in tithe paying.

Tax farmers (erroneously called "publicans") were people who purchased from the government the right to collect "indirect taxes" such as tolls and other local levies on goods that were in transit. The tax collectors had to pay set amounts to the government but were free to levy charges far in excess of that amount—to line their own pockets. People quickly caught on to their extortion but had no recourse other than to pay it . . . or else.

The normal posture Jews took when praying was to stand with arms crossed and eyes down. The Pharisee assumed this posture but prayed "to himself" (Luke 18:11, New Jerusalem), saying, "I thank you, God, that I am not grasping, unjust, adulterous like everyone else, and particularly that I am not like this tax collector here. I fast twice a week; I pay tithes on all I get" (verses 11, 12, New Jerusalem). According to rabbinical tradition, people who scrupulously paid tithe were called *ne 'eman*. His thankfulness consisted in his own self-gratification.

The taxman hovered by the perimeter of the courtyard. Looking downward, he prayed, "God, be merciful to me, a sinner" (verse 13, New Jerusalem). He'd extorted more than was reasonable. His handling of foreign money and contact with Gentiles kept him ritually impure. Everyone knew he was a sinner. He had nothing to commend him to God but his sinfulness.

Yet it was the unscrupulous taxman rather than the scrupulous Pharisee who left justified in God's sight. "God opposes the proud but he accords his favour to the humble" (James 4:6, New Jerusalem). Perhaps the Pharisee needed to be reminded of what Micah 6:8 says: "Do what is right. . . . Love loyalty and . . . walk humbly with your God" (New Jerusalem). One or two out of three isn't enough!

243

Little Man; Big Heart

Zaccheus . . . said . . . , "Behold, Lord, half of my possessions I will give to the poor, and if I have defrauded anyone of anything, I will give back four times as much." Luke 19:8, NASB.

It's one of those stories we learned in cradle roll or kindergarten—the story of Zacchaeus. Zacchaeus lived comfortably in Jericho—a city of palm trees and roses. At 825 feet below sea level, it had a nearly tropical climate. Little wonder, then, that Jericho was the site where Herod the Great built a fabulous country home with an elaborate sunken garden and a 138' x 295' swimming pool. Jericho was also where wealthy Jews spent their winters and where an enclave of priests, who went up to Jerusalem to minister in the Temple, also lived.

Zacchaeus gained his wealth as a tax farmer. But he was not just an ordinary tax collector. He was "a chief tax collector" (Luke 19:2, NASB). This meant that he'd paid a handsome sum for the privilege of collecting tolls and duties from merchants transporting goods in and out of the region of Jericho. Indeed, he would have had to pay the government in advance the amount of tolls expected. He then subcontracted the collection of "taxes" to numerous other individuals. They would pay the requisite amount (what the government expected plus a tidy profit) to Zacchaeus.

When Zacchaeus heard that Jesus was coming to Jericho, he wanted to see Him. But because he wasn't very tall, Zacchaeus wouldn't be able to see over the heads of the crowd. Resourceful as he was, he anticipated where Jesus would be walking and climbed a sycamore tree, where he could get a bird's-eye view. Jesus noticed Zacchaeus in his precarious perch and said, "Zaccheus, hurry and come down, for today I must stay at your house" (verse 5, NASB).

Jesus' self-invitation to Zacchaeus' place must have come as quite a shock, but he slithered down the tree and told Jesus, "Behold, Lord, half of my possessions I will give to the poor, and if I have defrauded anyone of anything, I will give back four times as much" (verse 8, NASB). His implication was that he always tried to be aboveboard in his work, but if he'd slipped up he'd repay four times as much. Additionally, he'd donate 50 percent of his belongings to the needy. Impressed by Zacchaeus' sincerity and generosity, Jesus announced, "Today salvation has come to this house" and proclaimed him a "son of Abraham" (verse 9, NASB).

Good deeds and faithful stewardship, of course, don't cause salvation, but are its results.

Render to Caesar . . .

Give to Caesar what is Caesar's, and to God what is God's.
Luke 20:25, NIV.

Once again some of Jesus' contemporaries engaged Him in a "game" of challenge and riposte. The chief priests (Sadducees) and scribes (Pharisees) joined forces in an attempt to "catch Jesus in something he said" (Luke 20:20, NIV). Perhaps if they could lure Him into saying something politically incorrect, they could then "hand him over to the power and authority of the governor" (verse 20, NIV). So they came up with a supposedly foolproof plan. "They sent spies, who pretended to be honest" (verse 20, NIV), but they had a trick question: "Is it right for us to pay taxes to Caesar or not?" (verse 22, NIV).

Wow! They had Jesus right where they wanted Him—on the horns of a dilemma. If He stated that they shouldn't pay taxes to Tiberius Julius Caesar Augustus, they could turn Him over to the Roman authorities for treason. If Jesus advocated taxpaying, then the common people would turn against Him, because they loathed paying taxes to Rome, which they regarded as unbecoming to God's chosen people.

But Jesus wasn't easily duped, and turned the tables, countering with His riposte: "Show me a denarius" (verse 24, NIV). He had no silver denarius on Him, but apparently they did—an embarrassing predicament. He asked them, as they showed Him the coin, "Whose portrait and inscription are on it?" (verse 24, NIV).

"Caesar's" (verse 25, NIV).

Oops! They had in their possession a piece of unclean heathen money! By carrying Caesar's likeness, they had violated the second commandment, which forbids images. Furthermore, its idolatrous wording, which read, "Tiberius Caesar, Augustus, son of the divine Augustus," violated the first commandment. They were complicit in lawbreaking.

Jesus retorted, "Give to Caesar what is Caesar's, and to God what is God's" (verse 25, NIV). Publicly, as was necessary in such a challenge-riposte situation, Jesus had shamed His opponents, which resulted in His gaining honor for Himself! And what did He imply? The coin, bearing Tiberius' image, belonged to him. Humans, bearing the likeness of God, belong to Him. It is legitimate for us to return to Caesar that which is rightfully his. Likewise, it is legitimate for us to return to God that which is rightfully His— ourselves. To do otherwise would be stealing.

The Widow's Mites

*All these out of their abundance have put in
offerings for God, but she out of her poverty
put in all the livelihood that she had.*
Luke 21:4, NKJV.

From the time Jesus was 12 years old, one of His favorite haunts was the Temple. We can't say for certain, but it seems a fair assumption that whenever He visited Jerusalem, He ended up at the Temple.

Once again Jesus found Himself in the Temple precincts—this time in the forecourt. Here stood 13 receptacles, shaped like ram's horns, into which money was collected. Each "treasury" had an inscription indicating what the funds were for: "New Shekel Dues," "Old Shekel Dues," "Bird Offerings," "Young Birds for the Holocaust," "Wood," "Frankincense," "Gold for the Mercy Seat," and six bore the notice: "Freewill Offerings."

A number of well-to-do people, dressed in their ostentatious finery, made a big show of dropping in their contributions. Jesus watched, silently standing by. Soon a widow, dressed in the simplest of garments (maybe moth-eaten ones at that), shuffled up to one of the receptacles and surreptitiously slipped two lepta into the "treasury." (The bronze lepton was the smallest and least valuable coin in circulation and was less than a hundredth of a denarius, which was the standard wage for a day's work.) Since it was all she had, she left facing certain starvation.

Jesus said, "All these out of their abundance have put in offerings for God, but she out of her poverty put in all the livelihood that she had." Scholars aren't agreed as to what Jesus meant. Some argue that He commended the widow for her generosity, because the real worth of a gift is not its inherent value but how much one has left afterward. Others think that Jesus recommended giving to God everything we have—regardless of the consequences.

If the immediate context controls our interpretation, then perhaps the widow's action of giving away all that she had wasn't appealing to Jesus but appalling! Just prior to this story Jesus denounced the scribes who took advantage of vulnerable widows by devouring their houses (Luke 20:47). The situation was comparable to the unscrupulous televangelist, for instance, who puts guilt trips on the destitute, assuring them that if they donate generously to the cause they'll receive back far more than they contribute. Such a "religious" leader is just as despicable as the scam artist who cons the elderly out of their retirement funds.

The Meaning
of the Crucifixion

Father, forgive them; for they know not what they do.
Luke 23:34.

It was an unthinkable turn of events. First, Jesus had been betrayed by one of His companions . . . for 30 pieces of silver, the going price of a slave! Next, the disciples fled like skittering cockroaches when a light is turned on. Third, He was subjected to a couple of sham trials, during the first of which Peter took a solemn oath that he didn't know Jesus. Fourth, Jesus was dragged before both Pilate and Herod and falsely accused as well as mocked. Fifth, Pilate, despite proclaiming Jesus' innocence, had Him flogged, an ordeal some people never lived through. After that, they heaved the crossbeam of the cross onto His shoulders as Jesus manfully stumbled off toward Golgotha, amid the jeers of the sarcastic rabble. Seventh, brutish soldiers stripped Him naked and hammered nails through His wrists and ankles and into the cross.

The physical agony of having His back shredded to ribbons from the scourging, of having a diadem of thorns scrunched down onto His head, of being nailed to the cross, and of hanging on the cross in the heat of the day can hardly be imagined. Crucifixion was a grizzly form of capital punishment, and it often took several days for the victims to succumb to their hunger, dehydration, exhaustion, exposure, loss of blood, cardiac failure, and possibly asphyxiation.

Additionally, Jesus' emotional anguish, which had begun in the Garden of Gethsemane with His betrayal and was followed by the desertion of His disciples, the fabricated testimony of lying witnesses, the ranting of the mobs incited by the religious leaders, and the sense of God's abandonment, can scarcely be understood.

In the face of such physical and psychological torture, that Jesus maintained any semblance of sanity boggles the mind. Yet at the height of His misery His thoughts turned to His mother, whom He entrusted to John's care.

Even more amazing, it seems to me, was what Jesus said as the Roman soldiers nailed Him to the cross: "Father, forgive them; for they know not what they do." How could Jesus feel so benevolently toward those capable of such brutality? Maybe He'd lost His mind after all! Surely a "normal" person would have wished for their comeuppance, especially when He had the power to summon 12 legions (50,000 to 80,000) of angels (Matt. 26:53) in His defense.

Then it dawned on me—that's what Jesus' ordeal was all about . . . forgiveness.

The Living Word

*In the beginning was the Word, and the
Word was with God, and the Word was God.
John 1:1, NIV.*

Awareness of the divinity of Jesus evolved over the years. This probably shouldn't surprise us, since good Jews were ardent monotheists and every day repeated the *Shema'*, saying: "Hear, O Israel: The Lord our God, the Lord is one" (Deut. 6:4, NIV).

Jesus' neighbors apparently saw nothing but a human being, one who had grown up among them. "Isn't this the carpenter's son? Isn't his mother's name Mary, and aren't his brothers James, Joseph, Simon and Judas?" (Matt. 13:55, NIV). In his letters to the various churches (these predate the Gospels) Paul differentiated between "God, the Father" and "our Lord Jesus." "Grace and peace to you from God our Father and the Lord Jesus Christ" (Gal. 1:3, NIV). The Synoptic Gospels (Matthew, Mark, and Luke) usually sought to identify Jesus' divinity by telling stories about Him, according to which He did something similar to what YHWH did in the Old Testament—controlling chaotic waters, providing food for thousands, etc. It's not until the later New Testament books (John and Hebrews, for example) that the authors boldly spoke of Jesus as God. Our passage for today is one of those scriptures.

The first chapter of the Gospel of John makes it clear in no uncertain terms that Jesus was divine. The preexistent Word not only was "with" God but was indeed God. Furthermore, echoing the opening words of Scripture, John wrote that "he was with God in the beginning" (John 1:2, NIV). And that's not all. The ultimate "proof" of the status of YHWH was His ability to create. Similarly, John unabashedly states that "through [the preexistent Word] all things were made; without him nothing was made that has been made" (verse 3, NIV). And as with YHWH, so with the preincarnate Word: "In him was life" (verse 4, NIV). The idea here is that the Word not only was self-existent but also was the source of life for all life forms. He is both Creator and Sustainer.

Should anyone reading the Gospel of John wonder about the identity of the Word, the author makes it clear. "The Word became flesh and made his dwelling among us. We have seen his glory" (verse 14, NIV). Jesus of Nazareth—Jesus Christ—was the preincarnate, preexistent Word. He may be human, but He is also divine. Theologians call Him the God-man.

The Lamb of God

The next day he saw Jesus coming toward him, and said, "Behold, the Lamb of God, who takes away the sin of the world!" John 1:29, RSV.

John the Baptist served as Jesus' forerunner. John claimed that he'd come to prepare the way for Jesus. What's interesting is that his proof text was Isaiah 40:3: "In the wilderness prepare the way of the Lord, make straight in the desert a highway for our God" (RSV). The preparation of a road was for "the Lord . . . for our God." If that's what John the Baptist was doing and if he was doing it for Jesus, then here's another innuendo about Jesus' divinity.

John also identified Jesus as "the Son of God" (John 1:34, RSV). (Some of the manuscripts use "the Chosen One" instead of "Son of God," but most of the sources use the latter terminology.) However, as they say . . . that's not all! John also called Jesus "the Lamb of God."

Scholars debate John's meaning. The imagery of a lamb pointed to several things.

Jewish apocalyptic writings spoke of a victorious lamb that would overturn evil at the end. Also, in the book of Revelation, we meet the same apocalyptic lamb, which would ultimately conquer the forces of evil. Satanic powers "will make war on the Lamb, and the Lamb will conquer them, for he is Lord of lords and King of kings" (Rev. 17:14).

Others identify the lamb with the Suffering Servant of Isaiah. The Suffering Servant was "like a lamb that is led to the slaughter, and like a sheep that before its shearers is dumb, so he opened not his mouth" (Isa. 53:7, RSV). It's true, of course, that Jesus suffered and died, but did John the Baptist expect that? Maybe—maybe not.

Some think that the referent for the imagery of the lamb was the Passover lamb. In the larger context of the Gospel of John we learn that Jesus' passion occurred on "the day of Preparation of the Passover" (John 19:14, RSV). And Paul identified Jesus Christ as "our paschal lamb" that had "been sacrificed" (1 Cor. 5:7, RSV).

Another possibility is to identify John's imagery with the lamb for the continual burnt offering. "This is what you shall offer upon the altar: two lambs a year old day by day continually" (Ex. 29:38, RSV).

Since the metaphor of a lamb had so many referents, maybe we need not choose among the options. Perhaps Jesus' work is the reality behind each of these possibilities.

The Gospel in a Nutshell

For God so loved the world, that he gave his only begotten Son, that whosoever believeth in him should not perish, but have everlasting life. John 3:16.

Probably most people would say that Psalm 23 is their favorite Old Testament passage of Scripture, and when it comes to the New Testament, most would likely identify John 3:16 as their favorite. It's usually not a good thing to pass judgment on people's tastes, but surely favoring these two biblical passages can hardly be faulted.

According to some schools of Christian thought, God is impassible. (No, the word isn't *impossible*.) Stemming back to Aristotle's concept of God, the idea is that God's perfection entails no "movement" within or for Him. Anselm said of God: "You are impassible. . . . You do not sense our affliction. . . . You are not afflicted by any share in our misery" (*The Proslogion*, Chap. VIII).

As a result, the argument goes, God cannot love, because love is an emotion. (Note that word "motion" embedded in "emotion.") But what about John 3:16 and other biblical passages that tell us God is love? Those who hold to God's being impassible argue that Bible authors didn't *really* mean what their words said. Instead, wherever Scripture asserts that He has any sort of emotion, the inspired writers were using anthropomorphisms. In other words, they were talking about divinity as if they were talking about humanity.

It's pretty hard, though, to explain away all the Bible verses that speak of God's love, mercy, pity, or compassion. As a result, many theologians now deny the doctrine of God's impassibility. Evangelical theologian Clark Pinnock insists: "Love is the very essence of [God's] being. . . . Love is more than an attribute; it is God's very nature" (*The Most Moved Mover*, p. 81).

Love, as an emotion, moves us . . . and moves God. It moves God to give, just as love moves us to provide good gifts to those we love. It's safe to say that one cannot love without giving. And what does God give? Many things, of course, but John 3:16 tells us that His love moved Him to give Jesus, His uniquely special Son. However, there's more to this gift. God has given us a double gift—Jesus, His Son, who in turn gives eternal life to all who believe in Him.

That's a snapshot of God that we can carry with us all the time.

Eternal Life

*It is my Father's will that whoever sees the Son
and believes in him should have eternal life, and
that I should raise that person up on the last day.
John 6:40, New Jerusalem.*

Of all the various authors of Scripture, John uses the expressions "eternal life" or "everlasting life" (the words are identical in Greek) the most. The terminology appears 13 times in the Gospel of John and six more times in the First Epistle of John. It appears only once in the Old Testament—Daniel 12:2.

According to the fourth Gospel, Jesus came specifically to provide eternal life. First, this implies, of course, that it isn't something we inherently have. There's nothing about human beings that's eternal—no soul (or spirit) that harks back to eternity or that will continue forever. We don't naturally have everlasting life; it's something that comes from above. Second, eternal life is reserved for a special group of people—those who believe in or on Jesus Christ. Eternal life is for believers only. "Everyone who believes has eternal life" (John 6:47, New Jerusalem). "Anyone who believes in the Son has eternal life, but anyone who refuses to believe in the Son will never see life" (John 3:36, New Jerusalem).

When Jesus spoke of our having eternal life, He used the present tense, which indicates that eternal life is something that Christians have here and now. However, we learn something surprising about those who have everlasting life—now, at this point in time. Just because we have eternal life right now, we can still die! "It is my Father's will that whoever sees the Son and believes in him should have eternal life, and that I should raise that person up on the last day" (John 6:40, New Jerusalem). Although believers die, they do not perish. They will rise in the resurrection because Jesus is "the resurrection. Anyone who believes in [Him], even though that person dies, will live" (John 11:25, New Jerusalem).

From Jesus' statements we can infer a difference between immortality and eternal life. Immortality in Scripture has a *quantitative* sense and refers to unceasing existence, whereas eternal life has a *qualitative* sense. It's eternal because it comes from the eternal God. As a result of this everlasting life that Jesus gives to His believers, "they will never be lost and no one will ever steal them from [Jesus'] hand" (John 10:28, New Jerusalem).

Death is only an interim state for believers; it doesn't destroy the gift of eternal life.

First Stones

He straightened up and said to them, "If any one of you is without sin, let him be the first to throw a stone at her." John 8:7, NIV.

An important role that women filled in the ancient Near East was to weld two males together. By becoming a wife, the woman served as a unifying link between her father and her husband. If a man wanted to defame the honor of either the father or the husband (or both), he could dishonor the woman who linked the two together by engaging in an adulterous relationship with her, thus tearing the social fabric. The way to restore the honor of the two violated males and thus to mend the social fabric was capital punishment—for both the adulterer and the woman (Lev. 20:10; Deut. 22:22-27).

On one of His visits to Judea Jesus visited the Temple, as was His habit. While He sat there teaching the people, the scribes and Pharisees plotted to dishonor Jesus by putting Him on the horns of a dilemma—to agree or disagree with the Mosaic law. They set their trap by dragging before Him a shamefaced woman whom they'd caught *in flagrante delicto*. "In the Law Moses commanded us to stone such women. Now what do you say?" (John 8:5, NIV). Interestingly, their concern was not with the honor of the shamed father and husband (or betrothed husband), because they'd ignored the male lover, who also should have been killed. Their intent was not to mend the torn social fabric, but to humiliate Jesus publicly.

Jesus stooped and began doodling on the Temple floor. "When they kept on questioning him, he straightened up and said to them, 'If any one of you is without sin, let him be the first to throw a stone at her'" (verse 7). Once again Jesus bent over and traced letters on the floor.

Scripture doesn't tell us what He wrote, but whatever it was, the accusers became embarrassed and began slinking away.

Jesus and the humiliated woman were by themselves, sans accusers. With no witnesses, there could be no capital punishment, so Jesus closed the case. "'Woman, where are they? Has no one condemned you?' 'No one, sir,' she said. 'Then neither do I condemn you. . . . Go now and leave your life of sin'" (verses 10, 11, NIV).

If Jesus, the only one without sin, refused to condemn the guilty woman and cast the first stone, surely we must demur from passing judgment on others.

Who Sinned?

"Teacher," his disciples asked him, "why was this man born blind? Was it a result of his own sins or those of his parents?"
John 9:2, NLT.

September 7
John

In September of 2007 Nebraska state senator Ernie Chambers initiated a lawsuit against God in Omaha's Douglas County Court. In the documentation Chambers accused God of "making and continuing to make terroristic threats of grave harm to innumerable persons" and producing "fearsome floods, egregious earthquakes, horrendous hurricanes, terrifying tornadoes, pestilential plagues, ferocious famines, devastating droughts, genocidal wars, birth defects and the like." As a result, the Defendant had caused "widespread death, destruction and terrorization of millions upon millions of the Earth's inhabitants including innocent babes, infants, children, the aged and infirm without mercy or distinction."

While at first thought the senator's lawsuit strikes us as frivolous and nonsensical, it does make sense if insurance policies are correct in their description of natural disasters as "acts of God." Despite our understanding of germs and genetics, of cause and effect, otherwise rational people resort to mystical explanations such as "It's of the devil" or "It's an act of God" in the face of what seems to be irrational suffering.

So when Jesus and the twelve happened upon a man who was blind from birth, they asked, "Why was this man born blind? Was it a result of his own sins or those of his parents?" After all, we want explanations for such pointless misery. We want to know why innocent people suffer. Even today it's tempting to surmise that people bring all suffering on themselves, that disease, disaster, and death are somehow God's verdict on personal evil.

Jesus' response both illuminates and puzzles. "'It was not because of his sins or his parents' sins,' Jesus answered. 'He was born blind so the power of God could be seen in him'" (verse 3, NIV). Suffering need not be construed as revealing sin. Jesus' words are instructive in that He denied any direct link between infirmity and sin—the parents' or the fetus'. Innocent people do suffer. They're perplexing in that as a typical ancient Near Easterner, He blurs the result of the ensuing healing as the cause—the man's birth defect existed so that God could be glorified when Jesus cured him. But when Jesus healed the man's congenital blindness, He provided us with a picture of a God who cures suffering rather than causes it.

The Bethany Syndrome

I am the resurrection and the life.
John 11:25, NLT.

Part 1—**The joy of intimacy with God**—"Martha welcomed [Jesus and His disciples] into her home" at Bethany (Luke 10:38, NLT). She enjoyed His presence by preparing for Him a satisfying meal. And Mary "sat at the Lord's feet, listening to what he taught" (verse 39, NLT). Sitting at someone's feet was the position of a learner, and the Greek verb here is in the imperfect tense, which means that Mary kept on drinking in everything Jesus said.

Part 2—The blight of God's cumbersome silence—In John 11 we again hear about the two sisters of Bethany, but this time we also meet their brother Lazarus, whom Jesus loved (John 11:3, 5). Mary and Martha were well, but Lazarus was sick—very sick. Immediately the sisters' thoughts turned to Jesus. Since He *loved* Lazarus, unquestionably He'd unleash His healing power in Lazarus' behalf. So they sent word to Him while He was in Perea, some 25 miles away. One would think that Jesus would have hiked those 25 miles as quickly as possible, but instead He dillydallied for two days. And back at Bethany you can hear the sisters whispering Jesus' name to Lazarus. "Don't worry, Lazarus. We've told Jesus." "Shhh! It's OK. Jesus is on His way." "Remember, Lazarus, you're the one whom Jesus loves—His favorite."

With each passing hour they expected to hear Jesus' welcome greeting at any moment. But what did they hear instead? Silence—and God's silence is well-nigh unbearable.

Part 3—The relief when God finally acts—When Jesus showed up outside Bethany, Lazarus had been dead for four days. The illness had won, despite all that the sisters had done. But at least Jesus had finally shattered the silence and the absence. First, He spoke, offering assurance of the resurrection (verse 25). Second, He became agitated, even indignant (verses 33 and 38). Third, He wept (verse 35). Fourth, He took action, raising Lazarus from the dead (verse 43).

All three episodes—the joy of intimacy with God, the blight of God's ponderous silence, and the relief when God finally acts—constitute the Bethany syndrome. And the Bethany syndrome—in its three aspects—is a paradigm of what most of us experience at one time or another. The day is coming (maybe only at time's end) when we'll finally experience the relief when God finally acts, and once again we'll be able to sing with gusto, "Yes, Jesus loves me!"

The Father's House

In my Father's house are many mansions:
if it were not so, I would have told you.
I go to prepare a place for you.
John 14:2.

Ask most Christians what they expect to live in when they get to heaven, and they'll utter a single word: mansions. Indeed, you've seen the illustrations in Adventist publications of palatial dwellings—large, elegantly appointed estates. We get that imagery, of course, from the King James Version's rendering of our scriptural passage for today. Unfortunately, our fantasies are based on a misreading of the text.

Jesus wanted to prepare His disciples for the tough times that lay ahead—His farcical trials, His brutal scourging, His shameful crucifixion, and His astonishing ascension. What could He say to prepare them for these unexpected events in the near future? What could He say to allay their feelings of abandonment?

He began by encouraging them to hold on to their faith. "Ye believe in God, believe also in me" (verse 1). The form of the verbs is ambiguous, but A. T. Robertson suggests that the best rendering is probably: "Keep on believing in God and in me" (*Word Pictures in the New Testament*, vol. 5, p. 248). The difficult times ahead necessitated ongoing trust.

He then tried to prepare them for the bombshell—His ascension. His Father's house (where He'd be going) had many mansions. He'd be leaving them, but only because He'd be preparing a place for them in His Father's house.

Note that Jesus spoke of His Father's house—singular. However, it was large, having many "mansions." The word He used, which the King James calls "mansions," is *monē* and means a place to stay, a room. And back in 1611 the English word "mansion" meant the same thing—a place to stay, an apartment in a larger building. It needn't mean a palace. He'd go and "prepare" a place—tidy up a room, so to speak—for them. Once all was in readiness, He'd return for those who'd maintained their trust in Him, and they'd live together happily ever after.

In other words, in preparing His disciples for the unexpected events just ahead, Jesus painted a picture of His lonesomeness once He'd leave them. He might not be there by their side, but He'd give them His Spirit until He could get a room ready for them in His Father's house. Then He'd return for them so that "where I am, there ye may be also" (verse 3).

Like Father, Like Son

He who has seen Me has seen the Father.
John 14:9, NASB.

Jesus had just attempted to prepare His disciples for His departure—His ascension to heaven. It was a difficult concept for them to get their minds around since in their experience the only final departure of people took place when they died. But Jesus wasn't talking about His death. He also spoke about the "way" to where He was going (John 14:4). Thomas countered that he wanted to know not only Jesus' destination but also the "way" to arrive there (verse 5). Jesus replied with His famous statement that He Himself is the "way" (verse 6).

Then, in His attempt to clarify matters further, Jesus seems to have only confused the disciples more. "If you had known Me, you would have known My Father also; from now on you know Him, and have seen Him" (verse 7, NASB).

Philip, puzzled, as were the others, responded: "Lord, show us the Father, and it is enough for us" (verse 8, NASB). What Philip asked for echoed Moses' request so many thousands of years previously: "I pray You, show me Your glory!" (Ex. 33:18, NASB). It's something most of us have wished for at one time or another—if only we could *see* God, our faith would be strengthened and surely our doubts quelled.

The pang in Jesus' voice comes through in His words: "Have I been so long with you, and yet you have not come to know Me, Philip? He who has seen Me has seen the Father; how can you say, 'Show us the Father'?" (verse 9, NASB).

Ancient Near Easterners' identity was embedded in others—implanted in what others thought about them and embedded in their forebears. Jesus reminded His followers that His personal distinctiveness didn't spring from His psyche but derived from God, His Father. Who and what His Father was is who and what He was. And Jesus wasn't talking about Joseph.

Personally, I sometimes think it would strengthen my faith if I could see God as Moses did—even if it was God's back. But that isn't possible. So what recourse do I have to know God? Clearly it's a venture of faith rather than knowledge. But Scripture does help us understand what God is like. It shows us what He stands for, what He does, what He doesn't like. But then some of the snapshots of God, especially in the Old Testament, seem a bit fuzzy. Jesus, however, offers our best picture of God. He's the corrective to those old, indistinct pictures.

Friends

I no longer call you servants, because a master doesn't confide in his servants. Now you are my friends, since I have told you everything the Father told me.
John 15:15, NLT.

A common biblical metaphor for those who believe in God—Jews and Christians—is that of slave. (Sometimes the Greek word is translated "servant," but it's the same Greek noun, which doesn't make a distinction between a servant or a slave.) In fact, in the New Testament alone, God's people are described as slaves or servants nearly 30 times, including references in which Paul, Peter, James, and Jude call themselves a slave of either God or of Jesus Christ.

It's a good metaphor, of course, and highlights the idea that men and women of faith are also people of obedience. It's not a matter of faith over against works. Rather, it's a matter of faith accompanied by works. Those who love and trust God consider it a privilege to serve Him.

Slavery as a metaphor hardly appeals to us today. It was abolished in the United States after a long struggle, and rightfully so because it brought out the worst in human nature. But to our shame, the stigma still lurks in the dismal corners of contemporary culture, manifesting itself in various forms of discrimination. Nevertheless, because submissive obedience is a direct consequence of gratitude, the metaphor of slavery would be appropriate if it were the only metaphor the Bible uses to describe the life of faith. But it isn't.

Jesus used another metaphor for people of faith that, despite the passage of nearly 2,000 years, still appeals to our taste. It's the metaphor of friendship, as addressed in our passage for today. "I no longer call you servants, because a master doesn't confide in his servants. Now you are my friends, since I have told you everything the Father told me."

Friendship is a much warmer metaphor, and it's refreshing to learn that Jesus Himself considers His followers to be His friends, confiding all that His Father had shared with Him. And it isn't just Jesus who sees us as friends. "The Father himself loves you dearly because you love me and believe that I came from God" (John 16:27, NLT). The verb translated "loves . . . dearly" comes from the same root as does the noun "friend."

Our relationship with God the Father and the Son, Jesus Christ, is far more privileged than that involved in servitude. It's our delight that They regard us as Their friends.

Same . . . Same

*Men of Galilee, why do you stand here looking
up into the sky? This same Jesus who has been
taken up from you into heaven will come back
in the same way you saw him go into heaven.
Acts 1:11, NET.*

In their worst nightmares the twelve would never have seen the events
that they'd just gone through. The Teacher upon whom they'd pinned
their messianic hopes had been betrayed—by one of them! He'd been man-
handled like a common criminal. A brawny Roman soldier had flogged Him
until His back was like raw meat. Jesus was then crucified, the most shameful and torturous form of capital punishment administered by the Roman
Empire. They'd spent an emotionally devastating Sabbath. Then they'd
learned about Jesus' resurrection—an empty tomb despite the Roman sen-
tinels commissioned to guard it. The resurrected Christ had at will appeared
and disappeared in their midst.

What an emotional roller coaster ride! Things had calmed down for
them as they spent 40 days enjoying their Lord's presence once again.
They'd been reunited in Galilee—by Lake Gennesaret—and had enjoyed a
campfire breakfast prepared by Jesus. Now it was Thursday, and they stood
with Him on the Mount of Olives, not far from Bethany, the town where
Mary, Martha, and Lazarus lived. This was one of Jesus' favorite retreats, especially the section known as Gethsemane.

Life was good . . . once again. Existence had returned to normal.

They became emboldened enough to ask Him if now He would restore
the kingdom to Israel. Jesus responded that this was classified information.
Then He added: "But you will receive power when the Holy Spirit has come
upon you, and you will be my witnesses in Jerusalem, and in all Judea and
Samaria, and to the farthest parts of the earth" (Acts 1:8, NET).

As they tried to wrap their minds around this latest information and
"while they were watching, he was lifted up and a cloud hid him from their
sight" (verse 9, NET). As they stood there gawking into an empty sky, they became even more startled to discover that two "men" had materialized out of
nowhere. These two strangers assured them that although they were now on
their own, the same (*oútos*) Jesus would return to them in the same (*outōs*) way
that He'd left them. That's still His followers' blessed hope.

The Unknowns

They put the names of two men before the group.
One was Joseph Barsabbas, who was also called
Justus. The other was Matthias.
Acts 1:23, NCV.

The Tomb of the Unknowns in the National Cemetery houses the remains of America's fallen war heroes beginning with World War I. Specially trained soldiers from the Old Guard watch over the tomb 24 hours, 365 days a year. Although we don't know the identity of these nameless men and women, we honor them for making the supreme sacrifice in serving their country.

Sometimes it's possible to know the name of someone yet still regard them as unknown. How? Because the name is the only information we have about such individuals. We encounter two such unknowns early in the book of Acts—Joseph Barsabbas and Matthias. In the Synoptic Gospels and the Gospel of John we learn a lot of information about Jesus and His disciples. We know the names of the twelve and can glean information about them and their personalities from reading the Gospel accounts. We also know that Jesus had a wider following of 70 disciples, but that's all we know about them since they remain nameless (Luke 10).

After Judas' death and Jesus' ascension, the 11 apostles decided they needed to replace Judas so that once again there would be the twelve. "So now a man must become a witness with us" (Acts 1:21, NCV). "He must be one of the men who were part of our group during all the time the Lord Jesus was among us—from the time John was baptizing people until the day when Jesus was taken up from us to heaven" (verse 22, NCV). So they prayed and cast lots to help them choose between Joseph Barsabbas and Matthias. "The lots showed that Matthias was the one" (verse 26, NCV).

With those qualifications, you'd think we'd have met them in the Gospel accounts, but no, the Gospels remain silent about these two men, even though they'd been among Jesus' followers from the very beginning. Why the Gospel writers said nothing about Joseph Barsabbas and Matthias, we have no idea.

Not all of us enjoy the same prominence as others. Some of us may remain in the shadows of those with more flamboyant personalities. Not all of us enjoy star billing. Nevertheless, we "unknowns" are important in God's sight. Being "unknown" is not a weakness.

Simony

Peter answered, "May your silver be lost for ever,
and you with it, for thinking that money
could buy what God has given for nothing!"
Acts 8:20, New Jerusalem.

Deacon Philip went to Samaria, where he performed numerous miracles, overawing the locals. Among those who were duly impressed was Simon. A practitioner of the magical arts, he had been regarded by the Samaritans as "the divine power that is called Great" (Acts 8:10, New Jerusalem). Scholars aren't sure what to make of this title, if it indeed was a title. Later Christian writers alleged that Simon claimed to be an incarnation of God, even the Messiah Himself.

Despite his reputation as a magician, "Simon himself became a believer" (verse 12, New Jerusalem), and Philip baptized him. Simon so admired Philip that he dogged his footsteps "and was astonished when he saw the wonders and great miracles that took place" (verse 13, New Jerusalem). And if Philip's miracle-working power wasn't enough to overwhelm Simon, Peter and John showed up. They'd been sent by the brethren at Jerusalem to assess what was taking place in Samaria.

The two apostles were pleased to find so many new converts, but quickly learned that they hadn't received the Holy Spirit. So they "prayed for them to receive the Holy Spirit" (verse 15, New Jerusalem). Next, they "laid hands on them, and they received the Holy Spirit" (verse 17, New Jerusalem). Simon was undoubtedly one of those who had "received" the Spirit. Now Simon became even more impressed. He may have admired Philip, but Peter and John were even more impressive.

So Simon broke out his wallet and begged, "Give me the same power so that anyone I lay my hands on will receive the Holy Spirit" (verse 19, New Jerusalem). He didn't want to buy the Spirit for himself. After all, he'd received the Spirit at Peter and John's behest. What he wanted was the ability to confer the Holy Spirit on others.

Peter reacted strongly, cursing Simon, but, to his credit, Simon immediately repented. Despite his quick turnaround though, Simon has come down through history as the father of heresy.

Whether his lasting reputation is merited, Simon gave his name to spiritual greed—*simony*, "the buying or selling of a church office or ecclesiastical preferment" (*Merriam-Webster's Collegiate Dictionary*, Eleventh Edition). Religion isn't a commodity to be bought and sold.

The Ethiopian Eunuch

The eunuch said, "Look! There's some water! Why can't I be baptized?"
Acts 8:36, NLT.

At this point in his life Deacon Philip was a busy man. His evangelistic endeavors had just met with great success in Samaria. Now the Holy Spirit pointed him in the direction of Gaza. An ancient caravan road wound from Jerusalem to Gaza, through Egypt, and to Ethiopia.

Along this old trade route Philip espied a wealthy Ethiopian reading as he bounced along in his chariot. Indeed, this was no ordinary Ethiopian, wealthy or not. He was the treasurer for the Candace of Meroë. (Although the word is usually capitalized—Candace—it was actually a title for the queens and/or the queen mothers of Meroë, which was situated primarily in what is now known as Sudan but also reached into the nation now known as Ethiopia.)

The man was returning home from Jerusalem, where he'd worshipped (verse 27). Many scholars argue that although he'd gone to Jerusalem to worship, he could hardly have been a proselyte because eunuchs, according to the Mosaic law, could never become a member of the covenant community. Perhaps, then, he was a "God-fearer," a Gentile sympathetic to Judaism.

Like most ancient readers, the treasurer was reading aloud. And he was poring over a scroll of Isaiah. At the moment Philip approached and overheard him reading, he was trying to understand Isaiah 53:7, 8. Philip asked, "Do you understand what you are reading?" (Acts 8:30, NLT). The Ethiopian eunuch admitted that he didn't and "begged Philip to come up into the carriage and sit with him" (verse 31, NLT). Philip wasted no time in complying and told "the Good News about Jesus" (verse 35, NLT).

Philip's impromptu Bible study must have been convincing, because as the chariot neared some water, the eunuch asked Philip to baptize him, which he did. As they both rose from the water, the Holy Spirit wisked Philip away to Azotus.

The man's skin color, rank, or physical condition didn't discourage Philip from baptizing him. Christianity is an inclusive religion. The criterion for membership isn't ethnicity, culture, social position, or physical state. It wasn't necessarily an easy lesson for those early Jewish Christians to grasp, and they learned the lesson only after direct divine intervention. Christianity embraces all—male and female; free and slave; Jew and Gentile; wealthy and poor, because God is no respecter of persons (Acts 10:34).

Who'd Have Guessed!

The scribes who were of the Pharisees' party arose and protested, saying, "We find no evil in this man; but if a spirit or an angel has spoken to him, let us not fight against God."
Acts 23:9, NKJV.

The four Gospels paint a dismal picture of the spirituality of the Jewish priests, the very people who should have been paragons of piety. It was they who showed the most animus toward Jesus. It was they who gave Judas 30 pieces of silver to betray Jesus. It was they who whipped up the mob into a frenzy as they shouted, "Crucify Him!" It was they who bribed the Roman soldiers to lie about the Resurrection. Yet in Acts 6:7 we read that "a great many of the priests were obedient to the faith" (NKJV)—became followers of Jesus. Who'd have guessed it!

Then there were Philip's forays as an evangelist. First, his preaching led to the conversion of many Samaritans, people the Jews loathed (and vice versa). Second, he baptized Simon, the man who was said to have been God! Third, Philip crossed paths with the Ethiopian eunuch, treasurer of Meroë, and baptized him—a man who was a castrated African, someone the Law categorically ruled out. Who'd have guessed it!

And let's not forget that hotheaded Pharisee who did his utmost to eradicate Jesus' followers. We first learn about Saul/Paul when he checked the coats of those who stoned Stephen. Later he obtained authorization to hunt down Christians in Damascus. But after the resurrected Christ stopped him dead in his tracks, Saul/Paul's zeal to demolish Christianity morphed into fervor to build it up. Not only that, but he was the first author to write portions of what we call the New Testament. Who'd have guessed it!

The Pharisees don't get good press in the Gospels, either. It was they who accused Jesus of ignoring the Law of Moses, which they tried to obey in minute detail. Yet in Paul's trial before Claudius Lysias, chiliarch and tribune of the Roman soldiers stationed in the tower of Antonia adjoining the Temple Court of the Gentiles, the Pharisees suddenly rallied round Paul. They proclaimed, "We find no evil in this man." Why? Because Paul claimed he was on trial "concerning the hope and resurrection of the dead" (Acts 23:6, NKJV). Who'd have guessed it!

Just when we think we have things figured out, God throws us a curve! With Him "all things are possible" (Matt. 19:26, NKJV), and improbability turns into actuality. Who'd have guessed it!

In Hock

That you and I may be mutually encouraged
by each other's faith.
Rom. 1:12, NIV.

The word "disciple" refers to someone in a position of learning—a student. The word "apostle" comes from a root word meaning "to be sent." The disciples sat at Jesus' feet, drinking in His instructions. When He commissioned them to teach others, they became apostles because He was sending them out to share. They were His ambassadors. In the New Testament the local churches sent envoys (apostles) to represent them (2 Cor. 8:23). But in a special sense, Jesus sent out missionaries (apostles), especially the twelve.

Paul, though not one of the twelve, often referred to himself as an apostle. He'd had a special encounter with the risen Christ, who had commissioned him to serve as the premier missionary to the Gentiles while the other apostles evangelized the Jews.

Apostles carried a certain amount of authority because they were the envoys of Jesus Himself, taught by Him and sent out by Him. Such apostolic authority, however, didn't require prideful authoritarianism. At the outset of his letter to the Christians at Rome, Paul revealed appropriate humility. As an apostle, he had something specific and important to share with them. Nevertheless, it would be a two-way street. As Christ's envoy, he expected to help "encourage" them and vice versa. Together they would enjoy a mutual experience of supporting one another.

Paul's same attitude of being both teacher and learner crops up again in Romans 1:14: "I am obligated both to Greeks and non-Greeks, both to the wise and the foolish" (NIV). Paul used a word meaning "debtor" to describe himself, despite his status as an apostle. And to whom was he in debt? Greeks and Barbarians (translated in the NIV as "non-Greeks") and wise and foolish (those who are in the know and those who are ignorant). In other words, Paul felt indebted to all.

Paul was in hock to others on two counts. First, as an apostle of Jesus Christ, it was his duty to share the good news of salvation with others, especially the Gentiles. He owed it to them to share his faith with them. Second, he himself wasn't an island, and had learned from others—even from those who weren't especially insightful. Learning is a lifelong experience.

Paul set a great example for everyone in positions of leadership—and for us, even if we aren't apostles.

The Centrality of Faith

*The gospel . . . is the power of God for salvation
to everyone who believes. . . . In it the righteousness
of God is revealed from faith to faith.*
Rom. 1:16, 17, NASB.

Paul now states the heart of his message to the Roman Christians—the good news. God through Jesus has provided the means to bring reconciliation between humanity and divinity. When we talk about this activity on God's part and what it means to each of us, we need to make sure that we don't turn the good news into bad news . . . or just plain old ordinary news. Good news makes one's heart skip a beat! It produces relief (aah!) as well as rejoicing (aha!).

Paul's next point is that the good news is power. Now, there are all kinds of power—solar power, nuclear power, steam power, horse power, etc. But the gospel is about a different kind of power—divine power, which makes all other kinds of power pale in comparison.

The effect of this power is salvation—salvation for believers. Paul uses a present active participle, which means he's referring to people who are believing—people who keep on having faith. Believing isn't something we experience once and then forget about. It's a way of life that involves trusting God . . . always. But faith isn't a work that produces salvation. "It is not man's faith that gives the gospel its power. . . . It is the power of the gospel that makes it possible for one to believe" (Anders Nygren, *Commentary on Romans*, p. 71).

Through salvation God's righteousness is revealed—not our righteousness, but His. God's uprightness—rightdoing—is made manifest through the salvation He provides for those who maintain their trust in Him. Salvation is relational—not legal, not meritorious. The word "salvation" describes the experience of God's righteousness becoming ours.

God's uprightness is "revealed from faith to faith." On the one hand, Paul's wording can mean that faith is both (1) the way we enjoy salvation and (2) its ultimate purpose. On the other hand, the expression "from faith to faith" may mean here in Romans 1:17 what it means in 2 Corinthians 3:18— passing from one degree to an even higher degree. Faith, then, grows stronger and stronger from an initial faith to a faith that deepens into a way of life.

Whichever meaning Paul had in mind, the point is this: salvation, from beginning to end, is a matter of trusting God. Salvation doesn't begin with faith and end with works. Faith, like Jesus Himself, is the beginning and the end of salvation.

All Have Sinned

All have sinned and fall short of the glory of God.
Rom. 3:23, NRSV.

In the Hebrew Scriptures YHWH clearly indicated that He had chosen the descendants of Abraham through Isaac as His special people. It's little wonder, then, that throughout the centuries the Jews came to take great pride in their special status. Not only was Abraham their predecessor, the friend of God, but also YHWH, Creator and Proprietor of the cosmos, had chosen them as His special people. Because of this pride in their spiritual status, Jesus had warned them to refrain from referring to Abraham as their father since they weren't behaving as he did, as would befit his descendants.

As Paul presented the gospel of Jesus Christ to both Jews and Gentiles, he needed to effect two things: (1) reduction of Jewish spiritual self-importance and (2) reduction of Gentile spiritual self-contempt. He needed to do this because when it comes to God's provision of salvation, no one is advantaged or disadvantaged.

And so here in Romans 3, Paul continues building his case that human achievement doesn't merit God's blessings. The Jewish advantage—the Law—is, of course, a reality. God privileged the Jews by entrusting them with the Law, something the Gentiles didn't have. And the Law brings knowledge, but it's merely the knowledge of sin that it produces (verse 20). That's how he went about reducing Jewish spiritual self-importance.

His method of reducing Gentile self-contempt entailed pointing out that knowledge—no matter how elevating—doesn't save. It merely adds to one's responsibility. Anyway, "there is no one who is righteous, not even one" (verse 10, NRSV). Indeed, "all have sinned and fall short of the glory of God" (verse 23, NRSV). This recognition that all have sinned (past tense) and are falling short (present tense) of honoring God levels the playing field. Jew or Gentile—all are in the same spiritual predicament. Nonetheless, these "all" "are now justified by [God's] grace as a gift, through the redemption that is in Christ Jesus" (verse 24, NRSV).

Spiritual ancestry (or lack of it) really doesn't matter. So what if Ellen White is in your family tree? So what if you're a preacher's kid? So what if you're a third- or fourth-generation Adventist? Being a religious "somebody" doesn't save us. Religious "somebodies" need God's grace just as much as religious "nobodies."

Clientela

We see now that a man is justified before God . . . not by what he has managed to achieve under the Law.
Rom. 3:28, Phillips.

Gallons and gallons of ink have flowed from pens as Christians past and present have misunderstood the relationship between faith and works or grace and law.

Ancient society consisted of two major classes—the elites and the nonelites. The elites, who constituted somewhere between 1 and 10 percent of the population, enjoyed 66 percent of the wealth and 50 percent of the land. The nonelites made up the rest of the population.

In the Greek and Roman cultures the practice of *clientela*—patronage and clientage—helped keep society on an even keel. Patrons were well-to-do individuals—among the elites—who gave benefactions to the less fortunate—the nonelites. The benefactions might be monetary aid, provision of food, personal protection, job advancement, manumission (freeing slaves), fairness in taxation, help with legal issues, employment, or other valuable gifts.

Clients were not expected to reciprocate with material benefits, but they were supposed to offer public gratitude. In Rome, for instance, clients would show up early in the morning at the patron's house and announce publicly how generous the patron was and how impossible it was for them, the clients, to repay such kindness. They would also run errands for their patrons or gather information through the gossip channels or attend funerals of the patrons' family members or even testify in court on behalf of their benefactors. Patrons would never mention the gift once the benefaction had been received, but the clients would always mention it—to anyone who would listen. Although no law legislated against ungrateful clients, just as patrons provided benefactions freely, so clients provided honor freely in return.

Arguments over faith and works become readily resolved when one understands salvation as the benefaction that (1) God, the patron, offers to (2) sinful humans, the clients. We didn't do anything to merit His benefaction, and we can't do anything to reimburse God for it. By accepting His patronage, we become part of His clientage. So each morning, at the start of the day, we ask our divine Benefactor if there's anything we might do for Him that day—not that we're trying to reciprocate in kind, because we can't, but that from deep-felt appreciation we feel obligated to serve Him and sing His praises whenever and wherever we can.

God's Sons

All who follow the leading of God's Spirit are God's own sons.
Rom. 8:14, Phillips.

We're so accustomed to calling Jesus Christ "God" or "Son of God" that we don't realize that certain human beings have been called "God" or "Son of God" for thousands of years. In the ancient Near East it was common for rulers to bear the title of "Son of God" or "God." From the first dynasty, the pharaoh was called "Son of Isis," and from the fourth dynasty on, another name for the pharaoh was "Son of Re." Thutmose III said he was God's son. The first Mesopotamian king to claim divinity was Naram-Sin of Akkad, who referred to himself as "God of Akkad." From the time of Mesilim of Kish, Sumerian kings were known as the son of the patron god or goddess. The Canaanite story of Keret refers to the king as "Son of El."

In the Roman culture, calling the emperors "Son of God" or "God" was a common way of showing them honor. For example, the Ephesians called Julius Caesar "God Manifest" and "Savior." Two years after he died, he was proclaimed "Divine Julius." Octavian, Caesar's adopted son, was called "Son of the Divine," and Virgil called him "God." In Pergamum a stone monument referred to "Emperor Caesar, Son of God."

It comes as an even greater surprise to discover that among the Hebrew people their king was called "Elohim" (Ps. 45:6) and God's firstborn son (Ps. 89:27). Other Old Testament referents for "son(s) of God" include angels/semidivine beings/offspring of Enoch/extraterrestrials (Gen. 6:2, 4; Job 1:6; 2:1; 38:7), the Israelite people (Hosea 11:1), King David (1 Chron. 17:13; Ps. 2:7), and King Solomon (1 Chron. 28:6).

New Testament authors honored Jesus Christ by calling Him "Son of God." But Jesus isn't the only one given this designation. Luke called Adam "son of God" (Luke 3:38). And perhaps most surprising of all, believers in Jesus Christ are called (as in our passage for today) "sons of God" by Paul, the author of Hebrews (if not Paul), and John. You see, we have become Jesus' siblings.

Every Christian, like Jesus, is a [child] of God (1) because of trust in Jesus, *the* Son of God (John 1:12), and (2) because of the Holy Spirit's guidance (Rom. 8:14). "What manner of love the Father hath bestowed upon us, that we should be called the sons of God" (1 John 3:1). Surely God couldn't honor us more!

When the
Holy Spirit Prays

*The Spirit also helps our weakness; for we do not know
how to pray as we should, but the Spirit Himself
intercedes for us with groanings too deep for words.
Rom. 8:26, NASB.*

I n the previous reading we noted that in the cultures of the ancient Near
East there was no higher honor for a human being than to be called a son
of God. We also noted that because of the Holy Spirit's leading we Christians
are given the status of "sons of God." In today's passage, also from Romans 8,
we learn of another blessing bestowed by God's Holy Spirit.

In this chapter Paul speaks of three groans or groanings: (1) groans by all
creation, (2) groans by Christians, and (3) groans by the Holy Spirit.

Although Jesus inaugurated the kingdom of God as a present entity,
there is also a future aspect to it. Theologians sometimes speak of the "now"
and the "not yet" of the kingdom. While we wait for the "not yet" to become
the "now," we suffer (Rom. 8:18). Most likely Paul refers to the suffering
caused by persecution, although perhaps we shouldn't totally rule out other
forms of suffering that we endure prior to the earth made new.

As a result Christians groan while "waiting eagerly for . . . the redemption of our body" (verse 23, NASB). And because the cosmos itself has also
been troubled by the reign of sin—the kingdom of evil, it "waits eagerly for
the revealing of the sons of God" (verse 19, NASB). That's why it too groans
(verse 22).

Even though we Christians are sons [children] of God, we're still frail
(verse 26) physically, mentally, and spiritually. This means that despite our
constant praying, we're deficient, and because of our limitations, we need
professional help with our praying since "we do not know how to pray as we
should" (verse 26, NASB). (The Greek indicates that it's not so much that we
don't know *how* to pray but that we don't really know *what* to pray for.)

"Without the Spirit, we are simply at a loss to know how to communicate with God" (Paul J. Achtemeier, *Romans*, p. 143). So it is that "the Spirit
. . . helps our weakness" (verse 26, NASB) in our communication with God.
He does this by interceding "for us with groanings too deep for words" (verse
26, NASB). Furthermore, the Spirit's ineffable prayers for us are in harmony
with God's will (verse 27). And that's what praying is all about—conformity
to God's will.

God Is for Us

If God is for us, who can ever be against us?
Rom. 8:31, NLT.

To hear some people talk, God is out to get us. He records our thoughts (though they're secret) and our actions (though we're alone) and our words (though we're dead tired and grumpy) and will fling them back into our teeth at a later date, especially the bad ones. Some Adventists have warned that the angels linger outside when we enter a cinema, although that may be the time when we need their influence and protection the most! Some have reasoned that the slightest moral lapse marginalizes us outside God's family. Colleagues of mine used to argue that someone would be lost if he uttered a cussword at the outset of an automobile accident in which he was instantly killed.

In church we sing: "tempests blow by order from Thy throne," and insurance companies talk about "acts of God," which are defined as destructive natural forces, such as lightning strikes or tornadoes or earthquakes. Some people allege that God refines us in the crucible of suffering (through such means as brain cancer, Huntington's disease, amyotrophic lateral sclerosis, etc.) until He sees His face reflected in us.

Oh, then there were the early Christians from Paul's time onward who suffered persecution—early on, some suffered at Paul's own hand. Others were evicted from the local synagogue. Some were turned into living torches by Nero. Later others were called "atheists" and condemned to death for refusing to put a pinch of incense on a fire and to say, "Caesar is Lord." These people who died for standing up for God must have wondered why God didn't stand up for them!

Paul himself, after becoming a servant of Christ, suffered greatly. He reported: "Five different times the Jews gave me thirty-nine lashes. Three times I was beaten with rods. Once I was stoned. Three times I was shipwrecked. Once I spent a whole night and a day adrift at sea" (2 Cor. 11:24, 25, NLT). Did he wonder if God was ignoring him?

Good news! Paul confidently assures us that God is for us and that nothing can separate us from His love. "Death can't, and life can't. The angels can't, and the demons can't. . . . Even the powers of hell can't keep God's love away. . . . Nothing in all creation will ever be able to separate us from the love of God that is revealed in Christ Jesus" (Rom. 8:38, 39, NLT).

Christ Is the End of the Law

Christ is the end of the law.
Rom. 10:4, NRSV.

Within Scripture we find some passages that are so ambiguous they have become fodder for argumentation. Did the inspired author mean this or that or something else? Sincere, well-meaning individuals take sides, and holding differing opinions in such instances is hardly an indication of perverseness. One of these unclear verses is our text for today. What did Paul mean when he wrote that "Christ is the end of the law"?

The word "law" is multivalent. Exactly which denotation of law did Paul have in mind? 1. The moral law (Decalogue)? 2. The ceremonial laws? 3. The health laws? 4. The Pentateuch (Mosaic law)? 5. The entire Hebrew Bible? 6. The oral law (supported by the Pharisees but denigrated by the Sadducees)? Our distinction among the moral, ceremonial, and health laws may have been lost on Paul, but at that time the other options were all legitimate denotations for the word "law." The word "end" is also ambiguous. What denotation did Paul have in mind? 1. Cessation or termination? 2. Last part or conclusion? 3. Goal, aim, or purpose?

The interpreter is left with 18 possible combinations of "law" and "end." Which of the 18 did Paul intend here in Romans 10?

From the entire book of Romans as context, it's probable that Paul had in mind either the entire Mosaic law (not the narrower understanding of certain parts of it and not the wider understanding of Old Testament Scripture as a whole), which included the requirements of circumcision and ritual purity, or the moral law, which defines sin. Whichever, Paul was pointing to the law that the Jewish people zealously tried to keep as the way to righteousness.

Of the three possible denotations for "end," the second one hardly makes sense in this context. And from other Pauline statements, it's hard to conclude that he thought the law had been terminated by Jesus Christ because in chapters 9-11 (the immediate context), Paul's references to the law are positive. So the aim of the law is Jesus Christ, the reason for it.

As a result, "there is no distinction between Jew and Greek; the same Lord is Lord of all and is generous to all who call on him. For, 'Everyone who calls on the name of the Lord shall be saved'" (verses 12, 13, NRSV). Thus, we are "justified by faith apart from works prescribed by the law" (Rom. 3:28, NRSV).

September 25
Romans

t

d,
God.

TO DO . . .
- The Dragon
  is attacking
  the commandments
  of God
  Heb 12:22
  The Heavenly
  Jerusalem
  We are on Mt
  Zion when we are
  in Jesus Christ
  144,000 are the
  ones who follow
  the Lamb
  Know The
  Truth
  Rev 14:14
  Who Will
  You Worship?
  Know The Gospel
  of Jesus Christ
  Obey God
  Do God's
  Will

themselves over whether or not they are
serious issue. If indeed we love the Lord, we
with what He wants. Indeed, obedience to
consequence of loving Him.

tters WWJD became a fad. WWJD appeared
ds, etc. The letters stood for the question:
question, don't you think? The problem is
tically different from ours. He had no radio
ch, no electronic games to play. He had no
e) to fret over, no rap music to listen to, etc.
ve.

e doing what God wants. Some go so far as
y they do because God told them to act in
r becomes criminal or even contrary to the
have serious questions about what it means
l.

od's will? Paul told the Christians in Rome
ed to this world: but be . . . transformed by
n. 12:2). J. B. Phillips translates the first verb
und you squeeze you into its own mould"
der constant pressure to comply with what
tead of succumbing to external pressures,
influence of God's Spirit. We need to "let
ole attitude of mind is changed" (verse 2,

ces of the world and succumb to the inter-
rove what is that good, and acceptable, and
e may not be one single divine will. When
it comes to God's will, some behavior may be good, other behavior may be acceptable, and still other behavior may be perfect. In other words, we sometimes
may need to choose among that which is good, better, and best. Obviously, that
which is best would be ideal, but we don't live in an ideal world. God will be satisfied even if we end up doing that which is better or simply good.

To Eat or Not to Eat

*The Kingdom of God is not a matter
of what we eat or drink.*
Rom. 14:17, NLT.

The church had sponsored a weekend of health lectures. One of the presentations dealt with what shouldn't be eaten—you know, items such as sugar, caffeinated beverages, raw cashews, salt, meat, etc. All these and more were on the list of banned food items. After 30 minutes of this, the pastor's wife, who was sitting toward the back of the room, turned to the person next to her and whispered, "Next thing they'll tell us we shouldn't drink water." You can imagine how surprised she was when the speaker added, "And we shouldn't drink soft water."

In Paul's letters to the Christians at Rome, he also addressed the matter of diet. Apparently some individuals were making a big issue over meat eating, advocating a vegetarian diet instead. Now, don't misunderstand me. I've been a lifelong vegetarian. To the best of my knowledge, not a morsel of meat has gone down my throat. The very thought of dining on a carcass causes me emotional distress. After all, I'm a human being, not a vulture!

The issue, however, in Paul's day was different. Nearly all meat on sale in the marketplace had come from animals sacrificed in the temple of a pagan deity. Some of this sacrificial flesh was burned on the altar. Some the officiating priest(s) ate. Some the family members consumed. The remainder was wholesaled to the local meat markets, where it was sold to customers, some of whom took comfort in the knowledge that the meat had been "blessed."

Certain Christians argued that because the meat had been offered initially to a pagan god, it wasn't fit for consumption by Christians. This position seems to have been in harmony with the decision made at the Jerusalem Council. However, it appears that this pronouncement hadn't been explained to Paul. He reasoned that idols are nothing. So flesh offered to them was no different from meat not offered to them. Those nongods didn't affect the meat at all.

It was those with a weak conscience who abstained from such meat by becoming vegetarians. Those with a strong conscience dined on it with impunity. However, the meat eaters shouldn't criticize the vegetarians, and the vegetarians shouldn't condemn the meat eaters. Loving tolerance should prevail. Nonetheless, "the Kingdom of God is not a matter of what we eat . . . , but of living a life of goodness and peace and joy in the Holy Spirit" (Rom. 14:17, NLT).

The Saints

*To the church of God that is in Corinth, to those
who are sanctified in Christ Jesus, called to be saints.
1 Cor. 1:2, NRSV.*

In the Adventist Church we seldom hear the word "saint" spoken, and when we do use the word, it's often with tongue in cheek. The reason for that is most likely our longstanding aversion to anything that smacks of Roman Catholicism. However, Paul wasn't afraid of the word and used it approximately 40 times.

The Greek word behind the English translation "saint" is *hágios*, which referred to something that was holy. In Scripture something became holy (1) by being set apart for sacred use and/or (2) by the immediate presence of God. For both reasons Paul could call the early Christians "saints." When they had accepted Jesus by faith, God had set them apart for special use as His people, and because God's Holy Spirit indwelt them, they were holy— saints. This despite the problems among the church members in Corinth (and in other cities, for that matter).

Paul, in his letter addressed to the "saints" in Corinth, referred to them as "those who are sanctified in Christ Jesus." Why is this significant?

First, the word translated "sanctified" is the Greek word *hagiázō*, which comes from the same root as the word translated "saint." Further, to use both terms of the same people was somewhat redundant. The chief difference is that one word is a noun (translated "saint") and the other is a verb (translated "sanctified").

Second, Paul used the perfect tense for the verb, which "implies a process, but views that process as having reached its consummation and existing in a finished state" (H. E. Dana and Julius R. Mantey, *A Manual Grammar of the Greek New Testament*, section 182). In other words, the Christians had already been sanctified and remained in the state of sanctification.

When we distinguish between justification and sanctification by insisting that justification is a past experience but sanctification is a future state that we spend a lifetime pursuing, we're out of sync with the biblical passages that speak in terms of both justification and sanctification being past experiences. They're two metaphors for the same saving work of God in Jesus. In the New Testament we also read about growing in grace, but the term "sanctification" is not used as its synonym. Next Sabbath, look around . . . at all the saints!

Unity

Now, dear brothers and sisters, I appeal to you by the authority of the Lord Jesus Christ to stop arguing among yourselves. Let there be real harmony so there won't be divisions in the church. I plead with you to be of one mind, united in thought and purpose.
1 Cor. 1:10, NLT.

Divided churches! In one of the churches my dad pastored, members were so divided that during one business meeting several men jumped into the aisle and almost duked it out as if they were in a saloon in the old West! After the meeting, the conference president shook his head in amazement and said, "I've never seen anything like that!" Mother used to alternate the sides of the church where she'd sit on Sabbath so that no one would have grounds to accuse her of favoring one faction over the other.

The Corinthian church was also divided into disparate sides. Paul had learned from members of Chloe's household that some people were saying, "I am a follower of Paul," while others claimed, "I follow Apollos," and others insisted, "I follow Peter," and yet others boasted, "I follow only Christ" (1 Cor. 1:12, NLT). It sounds picayune to take sides based on who had first evangelized them, but big troubles can spring from tiny issues.

But that wasn't the only basis for schisms among the Corinthian church members. Some missionaries with letters of recommendation had appeared on the scene and divided the church further—this time along doctrinal lines. These false teachers apparently espoused an early form of Gnosticism, the greatest theological threat to the growing movement. The Corinthians argued over whether or not the body was good or evil, whether there was such a thing as the resurrection of the body, whether or not one should eat food offered to idols, whether or not one should marry, whether or not husbands and wives should engage in marital relations, etc.

Also, some Corinthian Christians bickered over spiritual gifts. Which spiritual gift was most important? Speaking in tongues? Performing miracles? Being an apostle? Giving prophecies? Teaching others?

It's good to take seriously matters of theology and lifestyle, but when these produce enmity among the saints, something is seriously amiss. On the one hand, religion is wrongheaded when its adherents manifest more hate than love. On the other hand, unity doesn't entail parroting one another mindlessly. Nevertheless, infighting pierces the heart of our Savior.

The Temple of God, 1

Do you not know that you are a temple of God, and that the Spirit of God dwells in you? If any man destroys the temple of God, God will destroy him, for the temple of God is holy, and that is what you are.
1 Cor. 3:16, 17, NASB.

Metaphors are figures of speech that compare two things that are dissimilar in most ways but have at least one similarity. This commonality helps clarify meaning. One doesn't take a metaphor literally, even though it may clarify an idea. Here's a metaphor: Bill is a real pig. From the context, we would understand that this *Homo sapiens* named Bill really isn't *Sus domestica*. Speciation isn't the issue. Also from the context we'd learn either that Bill has a big appetite and will eat almost anything or that he's a sloppy housekeeper. Behavior is the issue.

Metaphors are "live" when they hold great meaning—even having a bit of an intellectual surprise that makes them engaging. Metaphors are "dead" when their meaning becomes unclear or obsolete and so they've lost insightfulness. Metaphors are "dying" when they become trite; meaning is still there, but so what. A "root" metaphor is a comparison that underpins one's worldview and influences personal understanding and behavior. Often we don't even realize that a root metaphor is a metaphor. Religion generally presses into service a number of root metaphors. The Adventist great controversy theme is an example of a root metaphor.

One of Paul's metaphors, which he repeated several times, is that we are God's temple. Most of us know what "temple" means even though we don't often encounter one—unless we're traveling around the world. (Our local churches are *not* temples.) Temples are sanctuaries—places where the deity dwells, even if it's in a representational form such as an idol or the glorious Shekinah presence in the Hebrew tabernacle.

We often have adopted Paul's metaphor here in 1 Corinthians 3:16, 17 as an example of how we should treat our bodies as individuals. Because the Holy Spirit indwells us, we should live healthfully. That's a good principle to live by—a good root metaphor—but it really isn't what Paul had in mind here. He was continuing the discussion about the importance of unity among Christian believers. He argued that maintaining serenity within the local church was important because the local church is the temple of God, where the Holy Spirit is active. Paul was thinking in corporate, not individualistic, terms.

Turn the Other Cheek

When we are cursed, we bless; when we are persecuted, we endure it.
1 Cor. 4:12, NIV.

How should Christians relate to injustice? If God gets irate over the injustice in our world—especially among His own people—and judges it, shouldn't we who bear His image behave in the same manner? Should we merely roll over and play dead in the face of unfairness?

Jesus seems to have argued that we should turn the other cheek when we're treated unjustly (Matt. 5:39). And Paul in today's passage indicated that the apostles didn't curse when they were cursed but instead blessed! He later scolded the Corinthian Christians for taking one another to court, where a heathen judge would give a verdict (1 Cor. 6:1). Yet the Seventh-day Adventist Church maintains a department of attorneys who sometimes initiate lawsuits in our secular court system. What's right to do? What's wrong to do? We can hardly resolve the issues here, but a few comments might add a little perspective.

First, Paul's immediate thought here is about persecution, a problem that early Christians faced from both Jews and Gentiles. When Paul spoke of the apostles' blessing those who cursed them, he put it in the context of persecution, which he said they endured. Numerous passages in the New Testament addressed the matter of persecution and martyrdom. When the Christians suffered persecution, it was a privilege because they were cosufferers with Jesus.

Second, when Jesus spoke about turning the other cheek and going the second mile in the face of unjust treatment, He was addressing individuals. He wasn't urging us to turn a deaf ear and a blind eye to those suffering from unfairness. Rather, He was encouraging personal endurance and patience in the face of unrighteousness.

Third, Scripture urges us to care for the marginalized and underprivileged among us—by ourselves. We (not someone else) should feed the hungry and clothe the naked.

Fourth, we have the example of Paul, who (1) cited his rights as a Roman citizen in order to avoid being flogged and (2) later exercised his rights as a Roman by appealing to Caesar for a fair hearing.

On the one hand, we should try to discern between good, better, and best behavior. On the other hand, we can fall back on divine forgiveness should we not live up to God's will.

Washed, Sanctified, Justified

October 1

1 Corinthians

You were washed, you were sanctified, you were justified.
1 Cor. 6:11, RSV.

Paul, in explaining their new status in Christ, brought up the Corinthian Christians' past lives. They'd previously not behaved in what most would consider an exemplary manner. They'd been "immoral . . . idolaters . . . adulterers . . . sexual perverts . . . thieves . . . greedy . . . drunkards . . . revilers . . . [and] robbers" (1 Cor. 6:9, 10, RSV). Something had made a difference in the way they lived, and Paul specified what had effected that change. Three "things" had revolutionized those Corinthians, and Paul lists them in our passage for today.

But wait! Sounds like Paul was a bit confused. Popular theology would have him rearrange his list of events to (1) you were (in the past) washed, (2) you were (in the past) justified, and (3) you are (in the process of) being sanctified. But not only is Paul's list of verbs in incorrect chronological order, but also the tense is wrong. He should have used two past tense verbs and one present tense verb. Instead, though, he used the past tense for all the verbs in our passage.

Paul's word order and choice of the past tense aren't wrongheaded. He was using three metaphors to describe the same life-changing experience. Additionally, the verbs he chose are correctives for three metaphors of the human condition.

Washed—Sin has made us unclean—polluted. Paul used a ceremonial metaphor. Isaiah said that even our best is like filthy rags (Isa. 64:6), which in Hebrew meant a used sanitary napkin—a source of ceremonial defilement. The antidote for spiritual uncleanness was washing. It was a past experience, having occurred at conversion.

Sanctified—Sin has made us unholy. The metaphor comes from the cultus, or domain, of the sanctuary/temple. The antidote is to be set apart by God for His use and to have His presence with us, both of which make us holy. It was a past experience, having occurred at conversion.

Justified—Sin has made us scofflaws and illegal aliens. The metaphor comes from the realm of jurisprudence. The antidote for this condition is that God, Lawgiver and Judge, has given us legal standing by proclaiming that we are not guilty. It was a past experience, having occurred at conversion.

Each metaphor of God's saving work—"in the name of the Lord Jesus Christ and in the Spirit of our God" (1 Cor. 6:11, RSV)—matches the human predicament.

277

The Temple of God, 2

*Do you not know that your body is the temple of
the Holy Spirit who is in you, whom you have from
God, and you are not your own? For you were bought
at a price. Therefore glorify God with your body.*
1 Cor. 6:19, 20, NET.

I n chapter 3 Paul used the metaphor of the temple to illuminate the status
of the Christian church, especially the community of believers in Corinth.
Now in chapter 6 he presses the same metaphor into service again but with
a different referent.

Gnostic thought, which had infiltrated Judaism as well as paganism, had
made inroads into Christianity. One of its chief emphases was knowledge—
something that was especially important to salvation. It might be fair to say
that in Gnostic thought knowledge had replaced faith as the condition for receiving salvation. ("Gnostic" comes from the Greek word *gnōsis*, which means
knowledge.)

One tidbit of knowledge emphasized was that material things are not
only inferior to spiritual things but are also inherently evil. Matter, of course,
is concentrated in the body, and so it followed logically that the body is likewise evil. Such a perspective could entail one of two opposite lifestyles. On
the one hand, because the body is evil, it should be spurned, treated badly,
beaten into submission. This could lead to various forms of asceticism. On
the other hand, because the body is evil, it won't be saved, and so anything
done in and to the body has nothing to do with salvation. This could lead to
various forms of licentiousness.

It appears that some Corinthian Christians had decided that it was im-
material how they lived in the body. Some seemed to have concluded that
prostitution was acceptable, and one member had had an affair with his
father's wife. Paul countered, however, that immorality isn't appropriate behavior for Christians. Why? Because their bodies are temples—temples of the
Holy Spirit. Immorality, then, is a sin against one's own body (1 Cor. 6:18),
which "is the temple of the Holy Spirit who is in you. . . . Therefore glorify
God with your body" (verses 19, 20, NET).

We Adventists have appropriated Paul's argument against immorality
and used it as a rationale for healthful living. Although that may not have
been what Paul had in mind, it's true to his line of reasoning. If the Holy
Spirit indwells Christians, then their bodies function as temples for God's
Spirit and should be treated with the care that temples warrant.

Marriage

The wife gives authority over her body to her husband, and the husband also gives authority over his body to his wife.
1 Cor. 7:4, NLT.

Several concerns formed the basis for Paul's comments in 1 Corinthians about marriage.

Gnosticism—Gnostics viewed matter as evil and spirit as good. Consequently they deemed the material part of humanity (the body) as evil, a prison for the spirit. Asceticism thus became the enlightened way to live, because it beat down the evil material body, helping emancipate the good spirit. It logically followed that marriage (a code word for intercourse) was spiritually deficient—no, evil. Paul countered that marriage wasn't evil and was so appropriate that divorce among Christians was banned.

Eschatology—The first Christians expected Jesus to return momentarily because He Himself had assured His disciples that their generation would be alive to see His return (Matt. 24:34). The concept of Jesus' immediate return permeates the New Testament. Paul argued that in light of the imminent Second Coming, the unmarried state was appropriate so that people would have no diversion of interest and energy as they served the Lord.

Concupiscence—Because libido exerts compelling power over our lives (our sexuality colors who we are and what we do), it can take considerable energy to repress or redirect the force of the libido unless we have the "gift" to do so. Marriage provides the moral release valve. So despite the nearness of the end, Paul felt that marriage was an appropriate lifestyle—good, although not the better or the best.

Parity—Paul and the Corinthians lived in a patriarchal culture. Male chauvinism suffused the ancient Near East. Hints of this crop up in Paul's discussions. Even today similar conditions mark the existence of many women in the world. Nonetheless, Paul was also ahead of his time in some respects. Our passage for today reveals the equality Paul envisioned between husband and wife. "It is often overlooked that the same privileges Paul gives to the man, he gives to the woman" (W. Larry Richards, *The Abundant Life Bible Amplifier: 1 Corinthians*, p. 119).

Regardless of one's circumstances—single, married, divorced—Paul's ethic focused on the other rather than on the self. "Don't think only of your own good. Think of other Christians and what is best for them" (1 Cor. 10:24, NLT).

The Committed Chameleon

Though I was not a slave to any human being, I put myself in slavery to all people, to win as many as I could. 1 Cor. 9:19, New Jerusalem.

Myth has it that chameleons change their skin color (brown, green, blue, yellow, red, black, or white) as a method of camouflage so that they'll blend in with their surroundings. Fact is that chameleons can modify their skin coloration, but not for the purpose of hiding. Rather, they change color in order to communicate messages, such as "I'm ready to mate," "I feel at peace," "I'm furious," or "I'm scared."

It's true, however, that octopi and cuttlefish can indeed change their skin color so that they look like their immediate environment and therefore escape detection. Their ability to change skin color is a form of deception, although it can also involve communication.

Paul felt that in order to communicate the good news of salvation in Jesus Christ he needed to be chameleonlike. "To the Jews I made myself as a Jew, to win the Jews; to those under the Law as one under the Law (though I am not), in order to win those under the Law; to those outside the Law as one outside the Law, though I am not outside the Law but under Christ's law, to win those outside the Law. To the weak, I made myself weak, to win the weak" (1 Cor. 9:20-22, New Jerusalem).

Was Paul wishy-washy? indecisive? spineless? Hardly. He wanted nothing to interfere with his ability to communicate, because the message that he wanted to share was of crucial significance. "I accommodated myself to people in all kinds of different situations, so that by all possible means I might bring some to salvation. All this I do for the sake of the gospel, that I may share its benefits with others" (verses 22, 23, New Jerusalem). He was a committed chameleon!

In our outreach endeavors as "missionaries," it's easy to want to impose our lifestyle onto others. Or we may preach the gospel in terms that may be quite opaque to our audience. A non-Adventist researcher in Salt Lake City recently told me about a Revelation Seminar he attended. The presenter's messages were quite out of sync with the worldview espoused by the Mormons he wished to reach. There was little connection between communicator and communicatees.

If we wish for others to hear us and respond positively, we need to be committed chameleons, as Paul was.

Spiritual Gifts

*Concerning spiritual gifts . . . I do not
want you to be uninformed.*
1 Cor. 12:1, NRSV.

Paul didn't want the Corinthian believers to be "uninformed" about spiritual gifts. (The word he used—*agnoeō*—lies behind our word "agnostic." It means lacking knowledge.) If he were alive today, Paul would undoubtedly say the same thing to all Christians. Yet some of the ideas we hear about spiritual gifts seem to reflect more ignorance (well-meaning though it may be) than knowledge. Perhaps we should remind ourselves of a few facts.

God is the source of the gifts—The ascended Jesus, according to Ephesians 4:7ff., bestowed these gifts. The channel for these gifts is the Holy Spirit (1 Cor. 12:4), which is, of course, why we call them *"spiritual* gifts."

Spiritual gifts appeared at a point in time—If these gifts had their beginning at Jesus' ascension, then they were not bestowed prior to the Christian Era. They're for the church.

Spiritual gifts are supernatural—If these gifts are of divine origin, they are for believers only and are *not* the same as those natural talents that have a genetic basis and can be improved by diligent effort. Having the "knack" to do something isn't a spiritual gift.

Paul's list of gifts includes: ability to heal (verses 9 and 28), performance of miracles (verse 10; cf. "deeds of power," verse 28, NRSV), prophesying (verse 10), discerning spirits (verse 10), speaking in tongues or glossolalia (verses 10 and 28), interpreting tongues (verse 10), and apostleship (verse 28). None of these gifts are of natural origin. So we should understand the remaining gifts to likewise be supernatural: wisdom (verse 8); knowledge (verse 8); faith—different from saving faith, which God gives to all (verse 9); teaching (verse 28); forms of assistance (verse 28); and forms of leadership (verse 28).

Spiritual gifts have one purpose—God provides them to build up not one's ego but the church. "To each is given the manifestation of the Spirit for the common good" (verse 7, NRSV). Once again Paul emphasizes the importance of the church and its unity.

Spiritual gifts are individualistic—The gifts are many, and no one has all of them. "All these are activated by one and the same Spirit, who allots to each one individually just as the Spirit chooses" (verse 11, NRSV).

If we keep these points in mind, we won't be ignorant about spiritual gifts.

Love Is . . .

Love suffers long and is kind; love does not envy;
love does not parade itself, is not puffed up.
1 Cor. 13:4, NKJV.

Margaret Walker said: "Love stretches your heart and makes you big inside." Do you agree? In the Talmud it is written: "Where love is, no room is too small." What do you think? According to Howard Thurman: "Love has no awareness of merit or demerit; it has no scale." Do you agree? Karen Sunde observed: "To love is to receive a glimpse of heaven." What do you think?

Enough of what you think or others think about love. In 1 Corinthians 13 we learn what Paul thought about love, and he wrote a masterpiece. He'd been addressing the matter of spiritual gifts—the facility to heal, to perform miracles, to speak in tongues, to prophesy . . . Wonderful, supernatural gifts that God gave to build up the church! Yet Paul insisted that as breathtaking as spiritual gifts are, something trumps every one of them. Love.

On the negative side, Paul explained what love does not do or is not. It isn't enviously resentful, doesn't toot its own horn, doesn't have an overly inflated sense of self, doesn't engage in odious behavior, doesn't fixate on self, isn't petulant and exacerbating, isn't quickly angered, doesn't tot up that which is bad, doesn't revel over injustice, and never forsakes or gives up. On the positive side, love suffers on and on and on, is tolerant, rejoices with truth, glosses over and/or endures everything and everyone, trusts everything and everyone, has high hopes for everything and everyone, and bears up under everything and everyone.

We sometimes assume that love comes naturally because it's inherent in the human psyche. Yet when we read Paul's description of what love does and doesn't do, what it is and isn't, such love strikes us as quite unnatural and difficult to come by.

Suddenly it dawns on us that when we juxtapose Paul's song of love with John's insistence that "God is love" (1 John 4:8), 1 Corinthians describes God—who He is and what He does. And Karen Sunde's observation that "to love is to receive a glimpse of heaven" is truer than we initially thought. God, who is love through and through, can work a miracle in our own lives so that we too can be loving and lovable—the greatest argument for Christianity (Ellen G. White, *The Ministry of Healing*, p. 470).

The Resurrection

It will happen in a moment, in the blinking of an eye,
when the last trumpet is blown. For when the trumpet
sounds, the Christians who have died will be raised
with transformed bodies. And then we who are living
will be transformed so that we will never die.
1 Cor. 15:52, NLT.

October 7
1 Corinthians

As a result of the Gnostic philosophy spread by missionaries, some Christians in Corinth concluded that there was no such thing as a resurrection of the body. The body was inferior and evil, made by the inferior deity called Demiurge. Thus, there was no justification for its resurrection. When it decayed, that was that. If there was any such thing as life after death, it was the ongoing existence of the spirit, which was eternal and made by the eternal God. Upon death it would escape from the body and join the other freed spirits in the heavens.

Paul had a spate of arguments and explanations that he threw at them to counter their misguided theology—anthropology, actually. First, the foremost part of the gospel that he'd proclaimed to them and that they'd accepted (1 Cor. 15:1) was that Jesus had been crucified, buried, and resurrected. This same resurrected Jesus had been seen by the twelve, 500 others at one time, James and the apostles, and Paul himself. "If there is no resurrection of the dead, then Christ has not been raised either" (verse 13, NLT). Second, if Jesus still lay in Joseph's tomb, then Paul's preaching was useless (verse 14). Third, if Jesus was still decomposing, then their hope of salvation was also useless, and their sins were unforgiven (verses 14, 17). Fourth, those Christians (in Corinth) who were deceased had perished (verse 18). Fifth, just as death and burial came by one man (the first Adam), so life and resurrection came by one Man (the Second Adam). Sixth, God was subjecting everything to Jesus, and the last entity He'd put under Jesus' feet was death (verses 26, 27). Seventh, their enigmatic practice of baptizing "those who are dead" (verse 29, NLT) made no sense if there were no resurrection. Eighth, would I keep putting my life on the line were there no resurrection (verse 32)? Ninth, Jesus is the firstfruits of those resurrected (verses 20, 23). Tenth, don't be so literal, thinking that same weak, corruptible body will come to life in the resurrection.

Resurrection may be enigmatic, Paul reasoned, but think about planting a seed. The "dead" seed hardly resembles the living plant that rises from the ground. So in the resurrection we'll all have bodies—not like those buried, but transformed and glorious bodies.

The Father of . . .

*Blessed be the God and Father of our Lord Jesus Christ,
the Father of mercies and God of all comfort.*
2 Cor. 1:3, NKJV.

Usually when we think of explaining who or what God is, we talk of His attributes, especially concentrating on omnipotence, omniscience, omnipresence, eternity, immutability, immortality, etc. We argue that any being without these characteristics cannot be divine.

The difficulty with such reckoning is that it fails to recognize that deities were and are worshipped without such qualities. Most of the gods of the world religions lack such attributes as omnipotence, omniscience, omnipresence, immortality, etc., yet were still regarded as gods. So the reasoning we typically use is flawed because it is circular. It assumes the conclusion from the outset by setting up a "definition" of deity based solely on the Judeo-Christian's God.

Paul takes a slightly different tack. He tells the Corinthian Christians three important things about the God whom they worshipped.

Father of our Lord Jesus Christ—The first identifying mark Paul singles out is that the One they worship is the Father of Jesus Christ, their Lord. Although Paul's writings include some hints about the divine nature of Jesus, he consistently refers to the Father as "God" and to Jesus as "Lord." At this early stage Christology was in the making. After all, it was a big step for Christians with a Jewish background to think about three persons in the Godhead. Nonetheless, the being whom they worshipped was a specific person—the Father of Jesus Christ.

Father of mercies—We tend to take the word "mercy" for granted when speaking of God, but not all deities were regarded as having this trait. The word Paul used can also be translated as "compassion" or "pity." In the Hebrew Scriptures God is almost always the one described as having compassion. However, this trait should also be manifested by Christians (Col. 3:12). God deals with us mercifully, and it's our privilege to show mercy toward others.

God of all comfort—The word Paul used for "comfort" refers to God's being by our side when we need Him. Additionally, the Holy Spirit is the one whom the New Testament calls by a noun form of the same root word. Sometimes during trying times we speak of God's silence, but silent or not, He hovers near us.

This Pauline snapshot reveals a God who cares . . . deeply. Now, that's good news!

God's Down Payment

Who also sealed us and gave us the Spirit
in our hearts as a down payment.
2 Cor. 1:22, NET.

Those of us not in the Pentecostal tradition generally don't make a big thing of the Holy Spirit. It isn't that we don't believe in the Spirit. We do. However, we feel a bit uneasy when talk turns to receiving the baptism of the Spirit.

Pastor Jerry and I were visiting people who had shown even a modicum of interest in Adventism. One of these persons was a middle-aged woman. She invited us into her home, and we quickly learned that she belonged to a Pentecostal church. We had a pleasant visit, and it was clear that this woman loved the Lord. Before we left, I made the mistake of saying, "Let's pray." This was a cue for her that all three of us were to pray aloud . . . together . . . at the same time. She prayed in a loud voice that Jerry and I would be baptized with the Spirit, and to myself I was praying, "Lord, no! Don't let it happen!" I'm not quite sure what I feared, but I guess I didn't want to fall prey to some sort of emotional experience for which I'd become embarrassed.

In Acts we read about a dozen Ephesians who hadn't yet received the Spirit. When Paul asked, they responded, "We have not even heard that there is a Holy Spirit" (Acts 19:2, NET). Paul rebaptized them, and "when [he] placed his hands on them, the Holy Spirit came upon them" (verse 6, NET). In the early church the reception of the Holy Spirit ("baptism of the Spirit") was the sine qua non of church membership (Acts 1:5; 11:16).

According to our Scripture passage for today, God established and anointed the early believers in Christ. Notice that God was the active agent who accomplished His work of establishing and anointing by means of Christ, who is the liaison between God and us. But the early Christians had a hope that embraced more than their day-to-day living here on Planet Earth. They had a firmly based hope in the Second Coming. Even more than hoping to see Jesus, they also had the hope of the final consummation of God's kingdom. They were already citizens of this kingdom, but they also felt convicted that they'd be part of the future revelation of that kingdom.

Their confidence was firm because God had given the Holy Spirit as the down payment, the earnest money assuring that the rest that He had promised would follow in due course.

We Become Like What We Behold

All of us, with unveiled faces, seeing the glory of the Lord as though reflected in a mirror, are being transformed into the same.
2 Cor. 3:18, NRSV.

Nathaniel Hawthorne wrote a short story titled "The Great Stone Face." He told about a visage that nature created by chance from rocks on a perpendicular mountainside. When observed from just the right perspective, the rocks formed the shape of a man's head. Legend had it that one day someone looking just like the old stone face would be discovered in that northern New England town.

In the valley lived little Ernest, who spent most of his spare time sitting on the porch of his modest home and gazing upward at the Great Stone Face. His mother had told him about the "prophecy" that one day a man would appear "with exactly such a face as that."

During Ernest's lifetime, on occasion someone would parade through town who supposedly resembled the Great Stone Face—Mr. Gathergold, Old Blood-and-Thunder, and Old Stony Phiz. But despite their superficial resemblance to the Great Stone Face, their characters didn't match the expectations.

Years later Ernest, the person who'd spent his life at the base of the Great Stone Face contemplating it, was the man who in looks and character truly did resemble the Old Stone Face. A visiting poet noticed the similarity and shouted to a crowd of bystanders, "Behold! Behold! Ernest is himself the likeness of the Great Stone Face!"

"Then all the people looked, and saw that what the deep-sighted poet said was true. The prophecy was fulfilled."

Paul related a similar story. He told the Corinthian Christians about Moses at Mount Sinai who had to veil his face after having received the Ten Commandments from God so that he could communicate with the Israelites, who themselves had a veiled heart. Then Paul said that all veils had been removed for those who had accepted Jesus as Savior and had become members of the new covenant. Furthermore, the Christians "with unveiled faces" were now viewing "the glory of the Lord" and, miracle of miracles, were "being transformed into the same."

It's our Christian privilege to contemplate the Lord—as Ernest had meditated on the Great Stone Face. And by so doing, we will be transformed into His likeness—as Ernest had been.

Charitable Giving

I don't mean you should give so much that you suffer from having too little. I only mean that there should be some equality. Right now you have plenty and can help them. Then at some other time they can share with you when you need it. In this way, everyone's needs will be met. 2 Cor. 8:13, 14, NLT.

Between A.D. 46 and 48 a famine devastated Jerusalem. It was so destructive that Queen Helena of Adiabene (Adiabene was a small independent kingdom in Mesopotamia), a relatively recent convert to Judaism, had sent emergency rations of grain and figs to Jerusalem. It may be that some of the church members in Jerusalem were suffering the aftereffects of this famine. Or it's possible that some early church members had become destitute because family had abandoned them when they'd converted to Christianity.

James, Peter, and John, leaders in Jerusalem, had earlier given Paul their blessing on his work among the Gentiles as long as he (and the Gentile converts) remembered to help the poor. Paul agreed and later affirmed, "I have certainly been eager to do that" (Gal. 2:10, NLT). So when Paul encouraged the Corinthian Christians to donate, he was simply upholding his end of the negotiations.

What's difficult when it comes to charitable gifts is knowing not only how much to donate but also how to give in such a way that the contribution will provide the most benefit. For example, 2.7 billion people live in poverty, which means they subsist on the equivalent of $2 or less per day. Should the two billionaire friends Bill Gates and Warren Buffett pool their billions and then divide the money ($108 billion) equally among poverty-stricken people, all would receive just $40 apiece—enough to keep them going for another 20 days. Hardly making a dent in poverty! Clearly, good stewardship entails ensuring that donations will have a significant impact. And what would happen if Gates and Buffett did give all their money to the poor? Wouldn't that add two more people to the poverty list?

Paul's perspective was clearheaded. While it's important that we be generous, we should give from our surplus and not put ourselves into dire financial straits similar to those of the people we wish to help. The goal Paul aimed for was a modicum of equality. "In this way, everyone's needs will be met."

Happy Givers

God loves a cheerful giver.
2 Cor. 9:7, RSV.

Money is money. What difference does my mood make when, for example, I toss some coins into the Salvation Army's red kettle outside the local Walmart? Does my contribution do less good if I'm grouchy when I write out a check for tithes and offerings?

True, money is money. Donations will buy the same amount of food or clothing regardless of whether we're grateful or complaining when we give. The end recipient won't know the difference. Right? Wrong. "As you did it to one of the least of these my brethren, you did it to me" (Matt. 25:40, RSV). God notices how we give—our motives, our attitudes.

The fact is that two distinct people can benefit from charitable gifts— the donor and the donee. When we give "reluctantly or under compulsion" (2 Cor. 19:7, RSV), we miss the subjective blessing, because "God loves a cheerful giver." The Greek word translated "cheerful" is the root from which we get our word "hilarious." Now, the word in Paul's day didn't have the same connotation as it does today—boisterously funny. He wasn't talking about people rolling in the aisles at church during the offering! Nevertheless, he was talking about people who gave in high spirits. What would it be like if collecting the offering was the most gleeful time of every church service?

Paul said something similar to the Christians in Rome when he spoke of him "who does acts of mercy, with cheerfulness" (Rom. 12:8, RSV). However, he included some additional elements to the act of giving by also referring to "he who contributes, in liberality; he who gives aid, with zeal" (verse 8, RSV). Liberality (sincerity with singleness of purpose), zeal (eagerly, with diligence), as well as joyfulness should mark Christian donations.

Paul didn't isolate the emotional aspects of giving, however. He also spoke of the cerebral side. "Each one must do as he has made up his mind" (2 Cor. 9:7, RSV). Meaningful giving involves both the mental and the sentimental faculties. Good stewardship doesn't mean spur-of-the-moment giving because we've been moved by some tear-jerking story. It means that we give thoughtfully—planning ahead. "Each of you is to put something aside and store it up, as he may prosper, so that contributions need not be made when I come" (1 Cor. 16:2, RSV).

God values sane and heartfelt giving, which can spring only from love.

Jesus' Fiancée

*You are like a fresh unspoiled girl whom I am presenting
as fiancée to your only husband, Christ himself.*
2 Cor. 11:2, Phillips.

Paul uses another striking metaphor, one we'd probably not be bold enough
to have coined ourselves. However, the figure of speech that there's a people who are God's fiancée, or wife, extends throughout Scripture.

In Isaiah 54:5 we read: "Your Creator is your husband, Yahweh Sabaoth is
his name" (New Jerusalem). And later: "Like a young man marrying a virgin,
your rebuilder will wed you, and as the bridegroom rejoices in his bride, so
will your God rejoice in you" (Isa. 62:5, New Jerusalem). Hosea's actual marriage to Gomer served as a metaphor for God's relationship to His people. "I
shall betroth you to myself for ever, I shall betroth you in uprightness and justice, and faithful love and tenderness. Yes, I shall betroth you to myself in loyalty and in the knowledge of Yahweh" (Hosea 2:21, 22, New Jerusalem).

Perhaps the most shocking use of the metaphor, though, comes to us
from Ezekiel, who uses the same marriage metaphor but in the context of incest between a father and his nubile daughter. God had adopted the child
when she'd been cast off at birth. But when she'd become a teenager, God
saw her and took her as his wife, "and you became mine," He said (Eze. 16:8,
New Jerusalem).

Paul picked up the metaphor and told the Corinthian Christians that like
a doting and proud father he was caring for them as for a betrothed daughter. During the yearlong betrothal, it was the father's responsibility to preserve the chastity of his betrothed daughter. At the end of the 12-month
duration he'd transfer the hand of the girl to the husband during a home-
taking ceremony, at which time the groom would discover the purity of his
bride. That's how seriously Paul took his responsibilities as the one who had
introduced the Corinthians to Christianity.

From another perspective the metaphor reveals how important the
church, with its individual Christians, is to Jesus. He views us as His chosen
bride, whom He will love and cherish. It's the groom's (hence Christ's) responsibility to maintain the well-being of His spouse, spelled out by the
Torah as "food, clothing [and] conjugal rights" (Ex. 21:10, New Jerusalem).

Scripture provides us with yet another lovely picture of God, our Creator
and Spouse.

Know Thyself

Examine yourselves to see whether you are in the faith; test yourselves.
2 Cor. 13:5, NIV.

The adage "Know thyself" was engraved in the forecourt of Apollo's temple at Delphi. It was Apollo's primary command. We don't know who originally coined the expression, and the original source has been given as Heraclitus, Chilon of Sparta, Thales of Miletus, Socrates, Pythagoras, or Solon of Athens.

Whoever came up with the advice was certainly a wise person, and most of us would agree with the sentiment that we should know ourselves. However, as Benjamin Franklin pointed out in his 1750 *Poor Richard's Almanack*, "There are three things extremely hard: steel, a diamond, and to know one's self."

Paul didn't give his advice to the Corinthian Christians with the thought in mind that they should know themselves inside out. He wasn't talking about personality or character or anatomy. He was talking about spiritual condition. It's easy for those with high spiritual ideals to be judgmental of others. Paul, though, was always a bit cautious when it came to judging others. He preferred leaving such judgment in God's hands.

Nevertheless, he felt that it was entirely appropriate (maybe even necessary) for each Christian (at least at Corinth) to scrutinize himself or herself—pretty much in the footsteps of the Greek thinker who came up with "Know thyself."

In today's passage, Paul used two verbs for the activity of Christian introspection. The first is *peirazō*. It referred to the process of testing something—tempting someone, not so they would sin, but so their true condition would become obvious. The second is *dokimázō*. It often was used to refer to the process of smelting silver or gold—to purify it and/or to prove its value. In the present context, both verbs denote pretty much the same thing. The chief outcome for this personal testing and assaying was to prove once and for all whether or not "Christ Jesus is in you" (2 Cor. 13:5, NIV). To fail the self-examination would mean that Jesus wasn't within.

Seventh-day Adventists have believed that since 1844 God has been in the process of judgment—the pre-Advent judgment. Some have become quite concerned and even distraught over what God might discover in the judgment. However, the fear of judgment won't bother any of us if we follow Paul's counsel to the Corinthians—"Examine yourselves . . . ; test yourselves."

All's Well That Ends Well

May the grace of our Lord Jesus Christ, the love of God, and the fellowship of the Holy Spirit be with you all.
2 Cor. 13:13, NLT.

Paul's pattern in writing letters was to begin with a salutation, such as the one he penned at the opening of this letter: "May God our Father and the Lord Jesus Christ give you his grace and peace" (2 Cor. 1:2, NLT). He also typically ended them with a benediction, as here: "May the grace of our Lord Jesus Christ, the love of God, and the fellowship of the Holy Spirit be with you all." Most of Paul's benedictions are short, but our text for today exceeds his others in length and includes three distinct and important elements.

The *grace* of our Lord Jesus Christ—The word "grace" was one of Paul's favorite terms. He used it nearly 100 times, which is more than two thirds of its occurrence in the New Testament. We sometimes blur the concept of grace with that of mercy, and it's true that the two ideas aren't opposed to each other. The other day at church the "Wit and Wisdom" feature was: "Mercy—When you don't get what you deserve. Grace—When you get what you don't deserve." Grace describes an attitude of generosity that is freely bestowed without regard to merit. Paul here speaks of Jesus' attitude of grace.

The *love* of God—As children, we all learned to sing "Jesus Loves Me," but as adults we sometimes forget that other gospel song, "The Love of God." We need to remember that the Bible refers to love as God's primary attribute: "God is love" and "God so loved the world . . ." We sometimes unconsciously assume that God got mad at us and was out to get us and Jesus stepped in between and saved the day . . . for us. That couldn't be further from the truth. Jesus didn't initiate the plan of salvation; God did. God "gave his only begotten Son" and "was in Christ, reconciling the world unto himself."

The *fellowship* of the Holy Spirit—The Greek noun behind the word "fellowship" is *koinōnía*, a word that came into vogue among Christian churches several decades ago. In classical Greek it referred to business partnerships. Later it came to mean any kind of close, sharing relationship, including close, personal companionship with one's spouse. The New Testament speaks of having such fellowship with God, Christ, and here with the Holy Spirit.

Clearly all heaven is engaged not only in saving us but in maintaining that condition.

Good News Turned Bad

*I solemnly assure you that the Good News
of salvation which I preach is not based
on mere human reasoning or logic.*
Gal. 1:11, NLT.

We sometimes refer to the "purity" of the early Christian church and talk about returning to "primitive Christianity," which serves as an ideal to be recovered, analogous to returning to the Edenic state. The fact is, though, that doctrinal aberration had infiltrated the early church.

Why did Paul write so many letters? Did he pine for pen pals? Hardly. He needed to address issues fracturing the church. As we saw, among the Corinthian Christians an early form of Gnosticism (or its precursor) had taken root. Additionally, those Christians had formed at least four distinct factions—those of Paul, those of Apollos, those of Cephas, and those of Christ.

Here in Galatians, we learn that another theological deviation was creeping in. This heterodoxy, though, sounded more "orthodox" than that in Corinth. The teachers from Jerusalem convinced some of the Galatians that the route to salvation involved becoming a Jew first. Once the Galatian Gentiles became circumcised and observed the time-honored religious festivals of Judaism, their commitment to Jesus Christ would carry them onward to salvation.

Paul himself would later admit that salvation was for the Jew first (Rom. 1:16), and Jesus had said something similar in John 4:22. Jesus also stated that God had sent Him to only the lost sheep of the house of Israel—Jews (Matt. 15:24)—and when He sent out the twelve as missionaries, He instructed them to confine their efforts to the same group (Matt. 10:6).

The church "pillars" in Jerusalem (James, Peter, and John) had agreed that Paul and Barnabas could preach the gospel (good news) to the Gentiles while they concentrated their efforts among Jews (Gal. 2:7-9). So it was that Paul had found many Galatians who gladly accepted the good news he proclaimed. They'd been baptized and formed the core of a community of Christian believers. They'd been enslaved to sin—lost, alienated from God— but had found reconciliation and freedom in Jesus, who had died on the cross . . . for them.

However, the "good news" that the teachers from Jerusalem had preached in Galatia—scrupulous observance of the law—was "another gospel," though not really (Gal. 1:6). It was "not based on mere human reasoning or logic" (verse 11, NLT). That "gospel" merely reinstated their slavery to the Law—pretty much the same as slavery to sin.

At the Cross or on the Cross?

I have been crucified with Christ.
Gal. 2:20, NASB.

I saac Watts wrote: "At the cross, at the cross where I first saw the light, and the burden of my heart rolled away." Two hundred fifteen years later Robert Harkness wrote a less-familiar song: "I met Jesus at the foot of the cross. . . . All my sins were washed away. . . . I found pardon at the foot of the cross." Both songs express noble sentiments. But . . .

From the Gospel records we can safely conclude that many people were there at the cross—at its foot: jeering priests, hardened soldiers, two bandits, curious crowds, a handful of Jesus' friends and relatives. Being there had little inherent meaning. Most probably received no benefit other than to fear and hate the Romans even more than they already did.

Paul agreed that something significant had taken place at Calvary. However, he didn't speak about being at the cross or at its foot. He declared that he had "been crucified with Christ." For him it wasn't a matter of being *at* the cross; it was a matter of being *on* it . . . with Jesus. Paul of course was speaking, not literally, but metaphorically. He wasn't physically present. Nevertheless, he could speak of being on the cross with Jesus.

Peter, who'd been visiting Antioch, had been happily taking his meals with the Gentile Christians there, but suddenly changed tactics when others from the Jerusalem church showed up. Suddenly Peter was eating with the Jewish Christians—at a separate table. Paul, who also was there in Antioch, scolded Peter for being so wishy-washy. It was this anecdotal experience that Paul used to remind the Galatians that in Christ there was no distinction between Jew and Gentile. All had been enslaved to sin (Gal. 2:17), but Jesus had ended that enslavement.

Christians should regard themselves as having been crucified *with* Christ— *on* the cross with Him, thereby dying to the Law. Through this solidarity with Jesus, they became justified not by works of the Law but by Jesus' faithfulness (verse 16). That's what Paul meant when he asserted he'd been crucified *with* Jesus. But he'd also been resurrected *with* Jesus. So "it is no longer I who live, but Christ lives in me; and the life which I now live in the flesh I live by faith in the Son of God, who loved me, and delivered Himself up for me" (verse 20, NASB).

Keep On Keeping On

*Are you so foolish? Having begun in the Spirit,
are you now being made perfect by the flesh?
Gal. 3:3, NKJV.*

The Galatian Christians had been baptized, becoming members of His church, and their decision for Christ had brought consequences. Life had become difficult. Paul said they had "suffered . . . many things" (Gal. 3:4, NKJV). No, it wasn't that their houses had burned down or that they'd contracted a horrible disease or that an earthquake had caused them loss.

Throughout the New Testament we meet the verb commonly translated "suffer" (as here) and the noun for "suffering." The verb appears nearly 50 times, and all but a handful of those times it refers to Jesus' crucifixion or the harassment Christians endured. The noun is used almost 20 times, and all but twice refers to Jesus' death or the persecution experienced by Christians. Just fewer than 10 percent of the uses denote either physical illness or emotional distress. Accepting Christ's name brought suffering—persecution. At first the persecution came from fellow Jews (remember how Saul had hunted down Christians with a view to exterminate them?) or from heathen neighbors or family. Later the Roman government sporadically persecuted Christians.

For most people today—at least in Western society—joining a Christian church involves no persecution. Occasionally new Adventists might lose their jobs because they can't work on Friday evening or during Saturday. But even then they often take recourse to the law (remember how Paul appealed to Caesar?) and win the lawsuit, because in nations such as America religious discrimination is illegal. In the States the employer bears the burden of proof that granting an exemption to working on Saturday would result in an excessive hardship on the business.

Despite the persecution that ensued, the Galatians had become Christians, and the results weren't all bad. Yes, on the one hand they'd encountered persecution, but on the other hand God had worked powerful miracles among them (verse 5). They had accepted *by faith* Jesus' sacrifice in their behalf. They had become justified in the Spirit—*by faith*. They hadn't become Jews first. Paul hadn't urged them to keep the law. He hadn't told the men to become circumcised. He hadn't instructed them to observe the Jewish festivals.

Although I've heard some Adventist preachers say it, we aren't justified by faith and sanctified (growth in grace) by works. All aspects of salvation are all of faith.

Adopted

*God sent [His Son] to buy freedom for us
who were slaves to the law, so that he could
adopt us as his very own children.
Gal. 4:5, NLT.*

What did Alexander the Great, Art Linkletter, Bill Clinton, Edgar Allan Poe, John James Audubon, Faith Hill, Gerald Ford, Lee Majors, Marcus Aurelius, and George Washington Carver have in common? All were adopted.

The practice of adoption is very old; the oldest laws regulating it come from Hammurabi's Code (c. 1750 B.C.). In ancient Mesopotamia, Egypt, and Greece, adoption usually entailed adults adopting adults into the family. During the Middle Ages the adoption of children came into vogue, although there were more ancient instances in which a child was adopted. In the ancient Near East adoption took place for various reasons but occurred most often (1) so that childless parents would have someone to care for them in their old age, (2) so that a childless parent could pass on the secrets of a skilled craft, (3) so that the family name could be perpetuated, or (4) so that real estate (and other assets) could be kept within the family. It wasn't uncommon for masters to adopt a slave as their heir, which meant that the slaves thus adopted gained their freedom. When land in Nuzi (an ancient Mesopotamian city near what is now Kirkuk, Iraq) was sold, the transaction involved a legal fiction of adoption in which the purchaser was adopted by the seller, who "gave" the land to his new child, who in turn presented his new parent with a "gift."

Among the ancient Jews adoption doesn't appear to have been commonly practiced. Esther had been adopted by her uncle. In Jeremiah 3:19 God speaks of adopting Israel. A document from Elephantine (in Egypt) records that a Jewish master manumitted and adopted his Jewish slave. Probably one could say that Joseph of Nazareth adopted Jesus, son of Mary.

Paul used the metaphor five times—in Romans, Galatians, and Ephesians—for those who become Christians. God—once again the active agent in rectifying the sin crisis—sent His Son to be born as all humans are in order to save us, we who are slaves to sin. Through this redemption process He emancipates us, making us His children—Jesus' brothers and sisters. As a result, we're now children of God and siblings of Jesus, who is "heir of all things" (Heb. 1:2). Thus, "everything [God] has belongs to [us]" (Gal. 4:7, NLT). We now have a place in the family picture of God.

Fruit Bearing

The fruit of the Spirit is love, joy, peace, patience, kindness, generosity, faithfulness, gentleness, and self-control.
Gal. 5:22, 23, NRSV.

We're all familiar with this passage of Scripture. Perhaps we memorized it as children. However, we may have overlooked (or forgotten) two significant aspects of these two verses.

First, Paul speaks of the fruit of the Spirit in the context of how Christians should behave. We "were called to freedom" (Gal. 5:13, NRSV). But Christian freedom isn't freedom for self-indulgence. Indulging the flesh isn't freedom but slavery. This newfound freedom means that we're not law-bound to a plethora of commandments but keep just "a single commandment, 'You shall love your neighbor as yourself'" (verse 14, NRSV).

While we were slaves to sin, we performed the "works of the flesh," which include "fornication [sexual license], impurity, licentiousness [wantonness], idolatry, sorcery, enmities [hostilities], strife [wrangling], jealousy, anger [blowing one's top], quarrels [selfish ambition], dissensions [taking sides in partisanship], factions [heresies], envy [feelings of ill will], drunkenness, carousing, and things like these" (verses 19-21, NRSV). Paul was convinced that "those who do such things will not inherit the kingdom of God" (verse 21, NRSV).

As works that slaves perform, such behaviors—contrary to the expression of doing what comes naturally—are hard. At least the results of such difficult works take a terrible toll on the human body and psyche.

Second, Paul speaks of the *fruit* [singular] of the Spirit. There are not many varieties of fruits of the Spirit among which we can choose as our tastes dictate. No, there's just one fruit that manifests itself in various attributes. In fact, the Greek allows the following alternative punctuation. "The fruit of the Spirit is love: joy, peace . . ." Either way, the life of freedom in the Spirit is marked by "love, joy, peace [internal security and tranquillity], patience, kindness [moral goodness], generosity, faithfulness, gentleness [leniency and clemency], and self-control [self-mastery]."

As fruit, which springs spontaneously from a healthy tree, this lifestyle should come naturally to Christians, and it will if the Holy Spirit is at work in our lives. We can safely say that this cluster of the fruit of the Spirit is equivalent to godliness.

He Ain't Heavy;
He's M' Brother

Bear ye one another's burdens.
Gal. 6:2.

Roe Fulkerson, author and editor, happened upon "a spindly and physically weak lad" who held a baby in his arms as he stumbled toward a playground. Fulkerson commented to the lad, "Pretty big load for such a small kid." But the youngster responded, "Why, mister, he ain't heavy; he's my brother." Fulkerson reported the episode in the September 1924 edition of *Kiwanis Magazine.*

Seventeen years later Catholic priest Edward J. Flanagan, founder of what is now known as Boys Town, noticed in the Christmas edition of the *Louis Allis Messenger* a picture of a similar lad carrying his younger brother. Titled "Two Brothers," the caption for the illustration read: "He ain't heavy, Mister—he's m' brother." Later it appeared in an *Ideals* magazine.

Because the picture and caption summed up the work done at Boys Town, Flanagan asked permission to colorize the picture and modify the caption to "He ain't heavy, Father . . . he's m' brother." From then on, the expression has served as the motto of Boys Town, headquartered in Omaha, Nebraska. The organization commissioned Enzo Plazzotta in 1977 to sculpt a six-foot modern rendering of the two boys. The Mariani foundry in Italy made bronze castings of it. Three of the statues adorn the campus of Boys Town and another the Boys Town National Research Hospital.

Paul, concerned about practical Christianity, urged the Galatians to care for one another.

"Bear . . ."—The word itself refers to taking into one's hands—lifting up—something that is heavy. Paul used the present tense, which urges that we keep on lifting up. He envisioned not a one-time lending a hand but a consistent practice of helping others.

"Burdens . . ."—The root for Paul's word is the same one behind our "barometer," an instrument that measures air pressure. Paul's term refers to a hardship that's especially difficult.

It's appropriate for us to help anyone struggling under any heavy burden—physical, mental, emotional, or spiritual. However, the context gives Paul's command special color. He's talking particularly about how we should deal with "a man . . . overtaken in a fault," whom we should "restore" (verse 1). In fact, restoration—mending broken lives—should be our specialty.

God's Seal

*You have been stamped with the seal
of the Holy Spirit of the Promise.
Eph. 1:13, New Jerusalem.*

For thousands of years before Paul wrote to the Christians at Ephesus, ancient Near Easterners had used seals. Seals came in two formats: signet rings, which could be worn on the finger or on a string around the neck, and cylinder seals, which typically had a hole drilled lengthwise through them so that they could be hung around the neck. Signet seals were pressed into clay, whereas cylinder seals were rolled across the clay.

Archaeologists have found thousands of seals. The average seal was made from a semiprecious gem (early ones were crafted from clay or bone) and was engraved backward so that the impression would read properly. Because they were small, seals couldn't contain a lot of information—usually just the person's name and position and sometimes a small picture or icon. For example, a seal from Old Testament times says "Jaazaniah servant of the king." And a jasper seal says "Shema servant of Jeroboam." An amethyst seal reads "Abijah servant of Uzziah." Another says "Belonging to Abijah (son of) Jeroboam."

Seals functioned as a surrogate of the person whose name they bore. They attested to ownership and also guaranteed authenticity. Scripture identifies several metaphorical seals: one's lover (S. of Sol. 8:6), circumcision (Rom. 4:11), and converts to Christianity (1 Cor. 9:2). Then in our passage for today Paul identifies the seal as the Holy Spirit.

In each of these metaphorical usages the "seal" involved demonstrated ownership and authenticity—the seal of circumcision signified that Abraham belonged to God, the lover as a seal on the beloved's arm indicated that the lover was the real thing and belonged to the other lover, and the Corinthian Christians served as the proof of Paul's apostleship.

Similarly, when God gave Christians the Holy Spirit—an experience that was identical with becoming a believer in Jesus Christ—as a seal in their lives, it demonstrated their genuineness as those who belonged to God. Christians were *His* people.

Many people throughout the history of Christianity have undergone baptism, but not all have been genuine Christians. It isn't enough to look like a Christian or even to talk like a Christian. There's such a thing as a false believer. However, the Holy Spirit at work in the life proves the genuineness of one's religion.

Saved by Grace

For by grace you are saved.
Eph. 2:8, NET.

October 23
Ephesians

E very Adventist surely knows this biblical passage. Grace is a key word in Christian theology, and we've heard references to it in many sermons. Did you know that the Greeks spoke about the three Graces, daughters of Zeus? The Greek poet Hesiod, who lived around 700 B.C., gave their names as Aglaea (goddess of brightness), Euphrosyne (goddess of joy and mirth), and Thalia (goddess of banquets). These three goddesses personified grace, beauty, and charm.

In fact, there was an ancient sculpture known as *The Three Graces.* It depicted the three goddesses, dancing hand-in-hand in a circle. Of this piece of art, Seneca, a Roman philosopher, wrote: "Why do the sisters hand in hand dance in a ring which returns upon itself? For the reason that a benefit passing in its course from hand to hand returns nevertheless to the giver; the beauty of the whole is destroyed if the course is anywhere broken, and it has most beauty if it is continuous and maintains an uninterrupted succession. . . . Their faces are cheerful, as are ordinarily the faces of those who bestow or receive benefits. They are young because the memory of benefits ought not to grow old. They are maidens because benefits are pure and undefiled and holy in the eyes of all; . . . [their robes] are transparent because benefits desire to be seen" (*De beneficiis* 1. 3. 2-5).

The Greek word *cháris*, which is most often translated "grace," had multiple meanings. It described (1) the attitude of the giver, (2) the gift itself, and (3) the attitude of the receiver. As Sophocles, Greek priest and playwright (c. 496–406 B.C.), put it: "Favor [*charis*] is always giving birth to favor [*charin*]" (*Ajax* 522).

According to Paul here in Ephesians, salvation is the benefit of grace—God's grace, of course. Grace is the divine mind-set springing from deep within God's character. But it's more than that. It also describes the gift of salvation that God freely bestows. We lay hold of God's gift "through faith," but faith doesn't produce salvation. Salvation "is the gift of God" (Eph. 2:8, NET). Additionally, grace refers to the attitude we manifest as the recipients of God's gift.

Because of the various nuances of grace, the squabble over law versus grace and works versus faith is fundamentally flawed. These terms are not really antonyms, though they may be paradoxical. Grace is the appropriate word for all aspects of salvation.

Then but Now

*At that time you were separate from Christ,
excluded from citizenship in Israel and foreigners
to the covenants of the promise, without hope
and without God in the world.
Eph. 2:12, NIV.*

The Ephesian Christians exemplified a before-and-after experience.
First, Paul pointed out their "then" experience—their condition *before* conversion.

They had been "separate from Christ." This, of course, is the condition of all before conversion. But there was more.

They had been "excluded from citizenship in Israel." Enmity marked the relationships between Jews and Gentiles. The Jews, as happens with many societies, considered themselves "the people" who lived in "the land." And they made the Gentiles to understand that all Gentiles were people without a country—undocumented aliens.

They had been "foreigners to the covenants of the promise." Because the Gentiles couldn't trace their ancestry back to Abraham or to Mount Sinai, they couldn't benefit from the covenant promises.

They had been "without hope." As a result, the Gentiles were hopeless—by birth. After all, salvation was of the Jews.

They had been "without God." It wasn't that Gentiles had no gods. They did. But they worshipped idols—ungods.

Second, Paul pointed out their "now" experience—their condition *after* conversion.

They had been "brought near through the blood of Christ" (Eph. 2:13, NIV). Their marginalization was past. They had "access to the Father by one Spirit" (verse 18, NIV).

They had become "fellow citizens with God's people" (verse 19, NIV). God's kingdom now included them.

Jesus had "preached peace to you who were far away and peace to those who were near" (verse 17, NIV). Jews and Gentiles had become one in Jesus Christ. No more enmity!

Jewish and Gentile Christians had been incorporated into "a dwelling in which God lives by his Spirit" (verse 22, NIV). No longer were they without God. They were all part of God's living temple.

And this transformation had taken place because of God's gracious benevolence.

Spiritual Growth

*We must grow up in every way into him
who is the head, into Christ.
Eph. 4:15, NRSV.*

In our readings for September 27 and October 1 it may have bothered some to read that sanctification is a past experience that occurred at conversion. However, that affirmation is based on such Bible verses as: "You were sanctified [aorist, or past, tense]" (1 Cor. 6:11, NRSV); "the inheritance among all who are sanctified [the perfect tense used here means that the act of sanctification took place in the past but has continuing efficacy]" (Acts 20:32, NRSV; see also Acts 26:18); "sanctified by the Holy Spirit [perfect tense]" (Rom. 15:16, NRSV); "those who are sanctified in Christ Jesus [perfect tense]" (1 Cor. 1:2, NRSV); "by God's will . . . we have been sanctified [perfect tense]" (Heb. 10:10, NRSV); "by which they were sanctified [aorist, or past, tense]" (verse 29, NRSV); and "those who are . . . sanctified by God the Father [perfect tense]" (Jude 1, NKJV).

Yet we all have heard preachers insist again and again that (1) justification is a *past* experience—a once-and-for-all event, (2) sanctification is a *present* experience—an ongoing occurrence, and (3) glorification is a *future* experience—another once-and-for-all event. Now, systematic theologians from various denominations have emphasized that salvation has three tenses—past justification, present sanctification, and future glorification. But the fact is that the New Testament authors more often than not refer to both justification and sanctification with the past or perfect tenses and not the present tense. Because of this fact, Adventist Bible scholar Arnold Wallenkampf in one of his books spoke in terms of *"theological* sanctification" (an ongoing present experience) and *"biblical* sanctification" (a one-time past event).

What Wallenkampf referred to as "theological sanctification" is also called "growing in grace." Now, *that* is a good biblical metaphor for the Christian's *present* ongoing experience. We come across this metaphor of growth not only in our passage for today but also in 2 Corinthians 10:15; Ephesians 2:21; Colossians 1:10 and 2:19; 1 Peter 2:2; and 2 Peter 3:18.

Whether the concept of growth is a biological or architectural metaphor, the truth of the analogy is that the Christian life (or the church, for that matter) isn't static. Greek philosophers such as Aristotle may have thought that perfection entailed being static, never changing. But we understand today that *becoming*—rather than *being*—connotes perfection.

Live Like a New Person

You were taught . . . to become a new person.
That new person is made to be like God—
made to be truly good and holy.
Eph. 4:24, NCV.

I f anyone has any doubts about the efficacy of Christianity, they need to take a long, hard look at the life of a truly converted Christian. Indeed, if Christianity doesn't make a difference in those who claim the name of Christ, then their religious experience—despite being called Christianity—is a charade.

In Ephesians 2 Paul spoke of the before-and-after experience of the Ephesian believers. But he couched the discussion in *sociological* terms as he wrote about them being marginalized—outside of Christ and outside the covenants made with Abraham and at Mount Sinai. They'd been without hope and without the Jewish God. As important as that metamorphosis had been, Paul couldn't let the matter drop without addressing the *ethical* differences that conversion makes in the life. And he broaches the topic in chapter 4.

By becoming one with Christ, each Ephesian believer had become "a new person." Through the salvation bestowed by their generous God, Christians are "made to be like God." Now, we mustn't misunderstand. The Bible doesn't teach that we're naturally divine. Neither does it teach that someday humanity and divinity will be blended into a harmonious whole—with no distinction between us. God will always remain God, and human beings will always remain human beings—albeit with glorious resurrection bodies.

However, God does intend to restore the divine image that we all bear—despite the blurring of that image as a result of sin. That's what it means to be "like God." Paul even clarified things for us: we're "to be truly good and holy." That means we're to lead moral lives.

Need more clarification? Paul provides it. "You must stop telling lies" (Eph. 4:25, NCV). "When you are angry, do not sin" (verse 26, NCV). "Stop stealing and start working" (verse 28, NCV). "Do not say harmful things" (verse 29, NCV). "Do not be bitter" (verse 31, NCV). "Never shout angrily or say things to hurt others" (verse 31, NCV). "Never do anything evil" (verse 31, NCV). Oh, want some positives? OK. "Be kind and loving . . . , and forgive each other" (verse 32, NCV).

If as new persons we live like that, then truly our religion *does* make a difference.

Model Marriage

Submit to one another.
Eph. 5:21, NLT.

In most of the ancient Near East, if a woman wasn't under the thumb of her father, she was under the heel of her husband. In the Roman culture an infant girl didn't receive a name of her own but went by a feminized form of her father's name—her father was her identity. Women were typically viewed as good for one thing—childbearing, which often ended in death. The father told his daughters whom they would marry and whether or not their marriage should be dissolved. Women were deemed to be inferior to men.

But scattered here and there were outbursts of feminism. In 195 B.C. a group of women marched into the forum and insisted that the Oppian Law, which made it illegal for them to purchase luxury items, be repealed. The male lawmakers grumbled but ultimately repealed the laws. In 42 B.C. the triumvirate enacted a law to tax 1,400 of the richest women. (Yes, some women managed to get wealthy.) The women rallied around Hortensia, who was one of their own, and barged into the forum, where the triumvirs unsuccessfully tried to oust them. Hortensia gave an impassioned speech—something that had never occurred before in the forum. As a result, 1,000 women gained an exemption.

It was in this cultural context that Paul offered marital advice to the Ephesian Christians. He counseled a moderate mutuality by urging, "Submit to one another." "You wives will submit to your husbands" (Eph. 5:22, NLT), and "You husbands must love your wives" (verse 25, NLT). This model of marriage was quite a revolutionary idea—especially for the men. "Husbands ought to love their wives as they love their own bodies. For a man is actually loving himself when he loves his wife" (verse 28, NLT).

Paul's counsel involved another sort of model. Marriage with mutuality modeled Christ's relationship with the church. Christ may have been the head of the church (verses 23, 24), but this relationship was based on love (verse 29), which sacrifices self (verse 25). Because marriage means becoming "one flesh," it entails mutual care on the part of both partners.

Mutual love characterizes Christ and the church. It also should characterize husband and wife. Understand Christ's relationship with the church and subsequently understand marital life. Understand marital life and consequently understand Christ's relationship with the church.

Armored and Armed

Take up the full armor of God.
Eph. 6:13, NASB.

Roman soldiers, decked out in their battle array, were a common sight in Paul's day.

Girdle—Roman soldiers had three different kinds of belts (*cinctura*): (1) a leatherlike garment that covered the lower abdomen, (2) a buckled belt to which the sword was attached, and (3) a sash identifying officer rank. Whichever of the three Paul had in mind, he said that it stood for truth— veracity, honesty, integrity.

Breastplate—This was the cuirass (*lorica*). At this time it would have been either a metal breastplate or the more costly chain or link mail that protected both chest and hips. Paul compared it to righteousness—the gift of salvation, which makes us right before God.

Footwear—Many soldiers in the ancient Near East fought barefoot, but Roman soldiers generally wore a half boot (*caliga*). Made of leather, these clod-hoppers had a studded sole. They provided surefootedness during the 20-plus miles soldiers marched in a day. They also made for a solid foothold in combat. Paul referred to the Christian's army boots as the "gospel of peace."

Shield—Legionnaires used several kinds of shields. Paul spoke of the *thyreós*, which was a large implement shaped like a door. It was constructed from iron, wood, and multiple plies of leather, which was soaked in water prior to battle to put out any flaming arrows and spears from the enemy. Paul identified the shield as faith—trust and faithfulness.

Helmet—The headgear worn by Roman soldiers was constructed from leather or metal. It weighed a lot and was richly decorated and costly. Paul compared it with salvation.

Sword—Romans used two kinds of swords—a short one (*machaira*) and a long one (*rhomphaiâ*). Paul here spoke of the former, which was easier to use in close combat. He likened it to God's Word, which the Spirit provides.

Most Roman soldiers had to buy their own armor and arms. But Paul spoke about the "armor of God." He meant not the armor God wore but rather the armor (and arms) He provided. Unlike the Roman legionnaires, Christians fought in a great cosmic conflict involving "not . . . flesh and blood, but . . . the spiritual forces of wickedness in the heavenly places" (Eph. 6:12, NASB).

Preserved

I am confident of this, that the one who began a good work among you will bring it to completion by the day of Jesus Christ.
Phil. 1:6, NRSV.

From time to time someone illustrates the relationship of faith and works with the metaphor of a rowboat. In order to reach the other shore we must use both oars equally—the oar of faith and the oar of works. The illustration highlights the importance of both faith and works. Unfortunately, the metaphor has two significant flaws.

First, it gives equal consequence to both faith and works: Both must be used with equal force in order to keep from going in circles. The New Testament, while encouraging good works, gives primacy to faith. And the Christian writers make it clear that works of any kind (Paul often uses the terminology "works of the law") express gratitude for salvation but do not generate it.

Second, the imagery portrays both faith and works as of human origin: We sit in the rowboat and ply the oars of faith and works with our own muscles. The New Testament, however, makes it clear that both faith and works are of divine origin. We all have a "measure of faith that God has assigned" (Rom. 12:3, NRSV). Our "good works . . . God prepared beforehand to be our way of life" (Eph. 2:10, NRSV).

It's clear that Paul would not find the metaphor of a rowboat helpful; in his epistles he repudiated the idea of works—good works, adherence to the law—supplementing faith. He had harsh words for those teachers who tried to convince new Gentile Christians that having begun the Christian life with faith they needed to complete their spiritual odyssey by keeping the law—celebrating the traditional Jewish religious holidays and becoming circumcised. There's a name for this aberration of theology and lifestyle that Paul countered: legalism. It's nothing to be proud of, although many years ago I heard a General Conference speaker assert at camp meeting, "I'm a legalist and proud of it!"

Yes, Paul would find the rowboat illustration repulsive. He scolded the Galatian Christians: "Are you so foolish? Having started with the Spirit, are you now ending with the flesh?" (Gal. 3:3, NRSV). And read again his words in today's passage: "I am confident of this, that the one who began a good work among you will bring it to completion by the day of Jesus Christ." All aspects of salvation are all of faith. God does the saving; we do the thanking.

Wiser and Wiser

I pray that your love for each other will overflow more and more, and that you will keep on growing in your knowledge and understanding.
Phil. 1:9, NLT.

Paul often assured his readers that he'd been praying for them, what we call intercessory prayer. It's a good habit to cultivate—praying for others. Too much of the time we pray for ourselves, which isn't necessarily bad but can be regarded as pretty egocentric because self is the center of concern. Here in our passage for today, Paul tells the Christians at Philippi that he prays for them, using the present tense, which meant that his praying for them was something he did all the time. It can be translated as "I keep on praying . . ."

What did Paul pray for?

Love—He wanted their love (*agapē*) to overflow. Because God is love—His fundamental attribute—and because He created humans in His image, it stands to reason that our characters should likewise have love as the basic trait. But Paul didn't want them to have just a small amount of love. He prayed for their love to "overflow." The word he used describes quantity—a measure that far exceeded the norm and so was an unexpectedly generous amount. Furthermore, he wanted this overflowing to continue on and on (present tense). And if that weren't enough, Paul added the words "more and more." He wanted the Christians at Philippi to have a never-ending supply of love.

Knowledge—Paul wanted them also to have knowledge and used an intensive form of the typical Greek word for knowledge. Theologians have long debated how much knowledge Christians should have, and in a religious setting the knowledge refers not to secular data—trivia—but to saving knowledge based on careful thought.

Understanding—Finally, Paul kept praying that the Philippians would have all understanding. He used a word that referred to perception that experience had sharpened. It was insight—horse sense. Once again, he didn't want them to have a modicum of insight. He prayed that they'd have all the various kinds of practical insight available.

In the context of Paul's sentence, it's possible that knowledge and understanding are like the banks of a river that would channel their abundant love. In other words, he wanted their limitless love to be channeled.

A Matter of Perspective

Consider others better than yourselves.
Phil. 2:3, NIV.

Although in Paul's epistles theological matters occupied his mind, he typically ended his messages with what academics call "paraenesis." (Biblical scholars use a special vocabulary that they understand but that puzzles the rest of us.) Paraenesis transliterates a Greek word meaning "counsel" or "advice." In other words, after explaining how Christians should think, he elucidated how Christians should behave. Proper theology should lead to proper actions. Indeed, a Christianity that influences how one thinks but has no impact on how one lives is worthless.

In our passage for today Paul urged that the Philippian believers embrace a particular perspective as they looked around them at others sitting in church. Jesus Himself had talked about a proud Pharisee who prayed "about himself" when he boasted, "I am not like other men" and seeing a publican added, "or even like this tax collector" (Luke 18:11, NIV). Paul here urged the opposite attitude. Instead of belittling others, we should prize them and praise them.

Paul recommended a perspective that regards others as more important than oneself—a noble goal that is difficult to attain. Nevertheless, John the Baptist and Jesus manifested this perspective. John said that he wasn't worthy to untie Jesus' sandals (Mark 1:7), and Jesus said that no one was greater than John (Matt. 11:11).

What did Paul think that admiring other Christians meant? He explained—just in case the believers at Philippi would misunderstand.

They should "do nothing out of selfish ambition or vain conceit" (Phil. 2:3, NIV). The term translated "selfish ambition" came to describe the behavior of people running for office—rivalry. Those who behaved this way asked, "What's in it for me?" The word for "vain conceit" meant literally "empty glory"—hollow honor. Honor kept society glued together in the ancient Near East, but when it had no basis it meant nothing.

When the Christians at Philippi complied with Paul's instruction to "consider others better than yourselves," they had to do so sincerely, or as Paul put it, "in humility," using a word that meant lowly or lowdown—a condition not considered enviable outside of the church. However, Christianity transformed the word into a desirable mind-set.

Jesus' Mind-set

*Your attitude should be the same that Christ Jesus had.
Phil. 2:5, NLT.*

Paul urged the Philippian believers to "be humble, thinking of others as better than yourself" (Phil. 2:3, NLT). But he wanted to illustrate further the kind of attitude that they should cultivate. So he told them that their mind-set should emulate that of Jesus. To get his point across, Paul cited an early Christian hymn—perhaps one that the new church in Philippi sang on many Sabbaths.

"Though he was God, he did not demand and cling to his rights as God. He made himself nothing; he took the humble position of a slave and appeared in human form. And in human form he obediently humbled himself even further by dying a criminal's death on a cross. Because of this, God raised him up to the heights of heaven and gave him a name that is above every other name, so that at the name of Jesus every knee will bow, in heaven and on earth and under the earth, and every tongue will confess that Jesus Christ is Lord, to the glory of God the Father" (verses 6-11, NLT).

This early hymn encapsulated themes Christians have tried to unpack ever since. It referred to Jesus' preexistence, incarnation, crucifixion, ascension, and glorification. It raised issues about what both the preincarnate Christ and the incarnate Jesus were like. We won't crack these theological chestnuts here—space won't allow it, even if we could! You see, hymns don't provide good mining for theological gems. They exemplify affective language, which shares and evokes emotion. We shouldn't confuse lyrics with cognitive communication, which shares theoretical constructs, or with informative speech, which presents empirical data.

The wording of the hymn Paul cited sings about Jesus' self-effacing attitude. Despite His ascribed honor as a divine person, Jesus willingly set aside that honor of endowed privilege and traded it for the shame entailed with becoming a human servant, and worse, one who'd been hung on a cross—a poignant picture of God. It is *this* mind-set that Paul urged Christians to embrace—self-effacing love. We sing about it even today: "Be like Jesus, this my song, in the home and in the throng; be like Jesus, all day long! I would be like Jesus" (James Rowe).

For a while the expression WWJD was popular—**W**hat **W**ould **J**esus **D**o? That's a good question. We may never be able to emulate Jesus' mind-set fully, but we can strive to do so.

Imperfectly Perfect

Not as though I had already attained, either were already perfect. . . . Let us therefore, as many as be perfect, be thus minded. Phil. 3:12-15.

November 2
Philippians

If you've been an Adventist for many years, you know that the topic of perfection—namely, sinless perfection—has been a hot-potato issue decade after decade.

"Historic" Adventists typically argue that perfection—sinless perfection—is not only a goal to strive toward but an attainable possibility now. One such individual announced, "I haven't sinned for years." Other Adventists cannot accept the concept of perfection—sinless perfection. They say that they've watched the mischief such a theology has produced—a focus on self that leads to either hubris or hopelessness.

Closely tied to the two theologies is an understanding of the nature of Jesus Christ, the Incarnate One. On the one hand, those who agree with the doctrine of sinless perfection view Jesus as our perfect Example, who upon His incarnation took the postlapsarian nature of Adam—the nature Adam had *after* the Fall. We can follow in His steps. On the other hand, those who disagree with the doctrine of sinless perfection view Jesus as our perfect Savior, who upon His incarnation took the prelapsarian nature of Adam—the nature Adam had *before* the Fall. His perfection substitutes for our imperfection.

Recognizing the need for spokespersons on either side of the issue to make their position clear, in 1975 Southern Publishing Association released a book titled *Perfection: The Impossible Possibility*, which presented thoughtful chapters written by four veteran theologians—two on either side of the subject.

The issue, though, isn't so much perfection itself. Both sides actually believe in Christian perfection. The divide comes over the matter of sinlessness. Can Christians attain a sinless state here and now, or does that experience occur only in the future—from glorification on?

Strange as it may seem, Paul avows both the unfeasibility and feasibility of perfection. In practically a single breath, he wrote to the Philippian believers that he didn't regard himself as already perfect (Phil. 3:12; see also 1 Cor. 13:10; Heb. 11:40), but then shortly spoke of Christians, including himself, as being perfect (Phil. 3:15; see also 1 Cor. 2:6; 2 Cor. 13:11). Might the solution to the paradox be this: We are perfect . . . *in Christ Jesus* (Col. 1:28)?

What to Think

Finally, brethren, whatever things are true, whatever things are noble, whatever things are just, whatever things are pure, whatever things are lovely, whatever things are of good report, if there is any virtue and if there is anything praiseworthy—meditate on these things.
Phil. 4:8, NKJV.

We've all heard someone say, "I just don't know what to think." The speaker felt in a quandary about something. Probably all of us have felt the same way at one time or another. But when it came to lifestyle, Paul told the Philippian recipients of his letter what to think.

That which is *true*—Paul used an adjective that described something real, something authentic, that comports well with reality. He wasn't implying that fiction is unacceptable to Christians. Good fiction, although an imaginary story, gives insight into reality.

That which is *noble*—This adjective referred to that which has dignity. It denoted a quality of life that evoked awe and respect from others. In secular Greek the term was used of people, especially older ones, who were levelheaded and stable in character. Excellence marked their lives. They were serious but not eccentric.

That which is *just*—Paul used another adjective in common use among the pagans. It denoted the quality of conforming to society's norms—that which was widely regarded as equitable and fair. It described being both law-abiding toward others and pious toward God. It also had overtones of integrity.

That which is *pure*—This term meant clean—not so much physically as morally. It referred to freedom from defilement and could be translated "chaste," "modest," or "sincere."

That which is *lovely*—The word Paul chose has the idea of that which caused people to be pleased. Negatively, it referred to that which is not repulsive. Positively, it referred to that which is alluring—in the good sense of the term.

That which is of *good report*—Some things merit disapproval because they're so disgustingly abhorrent, but this adjective described that which was meritorious—deserving of praise. The noun form could be translated as "that which people [should] admire or applaud."

In summary, Paul wrote, the mind can safely dwell on anything morally excellent and attractive (last part of Phil. 4:8).

Change of Citizenship

He . . . has rescued us from the ruling force of darkness and transferred us to the kingdom of the Son . . . , and in him we enjoy our freedom, the forgiveness of sin.
Col. 1:13, 14, New Jerusalem.

When a king in the ancient Near East invaded another land and con-quered it, he often would relocate the conquered peoples to another part of his empire. Despite the inconvenience and hardship (on the part of both the conqueror and the conquered) of such a practice, it served to help the defeated keep in mind their new citizenship. For instance, when King Tiglath-pileser III subjected various areas in Palestine, he moved large per-centages of the subjugated population to Mesopotamia, which he also did when he subdued the northern kingdom of Israel. Later King Nebuchadnezzar followed the same practice when he conquered Jerusalem, exiling large numbers of Judahites to Babylon (including Daniel).

Paul, perhaps borrowing a figure of speech from the Essenes at Qumran, who owned the Dead Sea scrolls, talked about the "ruling force" of darkness. Among the Jews, darkness was an analogy used to describe the condition of those enslaved to the powers of evil. In contrast to the evil realm of darkness, there was the kingdom of light—the kingdom of righteousness ruled by the righteous God Himself.

According to Paul, God had rescued the Christians at Colossae from "the ruling force of darkness." The Greek verb he chose to use, *rhýomai*, referred to dragging someone from danger. The connotation included the idea that (1) the danger was dire and that (2) the snatching of the victim was to one-self. Paul added the preposition meaning "out of." In other words, God had dragged the Christians out of the domain of darkness, drawing them to Himself. God had moved them into the kingdom of His dear Son, Jesus Christ—the kingdom of light.

They now had a different citizenship. Jesus Christ now ruled over them, and as their monarch, He had provided them with a new status. They now enjoyed "freedom" because He'd ransomed them from slavery. And this new liberation entailed "the forgiveness of sin." In secular Greek the word trans-lated "forgiveness" had many nuances, but in the New Testament it always refers to the act of overlooking and/or pardoning sin(s). And although Paul doesn't specifically say so, it's fair to assume that all Christians—including us—have received the same benefits.

Christ's Identity

He is the image of the invisible God, the first-born
of all creation; for in him all things were created,
in heaven and on earth, visible and invisible . . .
—all things were created through him and for him.
Col. 1:15, 16, RSV.

As in Philippians, so here Paul cites a Christian hymn (verses 15-20). Its lyrics overflow with emotional tags that point to Christ's identity.

"Image of the invisible God"—We've used as a theme in this book the metaphor of a photo album—of God. However, God Himself can't be photographed . . . because He's invisible. Although we find word pictures of God in the Old Testament, the clearest snapshot of God is Jesus Christ, who made the invisible God visible.

"First-born of all Creation"—The hymn used a term that emphasized the superiority and primacy of a person. The preincarnate Christ was not part of creation but prior to it.

"In him all things were created"—The preincarnate Christ could be called "firstborn" because He was God's agent for creation. Since "he is before all things" (verse 17, RSV), "all things were created through him and for him" (verse 16, RSV).

"In him all things hold together"—According to the lyrics, Christ not only made everything but also sustains it all. The perfect tense used here means that the preincarnate Christ at a past point in time brought the cosmos into being and continues to keep it in existence. Being the Creator wasn't sufficient; He's also the Sustainer.

"The head of the body, the church"—The hymn continued in verse 18 (RSV) to extol Christ's primacy by describing His relationship to another "thing" He created and sustains—the church.

"The first-born from the dead"—Because of the Resurrection, Jesus is the "first-born" (verse 18, RSV) out of the dead. Not only is He the firstborn of creation but also the firstborn of the dead. Oh, prior to Easter Sunday others had been resuscitated, but they faced death again. Not so with Jesus. It is this that gives Him primacy.

"In him all the fulness of God was pleased to dwell"—God indwelt Jesus (verse 19, RSV) with a completeness that distinguished Him from all the rest of us who've become God's children.

The point of the hymn is "that in everything [Christ is] pre-eminent" (verse 18, RSV). Ultimately, though, His supremacy becomes subjected to the Father Himself (1 Cor. 15:28).

Nailed to the Cross

Blotting out the handwriting of ordinances that was against us, which was contrary to us, and took it out of the way, nailing it to his cross. Col. 2:14.

Paul had informed the Christians in Galatia that his goal was to glory in just one thing—the cross of Jesus Christ (Gal. 6:14). And that is precisely what he set out to do in today's passage of Scripture, in which he colorfully described what God did at Calvary.

Paul called the Colossians' attention to "the *handwriting* of *ordinances*." The two words he used identify the object he had in mind. "Handwriting" translates *cheirógraphon*, which is a literal rendering. However, it had a technical meaning. When people borrowed money, they would personally write in their own penmanship an IOU in which they pledged to repay the debt. This document was called *cheirógraphon*. "Ordinances" translates *dógma*. Our word "regulations" is another suitable rendering. Although a general term, Hellenistic Jews used it for God's commandments, the regulations governing proper behavior.

In other words, Paul here indicated that the Old Testament law was the basis for indebtedness—the reason the *cheirógraphon* had been written. Humanity—both Jew and Gentile—had broken the commandments, thereby incurring a debt. (Sin among both Jews and Christians was sometimes spoken of as a debt. "Forgive us our debts . . .")

Having a debt hanging over one's head like the sword of Damocles wasn't pleasant, especially in a society in which most people barely eked out an existence, daily living from hand to mouth. That's why Paul described the IOU as being "against us" and "contrary to us." This documentation of indebtedness was our enemy.

But God, the one to whom we were indebted ("sin against God" [Gen. 39:9; cf. Ps. 41:4; 51:4]), took this *cheirógraphon* and blotted it out (*exaleíphō*). Museums of antiquity have numerous examples of IOUs from this period that were crossed out with a large X, which meant that the debt had either been forgiven or paid in full. This—and more—is what God did to our IOU. Not only did He cross it out, but also He nailed it to Jesus' cross (Paul's pun intended).

Consequently, "let no man . . . judge you" (Col. 2:16). You see, "if God be for us, who can be against us?" (Rom. 8:31).

Here's a picture of God worth treasuring!

Christian Haute Couture

You have stripped off the old self. . . . As God's chosen ones, holy and beloved, clothe yourselves with compassion, kindness, humility, meekness, and patience.
Col. 3:9-12, NRSV.

We often stereotype women as having well-stocked closets. But most men also have multiple changes of clothing. We either don't realize or forget that most ancient Near Easterners had just one set of clothes. Remember God's command? "If you take your neighbor's cloak in pawn, you shall restore it before the sun goes down; for it may be your neighbor's only clothing to use as cover; in what else shall that person sleep?" (Ex. 22:26, 27, NRSV).

Paul used the practice of removing one garment and donning another as a metaphor for the Christians' way of life. Prior to conversion their lifestyle was like an old, soiled garment (cf. Zech. 3:3). At baptism, however, they had "stripped off the old self with its practices" (Col. 3:9, NRSV). (Should we infer from this that early proselytes were baptized naked? Some early Christian documents seem to point in this direction.) From conversion on, however, "as God's chosen ones, holy and beloved, clothe yourselves with . . ." (verse 12, NRSV).

The new garments Christians were to wear consisted of a different fashion from what they'd worn previously. Here's how Paul describes the haute couture of Christians.

"Compassion"—The first item of clothing Paul mentions was *oiktirmós*—a sensitive compassion toward those who are suffering. It implies feeling distress at others' distress and has the connotation of an attitude that turns into action—providing relief.

"Kindness"—The next word, *chrēstótēs*, refers to a gentle disposition that manifests easygoing benevolence.

"Humility"—Christians are also to manifest *tapeinophrosúnē*, meaning a lowly self-opinion because of one's creatureliness and utter dependency.

"Meekness"—The next attitude is *praótēs*. Christians are to have inward calmness and mildness.

"Patience"—Finally, Christians must don *makrothymía*, meaning suffering long—not with their own problems but with others. People with this virtue are slow in reacting to others.

What's significant about this clothing is that Paul's terminology is used of the virtues shown by God and/or Jesus. It is truly haute couture—high style!

The Christian Household

*Wives, submit to your husbands, as is fitting in the Lord.
Col. 3:18, NIV.*

Paul's words here have all too often become the favorite proof text of husbands who strive to bolster their desire to dominate. We might justify such behavior if we ignored Paul's description of Christian behavior in verse 12 of this same chapter—to put on compassion, kindness, humility, meekness, and patience. Furthermore, verse 18 is only the tip of the proverbial iceberg. Paul's instruction to the Colossian Christians didn't single out the women. So we mustn't stop with verse 18. Notice what else Paul said . . . to the entire family.

Wives—"Submit to your husbands." We shouldn't overlook that Paul calls this subjection "fitting in the Lord." Was he implying that all manner of subjugation befitted Christians or that only a certain kind was fitting—the variety that the Lord would approve of?

Husbands—Paul next turned his attention to the dominant husbands: "Love your wives and do not be harsh with them" (verse 19, NIV). Any male dominance must be ameliorated with a love that had no harshness—love that had no bitterness and produced no bitterness.

Children—Paul even included the offspring. "Children, obey your parents in everything, for this pleases the Lord" (verse 20, NIV). In Ephesians 6:1 he restricted similar instruction by adding "in the Lord" (NIV), the same expression he used here as a modifier for the wife's submission.

Fathers—Paul singled out the males again, telling them to "not embitter your children" (verse 21, NIV). He didn't want the younger ones to become discouraged or despondent resulting from parental authority. (The *pater familias* could dole out even capital punishment.)

Slaves—Many households included servants who had been baptized along with the rest of the family. Paul instructed them to "obey your earthly masters in everything . . . with sincerity of heart and reverence for the Lord" (verse 22, NIV).

Masters—For the third time Paul turned his attention to the male, telling him to "provide your slaves with what is right and fair" (Col. 4:1, NIV). The two terms he used meant justice and equality or impartiality. Masters must recognize that they, too, had a Master—Jesus Christ.

Although our society is not patriarchal, the qualities of behavior that Paul prescribed are appropriate for any style of family.

A Triad of Christian Virtues

Remembering before our God and Father
your work of faith and labor of love and
steadfastness of hope in our Lord Jesus Christ.
1 Thess. 1:3, RSV.

Paul's letter to the Christians in Thessalonica is the oldest New Testament book and, of course, the first epistle Paul wrote. He had visited Thessalonica on his second missionary journey. The city had been founded by Cassander, one of Alexander the Great's successors. Paul had wanted to revisit the church he helped establish but wasn't able to. So he sent Timothy, who reported back that the Christians there still supported Paul and generally had remained faithful. Timothy's positive account prompted Paul to write the letter we now call 1 Thessalonians. In his introductory remarks Paul commended three aspects of their life as Christians.

Work of faith—The Thessalonian Christians had been saved through faith—the only way any of us enter the relationship with God that we call salvation. The noun embraces the ideas of trust and fidelity, and we'd be wise not to choose one connotation over the other or to pit one sense against the other. Those who trust in God for salvation in turn are faithful. Although Paul placed strong emphasis upon God's grace and the faith by which we accept His gracious gift of salvation, he never denigrated works as a response of gratitude.

Labor of love—Although faith plays a major part in becoming a Christian, love (*agapē*) plays a key role in our ongoing experience in Christ, who focused God's love for us. The believers in Thessalonica had love as well as faith.

It comes as a bit of a surprise that Paul used a term that we generally regard as a synonym for work—labor. Was he repeating himself? Maybe. However, the word translated "labor" is quite different from the word he used with faith. Paul chose a word that denoted not the physical activity of work but the results of such exertion. In other words, he referred to hard work that leaves the laborer exhausted. Behaving in a loving manner isn't always easy. Indeed, it can sap our physical, mental, and emotional energies.

Steadfastness of hope—Hope is the third trait the Thessalonians revealed. It is future-oriented. Christians not only celebrated the past event of God's salvation but also looked forward to its consummation with the return of Jesus Christ. Their hope didn't founder. It was steadfast—patiently constant.

Imitators

November 10

1 Thessalonians

You became imitators of us and of the Lord, when you received the message with joy that comes from the Holy Spirit, despite great affliction. 1 Thess. 1:6, NET.

For you became imitators . . . of God's churches in Christ Jesus that are in Judea, because you too suffered the same things from your own countrymen as they in fact did from the Jews. 1 Thess. 2:14, NET.

Did you know that in 1960 there were just 216 Elvis imitators? Ten years later that number had increased more than 10 times—to 2,400 registered Elvis imitators. (Yes, they can register!) In 1992 around 14,000 White males had registered. If his imitators continue to burgeon this way, by 2100 an incredible number of the world's population will be Elvis imitators! Having spurned such imitators for years, at the thirtieth anniversary of his death Graceland embraced them.

Paul observed that the Christians at Thessalonica were imitators. No, he didn't accuse them of being imitation Christians—phonies. Instead, he spoke of something admirable.

Imitators of the apostles—The earnestness of the apostles, who spread the good news about Jesus Christ, has probably never been duplicated. Those who had known Jesus personally and had hung on to His every word (including Paul, who, although he hadn't physically roamed Judea with Jesus of Nazareth, had seen the resurrected Lord) received the ultimate honor when Jesus commissioned them to go throughout the entire world to teach and baptize. The Thessalonian converts had become imitators of the apostles in this regard.

Imitators of the Judean churches—Paul praised the Thessalonian believers for becoming imitators of the Judean churches. Why? The Jews who had become Christians suffered much at the hands of their fellow Jews, and for a while Paul himself had spearheaded that persecution. Now the Thessalonian Christians were being persecuted by their neighbors. The New Testament writers consistently viewed persecution for Jesus as highly desirable.

Imitators of Christ—The best model of all to emulate is Jesus Christ. And Paul commended the believers in Thessalonica for their zeal in becoming imitators of Jesus. Paul later encouraged the believers in Philippi to have a mind—attitude—like Jesus' self-effacing behavior.

Are you and I good imitators—of the apostles, of the Judean churches, of Jesus Christ?

Dead, But . . .

*I do not want you to be ignorant . . . concerning
those who have fallen asleep, lest you sorrow
as others who have no hope.*
1 Thess. 4:13, NKJV.

Jesus had indicated during His lifetime that His second coming would be "soon." So Paul, along with the other apostles, clung to that expectation. It should come as no surprise, then, that the Christians at Thessalonica shared the same blessed hope in His imminent return. Then some of the believers died, which caused cognitive dissonance in the minds of those still alive. Paul felt compelled to help them deal with their confusion. Interestingly, his solution—the Second Advent—was what had caused their doctrinal perplexity in the first place!

The Gentile Christians at Thessalonica had once worshipped idols (1 Thess. 1:9). Among the beliefs widespread in Thessalonica was devotion to Fulvus, the son of Marcus Aurelius who had died at the tender age of 4. Subsequently, many believed that the deceased toddler had become a god. Another prevalent belief centered on Cabiros, a prince murdered by his own brothers. After his death he too became a god. So what about the deceased Thessalonian Christians, who hadn't lived to see the imminent return of Jesus? Now what? Would they be ignored at the Second Coming? Had they become gods? What about the survivors themselves? What would happen to them at the Second Coming? What should they think?

Paul's answer was the resurrection of the dead. The decedents were (metaphorically) asleep, so this condition wasn't permanent. Jesus would indeed return—and Paul still anticipated being among those alive when that event took place, hence his terminology "we who are alive and remain until the coming of the Lord" (1 Thess. 4:15, NKJV). He also explained the order of events connected with the Advent: (1) the Lord will return with great fanfare—"with a shout, with the voice of an archangel, and with the trumpet of God" (verse 16, NKJV); (2) "the dead in Christ" (verse 16, NKJV) will have no disadvantage for having died, since those who have remained alive "will by no means precede those who are asleep" (verse 15, NKJV) because the deceased "will rise first" (verse 16, NKJV); only then (3) those alive at the Second Coming will "be caught up together with them" (verse 17, NKJV); and (4) "we shall always be with the Lord" (verse 17, NKJV). So "whether we wake or sleep, we [will] live together with Him" (1 Thess. 5:10, NKJV).

As a result, today we use the word "cemetery," which means sleeping place.

How to Behave . . . Toward Others

Admonish the unruly, encourage the fainthearted, help the weak, be patient with everyone.
1 Thess. 5:14, NASB.

As in his other letters, Paul addressed orthopraxy (proper behavior) as well as orthodoxy (proper doctrine). In today's verse Paul encouraged the Christians in Thessalonica to do four things. Each verb is a present imperative, which indicates a command. Paul was speaking with authority. Also, he used the present tense, and in Greek this means not only something done now (in the present versus in the past or in the future) but also something done again and again and again—habitually, continually. In other words, Paul wasn't talking about behavior that took place once or only now and then. He wanted the church members in Thessalonica to keep on doing these four things.

Admonish the disorderly—Paul used the verb *nouthetéo*, meaning to exhort. It referred to instructing someone—especially those who were in the wrong. And whom should they warn? The "unruly." The noun Paul chose came from a compound root meaning "to break rank"—disorderly military conduct, which came to denote rioters. The people needing the instruction may have been sloppy, but more likely were against organization—against gospel order.

Encourage the fainthearted—Paul next told them to keep on encouraging—*paramythéomai*, which meant to speak soothingly to someone. And whom should they console? The "fainthearted." The noun Paul chose meant "small of spirit" and referred to those who are worried. (The King James Version's "feebleminded" misconstrues the idea Paul had in mind.)

Help the weak—Paul's verb meant to hold on firmly to something. In other words, to prop up. The people needing such support were the "weak." They may have been weak physically, but more likely Paul was thinking of those who are spiritually weak or even emotionally weak. Such people need a lot of shoring up.

Be patient with all—Perhaps Paul's last instruction sums up the others. It's probably the most difficult of all with which to comply. The verb translated "be patient" means to suffer long. The idea is to be constantly understanding and patient with *everyone*—not just one's spouse or children or friends or neighbors . . . but everyone.

These four behaviors characterize God's dealings with us through Jesus Christ.

How to Deal With Prophecy

Do not treat prophecies with contempt. But examine all things; hold fast to what is good. Stay away from every form of evil.
1 Thess. 5:20-22, NET.

From time to time "prophets" appear in the church—the Seventh-day Adventist Church. What are we to make of them? For instance, Margaret Rowen (self-proclaimed successor to Ellen White) predicted that the Second Coming would take place February 6, 1925, but she turned out to be a con artist and involved in a plot to murder one of her former supporters.

In more recent years there have been others: Elijah the Mantonite, an Adventist in Rhode Island's state hospital and member of the Boston Temple, who claimed the prophetic gift and said that when he got to heaven he'd be so close to God you'd be unable to put a piece of paper between them; a lady in Michigan who gained a following of true believers; Prophet Pearl, whose prediction of her tenant's murder failed (fortunately); and the list could go on.

It's tempting, of course, to dismiss these modern claimants to the prophetic gift as crackpots. After all, their behavior and claims can be quite bizarre. But Hosea's, Jeremiah's, and Ezekiel's behavior also appeared quirky—even wacky—at times. Paul, however, admonished the believers in Thessalonica: "Do not extinguish the Spirit. Do not treat prophecies with contempt" (1 Thess. 5:19, 20, NET).

But how do Christians avoid falling for people whose prophetic claims stem from mental or emotional aberrations? Good old common sense can help a lot, of course. But we mustn't be naive. That's why Paul encouraged the Thessalonian Christians to "examine all things" (verse 21, NET). The verb he chose was used for trying out oxen in order to determine their worth and for testing gold and silver by fire to ascertain their quality. Those who performed this appraisal process did so with the intent of demonstrating the genuine value of that which was tested—in this case, prophecy. Such testing had the potential of revealing substandard quality, as well.

Once the assessment process had been completed, the Thessalonians were either to (1) hold on to that which the assaying proved to be genuine or to (2) stay away from anything that seemed to be bad. Some Christians, according to Paul's instruction to the Corinthians, received the spiritual gift of discerning spirits, which made the assaying of prophecy more reliable.

Greetings

Grace to you and peace.
2 Thess. 1:2, New Jerusalem.

How do we know that the New Testament books written by Paul were epistles? Well, how do you know that the content of the envelope you receive from the post office is a letter? You recognize the format. First, it often has a date on it. Second, there's a salutation—"Dear So-and-so." Third, you notice the "body"—the message consisting of (usually) numerous paragraphs. Finally, there's a closing, such as "sincerely" followed by the sender's signature.

These conventions are quite similar to those of Greco-Roman letters. First, there was the *praescriptio*, or salutation, in which the sender sent greetings. Next followed the *formula valetudinis*, in which the sender hoped the recipient was healthy. Third, the *proskynema* assured the recipient of the sender's prayers. Fourth was the body of the epistle. Fifth, there was the *erroso*, or farewell, in which the sender wished for the recipient's prosperity. Finally, the writer added greetings from associates and friends.

The New Testament books bearing Paul's name followed the ancient epistolary format. However, his salutations contained two words, combining both the Gentile and Jewish forms of greeting—but with a twist. The typical Greek salutation was *chaírein*—"greetings" or "rejoice" or "be happy." The apostles and elders in Jerusalem used the same term in their letter explaining the decisions of the Jerusalem Council (Acts 15:23). James, Jesus' brother, later began his epistle with the same word (James 1:1). Such a usage is called phatic language, speech acts so commonplace that they've lost pretty much all significance, becoming just a stereotypical expression. Is the recipient of your letters really a dear—someone near and dear to you? Not necessarily.

Paul, unique person who he was, punned on the hackneyed *chaírein*, the usual salutation, penning instead *cháris*—grace. Furthermore, he doubled the usual salutation by adding the Jewish way of saying it—peace—even when the recipients weren't Jewish. Such phatic speech probably shouldn't be pressed for theological significance. Nevertheless, Paul's theological emphasis on grace undoubtedly lay behind his switching from writing *chaírein* to using a word that sounded rather similar but had a different meaning—*cháris*. For Paul's real theological emphasis, we need to concentrate on his other usages of grace—*cháris*—and there are many.

The Lawless One

Then the man of lawlessness will be revealed, whom the Lord Jesus will consume with the breath of his mouth and destroy by the splendor of his coming. This evil man will come to do the work of Satan with counterfeit power and signs and miracles.
2 Thess. 2:8, 9, NLT.

As we noted in the reading for November 11, the believers in Thessalonica had questions because some of their brothers and sisters in Christ had died. Paul tried to ease their concerns by referring to the doctrine of the resurrection, which would take place at Jesus' appearing. He admonished, "Comfort and encourage each other with these words" (1 Thess. 4:18, NLT).

Apparently his explanation helped, but the Christians in Thessalonica had yet more questions—likely because they had received a letter (maybe with Paul's name on it) asserting that Jesus had already appeared (2 Thess. 2:2). The term in question was *parousia*. It was a common word that referred to the festive arrival of a ruler to a city and his presence for the duration of his stopover there. A *parousia* was a gala occasion accompanied by much pomp and circumstance including banquets, athletic competitions, gifts, and sacrifices. During such an event sculptures were dedicated, edifices erected, coins minted, and prisoners set free. So it's easily understood why New Testament writers used the same word of the Second Advent.

But if Jesus' *parousia* had already taken place, why didn't they know about it? Paul had told them about the joyful shouting, the earsplitting voice of the archangel, and the blast of God's trumpet. He'd talked about the dead in Christ rising from their tombs and together with the living believers meeting the Lord in the air. If all this had happened, where had they been?

Paul assured the believers that Jesus' *parousia* was still future. Before His return the "man of lawlessness" would be revealed. He'd exalt himself as an object of veneration, claiming to be divine. The "man of lawlessness" would perform misleading miracles but would ultimately be destroyed at Jesus' *parousia*, a still future event but near at hand.

Throughout the history of Christianity certain overly zealous persons have distorted the doctrine of the Second Coming. They've either announced that it was now a past event or that it was to take place on a certain date (or year) in the near future. Such individuals have pointed excitedly to the "signs" taking place all around them—and reported in the daily papers, nightly newscasts, and monthly news magazines. They try to whip people into a frenzy. For shame!

No Work, No Food

Anyone who refuses to work should not eat.
2 Thess. 3:10, NCV.

What did Paul admonish—"Anyone who refuses to work should not eat"? Isn't this rather insensitive? What happened to feeding the hungry? Why, this same Paul much later told the Christians in Rome that they should feed even their enemies (Rom. 12:20). What about bearing one another's burdens (Gal. 6:2)? Didn't his mother teach him to share?

It seems that a few brothers and sisters had become fanatical there in Thessalonica.

You've heard about some Millerites who refused to dig up their ripe potatoes in October because they expected Jesus' second coming to take place on October 22. Why harvest the crops when in a few days Jesus would appear and they'd spend eternity with Him?

Apparently something similar was going on in Thessalonica. Some believers had quit working but expected some of their fellow Christians to feed them.

Why had they given up their usual employment? Maybe they felt that because Jesus had inaugurated the long-anticipated "Sabbath rest" they should live in "rest" themselves and so had quit their jobs. After all, if the prophesied Sabbath rest had begun when Jesus had established the kingdom of God on earth, shouldn't they refrain from labor during this end-time Sabbath? Perhaps they felt as did some of the Millerites—there was no need to work, because Jesus had either already appeared or would momentarily. Shouldn't one's lifestyle reflect one's theology?

Now, Paul had earlier agreed enthusiastically with the advice given by the church pillars in Jerusalem that he should convert the Gentiles to Christianity but that they, in turn, should remember their poor (and hungry) Jewish brothers and sisters. However, the situation in Thessalonica was different. Paul himself had set an example during his visit there. "We were not lazy when we were with you. And when we ate another person's food, we always paid for it. We worked very hard night and day" (2 Thess. 3:7, 8, NCV).

Jesus Himself uttered a blessing on those who, at the Second Coming, would be found working (Matt. 24:46). And Paul wrote to the Thessalonians: "We command those people . . . to work quietly and earn their own food" (2 Thess. 3:12, NCV).

How to Relate to Heretics

*If anyone refuses to obey what I have written
in this letter, take note of him and have nothing
to do with him, so that he will be ashamed of
himself, though you are not to treat him as an
enemy, but to correct him as a brother.*
2 Thess. 3:14, 15, New Jerusalem.

Paul was dead serious when he instructed "not to let anyone eat" who "re-fused to work" (2 Thess. 3:10, New Jerusalem), and he continued his admonition with the words found in today's verses. Let's dissect his instruction about how to deal with heretics, or at least those with fanatical ideas.

"Take note of him"—Paul's verb meant to label that person—identify him for what he was. Once again Paul used the imperative mood in the present tense, which meant that they should keep on noting this person. This was a big problem, and they mustn't ignore it or attempt halfheartedly to fix it. Of course, before an issue can be addressed it must be identified.

"Have nothing to do with him"—Once again Paul resorted to the same grammatical rendering—the imperative mood in the present tense. Don't mix it up with him, Paul commanded. From passages such as this the practice of "shunning" originated. Until 1983 the Catholic Church practiced shunning on occasion. Old Order Amish use shunning and call it *meidung*. Certain ultraconservative Mennonites also practice shunning. Jehovah's Witnesses shun apostates, refusing to greet them even on the street. In very close-knit societies shunning can have a devastating effect because it isolates individuals from their support system. But Paul's advice wasn't this extreme, as we shall soon see.

"You are not to treat him as an enemy"—Having identified the deviant Christian, they must not lead out in dealing with him as someone hated. Not all heretics or fanatics are enemies, especially when they're part of one's social group.

"Correct him as a brother"—Instead, they must admonish this person as they would their own birth sibling. (The root behind the Greek word for brother meant something like "united from the womb.") Reminds us of brotherly love, right?

And the purpose for all this? "So that he will be ashamed of himself." The verb Paul chose meant to turn against oneself. The heretical or fanatical brother needed to have second thoughts about himself and his behavior. It is our place, not to punish heretics and/or fanatics, but to discipline them, which means helping them see the error of their ways.

Young Upstarts

To Timothy, my loyal child in the faith.
1 Tim. 1:2, NRSV.

I f you've ever flown in a commuter plane, you've undoubtedly noticed that they hire "little kids" to maneuver these commercial aircraft, be they prop or jet propelled. When I first noticed the tender age of these pilots, I felt a bit concerned . . . until I recalled that these young adults had grown up playing video games and so had developed lightning-fast reflexes. Maybe it's not all that bad to entrust my life to this youngster, I consoled myself.

History has been replete with young people in responsible positions. King Tut died when he was just 18, after having ruled as pharaoh for a number of years. Alexander the Great was 16 when he became the regent of Macedonia. Two years later he led a cavalry band that wiped out an elite corps from Thebes. And at age 20 Alexander became king of Macedon upon the death of his father. Alexander the Great never lost a battle. Mozart was only 5 years old when he wrote his first musical composition.

Religious history has also had its share of young heroes. Joash became king of Judah at the juvenile age of 7. Much later Josiah became king of Judah when he was only 8 years old. William of Norwich had a reputation as a miracle-worker prior to his death when he was just 12. Joan of Arc was still in her teens when she suffered martyrdom. Ellen White in *The Great Controversy* spoke of the child preachers in Sweden. More recently Nelson Loris began preaching at age 12, and Uldine Utley began preaching in New York City when she was 14.

Timothy, as a young man, assisted Paul. Despite being "green," he served as Paul's representative, preaching and caring for churches when Paul couldn't do the job. Paul, referring to young Timothy, called him "my loyal child in the faith," "my child" (1 Tim. 1:18, NRSV), "my beloved child" (2 Tim. 1:2, NRSV), and "our brother" (Philemon 1:1, NRSV). Clearly he held Timothy in high regard.

But Timothy wasn't the only young person Paul "adopted." He also highly esteemed Titus and Onesimus. For a while he gave John Mark an opportunity to serve alongside him, but that didn't work out, resulting in a rift between Paul and his early associate Barnabas.

Paul apparently didn't feel threatened by younger colleagues and praised them for their dedication to God's work as ministers in the young but growing Christian church.

The Role of the Law and the Goal of the Gospel

The law is good, if one uses it legitimately. . . . The law is laid down not for the innocent but for the lawless . . . and whatever else is contrary to the sound teaching. 1 Tim. 1:8-10, NRSV.

From the emerging Christian church onward, the role of the law has constituted a bone of contention among believers. Indeed, it still constitutes a subject that Adventists, Baptists, and others dispute. Initially the discussion resulted from the social seedbed in which Christianity germinated—Judaism. Ever since the return from Babylonian captivity, the majority of Jewish leaders committed themselves to the strict observance of the Mosaic law as preventive medicine for yet another exile. Because nearly all the original followers of Jesus Christ were Jewish, the value of lawkeeping was taken for granted. Then Gentiles began streaming into the church, and the issue of how much commandmentkeeping they needed to espouse became a hot topic.

Later, because of the emphasis on good works within Roman Catholicism, the topic flared up again when the Protestant Reformation gained foothold. Then, in relatively more recent times, the same provocative subject reappeared when Adventists learned the "Sabbath truth," and in segments of our denomination the matter continues to foment.

Paul, in confronting the Jewish Christian supporters of the law, argued that the Christian theology wasn't antinomian (against the law). Law had its place, but . . . Here's where today's passage comes front and center: "The law is good, if one uses it legitimately" (1 Tim. 1:8, NRSV). And how did it function legitimately? It had been given "not for the innocent but for the lawless and disobedient, for the godless and sinful, for the unholy and profane" (verse 9, NRSV). Paul then proceeded to identify these people further: "those who kill their father or mother . . . murderers, fornicators, sodomites, slave traders, liars, perjurers" (verses 9, 10, NRSV). Clearly, then, Paul didn't regard the law as having abiding significance for converted Christians. (Does the behavior he described sound like the Christian lifestyle to you?)

That leads us to what Paul did see as the goal of the gospel. The logical conclusion from his words is that although the law was "laid down . . . for the lawless," the Christian lifestyle wasn't to be marked by behavior condemned by the law itself. No, "the aim . . . is love" (verse 5, NRSV). Love is the goal of the gospel—a love springing from three sources: "a pure heart, a good conscience, and sincere faith" (verse 5, NRSV).

Another Snapshot of God

Now to the King eternal, immortal, invisible, the only God, be honor and glory for ever and ever. Amen. 1 Tim. 1:17, NIV.

Throughout this book we've noticed numerous snapshots of God, and here in today's passage we find yet another. The picture is clearer than many because it comes to us not through a story but through a concrete list of words.

Before we take a closer look at this picture of God, we need to notice how Paul identifies God. He calls Him king. Some countries still have a king or queen, but not the United States. We tend to forget that in the ancient Near East kings had absolute power. They not only governed but also made the laws and executed justice. Much of the time kings also served in a temporary priestly capacity. If the king had an unselfish benevolent nature, the people were served well. If not, the peace and harmony of society were jeopardized.

Note the attributes Paul singled out.

Eternal—The Greek word Paul used is most commonly translated with terms meaning "forever." However, its semantic range included the denotations of unbroken rule or duration, perpetuity, a long period of time, the cosmos, or simply a significant period of time—such as when we speak of the Age of Reason or the jet age.

Immortal—The NIV agrees with the KJV in rendering the word Paul selected as "immortal." Strictly speaking, however, another Greek word had *that* meaning. Paul's word here means that God is incapable of becoming corrupted—not morally but physically. God cannot perish and become decayed as we can.

Invisible—We have eyes to sense those things that can be seen, but some things cannot be seen, such as molecules, atoms, protons, electrons, muons, pions, quarks, etc. Similarly, we have no access to God via our eyesight.

Only—While multitudes of deities have been worshipped throughout history, the Judeo-Christian perspective is that there is only one (true, real, genuine) God—YHWH—who is worthy to receive our honor and glory. And our deference and praise will go on eternally unbroken—in other words, just as long as God has existence, which is for ever and ever.

Pray for . . .

I urge that entreaties and prayers, petitions and thanksgivings, be made on behalf of all men, for kings and all who are in authority, in order that we may lead a tranquil and quiet life in all godliness and dignity. This is good and acceptable in the sight of God our Savior.
1 Tim. 2:1-3, NASB.

When it comes to prayer—especially intercessory prayer—all sorts of questions come to mind: Why should we pray? How should we pray? For what should we pray? For whom should we pray? When should we pray? In today's scriptural passage Paul addressed two of these questions.

For whom should we pray?—Paul first identified the objects of our prayers with the most general of terms: "all men" (1 Tim. 2:1, NASB). Can we assume, then, that we need not remember women in prayer? Not at all. Paul used the Greek word *ánthrōpos,* which referred to all human beings, rather than the word *anēr,* which denoted males. Paul urged that we pray for each and every *Homo sapiens.*

Then he narrowed the scope to those in positions of rulership, namely, "kings and all who are in authority" (verse 2, NASB). It's relatively easy to pray for generic humanity, but sometimes we find it difficult to pray (and even more particularly to pray with thanksgiving) for specific individuals—especially those in leadership positions with whom we disagree.

Nevertheless, Paul considered it an obligation to do so.

Why should we pray?—Undoubtedly Paul could have given several (maybe many) reasons for interceding on behalf of those in authoritative positions, but he concentrated on two.

First, "in order that we may lead a tranquil and quiet life in all godliness and dignity" (verse 3, NASB). Christian living involves (1) the outward demeanor of reverence toward God (here translated as "godliness") and (2) a character that pursues the golden mean between trying to please no one (arrogance) and trying to please everyone (sycophantic toadying). Such character traits can flourish only when those in positions of authority are benevolent.

Second, because such praying God commends and finds gratifying. In other words, praying for those in positions of power is what God looks for in our behavior.

What God Wants

*[God] wants everyone to be saved
and to understand the truth.*
1 Tim. 2:4, NLT.

M any Christians invest considerable thought and energy into understanding God's will. But what exactly does the divine will involve?
Does God will which socks I wear today? Does it really matter to Him which
banana I select from the bunch or which brand of tissues I buy or which
model of vehicle I purchase or which gasoline I use—Shell or BP or Texaco?

Although the intent to comply with what God wants is commendable,
the fact is that it focuses on self: *I* want to do God's will for *me*. While on first
impression such a mind-set seems to focus on the Other, in fact it's tinged
with egocentricism.

Paul saw God's will in terms that went far beyond individual self-interest. He
concentrated on God's will for humankind in general. And it appears that what
God wants doesn't entail the minutiae of life and lifestyle. If we understand Paul
correctly, we find that when he spoke of what God wants, he didn't think in
terms of choosing among Thousand Island, Ranch, Italian, or French salad dressing. And this brings us to our scripture for today, in which Paul spoke precisely
of what God wants—really wants. He wrote that God wants two things.

First, God wants "everyone to be saved." In a world that showed more
exclusivism than inclusivism, Paul's insistence that God's will embraced all
humanity was quite remarkable—even startling. (As we noted in the previous reading, Paul's "all men" meant each and every *Homo sapiens*.) It still affords a pleasant surprise! God doesn't play favorites. According to John
Calvin, brilliant Swiss Reformer, God has willed from eternity that some people will be lost and some saved, and it's humanly (and divinely) impossible
to change the divine will. Paul surely didn't believe that.

Second, God wants "everyone . . . to understand the truth." Paul saw the
acquisition of truth (he wrote generically here—"truth" instead of "the
truth") as a journey. Truth is something we come to—arrive at. And it's full
knowledge. (Paul used an intensified form of the noun.)

Both elements of what God wants have a present and future aspect.
We're saved here and now, but salvation is fully experienced in the future.
We can arrive at truth here and now, but we gain in-depth knowledge in the
future.

How to Relate to Old and Young

Do not rebuke an older man harshly, but exhort him as if he were your father. Treat younger men as brothers, older women as mothers, and younger women as sisters, with absolute purity.
1 Tim. 5:1, 2, NIV.

It isn't always easy to know how to treat others. When one holds a position of influence, the challenge becomes yet thornier, especially when others defy one's authority. And when persons in high positions are "young Turks," the foot-dragging of others can try their serenity.

Paul, fiery though he could be at times, wanted young Timothy to rein in his enthusiasm (for change or otherwise) and to behave as a true servant-leader. His advice is as cogent today as when he first penned it.

Males—Paul divided Timothy's male constituents into two categories—old and young. The word translated "older man" could refer to the local church elder, but the context of the discussion indicates that Paul referred to all older males and not just those in a position of leadership. He urged Timothy to avoid dealing "harshly" with such men—not to beat up on them. He spoke, of course, figuratively, and so meant that he shouldn't chide or rebuke them even though they might exasperate him.

As for the "younger men," Timothy should deal with them as he would with his own brother (if he had one). Cynically, one might say that Paul gave Timothy permission to duke it out with those his own age (sibling rivalry), but that really wasn't what Paul had in mind. Timothy, despite his position of authority, must treat the younger men as equals.

Females—Paul split Timothy's female parishioners into the same two groupings—old and young.

He urged him to treat the "older women" as he'd defer to his own mother. Although the ancient Near East was a patriarchal society, mothers were held in high esteem since they bore the brunt of bringing up the children until the boys could join their father in his business. Timothy should treat the elderly women with loving respect.

As to the "younger women," whose feminine charms might be all too alluring, Timothy should deal with them as if they were his own flesh-and-blood sisters—chastely, unerotically.

In other words, leaders must lead and not drive and should do so free of passion.

The Root of All Evil

The love of money is the root of all evil: which while some coveted after, they have erred from the faith, and pierced themselves through with many sorrows.
1 Tim. 6:10.

The relationship between a pious person and wealth has been something of a conundrum.

The Jews regarded wealth as a sign of God's blessing. "It is [God] that giveth thee power to get wealth" (Deut. 8:18). "The Lord shall make thee plenteous in goods. . . . Thou shalt lend unto many nations, and thou shalt not borrow" (Deut. 28:11, 12).

Yet Jesus said: "It is easier for a camel to go through the eye of a needle, than for a rich man to enter into the kingdom of God" (Matt. 19:24). But how could Jesus' ministry have succeeded without the generous support of those with means? And the Christians whom James addressed treated the wealthy with deference. "Ye have respect to him that weareth the gay clothing, and say unto him, Sit thou here in a good place; and say to the poor . . . sit here under my footstool" (James 2:3).

Paul only added to the confusion, it seems. In 1 Corinthians 10:24 he wrote: "Let no man seek his own, but every man another's wealth." Exactly what did *that* mean? Did he admonish covetousness? Hardly. What most of us don't realize is that the word "wealth" in the KJV isn't in the Greek text. Paul actually said something like this: "Let no one look out for number one, but for others." He was advocating unselfishness—just the opposite of what the KJV says.

In counseling Timothy he takes a swipe at those with riches . . . or does he? "The love of money is the root of all evil" (1 Tim. 6:10).

First, we must recognize that Paul overstates matters. The love of money was hardly the root of Adam and Eve's original sin. Money didn't exist in Eden, although one might understand Paul's terminology as code for self-centeredness.

Second, the context indicates why Paul seemed so negative when it comes to wealth. Money per se isn't evil and can even prove quite beneficial. However, loving money is part of coveting and through such inordinate desire for riches can lead to abandoning the faith. When our focus on money blinds us to other more important matters, we pierce ourselves through with much consuming grief—a kind of spiritual suicide. Little wonder Jesus instructed: "Lay up for yourselves treasures in heaven" (Matt. 6:20).

Faith of Our Mothers

I am reminded of your sincere faith, a faith that dwelt first in your grandmother Lois and your mother Eunice and now, I am sure, dwells in you.
2 Tim. 1:5, RSV.

aith of Our Fathers." Most of us have sung this familiar gospel song. "Faith of our fathers, living still, in spite of dungeon, fire, and sword; O how our hearts beat high with joy whenever we hear that glorious word! Faith of our fathers! holy faith! We will be true to thee till death." But why the faith of our *fathers*? Look around you at church, and chances are that you'll count more women in attendance than men.

Aren't we ignoring the faithful women who have served the Lord when we sing "Faith of Our Fathers"? Aren't we discounting the faithful female heroes (some have remained nameless) who have served as the backbone of our Judeo-Christian faith? Think of such stalwarts as Sarah, Miriam, Deborah, Jael, Hannah, Huldah, Esther, Mary, Martha, Dorcas, Lydia, and many others.

Even in a patriarchal society such as prevailed throughout the history of the ancient Near East, these and other staunch, God-fearing women had to be reckoned with. The chroniclers couldn't overlook them, even though sometimes they had no name, no voice, no face.

Paul referred to Timothy's sincere faith. The word he used meant without pretension or simulation. In other words, it was a true faith. This genuine faith, Paul said, was also shared by Lois, Timothy's grandmother (the Greek word is *mámmē*, baby talk), and Eunice, his mother. Paul described this true faith as having dwelled in Lois and Eunice, meaning that faith had taken up permanent residence in them, benefiting them because of its presence.

These early Christian women were stalwart believers and had passed along their faith from one generation to the next—Lois to Eunice to Timothy. Isn't that the way personal spirituality should be? It should be shared from one generation to another like a precious heirloom.

Surely we can celebrate the genuine Christianity of these women. Come to think of it, maybe we should sing, "Faith of our *mothers*, living still, in spite of dungeon, fire, and sword; O how our hearts beat high with joy whenever we hear that glorious word! Faith of our *mothers*! holy faith! We will be true to thee till death."

An Adage

*Here is a trustworthy saying: If we died with him,
we will also live with him; if we endure, we will
also reign with him. If we disown him, he
will also disown us; if we are faithless, he will
remain faithful, for he cannot disown himself.
2 Tim. 2:11-13, NIV.*

Some "sayings" are patently obvious. We call them adages, pithy proverbs that express a common sense idea. In fact, our word "adage" comes from a Latin word that means "proverb." In today's passage Paul expressed what he called a "trustworthy saying." Although it is pretty much self-evident, perhaps we should dissect it so that we can look at its individual segments. The saying has four elements, each of which has two parts. Each section begins with "if." Now, Greek had several kinds of conditions, and the word Paul used introduces what grammarians call a "simple condition." The "if" expresses an assumption and can just as easily be translated with "since," "because," or "although."

Element 1: "If we died with him, we will also live with him." Paul taught that Christians—all Christians—had died with Jesus. He wasn't speaking literally, of course, only metaphorically. Nevertheless, Paul used the concept with all seriousness. Jesus as the Son of man represented all humanity, and so when He died for sinners, we died corporately with Him. Paul used a verb in the past tense. Assuming that to be the case, then we shall also live together with Him in the here and now as well as in the future.

Element 2: "If we endure, we will also reign with him." If we keep on enduring bravely and calmly the sufferings that accompany our commitment to Jesus Christ, then in the future we shall be coregents with King Jesus.

Element 3: "If we disown him, he will also disown us." When we reject Christ, He rejects us. It's not that Jesus wants to be mean. However, salvation comes when we acknowledge Him as Savior. If we don't acknowledge Him as our Lord and Savior, we remain unsaved.

Element 4: "If we are faithless, he will remain faithful, for he cannot disown himself." Although we may remain (present tense) without faith, that doesn't mean Christ is unfaithful. There are some things God (and Christ) cannot do, and one of those things, according to Paul, is to be faithless. Paul said that He doesn't have the power or ability to be otherwise than He Himself is.

God's Slave

A servant of the Lord must not engage in quarrels, but must be kind to everyone, a good teacher, and patient.
2 Tim. 2:24, New Jerusalem.

Paul sometimes called himself a slave of Jesus, and in today's passage he included Timothy in that descriptive term. Slavery isn't something most of us know about firsthand, and in Western society it is so out of vogue that it's considered morally and ethically odious.

Slavery flourished in the Roman Empire, estimates suggesting that between 25 and 30 percent of the population consisted of slaves—millions and millions of people. Individuals became slaves in various ways—captured in battle, in need of money (indentured slaves), owing money (debt slaves), etc. Generally, the slaves at this time were "productive slaves" who worked in the mines or on plantations. (The one Greek term meant servant or slave.)

Regardless of the living conditions and treatment received, slaves had basically no personal autonomy. They did what their masters and overseers wanted and when they wanted. Manumission was a cherished goal for most, and some slaves actually saved up sufficient funds to buy their freedom.

Paradoxically, Paul described Christians as having been freed slaves (from sin and from Satan) yet continuing as slaves (to Jesus Christ). The idea behind both concepts, though, was hardly paradoxical. The main thrust of the two metaphors was lack of self-determination. As slaves of sin, they did whatever and whenever sin dictated. As slaves of Christ, they did whatever and whenever Christ wanted.

Paul told Timothy that slaves of the Lord must manifest four traits—one negative and three positive: (1) They must not (this was a necessity) fight ("quarrel"). Rather, (2) they must be "kind" (gentle and placid) when dealing with everyone. Additionally, (3) the Lord's slave should be a "good teacher." (Yes, some slaves functioned as teachers or tutors because some were well educated.) Finally, (4) they must be "patient." Instead of using the common Greek word for patience, Paul used a Greek word that means patiently putting up with evil—calmly enduring bad things and bad people.

Paul's description of the Lord's servant sounds a lot like God Himself.

The Goal of Scripture

All Scripture is given by inspiration of God, and is profitable for doctrine, for reproof, for correction, for instruction in righteousness, that the man of God may be complete, thoroughly equipped for every good work.
2 Tim. 3:16, 17, NKJV.

In today's passage Paul wasn't arguing about the extent of inspiration or how it works. To understand his point, we must examine the grammar, vocabulary, and context of the verses.

Grammar—Second Timothy 3:16 lacks a verb ("is"), posing the problem of where to place the "is" that is supplied. The KJV puts it in two places: "All scripture (1) *is* given by inspiration . . . and (2) *is* profitable . . ." That's grammatically acceptable. However, the translator needn't supply the word "is" twice. Once would suffice, and the text could read either: "All scripture given by inspiration of God *is* profitable for . . ." or "All scripture *is* given by inspiration of God and profitable for . . ." The former rendition is found in a number of translations.

Vocabulary—Paul used the Greek adjective *theópneustos*, which the KJV renders as "given by inspiration of God"—five words to translate one adjective. When I see the word *theópneustos*, my thoughts immediately go back to when God sculpted the first man from the earth and breathed the breath of life into his nostrils, causing Adam to come to life.

Paul also used the word *graphē*, here translated "Scripture." It's a general word referring to anything written and can legitimately be translated "writing" (as in Dan. 5:17). Although it could refer to writing other than Scripture, the New Testament uses the term often as a synonym of our term "Bible"—the Hebrew Bible, what we call the Old Testament.

Context—Paul wasn't trying to drum into Timothy's mind that the Bible—all Scripture—is divinely inspired. He was, rather, encouraging Timothy to read his Bible, because it's profitable to do so—useful in four ways: (1) teaching (doctrine), (2) reproof (refuting error), (3) correction (guidance in spiritual living), and (4) instruction in righteousness (discipline in right living).

That Scripture is inspired or how much of it is inspired is beside the point. Paul's point is that the inspired corpus is making one "wise for salvation through faith which is in Christ Jesus" (verse 15, NKJV). *That's* the goal of Scripture.

Ready to Depart

As for me, I am already being poured out as a libation, and the time of my departure has come.
2 Tim. 4:6, NRSV.

Just as people have illegitimately used yesterday's passage to argue about the process of inspiration and how much of the Bible is inspired, so they've used today's verse to argue that there is life after death—at least for Christians. They assume that Paul here used cognitive or informative language to give insight into what happens after death. As we read the entire discussion, however, it becomes fairly clear that Paul was using affective language—expressing his emotions in the face of his imprisonment and possible imminent death.

Most of us don't look forward to dying. But sometimes we have a sense of approaching death, and at such times it's possible to face our impending demise with mixed feelings. When we've been enduring excruciating pain, death can seem like a welcome relief. Nevertheless, we generally tend to cling to life despite the relief death might bring. Paul, in at least two passages, broached the topic of his fate—possible decapitation. Today's verse is one of them.

The discussion began his highly personal reflections by encouraging Timothy to "proclaim the message; be persistent . . . ; convince, rebuke, and encourage, with the utmost patience" (2 Tim. 4:2, NRSV). This was important, because a time was approaching when people wouldn't appreciate sound doctrine (verse 3). The present time was the opportune moment for Timothy to fulfill his responsibilities as a young preacher (verse 5). Timothy had a great future!

Paul, however, felt that he was nearing the end of his ministry. He was in prison, the place where people were held until they were tried and received a judicial verdict. Paul figured that he'd likely not survive. But imminent death didn't terrorize him. He was "already being poured out as a libation." (Note that Paul saw his confinement in spiritual terms—he was being poured out like a drink offering in God's temple.) The next step would be his trial and execution. But he was ready and bravely told Timothy, "I have fought the good fight, I have finished the race, I have kept the faith" (verse 7, NRSV).

Having shown himself a good Christian athlete, Paul coolly faced death, certain that God (not the emperor) would have the last word and bestow on him the winner's laurel wreath. Indeed, all victors in Christ will receive the same token of victory (verse 8). All Christians win!

Where Have All the Helpers Gone?

Demas has deserted me because he loves the things of this life and has gone to Thessalonica. Crescens has gone to Galatia, and Titus has gone to Dalmatia. Only Luke is with me. Bring Mark with you when you come, for he will be helpful to me. I sent Tychicus to Ephesus. 2 Tim. 4:10-12, NLT.

As Paul ended his letter to Timothy, he got even more personal than in his poignant reflections in the previous verses. He now sounds a bit melancholy while referring to six of his associates. Crescens, whom we meet only here, had gone to Galatia. (Some manuscripts say Gaul, as Galatia and Gaul were sometimes synonyms among the Greeks.) Titus, the recipient of another of Paul's letters, was in Dalmatia, also known as Illyricum. Luke, Paul's physician friend and associate, was still with him. Paul had sent Tychicus to Ephesus.

That leaves two others Paul listed—Demas and John Mark.

Demas—Paul mentioned Demas in two of his other letters—Colossians and Philemon. In those two epistles Demas was one of Paul's Gentile colleagues in Christian ministry. Now we learn that having loved "the things of this life" or this (present) age, he'd forsaken Paul and had retreated to Thessalonica. It's generally presumed that he'd abandoned Christianity—at least the eschatological hope. Demas may have taught that the resurrection had already taken place. The Christians at both Corinth and Thessalonica had had questions about the resurrection, so that may be why Demas ended up in Thessalonica—a place where his deviant views may have been considered acceptable.

John Mark—We know from the book of Acts that John Mark had joined Paul in his ministry when Paul and Barnabas had begun their missionary endeavors together. Mark, Barnabas' cousin, had gotten discouraged for whatever reasons and at Pamphylia had turned tail in the midst of Paul's first missionary journey. Paul and Barnabas subsequently had a falling out when Barnabas later wanted Paul to include John Mark on another mission trip. We learn that Paul and Mark eventually reconciled, and Paul considered him "helpful." Most likely this is the same Mark who later wrote the Gospel of Mark.

It's encouraging when hostility is defeated but saddening when collaboration dissolves into opposition.

How Golden-agers Should Behave

Older men are to be temperate, dignified, sensible, sound in faith, in love, in perseverance. Older women likewise are to be reverent in their behavior, not malicious gossips nor enslaved to much wine, teaching what is good, so that they may encourage the young women. Titus 2:2-4, NASB.

As a young pastor-teacher (Paul considered pastor-teacher as a single gift in Ephesians 4:11), Titus would find himself offering instruction to those considerably older than he. Here's how Paul thought older adults should behave.

Older men—Paul told Titus to encourage these senior citizens to manifest six traits. Older men should be "temperate." Paul didn't mean being a teetotaler, but used a word that connoted keeping one's emotions reined in—unlike the behavior of those besotted. They should also be "dignified" (in an appealing way) and "sensible," or of sound understanding, discreet.

Finally, their faith, love, and patient endurance should be healthy. Paul used the Greek word from which we get our term "hygiene." Alas, much of what passes as "old-time religion" is in reality neurotic spirituality. Paul argued that older men should exemplify a healthy religious perspective.

Older women—Paul didn't want Titus to overlook the elderly females in his congregation. He should admonish them to be "reverent in their behavior." Paul meant positively that their demeanor should befit those their age and spirituality. Negatively, the white-haired women mustn't be devils. Yes, that's the word translated "malicious gossips" in our passage! The Greek word *diábolos* referred to someone who went around accusing (falsely, of course) others. Older people can sometimes prove cranky, making allegations that cannot be proven.

Furthermore, the golden-age women mustn't be slaves to much wine. Once again, Paul didn't forbid completely the drinking of wine, which was a common beverage. (Fresh grape juice in that climate quickly achieved an alcoholic content.) It's sad enough to see a young person intoxicated, but it's even more off-putting to see an elderly person drunk as a skunk.

Finally, they should teach "what is good," with the objective that their young (female) "students" might be brought to their senses ("encourage"), living with self-control.

If you're among the largest percentage of those who read these daily devotional books, you're getting on in years—50 and above. How do you measure up?

What the Gospel Does

December 2
Titus

The grace of God has appeared, bringing salvation to all people. It trains us to reject godless ways and worldly desires and to live self-controlled, upright, and godly lives in the present age, as we wait for the happy fulfillment of our hope in the glorious appearing of our great God and Savior, Jesus Christ. Titus 2:11-13, NET.

Although it's true that salvation doesn't come as a result of good works, nevertheless experiencing salvation does indeed produce good works—the Christian lifestyle. In our passage for today Paul outlined some of the traits that characterize the Christian way of life.

God's grace negatively does . . . —God's grace, when it results in salvation, includes rejection and denial of two things. First, we must repudiate "godless ways." Paul used a word that indicated the absence or lack of reverence toward God. Second, God's grace disciplines us to disown "worldly desires," lusts that epitomize life in this present world in which we live. Although we inhabit this present world, that doesn't mean our behavior must be saturated with worldliness. By God's grace there's a better way to live.

God's grace positively does . . . —God's grace also teaches us to embrace a specific kind of lifestyle. Paul explained that we must *live*, using the term *záō*, which connoted more than mere physical life. It embraced the idea of life at its fullest, living out its great moral meaning. And our lives will exemplify three things: self-control, uprightness, and godliness. The order of these three terms has significance. "Schematically, each would refer to giving what was due: *sōphronōs*, to one's self; *dikaiōs*, to fellow human beings; *eusebōs*, to the gods" (Jerome D. Quinn, *Titus, Anchor Bible*, p. 167). In other words, Christians would behave in ways that both Jews and Gentiles would approve of. And they will do so now—in this present age in which we live, not waiting until the future coming age.

Nevertheless, we await "the happy fulfillment of our hope," literally, "the blessed hope." (The ancient Greeks and Romans didn't always regard hope positively because all too often it was baseless, leading to disappointment. But this hope is "blessed," a term once used pretty much exclusively of divine beings.) This blessed hope is the Second Advent. The grammatical structure can mean either (1) that both God and Jesus will return (Paul typically differentiates between God and Jesus) or (2) that Jesus is the God who will appear.

God's Personal Property

[Jesus] gave himself for us, that he might redeem us from all iniquity, and purify unto himself a peculiar people, zealous of good works.
Titus 2:14.

M any years ago at a camp meeting in Massachusetts the guest speaker delivered a sermon titled "Peculiar but Not Odd." His text was Titus 2:14, our scripture for today. Throughout his sermon Elder What's-His-Name kept repeating that as Adventists we must be peculiar but not odd.

The point of the sermon was accurate, but the preacher had no idea what Paul meant when he referred to Christians as "peculiar people." Neither the Greek word that Paul chose nor the English word selected by the translators of the King James Version denoted that which is odd or weird or even different. So let's take a closer look at what Paul meant.

The Greek word Paul chose is *perioúsios.* It meant "personal possession" or "private property." Actually, it described more than that. It didn't refer to just any personal property but to that which was a genuine asset—that which is treasured. *Perioúsios* referred to that which was cherished because of its great value. And that's precisely what the English word "peculiar" meant in 1611. It was derived from the Latin word *peculium,* which means "private property."

Although Paul used the word as a synonym for Christians, he didn't originate the concept. The idea goes back to the Old Testament. The author of Ecclesiastes referred to his amassing of wealth as the "peculiar treasure of kings" (Eccl. 2:8). Much earlier than that, however, God used the term of His chosen people—the people of Judah and Israel. In Exodus 19:5 and Deuteronomy 14:2 and 26:18 God called the Hebrews His "peculiar treasure" and His "peculiar people." The Hebrew word used in these passages, *cegullah,* had the same meaning as the Greek word that Paul used.

Christians, like the ancient Hebrews, are God's treasured possession. The reason that we are God's special treasure is that Jesus "gave himself for us" and by so doing has redeemed us from all iniquity, freed us—liberated us—from our lawlessness. Furthermore, He has purified us—cleansed us from our moral defilement. It is these divine actions that constitute us as His "peculiar people." As His special treasure, we are "zealous of good works"—burning with zeal to perform lovely and beautiful deeds.

Useless "Useful"

I am boldly asking a favor of you. I could demand it in the name of Christ because it is the right thing for you to do, but because of our love, I prefer just to ask you. So take this as a request from your friend Paul, an old man, now in prison.
Philemon 8, 9, NLT.

O nesimus, whose name meant "useful," was owned by Philemon, who lived at Colossae and had accepted Jesus as his Savior through Paul's preaching. Subsequently, the congregation of Colossian Christians met each Sabbath in the home of this wealthy slave owner (Philemon 2).

Apparently Slave Useful had fallen out of favor, perhaps having stolen some property, and had fled. On the one hand, it's possible that Slave Useful was a *fugitive*, a rebellious slave on the lam. This would have been a serious criminal offense, and Philemon may well have issued a warrant in which he pledged a monetary reward for the return of this runaway. Harboring such a fugitive was also a serious crime. Upon receiving Slave Useful back, Philemon had the legal right to brand him, flog him, or even crucify him. On the other hand, it's equally possible that Slave Useful, pagan though he was, had fled to Paul because he and Philemon had merely come to odds over something or another. In this case, he wouldn't have been considered a criminal. He wanted Paul, whom Philemon esteemed highly, to serve as *amicus domini*, friend of the master who would act in behalf of the slave.

Whatever the case, Slave Useful got together with Paul, who was under house arrest in either Ephesus or Rome. While there, Slave Useful became a Christian. Paul then, as *amicus domini*, penned a short epistle to Philemon. With great tactfulness Paul referred to Philemon as friend, coworker, and brother (verses 1 and 7). He explained that although Slave Useful had become useless to him, the slave master, the escapee had become useful to him, Paul, and should also become helpful to Philemon. So it was that Paul pleaded with Philemon, appealing to his best judgment and tenderheartedness, to accept Slave Useful back without recrimination.

Calling himself a prisoner and an old man (verse 9) and Slave Useful "my own son" (verse 10, NLT) and "my own heart" (verse 12, NLT), Paul begged Philemon to receive the runaway slave as his own brother (in Christ). "And whatever Slave Useful owes," Paul said, "send the bill to me" (see verse 18).

Sounds like the way God has treated us, doesn't it?

Adrift

*We ought, then, to turn our minds more
attentively than before to what we have
been taught, so that we do not drift away.
Heb. 2:1, New Jerusalem.*

Some Christians have concluded from biblical passages that speak of assurance in Jesus Christ the doctrine of once saved, always saved. However, other scriptures indicate that salvation can indeed be forfeited. Our passage for today similarly supports the idea that apostasy and loss of salvation can be an all-too-real experience for Christians. Lackadaisical Christians just might lose salvation, and our passage for today utilizes a nautical metaphor as a warning against spiritual recklessness.

"We ought" translates a Greek verb meaning "it is necessary." What type of behavior was indispensible? We should "turn our minds." The Greek word was used for keeping a sailing vessel on course and for bringing a ship to port. Additionally, this behavior mustn't be done haphazardly or lackadaisically but must be executed "more attentively" or with exceeding earnestness. If we don't exert due diligence, we just might "drift away," another maritime metaphor. The term implies almost imperceptibly gliding off course.

What should we rivet our attention on so as not to end up adrift? We must pay attention to what "we have been taught," or more literally, the message that we heard (Heb. 2:1). Not to do so would result in our carelessly neglecting the awesome salvation we previously accepted. In the book of Hebrews salvation has three aspects to it: (1) salvation from God's verdict of condemnation because of our sins, (2) salvation from the evil powers of this world that aid and abet us in our sinning, and (3) salvation for life in the kingdom of God, which Jesus inaugurated.

The word of good news under discussion "was first announced by the Lord himself, and is guaranteed . . . by those who heard him" (verse 3, New Jerusalem). Additionally, this great salvation had been attested to by "God himself . . . with signs and marvels and miracles of all kinds, and by distributing the gifts of the Holy Spirit" (verse 4, New Jerusalem).

The prospect of losing salvation stems not from a deficiency on God's part or Christ's part. They are faithful—ever and always active. The possibility and even probability of losing salvation exists because of human negligence. That's why the apostle refers here to drifting. Losing salvation and drifting into apostasy can be quite subtle.

Pray Boldly

Let us then approach the throne of grace with confidence, so that we may receive mercy and find grace to help us in our time of need.
Heb. 4:16, NIV.

December 6
Hebrews

M ost of us at one time or another have found ourselves nearly tongue-tied in the presence of someone we hold in great awe. We lose our poise, our saliva glands stop functioning, and we find ourselves searching for the right words if we aren't actually stammering. Similarly, although prayer is a privilege from which God's people can benefit, it can prove an over-whelming experience. Think about it. Frail and finite human beings can approach the omnipotent and infinite God!

In light of this great benefit, how should we behave in God's presence? Some assume that we should resort to Elizabethan English when we pray, saying "mayest," "giveth," "dost," "doeth," "haveth," "lovest," etc. Also, some think that we should use "Thee," "Thou," and "Thine." The assumption is that the old singular second person pronouns are somehow fitting when we address our "high" God. (We believe wrongly that these forms show respect for a superior. However, the old singular second person pronouns were actually used for one's peers, whereas the plural second person pronouns "you" and "your" were used to show deference.)

In today's scripture we learn that we can approach God's throne ("throne of grace" was a circumlocution for God's throne) with "confidence." The word used—*parrēsía*—means freedom and frankness in speech. It occurs approximately 30 times in the New Testament and is variously translated as "plainly," "publicly," "openly," "confidently," "boldly," and "fearlessly." When we approach God's throne, we need not be cheeky, but we can do so without halting speech. We can talk to Him freely and without inhibition.

When we pray in this manner, we will "receive mercy." God will respond with compassion—active pity—kindly. Additionally, freely spoken prayers will be met with "grace to help us in our time of need." The aid that God sends is well-timed: it arrives at just the right moment—at a favorable time.

How do you pray? How do I pray? As Christians, it's our privilege to speak with God without inhibition . . . and with ordinary language. He's not so high and mighty that He won't respond in a kindly and timely manner.

Baby Food

*Though by this time you ought to be teachers, you
need someone to teach you again the basic elements
of the oracles of God. You need milk, not solid food.*
Heb. 5:12, NRSV.

B ecause of certain physical maladies, some adults eat baby food. Most of
us regard such individuals with pity because we don't find baby food all
that appetizing and because it's emotionally humiliating for adults to dine
on Pablum or Gerber pureed peas. Even more drastic is the case of Howard
Cohen, who, after being diagnosed with cancer in 1999, took up drinking
mother's milk along with 28 other adults in California.

In the book of Hebrews we read about Christians who subsisted on spiritual baby food—milk—when they should have been ingesting solid food as
mature adults. Furthermore, these aged infants were "dull in understanding" (Heb. 5:11, NRSV)—dolts!

Spiritual milk, according to the book of Hebrews, consisted of "the basic
elements of the oracles of God." The terminology here means something like
"the preliminary ABCs of God's message." The educational system of the ancient world, whether Greek, Roman, or Jewish, included an elementary level
for children 7 years old and up. They studied the rudiments of reading, writing, and arithmetic. From age 14 onward they took up literary studies, which
included studying the classics (for Greek and Roman teens) or the Torah (for
Jewish adolescents). Upon completion of their education, they received the
attribution of *téleios* (mature, completed, or perfect), as in verse 14.

These Hebrew Christians were subsisting on spiritual milk rather than
solid food. This milk ("basic elements," "basic teaching," and "foundation")
consisted of such matters as "repentance . . . faith . . . instruction about bap-
tisms, laying on of hands, resurrection of the dead, and eternal judgment"
(Heb. 6:1, 2, NRSV). These were important issues to understand but shouldn't
be dwelt on as Christians spiritually and intellectually matured.

From the immediate context here in the book of Hebrews, it's clear that
the solid diet for those who'd graduated from elementary school consisted
of the work of Jesus Christ, who was both the once-and-for-all sacrifice for
sins and the high priest (after the order of Melchizedek) who ministers on
our behalf in the heavenly sanctuary (Heb. 4:14-16; 5:1-10; 7:11-28; 8; 9; and 10).

What is our spiritual diet—milk or solid food?

Without the
Shedding of Blood

Without shedding of blood there is no remission.
Heb. 9:22, NKJV.

I t may come as a surprise to some, but when we read anything—including the Bible—we need to engage in interpretation. For some, "interpretation" is a bad word, but no communication occurs without it. Everything we see and hear requires it, which means we must analyze messages, decoding their meaning. It shouldn't shock us, then, to admit that Hebrews 9:22 (along with the rest of Scripture) needs interpretation. Today's passage can be understood in two ways.

Universal principle—One way to understand the text is that sin(s) anywhere, everywhere, and at any time cannot be forgiven (atoned for) without bloodshed. This principle underlies the *lex talionis* of the Pentateuch: "Your eye shall not pity; . . . life shall be for life, eye for eye, tooth for tooth, hand for hand, foot for foot" (Deut. 19:21, NKJV; see also Ex. 21:24; Lev. 24:20). Among Christians this concept forms the basis for the longstanding substitutionary and satisfaction models of atonement.

Ancient Near Eastern principle—Hebrews 9:22 needn't assert a divinely ordained universal principle. It may merely reflect an ancient way of viewing matters. In the Hebrew cultus, atonement came about through substitutionary bloodshed—the offender brought to the tabernacle or temple a calf, goat, lamb, or bird, which was killed, dismembered, and burned. Some of the blood was sprinkled in certain locations, after which atonement occurred. "So the priest shall make atonement for him, and it shall be forgiven him" (Lev. 4:31, NKJV; cf. Lev. 17:11).

Which interpretation is correct? Perhaps the second. First, Hebrews 9:22 occurs in the immediate context of the Levitical requirements: "*According to the [Mosaic] law almost all things are purged with blood*" (NKJV). Second, the poor could obtain forgiveness by offering vegetable meal (flour), which entailed no bloodshed (Lev. 5:11-13). Third, our own experience of forgiving others reveals that forgiveness is a psychological act and requires no retaliatory violence, just an attitude of grace and mercy. Why should God—who personifies love, grace, and mercy—be any different, demanding bloodshed as the prerequisite for forgiveness?

Was it God who needed Calvary or us? Was the Crucifixion a necessity of divine justice or an exhibition of divine love?

The Three Tenses of Christ's Ministry

*Christ did not enter a sanctuary made with hands—
the representation of the true sanctuary—but into
heaven itself, and he appears now in God's presence
for us. And he did not enter to offer himself again
and again, the way the high priest enters the sanc-
tuary year after year with blood that is not his own. . . . But now he has appeared once
for all . . . to put away sin by his sacrifice. . . . Christ was offered once to bear the sins of
many, [and] to those who eagerly await him he will appear a second time, not to bear
sin but to bring salvation. Heb. 9:24-28, NET.*

Adventists have invested much time studying the book of Hebrews in
order to understand the work of Jesus Christ better. They have also
spent much time arguing about some of the fine points. In our concise comments here, we'll focus on the three tenses of His ministry: What He did in
the past, what He is doing now, and what He will do in the future.

Jesus' *past* work—In the context of the sanctuary rituals, Jesus served
as the sacrificial victim. On Calvary He died for humanity—the "Lamb of
God." Unlike the routine Jewish sacrifices, which were so ineffective that
they had to be offered daily, Jesus as sacrifice died "once for all . . . to put
away sin." That's why the repetitive sacrifice of the Mass distorts reality.
Christ needn't be offered again and again as in the Jewish cultus and in
Catholic rites.

Jesus' *present* work—Unlike the Jewish sanctuary ritual in which the
priests were distinct from the animal sacrifices, the spiritual reality is that
Jesus serves as both sacrifice and high priest. As antitypical high priest He entered "into heaven itself, and . . . appears now in God's presence for us." His
sacrifice on the cross was so effective that it need be done just once, but we
need His ongoing ministry to keep the effects of that once-and-for-all sacrifice alive for us. So, the crucified, resurrected, and ascended Christ is now in
God's presence, where He represents us continually.

Jesus' *future* work—What He did and is doing is truly awe-inspiring.
However, there's more—His future work, the blessed hope. "To those who
eagerly await him he will appear a second time, not to bear sin but to bring
salvation." By bearing our sin on the cross, He made salvation possible for us.
But when He appears in the sky, that's when He will really bring it to us!
When we sing Wayne Hooper's song "We Have This Hope," the hair on the
back of my neck stands up!

Faith Is . . .

Faith is the substance of things hoped for, the evidence of things not seen.
Heb. 11:1.

The well-known faith chapter begins with a graphic two-part definition of faith. Unfortunately, the vividness gets lost in translation.

"Faith is the *substance* . . ." The Greek word for "substance" is *hypóstasis.* It derived from a root meaning "stand under" and came to be a common philosophical term for the substructure of something—the underpinning of a building or the basis of a contract or promise. In commercial documents it referred to that which guaranteed a business deal. Because, materialistically, real estate (note the word "real") provided the basis for everyday existence, the word also meant property as well as the title deed that confirmed ownership of land.

"Faith is . . . the *evidence.*" The Greek word here translated "evidence" is *élegchos* (pronounced EL-eng-kos). It referred to the evidence used in a law court to buttress a case or decision. As such, it didn't necessarily involve incontrovertible proof, but it did refer to information sufficient for arriving at a judicial decision. Similarly, in the study of logic it referred to the demonstration of an argument under debate.

Faith, then, is the title deed to "things hoped for"—our home in heaven and the new earth. It is also that which confirms "things not seen"—our eschatological expectation. We don't live on the real estate now, and the object of our eschatological expectation remains unseen. Nevertheless, we are persuaded that our future remains true.

It's important to recognize that the basis for our conviction isn't knowledge but faith.

There's not a lot that we actually know, because knowledge involves certitude. That 2 + 2 = 4 is genuine knowledge and cannot be reasonably denied. Regardless of our language or culture, 2 + 2 always equals 4. Whether we're on Earth or Mars or Pluto or in another galaxy, 2 + 2 equals 4. On a commonsense and scientific basis, we also know that matter exists.

But much of what we think is knowledge is actually belief. There may be evidence for such faith, but it isn't absolute.

When we fail to differentiate between knowledge and faith, we end up sounding silly. It behooves us to speak of our faith in a way that won't offend thoughtful people.

It's Impossible to Please God

It is impossible to please God.
Heb. 11:6, NIV.

I f you're an Adventist of longstanding, then you've heard about all sorts of things that people say God doesn't like.

He doesn't want women to wear pantsuits or sleeveless clothing. He doesn't want us to go swimming or ride bicycles on Sabbath. He doesn't want monetary donations from drunkards. He doesn't want us to attend movie theaters.

He dislikes fiction. He dislikes jewelry. He dislikes wigs and toupees. He dislikes it when we take a nap on Sabbath afternoon. He dislikes jokes. He dislikes Disney World. He dislikes ball games. He dislikes lace and ribbons. Even Ellen White, despite her usual and frequent emphasis on grace, adds to the list. "[God] cannot love unruly children" (*Review and Herald*, Oct. 14, 1875). "Wicked children God does not love" (*An Appeal to the Youth*, p. 62). Oh, don't forget about the record books in heaven in which God writes down every evil thought or deed. We hear people talk about becoming sinless here and now, and sensitive people have given up in despair because they know from their own personal experience that they can't measure up and so God must frown on them.

The picture of God that we form after hearing all those (and other) comments is that He's an old grouch who's never happy. No matter what we do or don't do, He still grimaces. If something is fun, then He's against it! God has a perpetual scowl on His face. And if He's not glowering, then fury distorts His features. Why, some Christians believe that God has from eternity consigned all but a select few (whom He's predestinated) to unceasing torment in hell. American preacher Jonathan Edwards is remembered for his inflammatory sermon "Sinners in the Hands of an Angry God," which he delivered in Enfield, Connecticut, on July 8, 1741.

When we consider all the do's and don'ts that we hear about, surely "it is impossible to please God," just as our passage states. But wait a minute! Hebrews 11:6 says more than that. Note the introductory words that we've omitted: *"Without faith . . ."* So it *is* possible to please God . . . if we have faith. Faith is the key, "because anyone who comes to him must believe that he exists and that he rewards those who earnestly seek him" (verse 6, NIV).

Yes, God is delighted when we believe in Him and earnestly seek Him.

All Together

All these, having gained approval through their faith, did not receive what was promised, because God had provided something better for us, so that apart from us they would not be made perfect. Heb. 11:39, 40, NASB.

In 1965 Loretta Lynn sang a country song titled, "Everybody Wants to Go to Heaven." It mentioned the strange irony that despite our nearly universal aspiration to go to heaven, none of us wants to die! Of course, the underlying presumption is that upon death good people go immediately to heaven, where they enjoy everlasting bliss. When her husband, Mooney, died in 1996 at the age of 69, she wondered about where he went, because he hadn't been a paragon of virtue. Did Mooney go straight to hell or to heaven? One of her friends suggested to her that Mooney didn't go anywhere other than the grave.

Most Christians believe that when people die they go to their eternal reward. (Catholics believe that those not bad enough to end up in hell or good enough to go straight to heaven go to purgatory, where they're fitted for heaven. Some Protestants refer to a "middle [or interim] state.") That a deceased relative continues existence in the eternal bliss of heaven has afforded many people great solace, and when an Adventist advises them that such isn't the case, these believers often find themselves deeply perplexed. (It behooves us to present our teaching on the state of the dead with much care so as not to devastate the emotions of others.)

Today's passage sheds light on the matter of when believers receive their eternal reward, although we don't always take recourse to it. Chapter 11 of Hebrews, as we all know, presents a long list of people of faith: Abel, Enoch, Noah, Abraham, Sarah, Isaac, Jacob, Joseph, Moses, Rahab, Gideon, Barak, Samson, Jephthah, Samuel, David, the prophets, and others. Despite their strong and enduring faith, however, these men and women "died . . . without receiving the promises, but having seen them and having welcomed them from a distance, and having confessed that they were strangers and exiles on the earth" (verse 13, NASB). One aspect of these divine "promises" was "the city . . . whose architect and builder is God" (verse 10, NASB).

So what went wrong? Nothing, actually. "God had provided something better . . . so that apart from us they would not be made perfect." All believers go to their eternal reward together, not trickling in one at a time throughout the millennia of history.

The Christian Olympics

Therefore, since we are surrounded by such a huge crowd of witnesses to the life of faith, let us strip off every weight that slows us down, especially the sin that so easily hinders our progress. And let us run with endurance the race that God has set before us. Heb. 12:1, NLT.

The Olympics originated in Greece in 776 B.C. At the first meet there was only one event—a footrace. Koroibos, a cook, won the 600-foot-long race, running the length of the stadium. The first 13 Olympics consisted of just this single event. In 724 B.C. a second footrace, the *diaulos*, one complete lap around the stadium, was introduced. Four years later a third footrace, the *dolichos*, became part of the routine. It required contestants to run for about three miles, beginning and ending at the stadium. The games in 520 B.C. introduced the *hoplitodromos*—the last footrace of the day. In full armor that weighed between 50 and 60 pounds, the athletes would run either a single or double *diaulos*.

The general name for such contests was *agon* (from which we get our word "agony"), and the officials were *agonothetai*. At the sound of a trumpet the barefooted contestants would start from a standing position. Winners received a "crown" of twined olive twigs called a *stephanos*. They could also erect a statue of themselves in Olympia. Later these wreaths were constructed from gold. Athletes' hometowns also might add prizes of money, horses, gold tripods, free meals for life, or other material objects.

The book of Hebrews likens the Christian life to a footrace. In order to win, we Christians are admonished to "strip off every weight" that might slow us down—just as those ancient athletes ran unshod and naked or nearly so. (The word "gymnasium" comes from the Greek term meaning "nude.") We must divest ourselves of "the sin that so easily hinders our progress." Metaphorically urging us on are those men and women of faith mentioned in chapter 11.

Although the Christian Olympics may be exhausting, we must "run with endurance the race that God has set before us." And "we do this by keeping our eyes on Jesus" (Heb. 12:2, NLT). We should only glance at the crowd of faithful witnesses and keep our focus on Jesus, who is there in the stadium just as in ancient Greece a guest of honor on the sidelines (halfway down the track) proudly watched the runners.

The secret of success is what it always has been—discipline and stamina.

God Told Me to Do It

December 14

James

When tempted, no one should say, "God is tempting me." For God cannot be tempted by evil, nor does he tempt anyone; but each one is tempted when, by his own evil desire, he is dragged away and enticed. James 1:13, 14, NIV.

God has paid us a painful compliment by giving us free will. Our freedom constitutes the underlying basis for judgment, because in the judgment God holds us personally accountable for how we used our free will. Interestingly, we find this divine gift of free choice nearly intolerable and do our best to worm our way out of responsibility by blaming others for our behavior.

Comedian Flip Wilson (1933-1998) popularized one excuse by the famous line of his alter ego Geraldine: "The devil made me do it." Another copout is sometimes heard. In Hixson, Tennessee, Philip Badowski shot his parents to death and then mutilated their bodies, saying afterward that God told him to do it. And former president George W. Bush explained to two Palestinian leaders that God had told him to march into both Afghanistan and Iraq in order that the Middle East could enjoy peace and a Palestinian state could be formed.

Now, don't be too shocked. We find something similar in Scripture. God tempted Abraham to offer Isaac (Gen. 22:1). God hardened Pharaoh's heart so that he wouldn't free the Israelites. (Ex. 7:13). God tested the Israelites during their wilderness wanderings (Deut. 8:2).

James, however, provides a corrective. Using the same Greek word that appears in Genesis 22:1 and Deuteronomy 8:2 in the Greek version of the Old Testament that Jews and early Christians used, he wrote that God does *not* engage in such behavior. God has nothing to do with evil. He isn't tempted by it and doesn't tempt others with it.

Why, then, do we sin? James says that our sinning is quite explainable without recourse to supernatural intervention by the devil or God. "Each one is tempted when, by his own evil desire, he is dragged away and enticed" (James 1:14, NIV). It's our own innate propensity toward evil that tempts us, seducing us into sin. Continuing with his erotic metaphor, James continues: "After desire has conceived, it gives birth to sin; and sin, when it is full-grown, gives birth to death" (verse 15, NIV). If Satan and all his minions died tonight, sin would still exist.

God is willing to forgive our sins, but He can't if we refuse to take responsibility and blame either Him or the devil for our evil deeds.

When Sick

*Is any among you sick? Let him call for the elders
of the church, and let them pray over him,
anointing him with oil in the name of the Lord.
James 5:14, RSV.*

Illness isn't pleasant, yet sooner or later all of us suffer some sort of disease, and historically Christians have been foremost in pioneering the care of the sick. Although in the ancient world the ailing could be cared for in temples and later in facilities for ill and wounded Roman militia, hospitals as we know them originated within Christianity.

Today's passage underlies the religious practice of anointing the sick, but immediately several questions come to mind. Why call the church officers instead of a physician? Doesn't James's advice undermine the important role of medical doctors? Self-treatment is generally regarded as ineffective, but doesn't this practice encourage sham "healers"?

Perhaps we should take note of several important aspects of James's counsel. First, caring for the ill is a community concern—"call for the elders." Second, prayer is the elders' first duty. They're only laypeople when it comes to medical matters. Third, they anoint the patient.

Greek had two words for anointing: (1) *aleíphō*, a general term used for the everyday practice of rubbing olive oil on the body for either cosmetic or medicinal purposes; and (2) *chríō*, a more limited term used for the sacred or ritual use of olive oil as a means of dedication. According to Richard Trench, this distinction is maintained in both the New Testament and the Greek Old Testament (Septuagint). The first term "is the mundane and profane" expression; the second is "the sacred and religious word" (*Synonyms of the New Testament*, pp. 136, 137). Which word does James use here? The former—*aleíphō*.

In the ancient Near East (as in the Middle East even today), olive oil was valued as a medicine. For instance, Menander, Pliny the Elder, and Hippocrates thought it had curative power, and Jews regarded it as a "life elixir" that "possessed life and spirit" (Bo Reicke, *The Epistles of James, Peter, and Jude, Anchor Bible*, p. 59).

James advocated that the elders pray (the supernatural part) and have patients take their medicine (anointing, the natural part). If we think that being anointed exempts us from utilizing medical treatment, we misconstrue his intent. He recommended both prayer and medicine—not one or the other.

Seeing Isn't Believing

December 16

1 Peter

You have not seen him, yet you love him; and still without seeing him you believe in him.
1 Peter 1:8, New Jerusalem.

The scientific, or "empirical," method is a commonsense way of under-standing reality. A significant aspect of this method of study is reliance on the senses, although sometimes the senses have to be enhanced by use of instruments such as microscopes, telescopes, spectrometers, etc.

In much less rigorous ways, we believe our senses as is reflected in such statements as "I saw it myself" or "I heard him say that . . ." Most of us trust our senses without question. However, we often overlook that we have no "direct" contact with what's "out there." For example, what we see is the end result of a process: (1) light waves bounce off an object, (2) they are focused by the lens in our eyes, (3) they travel through the aqueous humor, (4) they fall on the retina, (5) rods and cones in the retina turn them into chemical-electrical impulses, (6) these impulses travel along the optic nerves, (7) impulses from the right eye end up in the left side of the brain, and those from the left eye go to the right side, and (8) the brain's occipital lobe forms an image. Similar processes take place for our sense of smell, hearing, taste, and touch.

However, these senses upon which we rely are not only mediated but are also limited. The light we detect is only a tiny portion of the electromag-netic spectrum; bees can see light waves that we can't! Similarly, we hear only limited frequencies of sound waves; dogs can hear more than we can! Furthermore, our senses can fail us. We've all seen optical illusions, but there are also audio, olfactory, and tactile illusions. Also, when brain chemistry is altered, we can have delusions—seeing, hearing, tasting, and feeling "things" that no one else senses.

With these limitations of our senses when it comes to detecting the ma-terial world, it's hardly surprising that they falter when it comes to detecting the spiritual world. We call what we learn about material things "knowl-edge." What we learn about spiritual things is "belief." Peter commends the recipients of his letter for their belief. They hadn't experienced Jesus by em-pirical methods; nonetheless they loved Him and believed in Him. His words remind us of what Jesus said to Thomas: "Blessed are those who have not seen and yet believe" (John 20:29, New Jerusalem). Because of their belief, they were "filled with a joy so glorious that it cannot be described" (1 Peter 1:8, New Jerusalem).

The Cover-up

December 17

1 Peter

Love covers a multitude of sins.
1 Peter 4:8, NRSV.

"Gossip" comes from two root words: god-sib, which originally referred to a godparent. It came into use in 1014, but the meaning shifted in 1811 to denote baseless chitchat among peers. Interestingly, the word needn't always denote hush-hush slanderous talk, but that's what we usually think of when today we hear the word "gossip." Eleanor Roosevelt said, "Great minds discuss ideas; average minds discuss events; small minds discuss people." Do you agree?

It seems as though it's an innate human tendency to enjoy sharing malicious tidbits about mutual acquaintances. "Did you hear that Bill's Camry was parked all night long at Sally's house last Sunday?" Even if Sally and Bill are an "item," there could be good reasons his car hadn't moved from her driveway for an entire night. She may have invited him over for supper, and when he tried to start the car the timing belt broke, so he had to call a taxi to take him home. Bill may have gone on a trip and didn't want to leave his new Camry parked unattended in his neighborhood. Sally's mother, who resides across the U.S., may have taken ill, and because of a spate of robberies in her subdivision, Sally asked Bill to house-sit while she tended her mother for a week. Thus, while the bit of gossip might have been literally true, its connotation was misleading and would sully Sally's and Bill's reputations.

Suppose, however, that both the denotation and connotation of the rumor were indeed true—that Bill had spent the night with Sally . . . in her bed. How would it help them to have such spicy news whispered from one person to another? True, Bill and Sally had fallen into immorality. And true, sin must be called by its right name. But does the responsibility of exposing their sin rest on the shoulders of the church gossip?

Today's passage explains the loving thing to do. "Love covers a multitude of sins." The word for "covers" means to plaster over and hide, to hinder knowledge of something. And what is kept from view? A plethora (yes, the Greek term lies behind our word "plethora") of sins. We behave this way because we "maintain constant love for one another" (1 Peter 4:8, NRSV). The term translated "constant" means expanded—our love is stretched out to hide sin. We're to sweep under the rug a multiplicity of sins. Sounds like God, who "will cast all our sins into the depths of the sea" (Micah 7:19, NRSV), doesn't it?

Be Happy

Think it not strange concerning the fiery trial which is to try you, as though some strange thing happened unto you: But rejoice, inasmuch as ye are partakers of Christ's sufferings; that, when his glory shall be revealed, ye may be glad also with exceeding joy.
1 Peter 4:12, 13.

Was Peter kidding? Is 1 Peter 4:12, 13 the right spiritual medicine for the diseased or the abused? No. Using this passage to console those suffering from such is like trying to twist a metric nut onto a nonmetric bolt. Note the following significant points.

1. Peter doesn't speak about trials—plural. The noun is singular—trial. It's inaccurate for us to apply this scripture to trials—in the plural. 2. The Greek noun can refer to a difficult and unpleasant experience as well as a temptation. 3. The original language uses the definite article with the singular noun—"*the* . . . trial" not "*a* trial." Peter refers to a specific trial—not trials in general. 4. He also modifies the noun "trial" with the adjective "fiery." The metaphor is of the smelting or assaying process by extreme heat that either purifies the metal or demonstrates its genuineness. 5. Peter emphasizes the kind of testing by repeating himself. The "fiery trial [singular] . . . is to try you"—referring to the recipients of this letter, who are "scattered all around . . . Pontus, Galatia, Cappadocia, Asia, and Bithynia" (1 Peter 1:1, NCV)—provinces of Asia Minor. This specific and unique fiery trial will demonstrate something about these early Christians in Asia Minor. 6. These Christian sufferers are to keep on rejoicing (present tense). 7. Verse 13 says they should keep on rejoicing because they were "sharing" (NRSV). 8. What is this sharing these brothers and sisters had? They were sharers in *Christ's* suffering—covictims with their Lord. 9. What sort of suffering did Peter identify as the suffering Jesus endured? He tells us that Jesus was an innocent victim (1 Peter 2:22; 3:18). 10. This biblical passage is talking about persecution—of being unfairly tried and unjustly punished. 11. Christians can endure their maltreatment because they "will be . . . full of joy when Christ comes again" (verse 13, NCV). Earlier Peter said that those being persecuted ought to keep on rejoicing in the here and now, but now he speaks of being "full of joy" in the hereafter.

Careful analysis thus reveals that we shouldn't quote 1 Peter 4:12, 13 to someone suffering from postnasal drip or cancer. The passage is intended to buoy up the spirits of those undergoing persecution. When the New Testament speaks of suffering, it means persecution.

What to Do With Worries

*Give all your worries and cares to God,
for he cares about what happens to you.*
1 Peter 5:7, NLT.

"Worry" has an interesting origin. In Old English the word was *wyrgan*, meaning "strangle." It evolved into the Middle English word *worien*, which meant the same thing but also took on the meaning to chomp with teeth, lacerating prey like an attacking wolf. During the seventeenth century the verb mutated to mean "persecute" or "distress." From there it came to denote in the nineteenth century the idea of anxiety.

Different temperaments make life interesting. Although a few of us appear to have been born with a predisposition to worry, it seems that most of us learn the fine art of fretting, which takes place in the part of the brain known as the amygdala. Maybe something in our upbringing contributed to our feeling insecure. A study by the National Institutes of Mental Health found that about 19 million Americans suffer from some sort of anxiety disorder. When a person has a chemical disorder related to worrying, certain medications can help restore the proper balance.

Anxiety, as most of us would suspect, can prove detrimental to one's health. (It's a basic Adventist belief that the mind, the source of our emotions, can affect the body.) From 1995 to 1997 the University of Bergen in Norway studied 62,591 people. Those in the investigation who scored high in an anxiety test turned out to be 25 percent more likely to develop precancerous cells than others in the research program.

Claude McDonald said, "Worriers spend a lot of time shoveling smoke." But not all worrying is frivolous or baseless. Some problems can prove nearly intractable or at least ominous. Nevertheless, many of the anticipated problems we fret over don't come to fruition.

Because most worrywarts don't have a genetic malformation that produces anxiety, the advice in today's passage is clearly appropriate. It's a habit that many of us can unlearn, although that might be more difficult than the process of having learned to fret. One response to worry is tied to faith in God. When we have a firm trust in Him, we can put our worries into His hands. Why, though, should this spiritual exercise work? Peter provides the reason: "He cares about what happens to you." The verb Peter used can also be translated "worry," and it's in the present tense: God is concerned—He keeps on worrying in our behalf!

Granville Sharp's Rule

To those who have received a faith as precious
as ours through the righteousness of our
God and Savior Jesus Christ.
2 Peter 1:1, NRSV.

Granville Sharp was born in Great Britain to Thomas Sharp. His significant contributions include his activism to abolish slavery, his agitation for reforming Parliament, his support for better wages for farmers, his defense of American revolutionaries, and his study of Greek grammar, which produced what Greek scholars know as "Granville Sharp's Rule." It's the latter that especially concerns us as we deal with 2 Peter 1:1.

From his study of biblical Greek, Sharp proposed six related but different grammatical rules, but it's his first rule—sometimes referred to as "TSKS"—that has been a tool for translating today's scripture into English. Stating Rule I has proved controversial, but a simplistic version will do here:

(1) *If* the Greek word for "and" separates two adjacent common nouns (*not* proper names such as Peter, Paul, Jesus, etc. ["God" and "Savior" in Greek aren't proper nouns]), and

(2) *if* the two nouns are singular (for instance, "book" rather than "books"), and

(3) *if* the first noun is preceded by the definite article (for example, "*the* man") but the second noun isn't,

(4) *then* the two nouns refer to the same thing (they're synonyms).

Sharp insisted that in the New Testament, this rule is ironclad—without exceptions. However, other grammarians have subjected Rule I to much scrutiny and argument. Some have claimed that it isn't inviolable, but despite the passing of more than two centuries since Sharp published it, the consensus is that the critics used faulty arguments and that the rule stands. The translators of the NET Bible report: "Sharp's rule stands vindicated after all the dust has settled" (footnote 5 for 2 Peter 1:1).

What does all this have to do with today's verse? It means that 2 Peter 1:1 is one of the clearest examples in the New Testament of Jesus being called God. As noted previously, Paul typically differentiated between God the Father and Jesus our Lord and Savior. However, the grammatical construction in 2 Peter 1:1 makes it pretty clear that the apostle here identifies Jesus as both our Savior and God.

Is God a Slowpoke?

The Lord is not slack concerning His promise . . .
but is longsuffering toward us, not willing that any
should perish but that all should come to repentance.
2 Peter 3:9, NKJV.

Some people take forever to get something done. Those who operate at a slower rate of speed are often, but not always, meticulous in their work. Many slowpokes not only behave unhurriedly but also think slowly even though they have no mental retardation.

Others are always in a hurry. They rush about with great energy. They can accomplish a given task in a fraction of the time that it takes others to perform the same job. Tell them a joke, and they anticipate the punch line (and start chuckling) before you complete your recitation.

What about God? Does He perform quickly or slowly? From what we learn in Scripture, we can answer with "It depends." Note what Nahum said: "The Lord is slow to anger" (Nahum 1:3). Yet in the same breath he added that He has "his way in the whirlwind." On the one hand, God sometimes acts speedily, as He warned Tyre and Sidon: "If you retaliate against Me, swiftly and speedily I will return your retaliation upon your own head" (Joel 3:4, NKJV). On the other hand, in "longsuffering [He] waited in the days of Noah, while the ark was being prepared" (1 Peter 3:20, NKJV).

Jesus spoke of His second coming as though it would occur within His own generation. Every New Testament writer who spoke of the Second Advent expected it to happen in their day, but as time dragged on, Christians began to wonder why it was taking so long for Jesus to return.

In today's passage Peter addresses that issue, assuring his readership that "the Lord is not slack concerning His promise." The word translated "slack" means to be slow or to loiter. When it came to Jesus' promise of His return, He wouldn't dillydally—at least in the human sense of the term. But if that is the case, then why hadn't Jesus returned?

Good question!

Jesus hadn't returned as anticipated because God "is longsuffering toward us, not willing that any should perish but that all should come to repentance." He puts up with human sinful nonsense because of His inward disposition ("willing") that *negatively* no one might suffer eternal loss and that *positively* all might find room for repentance. God puts up with some Christians dying the first death so that other people might not suffer the second death.

358

Hastening

You should look forward to that day and hurry it along—the day when God will set the heavens on fire and the elements will melt away in the flames.
2 Peter 3:12, NLT.

S ome words have several meanings, and translators can find it difficult to know exactly which of the alternative meanings is most appropriate. Sometimes the immediate context can help a translator choose between or among the possibilities. Occasionally the way an author uses the same term elsewhere can help clarify matters. At times one's theological perspective is the deciding factor.

Honest people disagree over how to render today's passage, namely, the term that is translated as "hurry it along" in the New Living Translation. The main topic appears clear enough—"the day when God . . ." Peter used the word *parousía*, a term used by other New Testament writers to describe the Second Coming. As noted previously, in the secular world the expression referred to the arrival and stay of an important person—a king or conquering general. Peter explained what would take place on that day, thereby further identifying it. The heavens would burst into flame, and the elements would disintegrate because of the intense heat. Clearly, the event Peter had in mind was Christ's return.

The Christians, Peter said, were to maintain two stances in light of this coming "day." First, they should keep on anticipating the arrival of the *parousía*. They shouldn't abandon their expectations. Second (and here's the thorny part), they should *speúdō* that day. The verb Peter chose could mean two things: (1) to speed up something or cause something to happen soon or (2) to await or desire eagerly. When Jesus said to Zacchaeus, "Quick, come down!" (Luke 19:5, NLT), He used the same verb (here translated "quick"), and in the next verse the very same verb describes what Zacchaeus did.

Did Peter teach (1) that Christians should speed up the Second Advent or (2) that Christians should eagerly desire it? If the latter, then Peter was repeating himself for emphasis—keep on anticipating and fervently wait for the *parousía*. If the former, then Peter was suggesting that Christians can speed up the time when Jesus returns (implying that we can also delay the Advent). Which option is proper? One's theology will help decide. Can human behavior influence divine activity? If so, then the former would approximate Peter's intent.

Does God Have a Dark Side?

God is light, and in him is no darkness at all.
1 John 1:5.

It seems that in recent years more and more people talk about the "dark side of God" or the "shadowy side of God." If these expressions mean that God is ineffable, then they're certainly on target. However, it seems that at least sometimes these words refer to an aspect of God that's evil—or at least not benevolent.

What are we to make of the idea that somewhere deep inside God's personality lurks some sort of unfathomable malevolence?

At a church I attended for 25 years, the pastor would say, "God is good," and the congregation would respond, "All the time." He'd then say, "All the time . . ." and the congregation would reply, "God is good." But what about those relatively rare biblical passages that seem to imply that God does have deep in His psyche a down side, a dark side? You've read them. "I will destroy man whom I have created from the face of the earth" (Gen. 6:7). "The Lord hardened the heart of Pharaoh" (Ex. 9:12). "Shall we receive good at the hand of God, and shall we not receive evil?" (Job 2:10). "Thou hatest all workers of iniquity" (Ps. 5:5). "I form the light, and create darkness: I make peace, and create evil: I the Lord do all these things" (Isa. 45:7). "I will bring evil upon this place, the which whosoever heareth, his ears shall tingle" (Jer. 19:3).

From these and other passages we might infer that God really does have a dark, shadowy side—like other deities, who were not only capricious but who also led immoral lives. (The Greek gods were said to behave in such wicked ways that some of the Greek philosophers teetered on the brink of atheism.) Another explanation, however, is possible. Because of the radical monotheism He wanted His people to espouse, He had to accept, temporarily, responsibility for all that happens—good and bad. (Some theologians speculate that the dualism of Zoroastrianism, to which the Hebrew exiles were exposed, paved the way for a limited dualism in which God is responsible for that which is good and Satan is responsible for that which is bad.)

Whatever our explanation for certain scriptural passages, John makes it clear that God not only created light, He *is* light, and in Him "is no darkness at all." Or as the psalmist sang: "The goodness of God endureth continually" (Ps. 52:1).

Confession Is Good for the Soul

December 24
1 John

If we confess our sins, He is faithful and righteous to forgive us our sins and to cleanse us from all unrighteousness.
1 John 1:9, NASB.

Today's verse is chock-full of meaning, but we'll be able to unpack just a portion of the inherent implications.

"If"—Greek has four different constructions for expressing a conditional situation, each with a different nuance. John here used the third class of condition, which stresses a future possibility. It's sometimes referred to as "the more probable future condition." This type of condition implies some uncertainty, but not much: "If (in case) you do so-and-so (I don't know if you will do it or not . . . it's up to you), then such-and-such will follow."

"Confess"—The word translated "confess" means "say the same thing as." The idea is agreement. In other words, to confess our sins (see below) means that we say the same thing about them as God and Jesus do. We agree with Them about evil.

"Sins"—The Greek word commonly rendered "sin" is *hamartía*. Originally it meant "missing the mark," as when an archer shoots an arrow at a target but misses, with the arrow falling either in front of, to the side of, or beyond the target. It denotes a mistake resulting from human weakness in contrast to high-handed rebellion.

"Faithful"—The Greek word means trustworthy. God in Jesus Christ can be counted on to do something because He and His Son are intrinsically dependable.

"Just"—God is also guiltless, always doing the right thing. Originally the term referred to doing that which is both customary and proper, and later took on moral overtones.

"Forgive"—The word John chose is *aphíemi*. It refers to the act of sending something away, getting rid of the object. It also includes overtones of letting something go from further notice—ignoring something. It was used of canceling debts as well as for divorcing a spouse, freeing a slave or prisoner, and even breaking wind. Jesus banishes our faults.

"Cleanse"—This term is the positive flip side of the coin of forgiveness. Not only does He forget about our mistakes, but He also cleans us up . . . morally and spiritually. "The blood of Jesus . . . cleanses us from all sin" (1 John 1:7, NASB). There are no exceptions.

Truly, confession *is* good for the soul.

A New Commandment

And now, dear lady, I am not writing you a
new command but one we have had from
the beginning. I ask that we love one another.
2 John 5, NIV.

What a surprise—a biblical epistle addressed to a female! We're used to reading New Testament letters written to churches (1 and 2 Corinthians, Ephesians, etc.) and to individual men (1 and 2 Timothy, Titus, etc.), but 2 John was sent to a lady. Just a minute, though! Scholars have suggested five different identities of the lady in question: (1) a lady named Electa (no such proper name is attested), (2) a lady called Kyria (a name in vogue among certain people), (3) My Dear Lady (a polite term)—an unnamed person, (4) an elect lady, which is really code for the church at large (as in the book of Revelation), and (5) an elect lady and her children, symbolizing the Johannine community. Whichever alternative is correct (*The Seventh-day Adventist Bible Commentary* leans toward a corporate identity), it still seems remarkable to have a New Testament epistle addressed to a female.

In this letter the apostle gave a command masquerading as a request— "I am entreating you . . ." John pointed out that this wasn't a new command but one known from the outset, so it shouldn't surprise anyone. What is this commandment? "Love one another." Sounds familiar, doesn't it? Jesus had told His disciples, "Love one another" (John 13:34).

That was Jesus' "new commandment," which He expanded so Peter, James, John, and the others wouldn't misunderstand: "As I have loved you, so you must love one another" (verse 34, NIV). Now, *that's* a tall order! Every Christian recognizes that Jesus personified God's love. Indeed, we celebrate that love today—Christmas. But how can we ever love as He did? Are we willing to die for someone else—not just loved ones but those who hate us and show it? The Greek word for love—*agapē*—doesn't mean we have to *like* these others. It does mean, though, that we'll treat them with respect and wish the best for them. Tough assignment!

John has yet another surprise for us. He explained what it means for us to love. "This is love: that we walk in obedience to his commands" (2 John 6, NIV). Sounds tautological, doesn't it? The commandment is to love, and to love means to keep the commandments! Nevertheless, it echoes 1 John 5:3, which says: "This is love for God: to obey his commands" (NIV). The second table of the Decalogue, as you recall, addresses how we should treat others: lovingly.

Good Health to All

*Beloved, I pray that you may prosper in all things
and be in health, just as your soul prospers.*
3 John 2, NKJV.

Adventists in the field of health care often use today's passage as a proof text to demonstrate that because God (via the apostle John) wants us to enjoy good health, we should adopt a lifestyle that contributes to physical well-being. It's likely, however, that 3 John 2 isn't a fitting proof text for buttressing our health message, appropriate as health reform may be. Besides, why do we need a proof text for something that common sense tells us is true—the idea that good physical health is worth preserving?

Third John, like 1 and 2 John, Galatians, Philippians, and other New Testament "books," is an epistle—a letter. As we've seen previously, letters follow a rhetorical formula. In fact, today's letters conform to a pattern similar to that of Greco-Roman letters. Here are the conventions of those ancient letters: (1) an opening formula that identified the sender and the recipient and greeted the addressee(s); (2) a statement of thanksgiving or appreciation, which could express a wish and often introduced some of the main themes that followed; (3) the body or message, which may have an opening, middle, and closing; and (4) a conclusion and/or farewell.

It's important to remind ourselves that such literary blueprints resort to *phatic* language. Linguist Eugene Nida explains that with phatic communication "the content . . . is almost zero, but the function . . . is to bring the receptor and the source together in a communicative relationship" (*Signs, Sense, Translation*, p. 27). Phatic speech acts serve as warm fuzzies to eliminate fear and/or resistance. When we open a letter with the word "dear," we aren't writing a Valentine's Day greeting to a sweetheart. And we may close a letter with the word "sincerely," even though within the body of the message we may have spoken ironically or sarcastically.

Writers in the ancient world commonly used phatic speech in the thanksgiving, which might include a wish that the addressee was in good health. The purpose of commenting on the recipient's health had one function: to erect a bridge of empathy between the sender (source) and the addressee (receptor). And that's precisely what John was doing when he said to Gaius, "I hope you're in sound health." The apostle was being polite, using phatic speech to "soften up" Gaius. That's why it isn't suitable as a proof text in support of a healthful lifestyle.

Old-time Religion

Beloved, being very eager to write to you of our common salvation, I found it necessary to write appealing to you to contend for the faith which was once for all delivered to the saints.
Jude 3, RSV.

How many Adventists are there? Fifteen million and growing daily. Not the answer I was looking for. African Adventists, Asian Adventists, South Sea Island Adventists, European Adventists, Latin American Adventists, North American Adventists, and . . . constitute the church. Yet even these groups can be further subdivided. There are South Sea Island Adventists who worship on Sunday and those who worship on Saturday (because of a quirk in the position of the international date line). There are European Adventists who play ball on Sabbath and those who lost their children because they refused to send them to school on Sabbath.

North American Adventists generally divide into (1) historic Adventists, whose sermons and books often contain more Spirit of Prophecy quotations than anything else; (2) self-supporting Adventists, who wear long cotton dresses and tend toward a more austere lifestyle; (3) conservative Adventists, who typically stress the Second Coming and think that wearing a wedding ring is sinful; (4) evangelical Adventists, who stress the gospel and accuse mainstream Adventism of being legalistic; (5) progressive Adventists, who innovate the Sabbath school lessons and would like to see women pastors ordained and an organization that gives more self-direction to local congregations; and (6) liberal Adventists, who characteristically emphasize the Sabbath and drink a little wine and often dine out for Sabbath dinner.

Which Adventists have the faith of their fathers and want to conserve the spirit or essence of Adventism? If you asked representatives from each of those subdivisions of North American Adventists, they'd most likely all affirm that they do. We shouldn't doubt the sincerity of members pigeonholed in these various subdivisions. We can take at face value their desire to preserve the best of Adventism, the heart of Adventism.

Jude felt compelled—even obligated—to encourage the early Christians to fight (contend) for "the faith . . . once for all delivered to the saints." The good news of salvation had been handed to them, not again and again but once, and their task from that time forward was to maintain the faith, which by this point in history had come to denote sound doctrine.

End of Sinners

And they came up on the broad plain of the earth and surrounded the camp of the saints and the beloved city, and fire came down from heaven and devoured them.
Rev. 20:9, NASB.

Ebola hemorrhagic fever, caused by the most virulent virus known, produces internal and external bleeding, and victims typically die from hypovolemic shock and/or organ breakdown. Dictators such as Stalin, Hitler, and Idi Amin have slaughtered literally millions of victims. Some babies lack a forebrain and cerebrum. Having no consciousness, they cannot see, hear, or feel. Millions of sex slaves (approximately 50,000 in the United States) find themselves physically and emotionally abused by both their pimps and johns.

Drunk drivers cause a traffic fatality about every 30 minutes in the United States. During the 25-year period between December 1981 and January 2006, more than 25 million people died from AIDs. In 2005 AIDS destroyed about 3 million men, women, and children. Some 70 percent of persons with necrotizing fasciitis (the generic name for the disease caused by flesh-eating bacteria) die a painful death if untreated, and 25 percent die even if treated. Every 2.43 seconds of every single day, someone dies from starvation, and 85 percent of these victims are children under the age of 5.

The existence—no, the prevalence—of suffering arguably provides the strongest case against the existence of God and for atheism. Indeed, as far back as the Greek philosopher Epicurus (341 B.C. to 270 B.C.), the reality of evil has put thinkers on the horns of a dilemma: (1) if God wants to avert evil but cannot, then He is impotent; (2) if God can prevent evil but doesn't, then He is Himself evil; (3) if God is both willing and able to put a stop to evil, then it shouldn't exist, yet it does; (4) if God both wills evil and causes it, then He isn't moral and hence not worthy of worship; (5) it's clear that God—at least a benevolently moral deity—doesn't exist.

Theologians have proposed rationales for the existence of evil and the agony it produces, suggesting that for reasons not always obvious to the human mind God has allowed the continuance of evil and its attendant suffering. Today's passage, though, makes it clear that despite the ongoing presence of evil, God *does* want to destroy it and has the capability to do so. Indeed, He shall destroy evil and evildoers. Would a beneficent deity destroy evil and its perpetrators? Absolutely! As a morally blameless person, He finds evil offensive—as do we.

The Invitation

The Spirit and the bride say, Come. And let him that heareth say, Come. And let him that is athirst come. And whosoever will, let him take the water of life freely.
Rev. 22:17.

Wedding invitations! It seems as though they're getting fancier and fancier. Many now come with a photo of the prospective bride and groom in a romantic pose. I received one the other day, and because I hadn't seen the groom since he was just a youngster, I found it intriguing to see how much he'd changed.

Matrimonial ceremonies exude joy and hope. Remember your own? The bride looks gorgeous in her gown, and the groom looks dashing in his tuxedo. The flowers add a festive touch. The music is inspiring, and even today hearing the traditional wedding march makes the hair on the back of my neck stand up! The officiating minister provides encouraging advice. The candles add a celebratory aura. The starry-eyed couple enters their new relationship with much bravado. The reception allows all to celebrate the new home just established.

Wedding celebrations in the ancient Near East—at least among the Hebrew people—were even more elaborate affairs than ours, although they didn't occur in a place of worship. They were basically secular celebrations that lasted for days. In addition to the bride price paid to the girl's father (frequently the bride was still in her teens), other gifts were exchanged, including a dowry given by the bride's father to his daughter. The wedding feast could last for a week or more, consisting of dancing, drinking, and dining.

Some of the Old Testament writers described YHWH's relationship to Israel as a marriage. "Thou shalt no more be termed Forsaken . . . but thou shalt be called Hephzibah ["my delight is in her"], and thy land Beulah ["married"]: for the Lord delighteth in thee, and thy land shall be married. . . . As the bridegroom rejoiceth over the bride, so shall thy God rejoice over thee" (Isa. 62:4, 5).

In the New Testament we find a similar metaphor. "I John saw the holy city, new Jerusalem, coming down from God out of heaven, prepared as a bride adorned for her husband" (Rev. 21:2). You and I can attend the wedding. We find the invitation in today's passage: "The Spirit and the bride say, Come." It's the last picture of God for our photo album. He wants us there— as part of the wedding celebration. Let's not forget to send ahead our RSVP.